Writer's Block

Writer's Block

Zachary Leader

The Johns Hopkins University Press

Baltimore & London

The Johns Hopkins University Press
701 West 40th Street
Baltimore, Maryland 21211
The Johns Hopkins Press Ltd., London

⊗ The paper used in this book meets the minimum requirements of
American National Standard for Information Sciences—Permanence of Paper for
Printed Library Materials, ANSI Z39.48–1984.

Library of Congress Cataloging-in-Publication Data

Leader, Zachary.
Writer's block / Zachary Leader.
    p.   cm.
Includes bibliographical references.   Includes index.
ISBN 0-8018-4032-5 (alk. paper)
1. Writer's block. 2. Creative writing—Psychological aspects.
3. Creation (Literary, artistic, etc.) I. Title.
PN171.W74L44 1991
808'.001'9—dc20.   90-4744   CIP

To Alice

Contents

Preface
ix

Chapter 1
Introduction
1

PART ONE
Psychoanalytic Theory

Chapter 2
The Freudian Account
33

Chapter 3
After Freud
55

Chapter 4
British Object-Relations Theory
82

PART TWO
Literary History

Chapter 5
Theories of Origin
115

Chapter 6
Wordsworth and Writer's Block
146

Contents

Chapter 7
The Case of Coleridge
186

PART THREE
External Prohibition

Chapter 8
Writing, Speech, and Culture
219

Chapter 9
Blockage and Externality: The Woman as Writer
232

Postscript
251

Notes
253

Index
315

Preface

The idea for this book first came to me when I was a graduate student at work on Blake. Anyone who thinks seriously about Blake has at some time to consider the question of his or her subject's sanity, and in my case the question arose at precisely the point I was having the most trouble with my own work. Blake rarely complained of such trouble. For all his eccentricity, he was an extremely productive, fluent writer. As far as we can tell from his letters and poems, the ease with which he dealt with difficult or intractable problems of composition—his ability, at several stages in his career, to let go, step back, move on—was crucial to his achievement. That this ease was also in marked contrast to the anxieties of authorship I myself was experiencing at the time—principally, a neurotic compulsion to revise every other word I produced—weighed heavily in my calculations as to his sanity.

Until, that is, I considered how sharply Blake's ease also contrasted with the experience of his contemporaries, particularly Coleridge and Wordsworth, both of whom not only suffered from prolonged periods of authorial agonizing but made such periods the very subject of their art. Not being able to write, after all, was a central theme in the early Romantic period, and its relative absence in Blake's life and work is an important ingredient of his oddity or otherness. Perhaps, I began to suspect, Blake's fluency, especially in the disfiguring accretions of the later prophetic books, was less a sign of health than of mania.

Such thoughts eventually led to the question of *writer's block* in general, and, the more I considered this question (from the safe perspective of a finished dissertation), the more richly problematic it became. Did it, to begin with, make sense to apply the term to writers as productive as Wordsworth and Coleridge? At what point—and why—did the term come into existence, and what were the terms it replaced? How was it to be distinguished from the sorts of difficulties most writers encounter in the act of composition? When, in other words, did a problem with writing become a block? The answers to these questions, I realized, could be sought in widely different fields—in psychology, of course, and literary history, but also in a long philosophical tradition of distrust of the written word, as well as in more general social and cultural speculation.

At which point, as the topic's implications began to proliferate, a nice self-reflexive moment of blockage threatened, and with it an urge to clamp down, to get the matter under some sort of control. The more I thought about this urge, the more I realized that it was characteristic. My fears of being swallowed up by the topic, on the one hand, and of imposing too rigid and potentially limiting a framework, on the other, were precisely those recounted by blocked writers themselves, as well as by the theorists—literary historical as well as psychoanalytic—I had begun to examine. A book on writer's block would have to steer carefully between such extremes—though the same could be said of writing of any sort.

Whether this book has done so is for the reader to decide. But if it has, credit is partly due to a number of people who helped and counselled me over the course of its composition. I am grateful, in particular, to P. N. Furbank, Neil Hertz, Christopher Ricks, and Tom Treadwell. Others who have read and commented on parts of the manuscript are John Beer, Rosemary Dinnage, Michael Ferber, Catherine Gallagher, Wendy Lesser, Mike Rose, Jean Strouse, and Peter Weston. My editors at the Johns Hopkins University Press—William P. Sisler, Eric Halpern, and Jane Warth—have been models of patient encouragement. I also have been fortunate in Jennifer Wills's skillful preparation of the typescript.

Finally, a word about expectations. This is not a book of case histories, and it does not forward—except in the most qualified and indirect fashion—a single theory of creative inhibition. It is a theoretical and historical enquiry. After an Introduction establishing the terms of the enquiry, the book moves on to a detailed critical account of a range of theories, providing only a small number of examples of blockage, including several that the reader may be surprised to hear spoken of as cases of writer's block at all. Some of the theories discussed in the book's psychoanalytic part are complicated (though I have tried to be as clear as possible in my accounts of them, relegating conflicts and complexities to the Notes), and in each case I have outlined the general features of the theory before discussing its specific application to questions of creative health. The book draws on diverse disciplines and techniques, and its claims to originality lie less in the theories themselves than in the way these theories are gathered together and used to elucidate a real, if tantalizingly protean, phenomenon.

Introduction

I begin rather narrowly, with the history and "literature" of the term *writer's block*. The first point to make about *writer's block* is that relatively little has been written about it. Although the phenomenon it means to designate can be found in a variety of times and places, the actual term is of recent and uncertain origin, and its air of psychological substance and authority is largely an illusion. A search through the relevant bibliographies reveals few useful citations, and only a single book before 1965, Edmund Bergler's *The Writer and Psychoanalysis* (1950), addresses itself directly, though not wholly, to the topic.[1] Since Bergler's book, only two others devoted to writer's block have appeared, excluding popular self-help manuals:[2] Tillie Olsen's *Silences* (1965), a frankly unsystematic or "impressionistic" compilation of suggestive anecdotes and quotations, with special emphasis on women writers; and Mike Rose's *Writer's Block: The Cognitive Dimension* (1983), a scholarly monograph on the inhibiting effects of "cognitive errors" or poor writing habits on American college students. Rose's book heralds a boomlet of research on the composing process, most of it by American educational psychologists and teachers of rhetoric and writing. In the last few years, this research has produced a number of articles associating or identifying writer's block in student composition with a variety of inhibiting factors.[3]

Bergler claims ("as far as I know") to have coined the term *writer's block*.[4] As far as *I* know, he may well have. When I first began work on this book, neither *writer's block* nor *writing block* appeared in the *Oxford English Dictionary* or its supplements, though the former did appear in the updated ninth edition of Webster's *New World College Dictionary*, with a citation date of 1953. This citation, though later than Bergler's, was an improvement on the 1954 citation, from Mary McCarthy's *A Charmed Life*, offered by the editors of the then-forthcoming *O.E.D. Supplement S-Z* (I was pleased, therefore, when the 1950 Bergler reference I sent the editors appeared in the *Supplement* upon its publication in 1986). Before the 1980s, a *writing block* meant simply "a pad of paper"—"which is much the same thing!" the senior editor added.[5]

Among psychoanalytic and more general encyclopedias, only the Collier Macmillan *Encyclopedia of Psychoanalysis* (1968) mentions writer's block. Its entry ignores Bergler (which is odd, given that its editor has coauthored an article with him)[6] and instead cites Otto Fenichel's *The Psychoanalytic Theory of the Neuroses* (1945), which predates Bergler. Fenichel, however, nowhere mentions writer's block (nor does the term appear in the book's earlier version of 1934, *Outline of Clinical Psychoanalysis*), though he does talk of *writer's cramp*, which is grouped with a variety of inhibitions associated with the psychology of work. *Writer's cramp*, in conventional usage, is a relatively aged and respectable term, one that the dictionaries trace to 1853; but its meanings are rarely psychological. According to the *O.E.D.*, it results from the exact opposite of creative blockage or psychological inhibition, being defined as "a form of cramp or spasm affecting certain muscles of the hand and fingers essential to writing, and resulting from *excessive* use of these" (my italics). Fenichel is not the first investigator to see writer's cramp as a psychological condition, but he is one of only a very few.[7] As for *block*, as psychological impediment or obstacle, the earliest citation is 1931.[8]

That Bergler should have coined the term *writer's block* and become its foremost theoretician is richly ironic. In his lifetime, Bergler published twenty-five books (some of them still in print), as well as three hundred or so articles. Between 1946 and his death in 1962, Bergler's books appeared at a rate of one or two a year; at the time of his death, approximately two dozen completed manuscripts, over one hundred projected manuscripts in various stages of completion, and dozens of articles remained unpublished.[9] He accomplished all this in the course of a psychoanalytic practice of thirty-five years, eleven in Vienna and twenty-four in New York City, to which he emigrated in the late 1930s, like so many European psychoanalysts. Among Bergler's books are studies of gambling, frigidity, laughter, fashion, divorce, money neurosis, middle age, and homosexuality. Early in his career in Vienna, Bergler established a reputation as a specialist in sexual dysfunction—in part for his work as assistant director of the Psychoanalytic Freud Clinic, in part for several papers he coauthored with its director, Eduard Hitschmann. But as Bergler's investigations diversified, a "discovery" or extension of Freudian theory, rather than any particular subject matter, began to characterize his work. Bergler terms this discovery "psychic masochism," or "the basic neurosis"[10]—the key, he believed, to a variety of disturbances, including writer's block, and the cornerstone of a theoretical and therapeutic edifice that he hoped would become "Berglerian psychotherapeutic treatment."

The peculiarities of Bergler's literary character and career reflect interestingly on the origins of the term *writer's block*. Within the psychoanalytic community, Bergler seems to have been largely ignored—something of a feat, given the number of articles and books he wrote and the prominence of some of the journals and presses that published his work. Dr. Melvyn Iscove, a trustee of the Edmund and Marianne Bergler Psychiatric Foundation, writes of Bergler's having been "the center of an ongoing controversy," but does so in a way that raises doubts. Bergler's theories, Iscove explains (and the weird italics are his own), "were hotly (and too briefly) contested within his circle of colleagues and *somewhat* beyond it, but they tended to be summarily *rejected*—seemingly on an emotional basis, and often with the flimsiest 'arguments' unworthy of their proponents—precisely because they touched on unconscious material too painful, too deeply repressed to become the subject matter of dispassionate discussion."[11] In other words, Bergler was mostly ignored.

What would it have been like, though, to have challenged so voluminous and indefatigable an antagonist? "The arguments promoted against the existence of writer's block," claims Bergler in defiance of what he calls the "supercilious ignorance" of hostile reviewers,

> are neither convincing nor intelligent. Critics, confronted with a new critical problem, reacted as might be expected: with naive superciliousness, mobilization of conscious rationalization, misunderstanding, and refusal to consume the appropriate diet: humble pie. With every ignoramus appointing himself a psychiatric-psychoanalytic expert, the results confirm my old conviction: the difference between people who know what they are talking about, and those who don't is that the latter tell the former what it is all about.[12]

Those critics who responded with comparable aggression, explains Iscove, "and challenged the Bergler theory in writing were apparently discouraged from continuing the exchange by the vigor with which Bergler, also in writing, defended his position and challenged their objections."[13]

None of which is to suggest that Bergler was *only* a joke or universally scorned. His articles and books, including *The Writer and Psychoanalysis*, can be ingenious and even tactful, as well as vigorous, in their modifications and extensions of Freudian theory. And several literary critics of repute have found them useful. Lionel Trilling, for example, thinks "Dr. Bergler has done good service in warning us against taking at their face value a writer's statements against himself, the more especially when they are frank"; Christopher Ricks approvingly quotes him on blushing, finding his theories "clearly apt to art though necessarily perilous for art"; and Norman Holland quotes him on Shakespeare, calling his interpretations "considerably more flexible" than those of his disciples.[14] Yet Bergler's works are rich in many of the most dubious and unsettling features of their kind. Consider, for example, the matter of evidence. Bergler founds his theories on clinical material; he has treated thirty-six writers in twenty years, all of them successfully. These writers, he tells us, were of substance: "At least half of my patients have been considered first rate by professional critics."[15] A remark such as this makes the heart sink, especially given the relative skepticism of Bergler's earlier treatment of psychoanalytic matters and his insistence that one move beyond or behind the orthodox Freudian view.[16]

Bergler's strengths and weaknesses are important because they are representative and because the term *writer's block* grows out of his sort of world; or, to be precise, out of a world of largely American—it is a very American term—psychoanalytic aesthetics. It became a part of the language, a well-known term, in the 1950s and early 1960s, its familiarity, appropriately, deriving from everyday speech rather than written record. These were times of intense American faith and interest in psychoanalysis, and of an intense interest within American psychology in general, as well as within American psychoanalysis, in creativity. The complaints of Alfred Kazin about "the purringly complacent formulas of Dr. Edmund Bergler"[17] are directed at a whole generation of psychoanalytic "pundits," as is his disapproval of Bergler's rigidity and reductivism. When Bergler claims that writer's block has but a single cause, that "every writer has had one basic conflict,"[18] his assurance is by no means unique or extreme. For A. A. Brill, long the acknowledged head of psychoanalysis in America, "the poet *invariably* [my italics] subordinates the thought to the feeling, the affect always comes first"; and "all persons analyzed by me who show poetic talent and who were recognized as poets by the world— all of them shared definite oral-erotic fixations."[19] Of course, reductivism and complacency of this sort are hardly American inventions; they merely flourish under proper conditions. Psychoanalysis encountered much less resistance in America than in Europe, and it was quickly (or relatively quickly) accepted by, and associated with, both medical psychiatry and medicine in general. The prestige and authority of "science" and its institutions in America smoothed and shaped its way. Hence the air of medical substance, of a treatable condition, assumed by writer's block; hence also the suspicion of something bogus or unearned about its claims.

Philip Roth is good and funny about these matters, in part because he appreciates the strengths, as well as the weaknesses, of Bergler's world. In *My Life as a Man* (1974), Roth's novelist hero and alter ego, Peter Tarnapol, recounts a dispute he has had with his analyst, Dr. Spielvogel (late of *Portnoy's Complaint*). One day, in the third year of his analysis, Tarnapol discovers that Spielvogel has written an article for the *American Forum for Psychoanalytic Studies,* in its special number on creativity. Spielvogel's article, "Creativity: The Narcissism of the Artist," features what Tarnapol quickly realizes is a portrait of himself, crudely disguised as "a successful Italian-American poet in his forties." Tarnapol is appalled at what he reads and says so in terms that echo some of what I have said about Bergler. The strength of this passage, though, derives not only from how funny and accurate it is in denouncing Spielvogel but also from its obvious excess and unfairness, so eventually—and Roth confirms this elsewhere—one sees something of strength in Spielvogel, or at least in some of the assumptions he represents.

> Up to this point in the article the patients described by Spielvogel had been "an actor," "a painter," and "a composer"—so this *had* to be me. Only I had *not* been in my forties when I first became Spielvogel's patient; I'd come to him at age twenty-nine, wrecked by a mistake I'd made at twenty-six. Surely between a man in his forties and a man in his twenties there are differences of experience, expectation, and character that cannot be brushed aside so easily as this. . . . And "successful"? Does that word (in my mind, I immediately began addressing Spielvogel directly), does that word describe the tenor of my life at that time? . . . And surely it goes without saying that to disguise (in my brother's words) "a nice civilized Jewish boy" as something called "an Italian-American," well that is to be somewhat dim-witted about matters of social and cultural background that might well impinge upon a person's psychology and values. And while we're at it, Dr. Spielvogel, a poet and a novelist have about as much in common as a jockey and a diesel driver. Somebody ought to tell you that, especially since "creativity" is your subject here. . . . You cannot begin to make sense about "creativity" or "the artist" or even "narcissism" if you are going to be so insensitive to fundamental distinctions having to do with age, accomplishment, background and vocation.[20]

"And so it went," Tarnapol continues, "my chagrin renewed practically with each word, I could not read a sentence in which it did not seem to me that the observation was off, the point missed, the nuance blurred—in short, the evidence rather munificently distorted so as to support a narrow and unilluminating thesis at the expense of the ambiguous and perplexing actuality" (p. 240). Finally, from a later passage:

> Just read on. Read the whole hollow pretentious meaningless thing, right on down to the footnotes from Goethe and Baudelaire to prove a connection between "narcissism" and "art"! "As Sophocles has written,"—and that constitutes *evidence!* Oh, you ought to go through this thing, line by line, and watch the ground shift beneath you! Between every paragraph there's a hundred foot drop! (Pp. 246–47)

Yet Spielvogel is, as Roth and Tarnapol acknowledge, capable of real insight and tact. When Tarnapol recovers from his tirade, he sends Spielvogel copies of two stories he has recently written:

> Not because I wish to open my case up to a renewed investigation in your office (though I see how you might interpret these manuscripts in that way), but because of your interest in the processes of art. . . . Your eminent colleague Ernst Kris has noted that "the psychology of artistic style is unwritten," and my suspicion (aroused by past experience) is that you might be interested in taking a crack at it. (P. 225)

The note to Spielvogel concludes with a request that the latter's "speculations" not be published without permission. It also contains a gentle chiding that recalls Bergler on "professional critics": "Yes, [the article on creativity] is still a sore point, but not so sore (I've concluded) as to outweigh this considered impulse to pass on for your professional scrutiny these waking dreams whose 'unconscious' origins (I must warn you) may not be so unconscious as a professional might like to conclude at first glance" (p. 225).

Spielvogel's response—this is the last of the passages I shall quote—is professional in an altogether different and more positive sense, and it makes Tarnapol wonder whether he was wrong to have left him:

> It was thoughtful of you to send on to me your two new stories. I read them with great interest and enjoyment, and as ever, admiration for your skills and understanding. The two stories are so different and yet so expertly done, and to my mind balance each other perfectly. The scenes with Sharon in the first I found especially funny, and in the second the fastidious attention that the narrative voice pays to itself struck me as absolutely right, given his concerns (or "human concerns" as the Zuckerman of

"Salad Days" would have said in his undergraduate seminar). What a sad and painful story it is. Moral, too, in the best, most serious way. You appear to be doing well. I wish you continued success with your work.

Sincerely,

Otto Spielvogel. (P. 225)

Whether or not Bergler was capable of such a letter, his writings often reveal shifts or discrepancies in critical acumen and tact comparable to those that puzzle and exasperate Tarnapol; sensibly qualified and skeptical passages (even witty ones, as when he concludes that "sometimes writing is the simplest way out—even for the writer")[21] nestle cheek by jowl with the Berglerian equivalent of "As Sophocles has written."

All of which is by way of suggesting that the term *writer's block* grows out of a particular place and time. Philip Roth and his fictional alter egos might think of themselves as suffering from writer's block; Philip Larkin, who produced poems at the snail-like rate of "about four a year, of which one is no good," [22] would not. (Nor, it could be argued, would any Frenchman or German—if only because there is no equivalent term in either of their languages.)[23] Larkin is not blocked, we might say, he is simply unprolific; but this is less of a distinction than it sounds, because if Philip Roth (or perhaps I should say Peter Tarnapol) was a poet and managed only three poems a year, he would be blocked. *Unprolific*, after all, is as much a metaphor as *blocked*; both are figurative and speculative terms, though with very different implications.

Before writers were *blocked*, they *dried up* or were *stuck in a rut*. Larkin's acceptance of his modest output resulted, I assume, from an appropriately conservative and chastening conviction that "that's all there is." Responsibility was assumed openly, with a sly pride. This is neither American nor psychoanalytic. When Larkin does use the word *block*, it is in a context rich in defensive irony, as in the following exchange with an American interviewer:

You didn't mention a schedule for writing. . . .

Yes, I was afraid you'd ask about writing. Anything I say about poems is bound to be retrospective, because in fact I've written very little since moving into this house, or since *High Windows*, or since 1974, whichever way you like to put it. But when I did write them, well, it was in the evenings, after work, after washing-up (I'm sorry: you would call this "doing the dishes"). It was a routine like any other. And it worked very well: I don't think you can write a poem for more than two hours. After that you're going round in circles, and it's much better to leave it for twenty-four hours, by which time your subconscious or whatever has solved the block and you're ready to go on.[24]

"Your subconscious or whatever" is the telling phrase here, along with "you would call this 'doing the dishes.'" These phrases, together with Larkin's frank (if not exactly un-self-conscious) acceptance of his state, make clear how unlikely he would be to think of himself as blocked, and how distant and alien he finds the culture that produced the term.

This, as I have suggested, may be in part because to think of oneself as blocked is to shift responsibility away from the self, to externalize and objectify the cause of one's difficulties. Lack of substance or flow is not the problem; the problem is an obstacle or impediment, like a growth or foreign body. Which is reassuring not only because it frees the subject from guilt (though try telling this to a blocked writer) but because it suggests something curable. No wonder the term has caught on so quickly. To be *stuck in a rut* is different again because it occupies a middle ground between blockage and desiccation. On the one hand, it is the rut that is to blame; on the other hand, the term suggests mindless or willful persistence: people who are stuck in a rut lack imagination or need to shift gears. A comparable duality attends *inhibition* (as in *creative inhibition*), a precursor to *block* in the psychoanalytic literature. Being inhibited is wrong, as well as a shame; it is something one works to overcome. The metaphor of creative powers as *frozen* also suggests both blockage and dearth because what causes the stoppage can be conceived of either as something external, a meteorological contingency, or as "frigidity" or lack—of warmth, or creative fire or spark, or life.

Such doubleness is suggested in the only other reference I have found to blockage in Larkin's writings, in "The Life with a Hole in It," which first appeared in print in the 1974 Christmas *Poetry Book Society Supplement*.

"THE LIFE WITH A HOLE IN IT"

When I throw back my head and howl
People (women mostly) say
But you've always done what you want,
You always get your own way
—A perfectly vile and foul
Inversion of all that's been.
What the old ratbags mean
Is I've never done what I don't.

So the shit in the shuttered château
Who does his five hundred words
Then parts out the rest of the day
Between bathing and booze and birds
Is far off as ever, but so
Is that spectacled schoolteaching sod
(Six kids, and the wife in pod,
And her parents coming to stay) . . .

Life is an immobile, locked,
Three-handed struggle between
Your wants, the world's for you, and (worse)
The unbeatable slow machine
That brings what you'll get. Blocked,
They strain round a hollow stasis
Of havings-to, fear, faces.
Days sift down it constantly. Years.[25]

What interests me about Larkin's use of "blocked" here is its subtle difference from the earlier reference. Once again, blame is not shifted: as the title suggests, the problem is ultimately a lack, not an impediment. What is new and interesting is the rhyme with "locked." As in expressions such as "inhibited" or "stuck in a rut," "blocked" here occupies a middle ground: something stands in the way, to be sure, but that something must be the self, "your wants," because what lies outside and opposes them—the world's wants and "The unbeatable slow machine / That brings what you'll get"—is given; hardly something you can cut away, like a growth. The "three-handed struggle" that immobilizes Larkin is really a two-handed struggle: between the self and "Life." Here also Larkin is conservative and chastening, though in this case "that's all there is to say about matters" replaces "that's all there is." And because this is a poem rather than an interview, and Larkin is a true poet (even in a minor poem), gone is the hint of sly, easy pride in "I was afraid you'd ask about writing."

Another way of talking about blockage involves a familiar comparison with nature. For example, in Wordsworth's "Resolution and Independence," a poem that is partly about the loss of "genial faith," by which is meant faith in genius or poetic power, as well as a more general optimism or good humor,

All things that love the sun are out of doors;
The sky rejoices in the morning's birth;

The grass is bright with rain-drops;—on the moors
The hare is running races in her mirth.
(8–11)

Almost at once, though, Wordsworth is cut off from this scene, as "fears and fancies thick upon me came." Such a contrast is found in several of Wordsworth's best-known poems, including "Tintern Abbey" and "Ode: Intimations of Immortality." In each case, the speaker's deadness or sterility—"the fear that kills" in "Resolution and Independence," loss of the "visionary gleam" in "Ode: Intimations," the "decay" of "genial spirits" in "Tintern Abbey"—is seen as unnatural and hence as a form of what today we would call blockage. The contrast with nature supports the *in*organic or abnormal character of inhibited or sterile states. This, at least, is how Gerard Manley Hopkins seems to have read Wordsworth, in "Thou art indeed just, Lord," in which the organic metaphor of drought is swamped or clogged by "unnatural" intimations, and in which Wordsworth's influence is obvious:

> . . . See, banks and brakes
> Now, leaved how thick! laced they are again
> With fretty chervil, look, and fresh wind shakes
> Them; birds build—but not I build; no, but strain,
> Time's eunuch, and not breed one work that wakes,
> Mine, O thou Lord of life, send my roots rain.
> (9–14)

The characteristic cramping or strain of the verse itself here, as of the buried suggestion of clogged banks and brakes in the opening lines ("leaved so thick!"), reinforces Hopkins's sense of the unnaturalness of his state and contradicts the concluding metaphor of parching or desiccation—unless rain, like the "fresh wind" that shakes the thick-leaved banks and brakes, will shake free or wash away what clogs. Like Wordsworth, in the 1805 version of *The Prelude*, Hopkins ultimately thinks of himself "as a clouded, not a waning moon" (10.918).

At which point other and more complicating metaphors arise. Sometimes when writers cannot write they are merely "lying fallow" or "priming the pump." "When the tank runs dry," explains Mark Twain, "you've only to leave it alone and it will fill up again in time."[26] In other words, fallow periods—to bump one metaphor up against another—can be grist for the mill. But how do you differentiate such a period—what Keats calls "delicious diligent indolence"[27]—from one of blockage? And at what point does a problem with a piece of writing become a block? When writers finds themselves, like Thackeray, "sitting for hours before my paper, not doing my book, but incapable of doing anything else,"[28] they may be at work, solving a problem. They are not necessarily victims of *writer's block* if the problem cannot be solved. This, at least, is the way E. M. Forster at one point chose to see matters, in a manner reminiscent of that of Larkin. Forster claimed, despite his relative inactivity, to find writing pleasant. When, after much agonizing, he decided he would never be able to figure out the plot of a work provisionally entitled "Arctic Summer," he simply gave up. He had a technical problem he could not solve.

But this account of the problem is too simple, too much something out of what Norman Mailer once called the "I am dumb" school of English intellectuals. To begin with, Forster himself was hardly immune to fears of blockage, or of what he called "going smash":[29] "You ask me about my work, I feel too sympathetic to keep silent, I am dried up. Not in my emotions, but in their expression. I cannot write at all"; "For a solid hour and a half have done nothing, and so it was this morning. Shall I force myself to begin a book and trust to imagination dropping in some time?" Nor was he without these fears while at work on "Arctic Summer": "I seem through at last, and others begin to suspect it. Idleness, depressing conditions, need for a fresh view of all life before I begin writing each time, paralyze me. Just possible I may finish *Arctic Summer,* but see nothing beyond."[30] It was only many years later that Forster characterized his problems as technical, as matters of plot ("I had not settled what is going to happen, and this is why the novel remains a fragment").[31] And the context of his remarks, unlike that of previous quotations, was public—an interview rather than a private letter. Privately, Forster was less composed and superficial, even while arguing the common-sense view. The doubleness of his attitude is seen clearly in this passage from a letter of 3 March 1920 to Forrest Reid:

I think that I've stopped creating rather than become uncreative: you are quite right there. I have never felt I'm used up. It's rather that the scraps of imagination and observation in me won't coalesce as they used to. Whether I'm happy or sad or well or unwell (and I've been all in the last eight years, *very* sad, *very* happy) the internal condition doesn't change. I'm sure that the Psycho-Analysts would nip on to it, and might possibly diagnose a toad. But I mistrust not so much their judgement as their influence. I should be very reluctant to let them meddle with me and make me change my estimate as to what is within myself. What they call a toad may be something that I call a precious stone. . . .

These people have no sense of literature and art and I regard with foreboding and resentment their offers to turn an artist upside down.[32]

Noteworthy here, in addition to Forster's distrust of psychoanalytic "meddling" and of the standard of psychoanalytic aesthetics, is the implied inadequacy or inaccuracy of metaphors such as "dried up" and "fallow." "I think that I've stopped creating rather than become uncreative. . . . I have never felt I'm used up." That Forster nonetheless resorts to metaphors of dearth and desiccation to describe his problems, and that they creep in again in the very next sentence (in "scraps" and the implication that the power to coalesce is lacking), suggests the need for a new—and more precise—terminology.

The simple answer, in other words, will not always do: sometimes technical problems arise for nontechnical reasons. For example, in 1876 Twain was "tearing along on a new book," the first sixteen chapters of which he wrote in a summer. It would be finished, he was certain, "in six working weeks."[33] He then stopped work on the book, leaving it for three or so years. When he took it up again in 1879 or 1880, he added another two chapters, and then another three; he then left off again until the summer of 1883. In 1884, eight years and seven books from that original summer, he completed *The Adventures of Huckleberry Finn*. Twain's problem was superficially technical, a matter of plot and structure. At the end of the summer of 1876, Twain had brought Huck and Jim to the mouth of the Ohio at Cairo, Illinois. The aim of their journey down the Mississippi had been just this point, for Cairo meant literal freedom for Jim: "He'd be a free man the minute he seen it [Cairo], but if he missed it he'd be in the slave country again and no more show for freedom."[34] But something in Twain resisted the logical move upstream: first he allowed Huck and Jim to float by Cairo in the fog at night; then, after Huck decides to "wait for dark, and start back in the canoe,"[35] the canoe disappears. All that is left for Huck and Jim is "just to go along down with the raft till we got a chance to buy a canoe to go back in"[36]—a scheme that allows Twain to transgress, even as he honors, the logic of his plot. Perhaps in recognition of the temptations to which he is succumbing, Twain ends the chapter with a steamboat "smashing straight through the raft."

This steamboat is unexpectedly—memorably—ferocious, as though freighted (or fraught) with all its author's irritation with *Huck Finn*, his anger and frustration:

> She was a big one, and she was coming in a hurry, too, looking like a black cloud with rows of glow-worms around it; but all of

a sudden she bulged out, big and scary, with a row of wide-open furnace doors shining like red-hot teeth, and her monstrous bows and guards hanging right over us. There was a yell at us, and a jingling of bells to stop the engines, a pow-wow of cussing, and whistling of steam—and as Jim went overboard on one side and I on the other, she came smashing straight through the raft.[37]

The narrative breaks off at this point.

When Twain took up *Huck Finn* two or so years later, he introduced the episode at the Grangerfords. This episode added two chapters, but it did little to advance Huck and Jim north, as the plot demanded. Some months later, Twain wrote chapters nineteen to twenty-one. These are the chapters in which Twain at last gives in to whatever pressures had been resisting the demands of the plot. The raft is resuscitated, the Duke and the King are introduced, and the current carries them all downstream. Twain reintroduces the raft because it perfectly suits the schemes of the Duke and King; these characters, who are smarter and stronger than Huck and Jim, provide an excuse to continue the journey downstream.

Once Twain comes to terms with his decision—or desire—to continue downstream, several of the finest and most famous of his descriptions of the beauty of the river and river life flow forth from him—followed by a surge of creative activity similar to that of the summer of 1876. "I'm booming these days," he writes to W. D. Howells, "it is no more trouble to me to write than it is to lie."[38] Twain finished the novel in a summer, working at the rate of three thousand to four thousand words a sitting. "What has happened," comments Henry Nash Smith,

> is that Mark Twain has abandoned his original narrative plan and has substituted for it a different structural principle. . . . [T]he action is not dictated by the reasonable if risky plan for Jim's escape but by the powerful image of Huck and Jim "a sliding down the river," "free and easy" on the raft. This image now embodies the only meaning which freedom and safety have in the narrative. It becomes the positive value replacing the original goal of actual freedom for Jim. The new goal is a subjective state, having its empirical basis in the solitude of the friends in their "home" on "the big river" but consisting in a mode of experience rather than an outward condition.[39]

The technical problem that prevented Twain from completing *Huck Finn* rose out of a desire to continue down the Mississippi. This desire has been explained in common-sense terms: Twain knew the lower Mississippi from his piloting days and did not know the Ohio.[40] But there is also a plausible psychological explanation, one that sees Twain as caught up in precisely the sort of conflict outlined by Freud and the early or orthodox psychoanalytic theorists discussed in the next chapter. According to this view, the logic of the plot and what Henry Nash Smith calls "actual freedom" or "an outward condition" stand ranged against an internal or "subjective" meaning, one associated with the author's past and with a realm beyond or outside logic and social restraint. Only when these earlier or inner pressures are admitted is the creative flow—how apt the metaphor at this point—released.[41]

Support for this view lies in the number and prominence of Twain's lapses from his new scheme or solution. For example, at the end of chapter eighteen, once Huck has been reunited with Jim on the raft, but before the Duke and the King have been introduced, Huck speaks of being "free and safe once more": "He said there warnt no home like a raft. . . . You feel mighty free and easy and comfortable on a raft."[42] Huck and Jim have forgotten the original plan of escape up the Ohio, but a new plan has not been introduced. In the next chapter, still before the appearance of the Duke and the King, Huck even finds a canoe, but says nothing of using it to return to the Ohio, as planned. "Thereafter," concludes Henry Nash Smith, "although thematically Huck and Jim might be expected to seize the first opportunity of escaping from their captors in order to head upstream, we are not surprised that they fail to do so. When they momentarily elude the Duke and the King after the Wilks episode (at the end of chapter twenty-nine), Huck says: 'away we went, a sliding down the river, and it *did* seem so good to be free again and all by ourselves on the big river and nobody to bother us.'"[43]

These instances suggest that the real problems confronting Twain in *Huck Finn* were psychological rather than technical, and that therefore it makes sense to refer to him as blocked. The term brings us closer to the nature of his difficulty, takes us beyond or behind problems of plot and structure. Its strength lies in its precision as a metaphor, its ability to describe economically a situation or problem for which no other comparably accurate means of description exists. Support for this view can be found in Twain's oft-expressed longing for escape or release in the letters of this period; in his failure to complete any book-length project between July 1875 and January 1880, "a much longer period than usual"; and in the relative unsatisfactoriness of what was published in the two years that followed.[44]

In one sense, of course, there is something absurd about associating Twain with writer's block: not only because he wrote so much and so fluently but also because, even in the case of *Huck Finn*, there is little evidence of authorial agonizing, except for a few sardonic references to the slowness of the book's progress—in addition, that is, to speculation about displaced authorial violence or frustration. The absence is telling, because misery is at least as important an index or distinguishing feature of writer's block as silence. Joseph Conrad, for example, was hardly an unproductive writer. The Canterbury, or Dent, edition of his complete works consists of twenty-six volumes, and he wrote numerous letters. But as anyone who has looked at these letters will attest, writing for Conrad was a type of purgatory. Here is an example—especially eloquent but by no means atypical— from 1898, while he was at work on *The Rescue:*

> I sit down religiously every morning, I sit down for eight hours every day—and the sitting down is all. In the course of that working day of eight hours I write three sentences which I erase before leaving the table in despair . . . it takes all my resolution and power of self-control to refrain from butting my head against the wall. I want to howl and foam at the mouth but I daren't do it for fear of waking the baby and alarming my wife.[45]

Passages such as these remind us that, for all its shadowiness and complexity, *writer's block* is neither a meaningless term nor one that applies exclusively to Americans. When Anthony Burgess declares, apropos of Dashiell Hammett, that "writer's block . . . is not calculated to impress British writers who have to regard literary paralysis as a luxury,"[46] we should recall Conrad. Similarly, when Burgess's model in these matters, Samuel Johnson, contends that "a man may write at any time if he will set himself *doggedly* to it,"[47] Conrad again provides an answer. "It is outrageous," he writes of a comparable, if implicit, accusation from his agent (*Under Western Eyes* was the work in question): "Does he think I am the sort of man who wouldn't finish the story in a week if he could? Do you? Why? For what reason? Is it my habit to lie about drunk for days instead of working? I reckon he knows well enough I don't."[48] The irony of Conrad's retort is that it recalls Johnson's own difficulties: not drunkenness, but what W. J. Bate calls a "massive . . . inner resistance" to writing—"especially after the accumulated fatigue from having fought that resistance for so long":

> He might say, and mean it, that "a man might write at any time if he will set himself *doggedly* to it." But as with Coleridge . . . the crushing burden of self-demand could make almost any other activity pleasant by contrast. Again, as with Coleridge, talking

was infinitely preferable. For there one's powers of expression could be exercised in the highest degree, and yet the result was constantly flying away instead of remaining there on paper to rebuke him. Hence his dislike of revision, and his eagerness (conceded under a certain bravado) to despatch a work to the press without rereading it, or his reluctance to reread it later.[49]

No one would deny that writing, like all forms of creative activity, requires work and the exercise of will power, or that some would-be writers are simply lazy or lack skill or facility. Nor would anyone deny that writing is full of difficulties and problems (a creative writer, according to Roland Barthes, is someone for whom language is a problem).[50] Nevertheless, as the example of Conrad suggests, writer's block need have nothing to do with lack of application. Nor need it "really," as others suggest, be a sign of incompetence or lack of talent; after all, the term can hardly apply to those who do not know how to write.

This is my objection to Rose's *Writer's Block: The Cognitive Dimension* and to all other attempts to attribute writer's block to cognitive errors or deficiencies. By *cognition* is meant those aspects of mental life concerned with knowing, including perceiving, comparing, contrasting, remembering, reasoning, and judging. It is traditionally contrasted with willing and feeling. *Cognitive science* is the attempt to study these phenomena as though they were separate from willing and feeling; thus it involves what George Miller calls "a necessary idealization, similar to ignoring wind resistance while working out the laws of gravitation."[51] When applied to writing, cognitive science examines, in Rose's words, "the way we carry out plans and strategies, or gauge information, and evaluate what we do."[52]

Cognitive science became particularly interested in creativity at approximately the time at which psychoanalysis was most popular and respected in America—the 1950s and early 1960s. A landmark in the history of creativity as a "field" (there has been a *Journal of Creative Behaviour* since 1967)—and a good way into it—is a speech given to the American Psychological Association in 1950 by its president, J. P. Guilford, at the time perhaps the world's foremost authority on cognition. Guilford's topic was the relation of creativity to general intelligence, as measured by IQ tests. Guilford began in the manner of predecessors such as Joseph Wallas and Joseph Rossman (and Hermann von Helmholtz and Jules Poincaré before them), by identifying a number of phases or stages in problem-solving. These were observation, memory, divergent thinking, convergent thinking, and evaluation. By divergent thinking, Guilford meant the ability to produce a variety or breadth of associations in response to ideas or stimuli; convergent thinking meant the ability to produce a single best or most complete answer to a problem. IQ tests, Guilford argued, measure only convergent thinking, whereas divergent thinking is much more likely to lie at the heart of creativity.[53]

When an approach such as Guilford's is applied to the genesis of a work of art or a piece of writing, a comparable but more specialized set or sequence of functions is outlined.[54] Cognitive psychology attempts to identify the necessary steps or stages in creation: *what* is required or needs to be done. Rose's study draws from this tradition, though it looks not at poets or novelists, but at a group of college students. These students possess what he calls "basic writing skills," which for some reason they cannot exercise. They therefore suffer from writer's block, which Rose defines as "an inability to begin or continue writing for reasons other than a basic lack of skill or commitment" (p. 3). Although Rose acknowledges the importance of psychological and sociological factors, he thinks that in some cases blockage can be attributed to cognitive causes—a cheering note for teachers of college writing and rhetoric (Rose's primary audience) because "cognitive problems are vulnerable to teaching and reteaching, conferencing, modeling" (p. xvii).

What, then, is a cognitive problem? Rose identifies six sorts, the harvest of a series of elaborately professional interviews and reconstructions (the students were videotaped while writing): the application of rigid, inappropriately invoked or incorrect rules of composition; misleading assumptions; premature editing; the absence of "appropriate planning and discourse strategies" (p. 4); conflicting rules or strategies; and inadequately understood or inappropriate evaluative criteria. "These are not," according to Rose, "primarily emotional difficulties; they are cognitive blunders and are thus clarified through cognitive psychology's conceptual lens" (p. 16). But if by cognitive blunders are meant errors or deficiencies in knowledge, then these are the blunders of unskilled writers. Writers *know* not to invoke inappropriate or rigid rules, or to edit prematurely—even if they persist in doing so; and they know—as they know how to use a pencil or a typewriter—because they are writers, and this knowledge is a tool of their trade. These are "basic writing skills." Rose claims that students can be taught or counselled into not committing cognitive blunders. This may well be true, in which case they are being taught how to write, rather than how to overcome writer's block. Although blocked writers may well edit prematurely, such editing results from "emotional" causes—be they psychological or sociological—rather than "cognitive" ones. The question that matters, to use the jargon of the field, is conative or affective, not cognitive: Why do blocked writers persist in habits they must know are counterproductive? The students Rose ought to be interviewing (if it is writer's block he is studying) are those who have already been taught and counselled, have shown they can write, and then reverted to bad habits. These students are blocked writers, and nothing Rose could tell them—nothing they could learn—about their cognitive errors would be likely to be of much use.

In one sense, of course, to call the students whom Rose discusses "blocked" is perfectly logical: were it not for "obstructing" cognitive blunders, they could write. But this sort of obstruction—a matter of ignorance or bad advice—is not what is usually meant by writer's block; nor does it really fit Rose's own definition. In other words, *writer's block* is not only a new and shadowy term but also (or therefore) a loose one, frequently misapplied. One aim of this book is to sort out the term's looser and more vulnerable applications from those that actually mean something—a task that entails looking as carefully at the terms *writer* and *writing* as *block*. Rose's book—and the approach it represents—makes the necessity for this clear, not only in the ways I have discussed but also because literature is not its concern. For it reminds us that *writing* can mean both literary creation and the simple presentation or expression of words in written form. Rose's account of writer's block applies to writing in this second and, as it were, more prosaic sense, whereas my book aims to examine both of them, though the latter will be examined after or apart from more specifically literary accounts. Finally, though I disagree with Rose's approach—or his understanding of writer's block—his book offers sensible advice for would-be student-writers and is doubtless accurate about their most frequently committed errors.

A different set of complications concerns questions of value or quality in creative writing. When we say someone cannot write, we may mean he or she is no good rather than unable to put words to paper. Nor is it immediately clear that only the second sort of inability is properly called a block. The later Wordsworth, it could be said, was blocked, though he wrote ceaselessly. So also, to borrow in part from another medium, was Browning's Andrea del Sarto, "the faultless painter." In both these cases, a once or potentially present power—whatever makes the difference between the technically competent and the more than technically competent—can be thought of not as "fled" (as in Wordsworth's "Whither is fled the visionary gleam?"), or "thwarted" by others or external circumstances (which is the view Andrea professes), but as blocked. A working assumption of many therapists is that questions of quality are not only outside their expertise but also irrelevant; that anyone who feels impelled to write can be called a writer, whether he or she finds writing easy, merely attempts to write, or suffers long periods of inhibition between periods of productivity. In Bergler's words, "a person treated psychoanalytically for writing block may prove, after his block has been removed, a poor writer and better suited to some other occupation. However, the function of the psychoanalyst is not that of a critic."[55] This view is fair-minded, practical, and orthodox. It is also properly attentive to suffering, which may be no less severe for bad blocked writers than for good ones. Its modesty recalls Freud on the limits of psychoanalytic aesthetics, his sense that "psycho-analysis throws a satisfactory light upon some of the problems concerning arts and artists, but others escape it entirely."[56]

Chief among the aesthetic problems Freud thought beyond psychoanalysis are those connected with the formal or technical properties of art works. These, though, are precisely the qualities that matter "first and foremost" ("The Moses of Michelangelo," 13:218) to the artist. "Meaning is but little to these men," Freud once told Ernest Jones, "all they care for is line, shape, agreement of contours."[57] Freud sometimes sees this ability to mold or determine a work's formal properties as the artist's distinguishing strength; a "mysterious power of shaping" (*Introductory Lectures,* 16:376), rather than any subject matter, sets the artist apart from other human beings. Nevertheless, in his "aesthetic," Freud often treats formal or technical qualities as a mere "bonus" or "bribe" in a work; they facilitate or sweeten the disturbing drives or fantasies that are the work's true or underlying motive and meaning. For the artist, though, the reverse is often the case: the emotions aroused by "ideational content," in the extreme formulation of Roger Fry's *The Artist and Psycho-analysis* (1924), one of the earliest attacks on Freud in this realm, should be regarded, in Jones's paraphrase, "as baits designed to attract the attention of the laity, who were not concerned primarily with art itself, though the baits might lead them toward that sacred arcana."[58] W. H. Auden makes the same point in specifically literary terms: what the poet or writer "is most aware of are technical problems. . . . [A]nd the psychoanalyst, concentrating on the symbols, ignores words; in his treatment of symbols and facts he fails to explain why of two works dealing with the same unconscious material one is aesthetically good and the other bad."[59]

This is not quite fair. First, it is not true that Freud's works are devoid of judgments of value: for instance, in "Psychopathic Characters on the Stage" (1942 [1905–6]), Freud offers clear reasons for preferring *Hamlet* to *Die Andere,* a play by the Austrian novelist and

dramatist Hermann Bahr; and in *The Interpretation of Dreams* Freud
makes a similar comparison between Franz Grillparzer's *Die Ahnfrau*
and *Hamlet*. These are not, I grant, especially difficult or daring discriminations, but they are discriminations. Second, it is not true that
Freud is inattentive to or "ignores" words. He is keenly aware of the
reach and power—and the enriching complication—of words; one
need only recall his treatment of parapraxes in Shakespeare—or its
influence, for instance, on William Empson.

In Empson's famous examination of Hopkins's poem "The Windhover," in *Seven Types of Ambiguity*, interpretation turns on the single
word "buckle" in line 10. The word can mean either "gird up" or
"collapse," which are almost opposite. Empson comments in a way
that makes clear his debt to Freud on words, as well as his sense of
Freud's importance to literary criticism:

> We seem to have a clear case of the Freudian use of opposites,
> when two things thought of as incompatible, but desired in-
> tensely by different systems of judgements, are spoken of simul-
> taneously by words applying to both; both desires are thus given
> a transient and exhausting satisfaction, and the two systems of
> judgement are forced into open conflict before the reader. Such
> a process, one might imagine, could pierce the regions that un-
> derlie the whole structure of our thought; could tap the energies
> of the very depths of the mind.[60]

Still, even granted the unfairness of Auden's particular charges,
Freud's criteria of value are usually implicit and not always what Auden or Roger Fry have in mind. Unity and complexity, for example,
are values not in themselves—not part of some "sacred arcana"—but
only insofar as they contribute to the acceptance of forbidden wishes.
Moreover, Freud's reticence about formal matters or "artistic technique" quickly became orthodoxy—and stayed so for some time.
Here, for instance, is Marie Bonaparte, in her book on Edgar Allan
Poe: "But there are men with a mysterious gift who can clothe these
daydreams . . . in forms which allow others, also, to dream their
dreams with them. How this is done, and what is the nature of the
pleasure premium of form and beauty which draws their fellows is
an aesthetic problem still unsolved."[61]

Of course, not all Freud's followers, even the earliest and most orthodox, were as modest or reticent. Hanns Sachs, for example,
sought to apply psychoanalytic theory to questions of beauty; Ernst
Kris and others influenced by ego psychology sought a reconciliation
of form and content; and so also (and to more effect, in my opinion)
did the post-Kleinian and object-relations theorists who make up the

so-called British school. Nor are post-Kleinian speculations about the formal or technical properties of art works confined to the realm of theory. For example, Hanna Segal has written of her treatment of several authors whose "blocks" (the term she uses is "creative inhibitions") are measured qualitatively as well as quantitatively, in terms of an "aesthetic significance" or "artistic maturity" [62] she is fully willing to anatomize and define, and in specifically psychoanalytic terms. Although some of the creative people she talks of treating are unable to write or paint, others come to her because they know their work is less than it could be, as in the case of the patient who "did decorative handicraft work in preference to what she sometimes called 'real painting' . . . because she knew that though correct, neat, and pretty, her work failed to be moving and aesthetically significant." [63] Segal treats the patient on the assumption that "the effect of superficiality and prettiness" is an aesthetic weakness and that in certain cases such weakness is "curable," a sign neither of lack of ability nor of knowledge.

Another of Segal's patients, a journalist and would-be novelist, often complains "that he has no style of his own," a remark that recalls Paul Federn's influential 1931 essay on "neurotic styles." [64] Disfiguring stylistic tendencies—be they the needless repetitions and meaningless abstractions that Federn points to in his essay, or other forms of cumbersomeness, or flatness, or agitation—can be thought of as psychological in origin (Federn talks of authors who are consciously convinced of the truth of what they are saying, but whose styles suggest that they *unconsciously* doubt it). There is plenty of evidence that blocked writers often see their problems as qualitative rather than quantitative: not no ideas, but no good ones; or, in stylistic terms, not a lack of words, but the wrong words. Being blocked can mean, as for Kafka, having "to see the pages being covered endlessly with things one hates, that fill one with loathing, or at any rate with dull indifference." [65] George Gissing is good on this form of blockage, as in the following account of poor Edwin Reardon from *New Grub Street*:

> The ordering of his day was this. At nine, after breakfast, he sat down at his desk and worked till one. Then came dinner, followed by a walk. . . . At about half past three he again seated himself, and wrote until half past six, when he had a meal. Then once more to work from half past seven to ten. . . .
>
> Sometimes the three hours labour of a morning resulted in half a dozen lines, corrected into illegibility. His brain would not work; he could not recall the simplest synonyms; intolerable

faults of composition drove him mad. He would write a sentence beginning thus: "She took a book with a look of—;" or thus "A revision of this decision would have made him an object of derision." Or if the period were otherwise inoffensive, it ran in a rhythmic gallop which was torment to his ear. All this, in spite of the fact that his former books had been noticeably good in style. He had an appreciation of shapely prose which made him scorn himself for the kind of stuff he was now turning out.[66]

The mention of Andrea del Sarto and of Segal's painter patient raises questions of another sort. Why does the term *writer's block* exist, but not, say, *painter's block*, or *composer's block*—or even *scientist's block*, as in the twenty-five year incubation of Charles Darwin's *The Origin of Species?*[67] One obvious answer is that many more people write—or have writing difficulties—than paint or compose (or discover the theory of natural selection); writers need not be artists. But there are historical reasons as well. For example, in Plato's time a distinction was made between poets, philosophers, and musicians, on the one hand, and sculptors, painters, and builders, on the other hand. (There were also, of course, important distinctions within these groupings, especially for Plato.) The painter or sculptor was thought of as an artisan or craftsman, a *technitēs*. He was a craftsman because his task, or *technē*, was to make existence visible; to give body to life. Painters and sculptors were grouped with inventors, mathematicians, scientists, and technicians, "members of a group," in Kris's words, "that investigates and controls the external world."[68] According to Rudolf Arnheim, by way of Heidegger, "*technē* was a form of cognition—that is, of perceiving what exists." Painters and sculptors drew their precepts from mathematics; the human figure was formed "according to traditional canons of measurable proportion."[69] The poet, however, was associated with a different realm entirely: that of prophecy and madness. "There is a third form of possession or madness, of which the Muses are the source," says Socrates in the *Phaedrus*, "if any man come to the gates of poetry without the madness of the Muses, persuaded that skill alone will make him a good poet, then shall he and his works of sanity with him be brought to nought by the poetry of madness."[70]

These associations still live. No one would talk of, for instance, "cabinetmaker's block" or "potter's block," because in both cases the tasks involved are perceived as wholly conscious, within the maker's control. Although painters have long since attained the status of poets (Kris locates the change "since the sixteenth century"),[71] they may still retain, in their own and others' minds, more prosaic or craftsmanlike associations. The source of these associations, according to Marion Milner in *On Not Being Able to Paint* (1950), may be the medium itself, the body or externality of paint, or even charcoal. Milner believes that the writer shares a crucial goal with the painter: both seek a reconciliation or marriage of subject and object, of the artist's needs and the needs of an "other," whether "the world" or another person. The other for artists is also always in part their medium, and their art or struggle is to respect the otherness of the medium—its "real objective qualities"[72]—while still shaping it to express an inner or subjective conception. Milner believes that this struggle sets the artist apart from the daydreamer or the neurotic. The artist, unlike the neurotic, "does not try to deny or forget about illusion, instead he seeks to affirm it and take responsibility for it, even in its most primitive aspects." At the same time, though, he has to attend to the outside world, by which is meant not only the essential or underlying features of the medium but also "the demands of the external reality which is society. He has to accept some public artistic convention, such as the outline or the musical scale or the grammar and vocabulary of a particular language, something that his particular time and place in history make available for him to use in conveying his private idea."[73]

The distinction between painter or visual artist and writer emerges for Milner in the course of an experiment with free drawings. These drawings often express "ideas" or "thoughts" ("reflections about the human condition, as well as experiences with a medium")[74] that might well have been put in writing of some sort. Yet for Milner these drawings "embraced a wider range of bodily experience than intellectual verbal statements. . . . By stimulating the sense of rhythm, balance, colour, movement, they seemed to give a sense of a solider, deeper-rooted kind of knowing."[75] By "deeper-rooted kind of knowing," Milner does not mean "deeper"; she is pointing to rootedness and solidity. The medium of drawing offers more of an "other," more resistance, than does the medium of writing; it is less susceptible to the controlling "I." This sense of the bodily integrity of the medium, of the weight or substance of outward reality, recalls the ancient Greek association of painters and craftsmen—and of craftsmen and external reality. *Painter's block* has about it something of *cabinetmaker's block.*

Which is a relief for me, given the complications already adduced for writer's block itself. Nor have these complications been exhausted. For example, the matter of types of blockage has barely been touched on. In addition to broad distinctions between quality and quantity, there are a variety of generic distinctions to be considered when discussing the term *writer's block*. Paul Goodman, for instance, has written an article on the reasons why otherwise productive essayists and lyric poets cannot write fiction or drama—cannot, that is, imagine a story (in Goodman's words, the blocked storyteller "cannot imagine other actualities as his own . . . or his own actuality to be otherwise").[76] Comparably suggestive speculations might arise out of consideration of the reverse case (fluent novelists, say, who cannot— not will not—write critical or expository prose); as of other sorts of what might be called generic inhibition. Nor is generic inhibition a matter only of broad distinctions. It is easy to conceive of types of blockage within genres, as in the inability of otherwise fluent lyric poets, authors also of shorter narrative poems, to write epic—despite a passionate conviction of its importance and centrality. "Why should we be owls, when we can be Eagles?" asks Keats rhetorically, on the eve of one of his own (ultimately unrealized) epic excursions. And elsewhere, "Did our great Poets ever write short pieces?" (The answer, of course, is yes, as Keats himself well knew.)[77]

Coleridge is an example of a prolific writer who suffered from several sorts of *block*. "A poet . . . or that which once seem'd he" is part of an epitaph (of Coleridge's own making) sustained not only by the relative slimness of his poetic output, much of it produced in a year and a half (1797–98), but also by its famously incomplete and apologetic character. In the field of philosophy, in which Coleridge was comparably able and ambitious, he was also *blocked*—in relation, again, to his capacities: unable to complete a much-projected philosophical synthesis or system, the "Opus Maximum"; breaking the *Biographia Literaria* off at just the point where his own metaphysics should appear (with the infamous "Letter from a Friend" in chapter thirteen). At the same time—or for much of it—he was fluent as a journalist and a lecturer and was a voluminous correspondent. The "smothering weight" of which he complains in "Dejection: An Ode" was selective, affecting only those sorts of writing he valued most. "I think there are but 2 good ways of writing," Coleridge explained to his friend Thomas Poole, "one for immediate, & wide impression, tho' transitory—the other for permanence—Newspapers the first— the best one can do is the second."[78] If Coleridge was unblocked when writing for newspapers and periodicals, this was in part because he was writing neither poetry nor philosophy. To have been our first "modern journalist" or "professional intellectual" or "man of letters," as Marilyn Butler has called him,[79] was hardly an *ambition*. Moreover, even at times when he published nothing at all, not even journalism, he was often most prolific privately. For example, the Notebook entries of an otherwise barren 1803 intersperse a wealth of natural and philosophic observation, "which in better times would have gone into his poetry"[80]—or his philosophy—with despairing utterances of creative loss and debility. Coleridge had not "dried up" at such periods, it could be argued, but was blocked; and blocked only in some genres and not in others.

Writer's block can also be looked at or classified in terms of chronology. Some writers, for instance, take forever to get started, both in their careers as a whole and in respect to individual works. "And all your notes," cries Dorothea to Casaubon in ardent puzzlement, "all those rows of volumes—will you not now do what you used to speak of?—will you not now make up your mind what part of them you will use, and begin to write the book which will make your vast knowledge useful to the world?"[81] Casaubon never gets to the first sentence of his "Key to All Mythologies." In Albert Camus's *The Plague*, Joseph Grand never gets past it, despite years of effort. When Grand invites Dr Rieux into his parlor, Rieux sees "a table strewn with writing in a microscopic hand, crisscrossed with corrections." "It's my opening phrase," Grand tells him, "and it's giving me trouble, no end of trouble."[82] Here is how the phrase reads: "One fine morning in the month of May an elegant young horsewoman might have been seen riding a sorrel mare along the flowering avenues of the Bois de Boulogne." This sentence, though, is "only a rough draft": "Once I've succeeded in rendering perfectly the picture in my mind's eye, once my words have the exact tempo of the ride—the horse is trotting, one-two-three, one-two-three, see what I mean?—the rest will come more easily" (p. 96). But, of course, the sentence is never completed; the rest never comes. First, "elegant" is replaced by "slim"; next Grand feels "some anxiety about the adjective 'handsome.' In his opinion it didn't convey enough." Some days later, Grand confesses that "the word 'flowering' was bothering him considerably" (p. 124). When this last difficulty is overcome ("flower-strewn" replaces "flowering"), Grand feels triumphant. But only for a moment, because "spoken aloud, the numerous 's' sounds had a disagreeable effect and Grand stumbled over them, lisping here and there. He sat down crestfallen; then he asked the doctor if he might go. Some hard thinking lay ahead of him" (p. 125).

When next we hear of Grand's manuscript, its author is deathly ill and the comic features of his dilemma are muted:

Rieux was horrified by the rapid change that had come over his face, ravaged by the fires of the disease consuming him. However, he seemed more lucid and almost immediately asked them to get his manuscript from the drawer where he always kept

25

it. . . . There were some fifty pages of manuscript. Glancing through them, Rieux saw that the bulk of the writing consisted of the same sentence written again and again with small variants, simplifications or elaborations. Persistently the month of May, the lady on horseback, the avenues of the Bois recurred, regrouped in different patterns. (P. 238)

In despair, Grand asks Rieux to burn the manuscript: "The doctor hesitated, but Grand repeated his injunction in so violent a tone and with such agony in his voice that Rieux walked across to the fireplace and dropped the sheets on the dying fire. It blazed up and there was a sudden flood of light, a fleeting warmth in the room" (p. 239). This fleeting light and warmth signal release for Grand, but also paltriness and waste. For a moment, his ridiculous obsession is treated seriously, so one might well think of him, in the words of Patrick McCarthy, a biographer of Camus, "both as an expression of Camus's fear that he will be unable to work and an illustration of the uncertainty of language."[83] This fear of Camus's is identified explicitly as writer's block by another of his biographers, Herbert Lottman (in the French translation of Lottman's book, the term used is simply "blocage").[84] But the moment does not last; the comic note almost immediately returns. Grand recovers ("I can remember every word"),[85] and when last we see him has made yet another fresh start: "I've cut out all the adjectives."[86]

Grand cannot truly count as a blocked writer because he has never shown that he can write (though there is nothing much wrong with his sentence, in any of its forms). Not only has he never got past the Bois de Boulogne, he also has trouble with letters, even ones that will rescue him from an obscure, ill-paid job or win back the woman he loves. It is absurd of Grand to want to be a novelist. Still, the manner in which he proceeds—or fails to proceed—is characteristic of many a blocked writer. Like Casaubon, Grand is the victim of what George Eliot calls "that chilling ideal which crowd[s] . . . laborious uncreative hours."[87] Casaubon, though also a nonstarter, has at least written something: scholarly tractates or "Parergons," the aim of which is to best and impress his rivals, the menacing Carp, Pike, and Tench. In these works, "references were extensive, . . . but not entirely shoreless; and sentences were actually to be written."[88]

As for blockage of the opposite sort—writers who are productive early on and then never write again—examples are legion. At the beginning of his career, Dashiell Hammett "read all kinds of magazines—poetry magazines; literary magazines; pulps—and sent them what they wanted."[89] He wrote the first four of his five novels—*Red*

Harvest, The Dain Curse, The Maltese Falcon, and *The Glass Key*—in addition to book reviews, poems, short stories, and a novella, in three years. All of this he accomplished by writing in the mornings and evenings; he held down an advertising job during the day. *The Thin Man,* Hammett's last novel, was published three years after *The Glass Key* and was followed, for the next twenty years, by silence. Yet he never gave up trying to write novels, "plugging away at it" [90] even after his output grew to resemble that of Grand: "I spend most of my time rewriting . . . most of what I had written. I bet if I worked hard enough on those few pages, I could whittle them down to a phrase." [91]

In cases such as Hammett's, of writers who start off well and then stop, it is especially difficult to distinguish blockage from creative exhaustion—from having nothing more to say. On occasion Hammett seems to have thought he had simply run out of gas: "He could not write, it seemed to him, because he had nothing to write about," explains Diane Johnson; at some moments it seemed to him that "his life, in some sense, had ended when he left San Francisco and obscurity, and his work and family, and the social class to which he owed allegiance but was uncomfortable in." [92] This is also, in part, how P. N. Furbank explains Forster's falling into silence as a novelist. After speculating, first, that Forster was of the type Freud identified as "those wrecked by success," and, second, that, as Forster himself averred, "being a homosexual, he grew bored with writing about marriage and the relations of men and women," Furbank names "a third consideration, more general than either, and that is that Forster was one of those who have 'only one novel to write.'" Furbank explains:

> I mean that he received his whole inspiration—a vision, a kind of plot, a message—all at once, in early manhood. He became an artist because of that early experience, an experience of salvation, and his inspiration as a novelist always harked back to that moment of enlightenment. For this reason he was content to use and re-use many of the same plot materials. . . . For the same reason the social types and manners which ruled his imagination were those of his Edwardian youth. This was no small difficulty for a realistic novelist, though it would not have arisen for a poet. He already found it so with *A Passage to India,* and evidently it was bound to grow with every year or decade. [93]

Furbank is careful and tentative here; his interpretation is partial or contributory. What goes against it is the sort of material presented earlier in the discussion of "Arctic Summer," especially Forster's admission that "I have never felt I'm used up"; what supports it is the relative equanimity of his later years. Far from "plugging away," as did Hammett, Forster seems only rarely to have considered writing a new novel, and the letters of the period are much less anxious about his silence than those of earlier days. This calm, though, can be interpreted in several ways: Forster could as easily be said to have succumbed to his block—to have "lost heart" or "given up the fight"—as to have run out of steam.

I want to be very clear about this. I am not suggesting that the notion of creative exhaustion or depletion—that simply running out of ideas, or novels, or poems—is impossible or inadmissible as an explanation of a writer's silence, but only that it is an interpretation, as speculative and arguable as other interpretations. Neither Hammett nor late Forster can be classed satisfactorily as a novelist who simply had no more novels in him—but other novelists might well be. There is, for example, the case of Herman Melville. In 1856, after completing his last novel, *The Confidence Man*, Melville told Nathaniel Hawthorne, in a conversation noted in the latter's journals, that he "had pretty much made up his mind to be annihilated." Later Lemuel Shaw, Jr., his brother-in-law, reports that "Herman says he is not going to write anymore at present and wishes to get a place in the New York Customs House."[94] For the remaining thirty-five years of his life, Melville wrote no new fiction except the posthumously published long short story, *Billy Budd*, completed just before his death. This silence is the most famous in American literature and has been attributed variously to American philistinism—the lack of recognition or acclaim accorded *Moby-Dick* and the works that followed it—and Melville's own deep-seated neuroses.

John Updike, in an admirably careful and caring essay suggestively entitled "Melville's Withdrawal," rejects both explanations. Or rather, he goes beyond them to a more fundamental one. After first demonstrating that Melville's silence "was not so instant or complete . . . as the mythic image of it,"[95] Updike makes the strongest possible case for an interpretation based on metaphors of natural decay or depletion. I quote from the closing paragraph of the essay:

> I am left with a sense that Melville was right to withdraw when he did, from a battle that had become a losing battle. His rapport had been broken with an audience that cared deeply about him chiefly as "the man who had lived among the cannibals." He had taken the sea tales as deeply into cosmic significance as he could, and had spent the treasure of experiences laid up in his youth. He had come to writing, at the age of twenty-five, rather sud-

denly, with scant record of earlier literary ambition. . . . By mid-
life, though not yet forty, he had come to care only about greatness, in the sense that Shakespeare or Dante possessed it, and
that Hawthorne—cool, slight Hawthorne—had once represented it to his fervent, impressionable prime. "Until I was
twenty-five, I had no development at all. From my twenty-fifth
year I date my life. Three weeks have scarcely passed, at any
time between then and now, that I have not unfolded within myself. But I feel that I am now come to the innermost leaf of the
bulb, and that shortly the flower must fall to the mould." By bow-
ing to that organic fall, and abstaining from a forced productivity,
and turning to public silence and private poetry, Melville preserved his communion with greatness, and enhanced with the
dignity of a measured abstention the communion we enjoy
with him.[96]

"Organic" is the perfect and revealing word here, picking up Melville's own metaphor of creative depletion, that of the innermost leaf
and the flower that "must fall to the mould." In the end, there was
nothing left: he "had spent the treasure of experiences laid up in his
youth." What lends strength to this reading is the manner in which
Updike coolly registers Melville's ambition. "To care only about greatness, in the sense that Shakespeare or Dante possessed it," raises
external—or commercial—rather than psychological problems for
Melville; though to many an other, and not necessarily lesser, writer
it leads to writer's block, as Updike well knows. (In the "Foreword"
to *Bech : A Book* [1970], Updike's protagonist wonders, in a letter to
his creator, "am I paranoid to feel my 'block' an ignoble version of
the more or less noble renunciations of H. Roth, D. Fuchs, and J.
Salinger?")[97] That Melville's problem, when carefully examined,
proved ultimately to be one of creative exhaustion, in the sense of
depletion, does not mean that all late silences are "organic" or inevitable. The metaphors of dearth or desiccation and blockage need not
be alternatives. When the contemporary American novelist Anne Tyler imagines that "any day now, I'll have said all I have to say; I'll
have used up all my characters," this does not preclude her from feeling, as she writes a sentence later, that "even when I feel I have no
ideas at all, and can't possibly start the next chapter, I have a sense
of something still bottled in me, trying to get out."[98]
These examples of the varieties and complications of writer's block
might well be multiplied; they are adduced here to suggest how rich
the topic is in problematic implications. To identify and analyze these
implications are among the main aims of this book. Another aim is to

provide a systematic critical inquiry into existing accounts. This inquiry is illustrated and tested by examples drawn from a variety of literary periods (though the English Romantics, for what I hope are seen as perfectly legitimate historical reasons, figure prominently). No attempt is made to quote or refer to everyone; the examples are chosen to serve and test theories. The book is neither therapeutic nor diagnostic, though I think some accounts are more plausible and intelligent than others.

The accounts themselves are grouped into the book's three parts: part one deals with psychoanalytic theories of blockage; part two, with literary historical accounts; and part three, with more general theories of writing, speech, and culture. The book moves outward in a series of widening contexts: from an initial focus on the individual psyche, one in which the writer is conceived of as at least potentially autonomous (or ultimately treated as such); to a variety of accounts of the inhibiting influence—the burdensome anxiety—of the literary past, both of the fact of what has been written and of the mantle or identity the writer inherits; to accounts of blockage which look less to the writer than to writing, and to the role to which culture or society consigns it. The structure also has a historical dimension, at least at the beginning: moving from an immediate history in part one—that of the psychoanalytic culture out of which the term *writer's block* grew; back to an examination in part two of the Romantic origins of that culture, in notions such as that of the author as autonomous genius, or the unconscious as the source of creative power; to part three's much greater leaps—back to Plato and the very origins of writing, fast forward to the technology that looks to some as if it might supplant it.

PART ONE

Psychoanalytic Theory

The Freudian Account

Freud's theories of literary blockage—he would say "inhibition"—have for the most part to be extrapolated from his accounts of unimpeded creativity: he wrote relatively little about writer's block per se. There are several possible reasons for this. To begin with, Freud seems not to have had many writers or artists as patients; he mentions only a single artist—the unnamed painter in "The Psychogenesis of a Case of Homosexuality in a Woman" (1920)—and no authors at all, though we know he treated at least one, the American poet H.D.[1] This absence may in part be a product of the history of the patient population of psychoanalysis: it was not until after World War II, and then only gradually, that psychoanalysis began to treat the merely uncreative as well as the "sick."[2] Then there is the matter of Freud's own fluency as a writer. Although several times he mentions wrestling with difficulties of style or complains of the inadequacies of language, all he ever said of blockage as a potential personal problem is contained in the following comment, about the importance of creative work in his life:

> I could not contemplate with any sort of comfort a life without work. Creative imagination and work go together with me; I take no delight in anything else. That would be a prescription for happiness were it not for the fact that one's productivity depends entirely on sensitive moods. What is one to do on a day when thoughts cease to flow and proper words won't come? One cannot help trembling at this possibility. That is why, despite the acquiescence in fate that becomes an upright man, I secretly pray: no infirmity, no paralysis of one's powers through bodily distress.[3]

That Freud should talk here only of "bodily" distress is a sign of the uncomplicated health of his life as a writer (though it might disguise a greater psychological fear). The extraordinary admission that "I take no delight in anything else" may in part be a product of age.

Writing and Wish Fulfillment

At the heart of Freud's sense of the writer or artist lies a conviction that art is "an activity intended to allay ungratified wishes—in the first place in the creative artist himself and subsequently in his audience or spectators" ("The Claims of Psycho-Analysis to Scientific Interest" [1913], 13:187). This view is maintained consistently. Freud first voices it in a letter of 31 May 1897 to Wilhelm Fliess, in which he asserts that "the mechanism of creative writing is the same as that of hysterical phantasies."[4] This is Freud's earliest recorded speculation about literary creativity. Eleven years later, in the crudest and most influential of his essays on writing, "Creative Writers and Day-Dreaming," he says that "the motive forces of phantasies are unsatisfied wishes, and every single phantasm is the fulfilment of a wish, a correction of unsatisfying reality" (9:146). Two years later, in *Leonardo da Vinci and a Memory of His Childhood*, Freud states that "kindly nature has given the artist the ability to express his most secret mental impulses, which are hidden even from himself, by means of the works that he creates" (11:107).

Why this should be so is elaborated in "The Paths to the Formation of Symptoms," the twenty-third of the *Introductory Lectures on Psycho-Analysis* (1916–17), in the course of a discussion of the relation between dreams, symptoms, fantasies, daydreams, and art. "The human ego," Freud writes,

> is . . . slowly educated by the pressure of external necessity to appreciate reality and obey the reality principle; . . . to renounce, temporarily or permanently, a variety of the objects and aims at which its striving for pleasure, and not only for sexual pleasure, is directed. But men have always found it hard to renounce pleasure; they cannot bring themselves to do it without some kind of compensation. . . . In the activity of phantasy human beings continue to enjoy the freedom from external compulsion which they have long since renounced in reality. . . . Indeed, they cannot subsist on the scanty satisfaction which they can extract from reality. (16:371–72)

In the pages that follow, much will be said of the inadequacy of this view, so it is well to remember that it not only has a long and distinguished pedigree but also is still very much alive today. Here, for instance, is John Updike again, maintaining that "the world, so balky and resistant and humiliating, can in the act of mimesis be rectified, adjusted, chastened, purified. Fantasies defeated in reality can be fully indulged; tendencies deflected by the cramp of circumstances can be followed to an end." And, later in the same essay: "Although as a child I lived what was to become my material and message, my wish to write did not begin with that material and message; rather it was a wish to escape from it, into an altogether better world."⁵

For Freud, the productions of fantasy are of several sorts: day-dreams, which are "imagined satisfactions of ambitious, megalo-manic, erotic wishes" (16:372); night dreams, of which daydreams "are the nucleus and prototype" (16:372); and art. The artist "desires to win honour, power, wealth, fame and the love of women; but he lacks the means for achieving these satisfactions. Consequently, like any other unsatisfied man, he turns away from reality and transfers all his interest, and his libido too, to the wishful constructions of his life of phantasy" (16:376).

"Honour, power, wealth, fame and the love of women"—these are the ungratified wishes allayed by art, the objects of those "most se-cret mental impulses" the artist is able to express "by means of the works he creates." They are the true or hidden subject matter of all art and creative writing, as well as the source, according to Ernest Jones, of all symbolism. "Only what is repressed is symbolised," says Jones in "The Theory of Symbolism" (1916), a work that Frederic Jameson calls "one of the most painfully orthodox in the Freudian canon,"⁶ "only what is repressed needs to be symbolised."⁷ In "Cre-ative Writers and Day-Dreaming," Freud groups these wishes into two categories:

> These motivating wishes vary according to the sex, character and circumstances of the person who is having the phantasy; but they fall naturally into two main groups. They are either ambi-tious wishes, which serve to elevate the subject's personality; or they are erotic ones. In young women the erotic wishes predom-inate almost exclusively, for their ambition is as a rule absorbed by erotic trends. In young men egoistic and ambitious wishes come to the fore clearly enough alongside erotic ones. But we will not lay stress on the opposition between the two trends; we would rather emphasise the fact that they are often united. (9:146–47)

This is not, at first glance, one of Freud's best moments, though less because of the passage's seeming sexism (Freud is not implying that women are naturally or always like this) than because of the ten-dency of its two categories to collapse into each other. For Freud, the vast preponderance of repressed wishes are erotic, and of erotic wishes the vast preponderance (though sometimes only after lengthy and ingenious interpretation) turn out to be Oedipal. Norman Holland lists such wishes as "primal scene fantasies, castration fears, Oedipal wishes, and the like,"[8] but all of these, ultimately, are "the like"—or the same. As for ambitious (sometimes "aggressive") wishes, these also reduce to Oedipal fantasies. Freud may be admitting as much in the "Preface" he wrote in 1919 to a volume of essays by Theodore Reik entitled *Ritual: Psycho-Analytic Studies*. In this "Preface," Freud commends Otto Rank's *The Incest Motif in Poetry and Saga* (1912), which "has produced evidence of the surprising fact that the choice of subject-matter, especially for dramatic works, is principally determined by the ambit of what psycho-analysis has termed the 'Oedipus complex.' By working it over with the greatest variety of modifications, distortions and disguises, the dramatist seeks to deal with his own most personal relations to this emotional theme" (17:261).

When Freudian aesthetics is termed *reductive,* a passage such as this is the sort of thing critics have in mind. All literature is reduced, in Frederick Crews's words, to "the primordial and monotonous fantasies of mankind."[9] But Freud would be quick to reply that various factors (those shifting "modifications, distortions and disguises") prevent art works, or the "products of imaginative activity," from being "stereotyped or unalterable" ("Creative Writers and Day-Dreaming," 9:147). Moreover, the Oedipus complex is hardly a narrow topic. "A person's emotional attitude to his family" is how Freud defines it in the Reik "Preface" (17:261), in which its prominence is seen as "an expression of the biological facts that the young of the human race pass through a long period of dependence and are slow in reaching maturity, as well as that their capacity for love undergoes a complicated course of development. Consequently, the overcoming of the Oedipal complex coincides with the most efficient way of mastering the archaic animal heritage of humanity" (17:261–62).

It is the Oedipus complex in this larger sense that can be said to determine the constitution or character of the personality, the choice of the love object, and the subject's growth into sexual maturity, "which biological maturation in itself in no way guarantees." In this sense, to quote J. Laplanche and J.-B. Pontalis, "the Oedipus complex is not reducible to an actual situation—to the actual influence exerted by the parental couple over the child. Its efficacy derives from the fact that it brings into play a prospective agency (the prohibition against incest) which bars the way to naturally sought satisfaction and forms an indivisible link between wish and law." The Oedipus complex thus expresses a triangular relation between the child, the child's natural object, and the figure who "blocks" him or her from that object. To quote Laplanche and Pontalis again, "it is the different types of relation between the three points of the triangle which—at least as much as any particular parental image—are destined to be internalised and to survive in the structure of the personality."[10]

Beyond Oedipus

All of which implies a single blocking agent: the internalized image of the father or whatever "part" stands for him. It is, however, possible to discover in Freud's writings a second motivating force in art and literature and thus the possibility of a second source of blockage. This source is the death instinct, which makes its first shadowy appearance in the 1913 paper "The Theme of the Three Caskets."[11] The paper begins by bringing together the stories of Cordelia, Aphrodite, Cinderella, and Psyche, each of whom is the youngest, but ultimately the most excellent, of a group of three sisters. Freud then identifies these sisters as "the Fates, the Moerae, the Parcae or the Norns" (12:296), having previously associated the third, because she is often mute (and muteness symbolizes death in dreams and stories), with "Atropus, the inexorable" (12:296), or Death. But there is a problem here: Death is ugly and undesirable, yet "in the Judgement of Paris she [i.e., the third sister] is the Goddess of Love, in the tale of Apuleius [i.e., Psyche] she is someone comparable to the goddess for her beauty, in *The Merchant of Venice* she is the fairest and wisest of women, in *King Lear* she is the one loyal daughter" (12:298). Moreover, if the third daughter is really Death, why is she not merely chosen but freely chosen, in each of the stories?

At this point Freud inadvertently and for the first time reveals the existence of what in *Beyond the Pleasure Principle* (1920) he calls the "death wish," or *Todestrieb*—a new basic category of wish and a second motive force in literature. He begins by discussing the myth of the Fates: "The Moerae were created as a result of a discovery that warned man that he too is a part of nature and therefore subject to the immutable law of death. Something in man was bound to struggle against this subjection" (12:299). Why? Because "man, as we know, makes use of his imaginative activity in order to satisfy the wishes that reality does not satisfy."

> So his imagination rebelled against the recognition of the truth embodied in the Myth of the Morae, and constructed instead the myth derived from it, in which the Goddess of Death was replaced by the Goddess of Love. . . . The same consideration answers the question how the feature of a choice came into the myth of the three sisters. Here again there has been a wishful

reversal. Choice stands in the place of necessity, of destiny. In this way man overcomes death, which he has recognised intellectually. No greater triumph of wish-fulfilment is conceivable. (12:299)

But what of the original form of the myth? How do we account for the existence of a myth in which what is embodied is not a wish but a "truth"? Was it not "imaginative reality" that created the original myth of the Fates, just as surely as it created the myths of Aphrodite and Psyche, which derived from it? All Freud says to meet this objection is that from the first there was an "ancient ambivalence" in the depiction of "the great Mother-goddesses of the oriental peoples" (12:299)—that they were thought of as goddesses of life and fertility, as well as destruction and death. But this explanation does not solve anything. The myth of the Fates is still an example of an imaginative creation that makes us *face* rather than avoid unpleasant or unwanted reality. In Freud's words, it was "created as a result of a discovery that warned man that he too is a part of nature and therefore subject to the immutable law of death" (12:299). This recognition is hard to see as anything for which one would wish.

Unless, of course, we think of the death instinct itself as being buried or hidden at the myth's heart. This is suggested when Freud moves from *The Merchant of Venice* to *King Lear*. In *The Merchant of Venice*, Portia's identity as a variant of the later modification of the myth of the Fates is clear. She is associated with the third of three caskets from which the suitors must choose (and caskets, Freud assures us, are female symbols); she must remain mute as to her own preference; and lead itself is "mute," though ultimately the most worthy or excellent of metals. In *King Lear*, on the other hand, "a reduction of the theme to the *original* myth is being carried out" (12:300; my italics). When Lear enters holding Cordelia's dead body in his arms, "Cordelia is Death": "External wisdom, clothed in the primaeval myth, bids the old man renounce love, choose death and make friends with the necessity of dying" (12:301). The only way to account for the genesis and acceptance of such a work in terms of the Freudian model is to posit for writer and audience an instinct or wish for the truth it embodies, which Freud does not do.[12] Even when the theory of the *Todestrieb* finally appears in print six or so years later, in "The Uncanny" (1919) and *Beyond the Pleasure Principle*, its implications, both for Freud's theory of writing and for a theory of blockage, remain unexamined. It is only with later writers that the theory is explicitly recognized as a potential source both of creativity and its inhibition.[13]

Writing and Neurosis

Second only to the objection that Freud's aesthetic is narrow—that it reverts monotonously to the Oedipal origins of art—is the objection that it is defamatory. In Trilling's words, Freud "made the error of treating the artist as a neurotic."[14] The trouble with this objection is that it is not altogether fair to Freud, because he almost always, and quickly, qualified his accounts of the neurotic character of the artist. "If a person who is at loggerheads with reality possesses an *artistic gift*," he tells us in *Five Lectures on Psycho-Analysis* (1910), "he can transform his phantasies into artistic creations instead of into symptoms. In this manner he can escape the doom of neurosis and by this roundabout path regain his contact with reality" (11:50). The distinction here between artist and neurotic is clear and explicit, as it is in the following familiar passage from "The Paths to the Formation of Symptoms":

> An artist is once more in rudiments an introvert, not far removed from neurosis. He is oppressed by excessively powerful instinctual needs. He desires to win honour, power, wealth, fame and the love of women; but he lacks the means for achieving these satisfactions. Consequently, like any other unsatisfied man, he turns away from reality, and transfers all his interest, and his libido too, to the wishful constructions of his life of phantasy, whence the path might lead to neurosis. . . . An artist, however, finds a path back to reality. (16:376)

Freud then discusses how he does so. Again, the pejorative impression is quickly and clearly countered.

Freud's essays contain, in addition to these direct or explicit accounts of the artist's or writer's nature, a variety of incidental references to art and artists, and the majority of these, in addition to references to wish fulfillment, are negative. The "narcotic" effects of art are noted in passing in *Civilisation and Its Discontents*, along with the "inner dishonesty" art shares with dreams (21:34); the hero of Wilhelm Jensen's novel *Gradiva*, discussed by Freud in *Delusions and Dreams in Jensen's "Gradiva"* (1907), is said to be "destined to become an artist or a neurotic; he was one of those whose kingdom was not of this world" (9:14); "a happy person never phantasizes," we are told in "Creative Writers and Day-Dreaming," "only an unsatisfied one" (9:146). Often the "childlikeness" of art, and so of artist and audience, is stressed. In "Psychopathic Characters on the Stage" (1942 [1905–6]), the enjoyment of the spectator at a drama is said to be "based on an illusion; that is to say, his suffering is mitigated by the certainty that, firstly, it is someone other than himself who is acting and suffering on the stage, and, secondly, that after all it is only a game, which can threaten no damage to his personal security. In these circumstances he can allow himself to enjoy being a 'great man,' to give way without a qualm to such suppressed impulses as a craving for freedom in religious, political, social and sexual matters" (7:306). Here, as elsewhere in his writings, Freud's wish to distance himself from the needs and experiences he explains is palpable.

A comparable distance or disapproval can be detected in the aesthetics of Freud's immediate followers. In Jones's 1916 essay "The Theory of Symbolism," a familiar distinction is made between the "desire for ease and pleasure" and "the demands of necessity." This opposition, in Marion Milner's words, gives the impression that the desire for ease and pleasure "is something that we could, if we were sufficiently strong-minded, do without. The phrase reflects perhaps a certain puritanism which is liable to appear in psychoanalytic writing." [15] The same note is even more clearly sounded in an early paper by Sachs and Rank, in which they distinguish between an original (or aboriginal) process of identification, the function of which was to help people adapt to reality, and a subsequent (or decadent) symbolism. The primary process of identification "becomes superfluous and sinks to the mere significance of a symbol as soon as this task of adaptation is accomplished," they write. Thus, a symbol becomes for them the "unconscious precipitate of primitive means of adaptation to reality that have become superfluous and useless, a sort of lumber room of civilisation to which the adult readily flees in states of reduced or deficient capacity for adaptation to reality, in order to regain his old long-forgotten playthings of childhood." [16]

The disapproving or patronizing note sounded here and in Jones derives ultimately from Freud; though Freud, as well as Milner, knows that human beings simply "cannot subsist on the scanty satisfaction which they can extort from reality" (16:372). How widespread the note became is suggested in the following passage from Doris Lessing's *The Golden Notebook*, first published in 1952. The blocked writer, Anna Wulf, has just told her psychoanalyst, the maliciously nicknamed Mother Sugar, that she feels she can no longer write:

> I am interested only in stretching myself, or living as fully as I can. When I said that to Mother Sugar she replied with the small nod of satisfaction people use for these resounding truths, that the artist writes out of an incapacity to live. I remember the nausea I felt when she said it . . . it is because this business about

art and the artist has become so debased, the property of every sloppy-minded amateur that any person with a real connection with the arts wants to run a hundred miles at the sight of the small satisfied nod, the complacent smile. . . . But extraordinary how this old stuff issued so fresh and magisterial from the lips of psychoanalysis.[17]

Mother Sugar's complacent nod suggests a genuine ambivalence about artists and art, a result perhaps of Freud's own uneasy sense of the relative claims of art and science, as well as of the problematic relation of psychoanalysis to both. Another and related explanation lies in Freud's personal psychology. In "The Moses of Michelangelo" (1914), Freud speaks of his own reactions to art works. If they "exercise a powerful effect," he tries "to explain to myself what their effect is due to. Wherever I cannot do this, as for instance with music, I am almost incapable of obtaining any pleasure. Some rationalistic, or perhaps analytic, turn of mind in me rebels against being moved by a thing without knowing why I am thus affected and what it is that affects me" (13:211). Such a "turn of mind" is bound to result in mixed feelings about artists or writers and their audience because what motivates the former and moves the latter is unconscious.

When the Writer Writes

How, then, is wishful fantasy transformed into art? What is the process that creates a work of art? The Freudian account of *Hamlet*, as expounded in the October 1897 letter to Fliess, *The Interpretation of Dreams*, and Jones's *Hamlet and Oedipus* (1912), offers a convenient starting point. Although in some works—*Oedipus Rex*, for example—the originating fantasy "is brought into the open and realised as it would be in a dream" (*The Interpretation of Dreams*, 4:264), in most cases, and especially in "modern" ones, it remains more deeply hidden or repressed. To find the originating fantasy, therefore, one must look to its aforementioned "inhibiting consequences," just as one would "in the case of a neurosis" (4:264)—another of those remarks that contribute to the negative impression of the artist with which Freud is associated. The inhibiting consequence in Hamlet's case is his delay, the inability to carry out the task of revenge set by his father's ghost. Freud's account of the delay issues from a refutation of two influential interpretations: the first sees Hamlet as excessively intellectual and is associated with Goethe; the second sees him as "a pathologically irresolute character" (4:265). Freud refutes these readings by citing scenes and lines in which Hamlet's strength and nobil-

ity are stressed. For his own interpretation, Freud looks to "the peculiar nature of the task" Hamlet faces. Far from being effete or sickly,
Hamlet is a man "able to do anything—except do vengeance on the
man who did away with his father and took that father's place with
his mother, the man who shows him the repressed wishes of his own
childhood realized" (4:265). In Jones's words, Claudius "incorporates
the deepest and most buried part of his own personality, so that he
cannot kill him without also killing himself." [18]

From here Freud moves beyond the play to Shakespeare himself,
noting that Hamlet's distaste for sexuality "was destined to take possession of the poet's mind more and more during the years that followed. . . . For it can of course only be the poet's own mind which
confronts us in Hamlet" (4:265). What, then, was bothering Shakespeare at the time of the composition of *Hamlet?* Freud's answer derives from a biography by George Brandes: "*Hamlet* was written immediately after the death of Shakespeare's father (in 1601), that is,
under the immediate impact of his bereavement and, as we may well
assume, while his childhood feelings about his father had been
freshly revived" (4:265). Freud also mentions that Shakespeare's son,
"Hamnet," had died at an early age. These are the bare bones of the
Freudian interpretation.

I present this familiar material because it offers a clear and representative instance of Freud's account of the genesis of a work of art.
"A strong experience in the present," as Freud says in "Creative Writers and Day-Dreaming," awakens in the creative writer "a memory of
an earlier experience (usually belonging to his childhood) from which
there now proceeds a wish which finds its fulfilment in the creative
work. The work itself exhibits elements of the recent provoking occasion as well as of the old memory" (9:151). The present experience—in Shakespeare's case, the death of his father—takes the writer
back to an earlier one for the same reason that the neurotic is fixated
on earlier memories. As Freud puts it in "The Paths to the Formation
of Symptoms," the reason neurotics look to their childhood is because
it represents "a period of the past in which their libido did not lack
satisfaction, in which they were happy. They search about in the history of their life till they find a period of that sort, even if they have
to go back as far as the time when they were infants in arms—as they
remember it or as they imagine it" (16:365). In the neurotic, the symptom "repeats this early infantile kind of satisfaction, distorted by the
censorship arising from the conflict, turned as a rule to a feeling of
suffering" (16:365). In the writer, such a function is served by the
work. In *Delusions and Dreams in Jensen's "Gradiva,"* Freud describes
the neurotic in terms that recall the artist: "The development of the
mental disorder sets in at the moment when a chance impression

arouses the childhood experiences which have been forgotten and which have traces, at least, of an erotic colouring. . . . [T]he childhood impression was stirred up, it became active, so that it began to produce effects, but it did not come into consciousness" (9:47).

The pattern of precipitating present experience, childhood memory, and compensating wish fulfillment in the work is also clearly visible in Freud's much more detailed discussion of *Leonardo da Vinci and a Memory of His Childhood*. At the summit of his life, when he was in his early fifties, an artistically dormant—a blocked—Leonardo was brought back to life by a strong present experience. This experience was the meeting of a Florentine lady whose smile of "bliss and rapture" (11:117) recalled or awakened in him a childhood memory of his mother. The memory had been repressed because it contained an especially strong erotic component, the product of his early circumstances. Leonardo was illegitimate and for the first few years of his life lived alone "with his poor, forsaken, real mother" (11:91). Freud imagines the Leonardo of these early years as "left . . . open to the seductions of a mother whose only solace he was"; he imagines Leonardo "being kissed by her into precocious sexual maturity" (11:131).

Sexuality awakened at so early a stage is often repressed with great violence; Leonardo "had long been under the dominance of an inhibition which forbade him ever again to desire such caresses from the lips of women" (11:117). Only later in life was this desire again allowed expression, and then only in art. What released it was a woman whose smile, recalling an earlier smile, inspired first the *Mona Lisa* and then the *Madonna and Child with St. Anne*. Freud's emphasis on the smile fits in with traditional notions of its meaning and importance: the smile had long been considered among the most—if not the most—memorable features of Leonardo's painting, "the most perfect representation of the contrasts which dominate the erotic life of women; the contrast between reserve and seduction, and between the most devoted tenderness and a sensuality that is ruthlessly demanding" (11:108). These factors lead Freud to conclude his account of Leonardo with a formulation that recalls "Creative Writers and Day-Dreaming": "With the help of the oldest of all his erotic impulses he enjoyed the triumph of once more conquering the inhibition in his art" (11:134).

The Writer's Art: Disguise

How, then, is it that the writer or artist makes his or her wishful fantasies and forbidden impulses acceptable? Is there really nothing to be learned—from psychoanalysis, that is—about the nature of the artistic gift? Freud usually suggested as much. But his practice often belied his pessimism, and it is possible to identify several different and, in some cases, contradictory attempts at an answer. To begin with, something must be said of the matter of disguise or distortion. "We were standing in front of . . . Goethe's works which filled three . . . bookshelves," reports Sachs in *Freud: Master and Friend* (1944), and "Freud said, pointing towards it, 'All this was used by him as a means of self-concealment.'" [19] In other words, the forbidden instinctual material at the heart of a piece of writing or a work of art must be disguised in some way if it is to be accepted. This is why, in a tragedy for instance, "the impulse that is struggling into consciousness, however clearly it is recognisable, is never given a definite name; so that in the spectator too the process is carried through with his attention averted, and he is in the grip of his emotions instead of taking stock of what is happening" ("Psychopathic Characters on the Stage," 7:309). The example Freud dryly points to is *Hamlet*, in which "the conflict . . . is so effectively concealed that it was left to me to unearth it" (7:310).

The art of disguise as a means of overcoming resistances is also mentioned in "Some Character Types Met with in Psycho-Analysis" (1916), in which Freud provides examples of the ways dramatists distract audiences by supplying plausible but, ultimately, superficial motives for their characters. The true or deeper motive behind Rebecca Gamvik's refusal of success in *Rosmersholm* (she is of the type "wrecked by success") "could not be explicitly enunciated. It had to remain concealed . . . otherwise serious resistances, based on the most distressing emotions, would have arisen" (14:329). So Ibsen erects a smokescreen of lesser or superficial motives, what Marie Bonaparte, talking of Poe, calls "that conscious, logical and aesthetic façade which we call creative writing." [20] Freud's ambivalence toward art may partly result from this sense of the distracting or duping it entails. In *Richard III*, for example, Shakespeare "engages our intellectual activity, diverts it from critical reflection and keeps us firmly identified with his hero. A bungler in his place would give conscious expression to all that he wishes to reveal to us and would then find himself confronted by our cool, untrammelled intelligence, which would preclude any deepening of the illusion" (14:315).

Aesthetic Bonus

Disguise is not the only means by which "the true artist" is able "to work over his daydreams in such a way as to make them lose what is too personal about them and repels strangers, and to make it possible for others to share in the enjoyment of them" ("The Paths to the For-mation of Symptoms," 16:376). To begin with, there is the second of the "methods" referred to in "Creative Writers and Day-Dreaming": in addition to altering and disguising proscribed fantasies the artist

> bribes us by the purely formal—that is, aesthetic—yield of plea-sure which he offers us in the presentation of his phantasies. We give the name of an *incentive bonus,* or a *fore-pleasure,* to a yield of pleasure such as this, which is offered to us so as to make pos-sible the release of still greater pleasure arising from deeper psychical sources. In my opinion, all the aesthetic pleasure which a creative writer affords us has the character of a fore-pleasure of this kind, and our actual enjoyment of an imaginative work proceeds from a liberation of tensions in our minds. (9:153)

This theory of aesthetic bonus or forepleasure derives from the phi-losopher and "scientific" aesthetician G. T. Fechner (1801–87), the author of a book on humor and of a number of the jokes Freud anal-yses in *Jokes and Their Relation to the Unconscious.* Freud openly ac-knowledges his debt to Fechner when he introduces the term "fore-pleasure" in connection with what he calls "tendentious jokes" (8:135). The initial or superficial pleasure in tendentious jokes, Freud explains, serves a second and greater pleasure, "by lifting suppres-sions and repressions." This is the "major purpose" of the tenden-tious joke: "combating suppression, in order to lift [the hearer's] in-ternal inhibitions by the 'principle of fore-pleasure'" (8:137). In Richard Wollheim's words, "the joker makes use of the joke in order to divert [the hearer's] attention from the impulse that seeks expres-sion, and the joke is expected to achieve this for him by the discharge of energy it can secure."[21] As these passages suggest, though, the aesthetic bonus or forepleasure is ultimately itself a means of dis-guise, of "diverting attention"; thus, it is not so much a second method of overcoming resistances as a type of the first.[22]

A similar confusion lies at the heart of Freud's remarks about the connection between beauty and the aesthetic bonus. In "The Claims of Psycho-Analysis to Scientific Interest," Freud says that the artist's wishful fantasies "only become a work of art when they undergo a transformation which . . . conceals their personal origins and, by obeying the laws of beauty bribe other people with a bonus of plea-sure" (13:187). But what Freud says elsewhere of "the laws of beauty" creates problems. In a 1915 footnote to *Three Essays on the Theory of Sexuality* (1905), he claims that "the concept of 'beautiful' has its roots in sexual excitation" (7:156n.2), and in *Civilisation and Its Discontents* he says that "all that seems certain [of beauty] is its derivation from the field of sexual feeling" (21:83). This view quickly becomes ortho-dox. According to Sachs, "the hypothesis [about beauty] which was considered to conform best with analytic viewpoints—especially in their earlier form—stated that beauty was a sublimation derived from the erotic attraction of a sexually desired person; in short, sublimated object-libido. . . . On this basis we can understand why we find beauty so often without any relation to sex: the libido component has to be sublimated, i.e. desexualised." This is why "the badge of true beauty is sadness";[23] beauty is instinct with a longing for all that is hidden or buried. But if art is for Freud the means by which an artist overcomes resistances to repressed wishes, the implications of the beauty/sex connection seem tautological: the aesthetic bonus—that which allows for the expression of proscribed fantasy material—turns out to be dependent upon the proscribed. This dependency seems not to have bothered Freud, perhaps because he would argue that the sexual feelings raised by beauty were somehow different (though how?) from those associated with the Oedipus complex.[24]

Freud's few remarks about *non*sexual components of the beautiful are comparably puzzling. Norman Holland, for instance, invokes "three canons that a great many critics have settled on to back up value judgements: unity, complexity, and intensity," and he then dis-covers them in a variety of Freud's incidental remarks or observations about "the perceptual pleasure of formal beauty."[25] According to Hol-land, unity is pleasurable and is part of the aesthetic bonus for Freud because it "gives us a sense of 'the discovery of the familiar.' All those loose ends, slightly disturbing and unsettling, fall into place"[26]—a conclusion he draws out of passages from "The Uncanny" and *Jokes and Their Relation to the Unconscious*. Complexity is seen as a value in the latter work because it "serves a defensive, disguising function, easing our inhibitions,"[27] as it also does in "Creative Writers and Day-Dreaming," in which Freud distinguishes between "writers most highly esteemed by the critics"—by which he means good or serious writers (perhaps I was unfair to Bergler)—and "the less pretentious writers of novels, romances, and short stories who nevertheless have the widest and most eager circle of readers of both sexes" (9:149). The latter writers focus attention on a single figure, whereas, in Holland's words, "more complex works [and, Freud seems to imply, 'better' ones] split up the ego 'into many part-egos, and in consequence . . . personify the conflicting currents of . . . mental life in several heroes.' Thus Freud seems to take complexity as itself a value in art"[28]—as part of that forepleasure which helps a reader overcome the objec-tionable or proscribed portions of the originating fantasy. As for in-tensity, all Holland can come up with are the same unconscious desires the aesthetic bonus is called forth to sweeten: "Intensity . . . seems to correspond to Freud's general view of literature as satisfying . . . unconscious desires or resolving unconscious tensions."[29] Of the three traditional criteria of aesthetic value, then, only the first—unity—is invoked by Freud as a distinct or separable value, and then only occasionally or in passing. Complexity and intensity matter to him, but they are subsumed under, or implicated in, notions of disguise and of the affective power of universal wishful fantasies.[30]

Writing as Play, and Flexibility of Repression

Two other facets of Freud's account of creativity remain to be discussed. Sometimes Freud associates forepleasure with what Wollheim calls "the pleasure in play that is provided by the medium of the art: the element of 'true play' that [has] been so heavily stressed in Idealist aesthetics."[31] According to this theory, the pleasure derived from play is aesthetic because, in Freud's words, it is marked "by the condition that in it we are not trying to get anything from things or do anything with them" (8:95). The enjoyment of play, and here Freud quotes Kuno Fischer on jokes, "lies only in itself . . . has its aim only in itself and . . . fulfils none of the other aims of life." This view is different from Johan Huizinga's notion of the connection between play and beauty: "the profound affinity between play and order,"[32] which assumes an affinity between order and beauty; though it may, as Anthony Storr suggests, have affinities with current biological notions of play, which see it as "a way of discharging superfluous energy."[33]

"Superfluous energy" or "gratuitous play" are not, however, notions with which Freud is likely to be comfortable, and, as soon as he voices them in *Jokes and Their Relation to the Unconscious,* he begins to back away, as in the following passage: "If we do not require our mental apparatus at the moment for supplying one of our indispensable satisfactions, we allow it itself to work in the direction of pleasure and we seek to derive pleasure from its own activity. I suspect that this is in general the condition that governs all aesthetic ideation, but I understand too little of aesthetics to try to enlarge on this statement" (8:95–96).

Jack Spector is good on the reasons for Freud's reticence here: "Given Freud's restless and interminable search for explanations within the dynamics of mental activities and his hunt for the motivations of human behaviour, it was inevitable that he would not tie himself to a view that allowed the activity itself to be self-sufficient or 'unexplained.'"[34] Or as Philip Rieff says, "he did not believe that art—or the play of children—could be the product of superabundance and spontaneity. Play itself is a practical effort."[35] Freud later saw value in play, but value of the sort Rieff describes, in which play serves a practical purpose: mastering experience.[36]

In addition to disguise, distortion, and the aesthetic bonus or fore-pleasure, whether conceived of as beauty or play, Freud mentions one other, and in some ways more basic, feature of the writer's make-up or character. He calls this feature "flexibility" or "looseness" or "laxity" of repression (the German word is *Lockerheit*). The artist possesses "a certain degree of laxity in the repressions which are decisive for a conflict" (16:376); this laxity frees the artist to work with and over what is repressed, transforming it into art. The creative writer, Freud tells us in *Delusions and Dreams,*

> directs his attention to the unconscious in his own mind, he listens to its possible developments and lends them artistic expression instead of suppressing them by conscious criticism. Thus he experiences from himself what we learn from others—the laws which the activities of this unconscious must obey. But he need not state these laws, nor even be clearly aware of them; as a result of the tolerance of his intelligence, they are incorporated within his creations. (9:92)

What matters here, and in the previous quote, is a greater *degree* of tolerance or laxity; this is what distinguishes the writer or artist. In *Leonardo da Vinci and a Memory of His Childhood,* Freud talks of the artist's "extraordinary capacity for sublimating the primitive instincts" (11:136), and in "The Paths to the Formation of Symptoms" he talks of the artist being oppressed "by excessively powerful instinctual needs" (16:376). This view of the writer or artist as being possessed of greater capacities than other people is partly a Romantic inheritance, and it feeds in to the notion of the artist as neurotic. It also, of course, relates to more positive Romantic notions of the artist as heroic outsider (notions Jung will make much of), in which emphasis is shifted from excess per se—of drive or the need to release repressed material—to the artist's greater freedom from cultural restraints. In any event, this belief is the necessary precondition for the artistic shaping—the disguise, distortion, embroidery (as in the aesthetic bonus), or play—that allows for creative expression.

Writer's Block

From the Freudian perspective, then, when writers lose flexibility of repression they cannot write, cannot employ their "special gifts." The strength of the repressive mechanism prevents the blocked writer from releasing powerful instincts and wishes, and writing takes on the character of a dangerous transgression, one which, because the fantasies that motivate it are usually or ultimately Oedipal, is associated with the parent. The writer's anxiety about the release of his wish—"his" because Freud mostly ignores women writers—is thus a version of castration anxiety, one that plays into the "fact" (to Freud, at least) that "there is no doubt that the creative artist feels towards his works like a father" (*Leonardo da Vinci and a Memory of His Childhood*, 11:121). A father, of course, can express his feelings (toward his wife); a son's feelings for his mother have to be repressed. Freud does not tell us why this happens. The need to repress simply reasserts itself, overpowering the sublimative compensations of art and resulting, if not in silence, then in other presumably more thorough sublimations.

Nowhere in Freud's writings is this process fully anatomized, nor is it applied to, or adapted for, women writers or artists. We must work from partial accounts, often employing different terminologies. In *The Interpretation of Dreams*, for example, Freud draws on an extended quotation from Johann Schiller to describe the role of repression in blockage, but says almost nothing of the proscribed character of what is repressed. The quote occurs in the course of a discussion of what attitude his patients should take to involuntary thoughts. These thoughts usually meet with violent resistance from what Freud calls "the critical function" (4:102), by which he means something like what I have called the repressive mechanism; Freud's aim with his patients is to get them to relax or abandon the critical function, and he quotes Schiller to prove that "the poetic creation must demand an exactly similar attitude." What sparks Schiller's comment is a letter from his friend the critic C. G. Körner. Körner complains of being blocked (Freud calls his problem "insufficient productivity"), and Schiller replies that

the ground for your complaint seems to me to lie in the constraint imposed by your reason upon your imagination. I will make my idea more concrete by a simile. It seems a bad thing and detrimental to the creative work of the mind if Reason makes too close an examination of the ideas as they come pouring in— at the very gateway, as it were. Looked at in isolation, a thought may seem very trivial or very fantastic; but it may be made important by another thought that comes after it, and, in conjunction with other thoughts that may seem equally absurd, it may turn out to form a most effective link. Reason cannot form any opinion on all this unless it retains the thought long enough to look at in connection with the others. On the other hand, where there is a creative mind, Reason—so it seems to me—relaxes its watch upon the gates, and the ideas rush in pell-mell, and only then does it look them through and examine them in a mass.— You critics, or whatever else you may call yourselves, are ashamed or frightened of the momentary and transient extravagances which are to be found in all truly creative minds and whose longer or shorter duration distinguishes the thinking artist from the dreamer. You complain of your unfruitfulness because you reject too soon and discriminate too severely. (4:103)

Schiller's "Reason," here, is Freud's "critical function," or the repressive mechanism, and blockage occurs when it is employed "too soon" or "too severely." As for the cause of this precipitousness, all we get is the unexpected strength of "ashamed" and "frightened," together with images of flood and anarchy, of ideas that "come pouring in" or "rush in pell-mell." What Freud has elsewhere taught us to see as the forbidden character of the "ideas" or "thoughts" Schiller talks of is only hinted at here, in images of shame and uncontrol.

The term Freud himself uses for blockage is "inhibition," which he associates with mania or hysteria, defined as the identification of the ego or sense of self with the superego, or repressive mechanism. "Inhibition," unfortunately, is one of the more problematic of Freud's terms. It is usually employed as a synonym for, or type of, symptom, as in common psychoanalytic usage,[37] but on at least one occasion, in *Inhibitions, Symptoms, and Anxiety* (1926), symptom and inhibition are contrasted. This contrast is structural and not, for our purposes, especially enlightening. A symptom is viewed as something beyond the ego's control; Little Hans's fear of horses, Freud tells us, is a symptom. An inhibition is a restriction that the ego imposes on itself "so as not to arouse the anxiety-symptom" (20:101), as in Little Hans's inability to go out into the streets for fear of encountering a horse. Because neither Little Hans nor the blocked writer seeks this inhibition, though, to talk of it as within his control is somewhat misleading.

Inhibitions, Symptoms, and Anxiety contains two important passages relating to writer's block, one of them Freud's only comment on writing in its larger or more general sense, as opposed to creative writing:

Analysis shows that when activities like playing the piano, writing or even walking are subjected to neurotic inhibitions it is because the physical organs brought into play—the fingers or the legs—have become too strongly eroticised. . . . [T]he ego-function of an organ is impaired if its erotogenicity—its sexual significance—is increased. It behaves, if I may be allowed a rather absurd analogy, like a maid-servant who refuses to go on cooking because her master has started a love affair with her. As soon as writing, which entails making a liquid flow out of a tube on to a piece of white paper, assumes the significance of copulation, or as soon as walking becomes a symbolic substitute for treading upon the body of mother earth, both writing and walking are stopped because they represent the performance of a forbidden sexual act. The ego renounces these functions, which are within its sphere, in order not to have to undertake fresh measures of repression—*in order to avoid a conflict with the id.* (20:89–90)

Inhibition occurs when the activity involved—not just, as here, "the physical organs brought into play"—is too strongly eroticized; and this is pretty much what has been said before about the creative writer's association of writing with forbidden fantasies.

Freud then mentions a second type of inhibition, though it can also be seen as a version of the first: "There are clearly also inhibitions which serve the purpose of self-punishment. . . . The ego is not allowed to carry on those activities, because they would bring success and gain, and these are things which the severe super-ego has forbidden. So the ego gives them up too, *in order to avoid coming into conflict with the super-ego*" (20:90). This is precisely the process Freud describes in *Dostoevsky and Parricide* (1928), in connection with Dostoevsky's gambling. Dostoevsky was a compulsive gambler, whose success at the tables affected his ability to write. His wife, writes Freud, "noticed that the one thing which offered any real hope of salvation—his literary production—never went better than when they had lost everything and pawned their last possessions. . . . When his sense of guilt was satisfied by the punishments he had inflicted on himself, the inhibition upon his work became less severe and he allowed himself to take a few steps along the road to success" (21:191).

These are Freud's only direct references to writer's block. In *Leonardo da Vinci and a Memory of His Childhood*, however, he offers a detailed account of a blocked artist, and this account is also relevant to the writer. That Leonardo was blocked is clear. On his deathbed, according to Giorgio Vasari, he reprimanded himself for "having offended God and man by his failure to do his duty in his art" (11:64). Leonardo's turn from art to scientific research was no easy or untroubled business; behind it lay a history of creative difficulties and incompletions. According to one eyewitness quoted by Freud, Leonardo "appeared to tremble the whole time when he set himself to paint, and yet he never completed any work he had begun, having so high a regard for the greatness of art that he discovered faults in things that to others seemed miracles" (11:66n.1). The works themselves bear witness: the unfinished last paintings, "the Leda, the Madonna di Sant' Onofrio, Bacchus, and the young St. John the Baptist" (11:66–67). Then there is the time that he took with what he did complete, a "slowness which had all along been conspicuous in Leonardo's work," according to Freud, and one which he sees as "a symptom of [his] inhibition and . . . the forerunner of his subsequent withdrawal from painting" (11:68). Freud attributes the fate of the *Last Supper* to this slowness: Leonardo chose to paint the scene in oils because "he could not become reconciled to fresco painting, which demands rapid work while the ground is still moist" (11:68). Although oil allowed him "to protract the completion of the painting to suit his mood and leisure" (11:68), it also ensured that the colors would not become incorporated with the plaster; hence the painting's present deplorable state.

I have already mentioned that period in Leonardo's life—his artistic prime—in which the inhibition of his art was lifted. The period was inaugurated by a present experience (his meeting with the Florentine lady, the model for the *Mona Lisa*), which reawoke or broke through to childhood memories of forbidden sexual experience, memories with which Leonardo seems to have associated his painting. According to Vasari, Leonardo's earliest works were facial studies of laughing women and children, and Freud implies that these sketches share with the *Mona Lisa* and the great works of Leonardo's maturity a fascination with "the contrasts which dominate the erotic life of women" (11:108). Because of what Freud calls "the accidental conditions of his childhood" (11:132), Leonardo located such contrasts in the figure or smile of his mother. In the first three or so years of the life of Leonardo, his mother "took her little son in place of her husband, and by the too early maturing of his eroticism robbed him of a part of his masculinity" (11:117). The results for Leonardo were threefold: an atrophied sexual life, "restricted to what is called ideal (sublimated) homosexuality" (11:80); its initial sublimation in art; and a second sublimation, in the form of an overpowerful instinct for research, an instinct first awakened in the period of infantile "sexual researches" common to all men, but especially powerful or memorable in Leonardo's case.

Although Freud does not say precisely why, he implies that research was for Leonardo a more acceptable sublimation—or a more thorough one—than artistic activity, and that somehow it brought him more safely into contact with his forbidden wishes. Freud also implies that the almost total repression of Leonardo's sexual life not only made this safer contact necessary—called forth a more violent sublimation—but also interfered with artistic activity and denied Leonardo the very flexibility of repression without which the artist cannot work. "In the bloom of his youth Leonardo appears at first to have worked without inhibition," Freud writes, but soon, with the continued repression of sexual life, signs of the other, more thorough (or at least satisfying) sublimation began to take over:

> His activity and his ability to form quick decisions began to fail; his tendency towards deliberation and delay [grew]. . . . Slowly there occurred in him a process which can only be compared to the regressions in neurotics. The development that turned him into an artist at puberty was overtaken by the process which led him to be an investigator, and which had its determinants in early infancy. The second sublimation of his erotic instinct gave place to the original sublimation for which the way had been prepared on the occasion of the first repression. He became an investigator, at first still in the service of his art, but later independently of it and away from it. . . . His infantile past had gained control over him. (11:133)

The complications of this history ought not to obscure a simple and familiar explanation: blockage or inhibition is brought about by the reassertion of repressive forces, a product presumably of increased pressure from the impulses being repressed. This is partly what Freud means by the last sentence quoted above: "His infantile past had gained control over him." For even if Freud is referring here to a return to an original sublimation—desire for the mother initially sublimated into scopophilic instincts, or what Freud calls "infantile sexual research"—it is pressure from the repressed wish for the mother, or "the infantile past," that brings it about.

Presumably the same pattern would assert itself when the wish in question was for death rather than the forbidden parent. The blocking agent would again be too insistent a pressure from the wish, with a consequent increase in the power of the repressive mechanism. Here again—as with so much associated with the death instinct—we have no way of knowing. What, for instance, did Freud make of the silence that overtook Shakespeare at the end of his career—a silence impossible to see as desiccation in so miraculously fertile a writer? Might not this silence be attributed to pressure from the death wish rather than Oedipal instincts? Could not one see the long looping returns of the late romances as images of stasis rather than rebirth, as signs of the author's own longing for rest or release, a longing too intense for the rough magic of artistic sublimation? Freud seems to have had nothing to say of these matters; just as he had nothing to say of blockage in the case of the women writers, when presumably the wish in question is for the father rather than death or the mother. As for those of his followers who discuss the late plays, their interpretations are depressingly "Freudian." Sachs detects Oedipal material in the four late romances (and connects the theme of a daughter's marriage to Shakespeare's relationship with his own daughter, Judith); Ella Sharpe concludes that "the stimulus for regression in the poet's maturity was the reactivation of the unconscious incest wishes towards his daughters, the buried hostility to the father being transferred to sons-in-law." [38]

At which point, and in conclusion, we should recall the partial and piecemeal nature of Freud's aesthetic, as well as the unfairness of assuming, as this chapter has, that there is one. What Freud had to say about writers and artists was provisional; the all-but-disabling narrowness of the accounts of creativity and blockage examined above is at least in part attributable to their synthetic or patchwork character, the fact that someone other than Freud has had to piece them together. Perhaps if Freud had seen his occasional essays and passing comments on writing and art collected, he would have realized just how limiting they can appear. However, too much attention to consistency, that "hobgoblin of little minds," can block. The influence of Freud's theories, moreover, is still very much alive, even in works that seek to revise or repudiate them.

After Freud

Three broad themes characterize the revision or extension of Freudian accounts of creativity and blockage: a turn back past the Oedipus complex to an earlier source of conflict, that of individuation; a denial of the ego's passive role in creativity; and a gradual rehabilitation of the writer's image. The first of these themes is crucial to the aesthetics of Carl Jung; the second figures prominently in the writings of Otto Rank; and the third is seen in them both, though somewhat less clearly in Jung, who often stresses the writer's necessary alienation from nonartistic or noncreative realms. Jung and Rank are probably the most influential of first-generation revisionists in the aesthetic realm, and their theories provide a useful context for the aesthetics of ego psychology, in which all three themes or trends are realized. Ego psychology and post-Kleinian object relations are the dominant movements of the second generation of psychoanalytic aesthetics, at least in the English-speaking world.

I focus on psychoanalytic accounts in this chapter (including—rather loosely—those of Rank and Jung), though other psychotherapies deal with blockage. This decision derives in part from the theoretically threadbare or derivative nature of such therapies, or at least of those with which I am familiar. Often they amount to little more than common sense and question-begging reinforcement: pull yourself together, be more confident, draw up and stick to a list of priorities. The nature and etiology of the condition the therapy purports to treat are either ignored or baldly assumed. What matters in most of these new or fringe psychotherapies is that the methods outlined work (the 100 percent cure rate claimed by Bergler is not unique). But faith healing also "works," as Freud himself was forced to acknowledge in deferring to the superior results obtained at Lourdes. Successful case histories demonstrate as little about what Frederick Crews calls the "propositional content" (often itself almost negligible) of the new psychotherapies as they do of psychoanalysis itself.[1]

Other exclusions in the pages that follow are more problematic—

in particular those of "deviant" theorists such as Alfred Adler and Harry Stack Sullivan, as well as of more established figures from what might be called the second generation of American ego psychology, including Edith Jacobson, Phyllis Greenacre, and Otto Kernberg. There are several reasons for these exclusions. Some figures are simply not sufficiently original, at least in the realm of aesthetics, to warrant separate discussion. Others, though interesting and innovative, are uninfluential, at least in comparison to their contemporaries (for example, W. R. D. Fairbairn in relation to Klein). The most problematic of the figures *in*cluded—and the least well known—is probably Rank, but his theories were so directly concerned with questions of creativity and blockage that to exclude him would have made no sense. He also provides a useful bridge to important aspects of ego psychology and object relations.

The present chapter moves from a brief consideration of Jung to Rank to ego psychology, leaving the British object-relations theorists to more extended treatment in chapter four. The story it tells is of a gradual deepening and sophistication in the psychoanalytic approach to creativity, one that moves progressively closer to a view of writing and writer's block echoed by writers themselves, including those who have written most eloquently about blockage. As for the larger question of the scientific status of psychoanalytic theory, I can only offer a very unscientific response. Although the theorists I discuss seem more rigorous and intelligent than many of those I have excluded, none of them, Freud included, meets the evidentiary standards of "hard" science. This is worth admitting from the start, while also insisting on the continuing power and interest of much psychoanalytic theory.

Carl Jung (1875–1961)

The central feature of Jung's account of artistic or literary creativity is the passivity of the artist, and in this respect his aesthetic is retrogressive or "Freudian." Poets and artists feel that the intention or message of a true work of art is forced upon them; it is alien, outside their conscious control. The artist "can only obey the apparently alien impulse within him and follow where it leads, sensing that his work is greater than himself, and wields a power which is not his and which he cannot command."[2] For Schiller, Jung notes, the artist is distinguished by his knowledge of "the secret of the middle way" between conscious and unconscious worlds. Not for Jung: "My own experiences," he writes in "The Role of the Unconscious" (1918), "led me to doubt this. I am of the opinion that the union of rational and irrational truth is to be found not so much in art as in the symbol *per se*" (10, par. 24). It is not so much the poet as the poetic or visionary force that effects the union. "The content clothed itself," he says of one of the fairy tales of his friend Otto A. H. Schmitz. "Schmitz himself did not really know what his tale meant" ("On the Tale of the Otter" [1932], 18, par. 1718). Creation for the true or visionary poet is thus a form or state of possession, numerous instances of which Jung and his followers offer from their own and others' experience.[3]

These states Jung identifies as "autonomous complexes" (15, par. 122), a term he associates equally with creative and pathological processes. Autonomous complexes arise from the unconscious, but not from that part of the unconscious Jung terms the personal, or Freudian, unconscious. The personal, or Freudian, unconscious is the realm of "the shadow"—that is, "the negative side of the personality, the source of all those unpleasant qualities we like to hide" ("The Psychology of the Unconscious" [1917], 7, par. 103n]). Autonomous complexes arise from a deeper collective unconscious, which is the realm of "primordial images" (5, par. 209), or archetypes. When the archetypal product of such a "complex" rises into consciousness, either in the form of a symptom or a poem, "its association with consciousness does not mean it is assimilated, only that it is perceived . . . it is not subject to conscious control, and can be neither inhibited nor voluntarily reproduced. Therein lies the autonomy of the complex: it appears and disappears in accordance with its own inherent tendencies independently of the conscious will" (15, par. 122). Such a condition suggests schizophrenia rather than neurosis, and, just as Freud has been accused (by Jung, among others) of identifying art with neurosis, so Jung has been accused of calling Joyce and Picasso schizophrenic. This charge Jung rather lamely rebuts in a revealing footnote to an essay on Picasso, explaining that "I regard neither Picasso nor Joyce as psychotics, but count them among a large number of people whose *habitus* it is to respond to a profound psychic disturbance not with an ordinary psychoneurosis but with a schizoid syndrome" (15, par. 208n.3). The word "profound" is the important one here: to Jung, the true or visionary artist is unlikely to be associated with anything so mundane as an "ordinary psychoneurosis"; blockage (if it exists at all in the case of visionary artists) is unlikely to be attributed, as in Freud, to the simple reassertion and repression of neurotic fears.[4]

All of which bodes ill for a Jungian theory of creative inhibition. If the artist can do nothing to get in touch with the collective unconscious, if his or her personal psychology is irrelevant to the exercise (already too active a term) of visionary powers, then blockage as conventionally conceived is meaningless. There are those who are capable of receiving the archetypes and of withstanding the isolation consequent upon their transmission (Jung makes much of this "isolation"),[5] and there are those who are not—and those who are not, are not writers. This distinction is implied in the following passage from "Analytical Psychology and Education" (1926), in which Jung belittles the artist's fear of psychology, the sort of fear E. M. Forster expresses in his remark about "psychological meddling":

> As if a whole army of psychologists could do anything against the power of a god! True productivity is a spring that can never be stopped up. . . . Creative power is mightier than its possessor. . . . If, on the other hand, it is a neurosis, it often takes only a word or look for the illusion to go up in smoke. Then the supposed poet can no longer write, and the painter's ideas become fewer and drearier than ever, and for all this psychology is to blame. (17, par. 206)

Only the "supposed" poet, in other words, can be blocked, and the supposed poet, Jung implies, is not a poet at all.

The assumptions that underlie Jungian therapy complicate this picture. For Jungian therapy assumes that the therapeutic process can, if properly guided, unblock access to the collective unconscious, and that what is hidden or partial can be brought out of shadow. The therapist "unblocks" the patient through the study and interpretation of dreams and the encouragement of creative fantasy. He or she encourages the patient to see dreams and fantasies as the psyche's attempts at self-regulation and compensation, as signs of health rather than inadequacy or evasion. Although the Freudian, or personal, unconscious might well be the realm of an inferior shadow, Jung and his followers are quick to repudiate "the totally erroneous supposition that the unconscious is a monster" ("Problems of Modern Psychotherapy" [1929], 16, par. 156). For Jung, the deeper levels of the psyche constitute a self-regulating system of balanced oppositions, in which "every process that goes too far immediately and inevitably calls forth compensations. . . . Too little on one side results in too much on the other" ("The Practical Use of Dream-analysis" [1931], 16, par. 330). The question patients must therefore ask of a given dream or fantasy—even of a neurosis—is "What conscious attitude does it compensate?" (16, par. 334), and the therapist helps them to do so not only through a generalized sympathy but through a knowledge of symbols.[6]

Because the writer also is in search of wholeness, Jungian therapy restores the notion of blockage. After all, the meaning and purpose of the unconscious materials upon which the writer needs to draw are the same as those of the patient in Jungian therapy; paintings and poems are no different from dreams and fantasies in their essential purpose, which is compensation or regulation. This is why Jung's descriptions of the developed individual—the successful patient in Jungian therapy—recall his accounts of the visionary artist. For example, in "The Development of Personality" (1934) Jung talks of the process of individuation "from the germ state to full consciousness [as] at once a charisma and a curse, because its first fruit is the conscious and unavoidable segregation of the single individual from the undifferentiated and unconscious herd. This means isolation" (17, par. 294). And, later on: "To develop one's personality is indeed an unpopular undertaking, a deviation that is highly uncongenial to the herd, an eccentricity smelling of the cenobite, as it seems to the outsider. Small wonder, then, that from earliest times only the chosen few have embarked upon this strange adventure" (17, par. 298).

The person who seeks individuation also resembles the artist in being *called* to wholeness, as if possessed. Individuation results from a vocation, and vocation for Jung "acts like a law of God from which there is no escape." The man who goes his own way "*must* obey his own law, as if it were a daemon whispering to him of new and wonderful paths. Anyone with a vocation hears the voice of the inner man; he is called" (17, par. 300). This is not to say that the developed individual is unconnected to the many; again, like the artist, he is also "part of the people as a whole, and is as much at the mercy of the power that moves the whole as anybody else. The only thing that distinguishes him from all the others is his vocation. He has been called by that all-tyrannizing psychic necessity that is his own and his people's affliction. If he hearkens to the voices, he is at once set apart and isolated as he has resolved to obey the law that commands him from within" (17, par. 304). And this isolation, as with that of the true artist, "makes us conscious of the evil [of suppression] from which the whole community is suffering, whether it be the nation or the whole human race" (17, par. 319).

Jung himself connects the developed personality and the visionary artist later in the same essay, when he admits the ultimate mysteriousness of their origins: "All the usual explanations and nostrums of psychology are apt to fall short here, just as they do with the man of genius or the creative artist. Inferences from heredity or from environment do not quite come off. . . . There is always something irrational to be added, something that simply cannot be explained, a *deus ex machina* or an *asylum ignorantiae*, that well-known soubriquet for God" (17, par. 31). The only important difference between Jung's account of the developed individual and that of the visionary artist (aside, that is, from an increased tendency to poeticize in describing the artist) is his stress on the importance of consciousness for the individual. Jung has little to say about cognitive or conscious elements in the creation of visionary works of art. The poet or artist is simply a vehicle, a person overcome or possessed. But in the case of the developed individual, Jung makes much of the importance of properly receiving and accepting—even working over and with—what arises from the unconscious:

> Only the man who can consciously assent to the power of the inner voice becomes a personality; but if he succumbs to it he will be swept away by the blind flux of psychic events and destroyed. That is the great and liberating thing about any genuine personality: he voluntarily sacrifices himself to his vocation, and consciously translates into his own individual reality what would lead to ruin if it were lived unconsciously by the group. ("The Development of Personality," 17, par. 308)

Nowhere is this crucial anomaly—between unconscious artist and consciously developed individuality—more dramatic than in Jung's "The Transcendent Function," an essay of 1916 that was posthumously published. Jung opens the essay with a clear distinction between artist and developed personality:

> The definiteness and directedness of the conscious mind are extremely important acquisitions which humanity has bought at a very heavy sacrifice, and which in turn have rendered humanity the highest service. Without their service technology and civilization would be impossible, for they all presuppose the reliable continuity and directedness of the conscious process. For the statesman, doctor, and engineer as well as for the simplest labourer, these qualities are absolutely indispensable. We may say in general that social worthlessness increases to the degree that these qualities are impaired by the unconscious. Great artists and others distinguished by creative gifts are, of course, exceptions to this rule. The very advantage that such individuals enjoy consists precisely in the permeability of the partition separating the conscious and the unconscious. (8, par. 135)

The essay then discusses ways of integrating or restoring a balance between conscious or directed and unconscious elements in the lives of the nonartistic, a process Jung calls "the transcendent function": "The tendencies of the conscious and the unconscious, are the two factors that together make up the transcendent function. It is called 'transcendent' because it makes the transition from one attitude to another organically possible, without loss of the unconscious" (8, par. 145). The therapist mediates the transcendent function by working over symbolic material; but this process is of use only at the beginning of treatment. Eventually the patient must take a more active and independent role in confronting his or her hidden nature.

Yet how is this to be done? The interpretation of one's own dreams does not work; "the difficulties . . . are too great" (8, par. 151). "Unconscious interferences in the waking state, ideas 'out of the blue,' slips, deceptions and lapses of memory, symptomatic actions, etc." (8, par. 154) are also considered too fragmentary. Although "spontaneous fantasies" are said to provide better material, the capacity to produce them is relatively rare in developed societies. All that is left are more "artificial" materials (8, par. 166), by which Jung means giving "visible shape" to one's emotional disturbances (these being the signals or symptoms of one-sidedness, of a need for integration or the restitution of balance):

> Patients who possess some talent for drawing or painting can give expression to their mood by means of a picture. It is not important for the picture to be technically or aesthetically satisfying, but merely for the fantasy to have free play and for the whole thing to be done as well as possible. . . . A process is created which is influenced by both conscious and unconscious, embodying the striving of the unconscious for the light and the striving of the conscious for substance. (8, par. 168)

The conscious Jung mentions here comes into operation in two ways: either by the patient's attempt to mold the unconscious product aesthetically, varying and refining it according to current aesthetic standards; or by an intensive struggle to understand its meaning. "The danger of the aesthetic tendency is over-valuation of the formal or 'artistic' worth of the fantasy productions; the libido is diverted from the real goal of the transcendent function and subsumed into purely aesthetic problems of artistic expression. The danger of wanting to understand the meaning is over-valuation of the content, which is subjected to intellectual analysis and interpretation, so that the essentially symbolic character of the product is lost" (8, par. 176).

It is obvious that these are the dilemmas of the artist, and it is no surprise that Jung's followers have made much of "the transcendent function" in their accounts of creativity. Rosemary Gordon, for example, likens the oscillation between conscious and unconscious elements in the above passage to the aesthetic theories of post-Kleinians such as D. W. Winnicott, Anton Ehrenzweig, and Marion Milner. For

Jung also, Gordon argues, "the power of creation demands first and foremost that a person be available to those freely moving oscillations between control and surrender, between differentiation and de-differentiation, that is between periods of active conscious work on the one hand and periods of passive acceptance on the other." As a consequence, blockage can ensue in one of two ways: "The hindrances to creative work and creative being may stem either from the self—which may then be idealized, or else the hindrances may come from an excessive distrust of the non-ego forces. Thus creativity does indeed seem to depend on the capacity to have and to tolerate the ebb and flow, the rhythms and the oscillations between conscious and unconscious, between control and surrender, between ego and non-ego."[7] And these hindrances, of course, can be overcome by the artist or writer, as they can be by the patient. Art is thus a conscious as well as an unconscious "striving for wholeness."

This application or extension of Jung's theories in "The Transcendent Function" makes sense, but ignores his deliberate exemption of the true artist or poet at the beginning of the essay, as well as the consistent belittling of the secondary process in his writings as a whole. The balancing and oscillation between conscious and unconscious factors, of which Gordon makes so much, is necessary for *non*-artistic creativity only, as Jung is careful to make clear at the start of "The Transcendent Function." About this exemption or distinction, Gordon and other Jungian theorists say nothing. Their silence points to a crucial division in Jungian aesthetics: on the one hand, Jung envisions creative writing as a process wholly independent both of conscious and "psychological" determinants, a view that makes writer's block an impossibility. On the other hand, Jung helps to weaken limiting Freudian notions of writing as purely defensive or evasive, and of the creative impulse as neurotic. When these latter aspects of Jung's writing are connected to his account of individuation or personal development—an account with obvious aesthetic application—creative inhibition or blockage resurfaces, and in a newer and more interesting light. It is only in this latter sense that Jung marks a stage in the development of post-Freudian theories of creativity and blockage.

Otto Rank (1884–1938)

The aesthetics of Freud and Jung were peripheral or secondary to their larger theories; they were "applications." But for Rank, aesthetic problems—especially problems of creativity and blockage—were absolutely central. Rank's career began with three works on art and literature: *The Artist* (1907), a characteristically opaque but orthodox extrapolation from Freud's earliest comments on artists and writers; *The Myth of the Birth of the Hero* (1909), to which Freud contributed paragraphs on the family romance; and *The Incest Motif in Poetry and Saga* (1912), to which Freud alludes in the preface to Reik's *Ritual: Psycho-Analytic Studies*. The two latter works by Rank are meant in part as "proofs" of the often gnomic formulations of *The Artist*. The effect of their accumulated instances is to bludgeon the reader into accepting the familiar truth of the epigraph (from the nineteenth-century German dramatist Friedrich Hebbel) to chapter one of *The Artist:* "It is surprising how far one can trace back all human drives to a single one."

In Rank's early works, it is possible to detect hints of a break with Freud, but the first explicit stage or phase of this break occurs with *The Trauma of Birth* (1924)—itself a traumatic birth for Rank, though at first neither he nor Freud saw it as such (it was dedicated to Freud, who accepted the dedication with a phrase from Horace: *Non omnis moriar* [I shall not completely die]).[8] *The Trauma of Birth* is Rank's major theoretical work, and in it questions of creativity are of crucial importance. But such questions also figure in his works on what might be called "The Practical Bearing of Psychoanalysis"—the title of a series of four lectures Rank delivered in New York in the same year.[9]

Rank's break with Freud was precipitated in part by clinical experiences, specifically of blocked artists, "individuals who, though they are really productive, . . . produce nothing, or else artistically productive men who feel themselves restricted in their possibilities of expression."[10] From the beginning, Rank's clinical practice, unlike Freud's, was with relatively "normal" subjects, as befitted not only his youth and nonmedical background but what one of his biographers calls "his lifetime preoccupation with wholeness and creativity rather than pathology."[11] These patients were drawn at first from Freud, as well as from Hitschmann and other senior figures in the psychoanalytic movement, and then from the fashionable, if somewhat bohemian, literary and artistic circles in which Rank and his wife began to move, first in Vienna and then in Paris, where they settled after 1926. Included among Rank's circle in Paris were Anaïs Nin and Henry Miller, the first of whom Rank not only analyzed but also asked to collaborate with him on his writings, to help clarify and simplify them. Nin writes of Rank and her therapy in the first and second volumes of her adult *Diary,* and she refers specifically to his having taught her, through the example of his own intuition and flexibility in the analytic session, to become more spontaneous in her writing. She credits Rank with freeing her as a writer, though oddly and interestingly Rank seems to have shared with Lessing's Mother Sugar a disapproval of the diary or notebook form. For Nin, though, Rank was the exact opposite of a doctrinaire figure such as Mother Sugar. "With [René] Allendy," she writes of an earlier and more or- thodox analyst (Jacques Lacan's great adversary), "I became aware that each thing I did fell into its expected place; I became aware of the monotony of the design . . . the logical chain-reaction of clichés." Rank, in contrast, "waits, free, ready to leap, but not holding a little trap door in readiness which will click at the cliché-phrase." [12]

What Rank's experiences with blocked writers and artists taught him—though this was a conclusion also influenced by more personal motives—was that "pure psycho-analysis of such types undertaken for the removal of inhibitions as indicated by Freud's therapy, did not help at all for the psychological understanding of the creative pro- cess." [13] To acquire such an understanding, Rank had radically to re- vise Freud's basic notions of the origin and nature not only of conflict and anxiety but also of the unconscious. Conflict, for Freud, origi- nates in the vicissitudes of instinctual life, the repression of wish and fantasy. The anxiety that makes for repression is the castration anxi- ety, which is ultimately or originally external. For Rank, though, anx- iety and conflict derive from birth and are independent of external factors or agents. "My conception of repression differed from Freud's," writes Rank in *Art and Artist* (1932), the most important of his studies in creativity, "for to him it is the result of *outward* frustration, while I trace it to an *inward* necessity." [14] We are born with fear, which exists, in Rank's words from *Truth and Reality,* "*independently* of outside threats whether of a sexual or other nature." [15]

That birth is the source of fear is an idea Freud himself voiced sev- eral times. As early as 1909, in a footnote to chapter six of *The Inter- pretation of Dreams,* he mentioned "the act of birth [as] the first expe- rience of anxiety and thus the source and prototype of the affect of anxiety" (5:400–401). In "A Special Type of Choice of Object Made by Men" (1910), he calls birth "both the first of all dangers to life and the prototype of all the later ones that cause us to feel anxiety." "The experience of birth," he continues, "has probably left behind in us the expression of affect which we call anxiety. Macduff of the Scottish legend, who was not born of his mother but ripped from her womb, was for that reason unacquainted with anxiety" (11:173). Although this last example, as Freud seems later to have recognized, is not a happy one (being ripped from the womb certainly *sounds* traumatic), the larger point is perfectly clear. Nor are these Freud's only pub- lished references to birth trauma: in the twenty-fifth of the *Introduc- tory Lectures on Psycho-Analysis,* he calls it "the first state of anxiety

. . . so thoroughly incorporated into the organism through a count-less series of generations that a single individual cannot escape the affect of anxiety even if, like the legendary Macduff, he 'was from his mother's womb untimely ripped'" (16:397).

Freud made no attempt to develop these suggestions, or even to integrate them into his larger theory of instinctual conflict, until after Rank's *The Trauma of Birth,* and even then the effort was rudimentary at best—with Freud arguing that later anxiety merely copied the *form* taken by the birth trauma, without being an "abreaction" of it. For Rank, though, these early references served as a sanction; they al-lowed him to think of *The Trauma of Birth* not as a departure, but "only as a contribution to the Freudian structure of normal psychology, at best as one of its pillars." [16]

Once one takes "literally and seriously," in Rank's words, Freud's suggestion that anxiety grows out of the trauma of birth, then "it is easy to realise how every infantile utterance of anxiety or fear is really a partial disposal of the birth anxiety." At first, Rank seems to have emphasized the physical origins of this anxiety, but eventually he shifted his focus away from the physical, to the more general psycho-logical consequences of separation from the mother—a change anal-agous to Freud's early volte-face over childhood seduction. In either case, though, the theory had disturbing implications for what Rank calls "the Freudian structure of normal psychology." To begin with, "just as the anxiety at birth forms the basis of every anxiety or fear, so every pleasure has as its final aim the re-establishment of the intra-uterine primal pleasure." But what, then, of the Oedipus complex? Rank does not deny the existence of forbidden sexual impulses or of the fears of castration which they generate; he sees them as based "on the primal castration at birth, that is, on the separation of the child from the mother." [17] "*Im gegenteil, die Mutter,*" Rank declared, [18] and this emphasis on the pre-Oedipal mother is decidedly un-Freudian. For Rank, in Ernest Jones's words, "the essence of life was the relation between mother and child," [19] a view he seems to have held at least as early as 1919. Freud, however, always placed less emphasis on the mother/child dyad than on the child's relation to the father. Nor did Freud have much to say of the mother's protective or nurturing functions, or of the child's maternal—by which is meant pre-Oedipal—needs.

Rank believes that conflict derives from humanity's essentially am-bivalent feelings about separation. These feelings, he argues, are "biological"; they are present or inevitable for all who undergo the experience—the trauma—of birth. This is because all individuals possess a will to independence—a creative impulse—as well as a comparably deep longing for incorporation or community, a state analogous to the above-mentioned "primal" condition or "intra-uterine primal pleasure," and one that recalls Freud's account of regressive longings in *Beyond the Pleasure Principle*. In the actual birth, writes Rank in *Will Therapy*, "the inner fear, which the child experiences . . . has in it both elements, fear of life and fear of death, since birth on the one hand means the end of life (former life), on the other, carries also the fear of the new life. . . . There is in the individual a primal fear, which manifests itself now as fear of life, another time as fear of death."[20] Rank identified this fear as early as his second book, *The Myth of the Birth of the Hero*, in which "the vital peril, thus concealed in the representation of birth through exposure, actually exists in the process of birth itself"[21]—so that birth is both a triumph against opposition and a fatal entry into a life of struggle, principally (or ultimately) against death. The result, not only for the hero but also for us all, is ambivalence, a pattern of conflict reproduced throughout one's life; a conflict between "individuation and involvement," to use Susanne K. Langer's analogous terms, or "emergence and embeddedness."[22] Because the opposing impulses of separation and merger account for all our conflicts, fears, and pleasures, and because their origins are physical or biological, "we are led to recognize in the birth trauma," Rank concludes, "the ultimate biological basis of the psychical."[23] The closeness of this theory to object relations is suggested in the following passage from a controversial lecture Rank delivered in 1928 to a large audience at the Boston Society of Psychiatry and Neurology. The "single great problem" of psychology, Rank argues, is "the contrast between the ego and the Thou, between the Self and the world, between the inner and the outer." Psychology is thus "a *science of relations*, which easily runs into the danger of overestimation of either the one or the other factor in itself instead of dealing with the relationship between the two."[24]

The Trauma of Birth traces the primal conflict or ambivalence in all ages and aspects of human life. Everywhere Rank looks, he finds its manifestations: in infantile anxiety, adult neurosis, sexual gratification, and all forms of sublimation, from the "symbolic adaptations" of normal men and women in dreams, to culture in all its forms, including myth, the structure of the state, religion, art, philosophic speculation, and psychoanalysis itself. This is also what happens in his subsequent books, especially *Art and Artist*, in which the archetypal opposition is uncovered in all aspects of creation. For Rank, the artist's problem is that of all humanity, which is why he referred to neurotics as failed artists. We must all, according to Rank, find a way of balancing contradictory impulses, the simultaneous wish for and

fear of individuation. But "whereas the average man largely subordinates himself, both socially and biologically, to the collective, and
the neurotic shuts himself deliberately off from both, the productive
type finds a middle way."[25] It is a way that all people seek, and the
ability to achieve it depends upon the extent to which one is like, or
makes oneself like, an artist. "The person," writes Rank in *Truth and
Reality* (1929), "is both creator and creature at once; from creature he
actually becomes the creator—in the ideal case, of his self, his personality."[26]

How, then, does writing or art call for "a middle way"? The writer
begins with an impulse "to immortalize his mortal life," "to eternalize
his individuality apart from the collective ideologies"[27]—that is, to be
original. This involves separation from a variety of potential entrap-
ments, the most insidious of which are often of the artist's own making. Not only must the artist "liberate himself from the earlier ideologies that he has hitherto taken as his pattern; in the course of his
life (generally at its climax) he must undergo a much harder conflict
. . . he must escape as well from the ruling ideology of the present,
which he has himself strengthened by his own growth and development" (p. 368). The irony of all this effort is that the individuating
impulse is itself, ultimately, a longing for community or merger, for
"the potential *restoration* of a union with the Cosmos, which once
existed and was then lost." The satisfactions of art recall "the prenatal
condition, which the individual in his yearning for immortality
strives to restore" (p. 113). Nevertheless, the artist experiences the
initial or inaugurating impulse as a wish for separation or emergence.

In the act of expressing this impulse to separate, dependence and
involvement are unavoidable; the escape from ideologies is impossible. The writer is dependent, for instance, on an audience and on
"canons of style, evolved from the collective consciousness" (p. xiv).
If the writer's experiences of individuality are to be eternalized in art,
they must have "form," which Rank defines as "the spontaneously
given expression of the particular human ideology prevailing at the
moment" (p. 359). This definition is Rank's version of the distinction
between primary and secondary processes. "The poetic process," he
writes, "divides more or less closely into two separate phases, which
have been called the conscious and the unconscious, but really correspond to the two phases of language-formation, the individual creative expression of an experience and the collective communication
of it" (p. 275). In the verbal shaping of the second phase occurs "a
fresh collectivizing of what was originally expressed personally, with
communicating and understanding as its object" (p. 279). Thus, the
middle way of the artist or writer involves both individual assertion

and collective communication, emergence and embeddedness, which is why Rank's account of it in *Art and Artist* attends to both components. Previous studies of the artist or writer, by which Rank means those of Freud in particular, "study the creative process in the artist himself [and are] too much inclined to underrate both his cultural dependence and his aesthetic effectiveness" (pp. xviii–xix)—an imbalance born of an earlier bias: the tendency to regard the art work not as the creation of the individual but as that of the *Zeitgeist*. In *The Artist*, Rank admits, he paid too little attention to cultural dependence; he tries to overcome this failing in his later works.

What, then, enables the writer to write? Rank's answer derives from a radically un-Freudian notion of will, his version of the conscious or the ego. *Will* is a term that plays almost no part in Freud's writings, except for a few early references in connection with hysteria. This absence is understandable, given Freud's theories of the unconscious origins of mental illness, what Charles Rycroft calls his "assumption of psychic determinism."[28] As for the ego in Freud's theory, in *Truth and Reality* Rank deplores it as helpless and dependent, a nonentity, for which there remains no independent function. For Rank, though, as for the later ego psychologists, the ego is—or can be—active: "instead of being caught between the two powerful forces of fate, the inner id and the externally derived super-ego, [the ego] develops and expresses itself creatively"—which is why he calls it "much more than a mere show place for the standing conflict between two great forces."[29] The ego is "the temporal representative of the cosmic primal force,"[30] by which is meant, according to a contemporary Rankian, "not some mystical power, but the energic nature of the universe, especially of the living universe"[31] (though "energic nature" is hardly a down-to-earth concept). In Rank's words from *Art and Artist*, "the individual will is a derivative of the biological life-impulse," though "a purely human derivative"[32]—that is, it is other than merely adaptive. As such, it is "primary . . . a given."[33] "I have always felt," Nin once said to Rank, "that there *is something beyond* lesbianism, narcissism, masochism, etc." "Yes," she recalls him responding, "there is creation."[34] This belief in creation—or the creative will or force—is hinted at in his earliest and most orthodox publications. Even in *The Artist*, he speaks of a primal energy source such as that referred to by Schopenhauer and the pre-Socratic philosophers Anaxagoras and Empedocles, who taught that plants grow from an inner desire.[35] Rank's later works merely give this source a new prominence.

The absence, then, of an active, independent impulse or force is what Rank laments in Freudian notions of creativity. What, he asks, is the agent in the process of sublimation?

When psychoanalysis speaks of a sublimated sexual impulse in creative art, meaning thereby the impulse diverted from its primarily biological function and directed towards higher ends, the question as to what diverted and what directed is just being dismissed with an allusion to repression. But repression is a negative factor, which might divert but never direct . . . I, for my part, am of the opinion that . . . positively willed control takes the place of negative inhibition, and that it is the masterful use of the sexual impulse in the service of this individual will which produces the sublimation.[36]

Here Rank anticipates Ernst Kris and the American ego psychologists in his stress on the active, conscious powers of the creator. Although Rank's theories of will derive ultimately from his early study of Schopenhauer, according to Fay Karpf, an early Rankian, there is also something characteristically American about them, something "not unlike the treatment incorporated in James' psychology and . . . introduced . . . for the same essential reasons that James did, namely, opposition to a completely atomistic, mechanistic, and deterministic view of personality and conduct."[37] This "American" quality is not surprising, given Rank's early and lifelong interest in American culture, particularly in the writings of Emerson and Twain, as well as his work (while a student at the University of Vienna) not only on William James's psychology but on the theories of the Harvard neurologist James Jackson Putnam. Freud also thought Rank's ideas "American": his bold but ultimately inimical "train of thought . . . was conceived under the stress of the contrast between the post-war misery of Europe and the 'prosperity' of America, and it was designed to accelerate the tempo of analytic therapy to suit the rush of American life."[38] A similar point might be made about the "Americanism" of ego psychology, with its concept of a healthy, or "unhampered," part of the ego, the ego as "conflict-free zone." Lacan's complaints against ego psychology make much of this connection, as though the need for "some stable value, some standard of the measure of the real" (i.e., the autonomous ego, that "down-at-heels mirage"), was peculiarly compelling for those "on the other side of the Atlantic."[39]

The function of Rank's version of the "down-at-heels mirage" against which Lacan rails is to overcome regressive forces, the first of which is fear, the inevitable byproduct of assertion. This function is necessary because assertion involves separation, which is simultaneously perceived as death as well as life. Fear of birth is fear of death, which is why Ernest Becker in *The Denial of Death* (1973) is able to place Rank in the company of Norman O. Brown. "Consciousness of death," writes Becker, "is the primary repression, not sexuality. As Rank unfolded in book after book and as Brown has recently again argued, the new perspective on psychoanalysis is that its crucial concept is the repression of death. *This* is what is creaturely about man, *this* is the repression on which culture is built."[40] It is the autonomous creative will that effects such a repression. In Rank's words from *Art and Artist*, "with the productive type the will dominates, and exercises a far-reaching control over (but not check upon) the instincts, which are pressed into service to bring about creatively a social relief of fear."[41] For Freud, such relief was tinged with escapism. "The demand for immortality," he writes in "Of Transience" (1916), "is a product of our wishes too unmistakable to lay claim to reality: what is painful may nonetheless be true" (14:305). For Rank and Becker, the impulse to immortality is seen more positively.

The will does not block out or obliterate fear; it overcomes it, in a manner that links Rank with the existentialists. "This overcoming," writes Rank in a phrase worthy of Kierkegaard, "is only possible . . . in one way . . . through volitional affirmation of the obligatory."[42] This is a familiar existentialist paradox: the obligatory, once chosen, ceases to be a hindrance. Rank's use of the Oedipus myth to explain this paradox is a measure of how far he had moved from Freudian orthodoxy. Rank sees the story of Oedipus just as Freud says one should not, as a tragedy of fate:

> It even seems to me as if the Oedipus myth itself if taken in the Greek spirit, were an expression of the same striving for independence in human development: namely, the deliberate affirmation of the existence forced on us by fate. That which is divinely but unequivocally preordained for the hero by his birth, in the mythical account, he deliberately makes his own by embodying it in action and experience. This experience is a creative experience, for it serves to create the myth itself, and the sagas, poems, and tragedies based on it, whose various representations of the one theme are determined by the collective ideological outlook of the moment and the interpretation appropriate thereto.[43]

This passage suggests a second affinity to the existentialist—in addition, that is, to the artist's (or productive type's) need to create value in his or her life: Rank sees the problems we face as inevitable products of the human condition, as problems that cannot be "cured" in the manner of neuroses. One final connection between Rank and the existentialist is his vision of the artist's (or will's) first task: the creation of an artistic identity. "The creative artistic personality," Rank writes in *Art and Artist*, "is . . . the first work of the productive individual, and . . . all his other works are partly the repeated expression of this primal creation, partly a justification by dynamism." Or, later: "The self-labelling and the self-training of an artist is the indispensable basis of all creative work."[44] In other words, to approve one's independence or individuation, to appoint oneself as maker and accept one's autonomy, is the precondition of a productive life. What this act of self-appointment calls for is what all subsequent creation calls for: a willingness to separate oneself, in the words of Rank's exponent Esther Menaker, "at the expense of 'the other'—be that mother, the family, or society at large."[45]

As the above quotation suggests, fear is not the only impediment to creativity: guilt also plays its part. Thus, Rank offers the same two sources or sorts of blockage as Freud. But guilt for Rank has nothing to do with forbidden sexual impulses, as it does, for example, in Freud's account of Dostoevsky; instead it is related to pre-Oedipal stages, what Freud would call oral and anal stages. Rank believes that guilt is as inevitable a byproduct of separation as fear. After all, the infant experiences the development of the ego or self—the will—as denial or opposition; all separation is separation *from* something. Hence the frequency with which self-willing in infancy is manifested in what Rank calls "not wanting to,"[46] as in the familiar contrary period between the ages of two and four: rejection and hostility are the infant's reactions to the inevitable deprivations entailed in growth. The feelings of hostility—or infant sadism—are directed inevitably against the prohibiting mother, but, because the infant is still dependent upon the mother, they cannot always be expressed. The result is Rank's version of the development of the superego. "The child incorporates the strict mother image as a part of his own ego," writes Menaker, "and demands self-punishment. . . . This internalization and the taking of the guilt upon oneself perpetuate the relationship to the mother and stand in the way of separation from her. It also forms the kernel of the superego for both men and women."[47] Rank sees this pattern repeated whenever individuals assert themselves, with the mother's role being taken by any number of opposed "others."

Rank's examples of the inhibiting effects of guilt are myriad and range from accounts of individuals to those of whole civilizations, the latter often retailed in disconcertingly abstract and generalized terms. Here, for instance, is his account in *Art and Artist* of the relation between will and guilt in Greek culture, which Rank sees, as does Nietzsche, as the eventual triumph of science ("truth") over art—a supplanting or transition that recalls Freud on Leonardo's abandonment of painting for "research" and, thus, serves as a macrocosmic instance of creative blockage. Rank begins by asserting that Greek art celebrates the individual or human at the expense of the collective or natural, the "earth" or "community" as nurturing mother. Greek art is the product of a "freedom-ideology" (why Rank believes this, or whether he is right to do so, is not in question here), and

> freedom-ideology, beyond a certain point, presumes the nega-
> tion of . . . dependence and is therefore also in a deeper sense,
> dishonest. This fundamental dishonesty towards nature then
> comes out as the consciousness of guilt, which we see active in
> every process of art. . . . This feeling of guilt, of human *hybris*—
> of which the Greeks were the first to become conscious . . . is
> acquired by the gradual growth and formation of another ideol-
> ogy, that of truth, which acts paralyzingly on the freedom of the
> ideology of beauty. This scientific ideology born of the feeling of
> guilt therefore first appears in Greece, where the ideology of ar-
> tistic beauty also attained its greatest freedom.

Rank thus attributes Plato's hostility to art to its "dishonesty" or *"hy-bris,"* his opposition being a manifestation of "this scientific guilt-feeling in the Greeks."[48] The art-ideology is "blocked" by guilt at the abandonment or denial of humanity's animal or natural dependence.

Menaker, who is herself a Rankian therapist, offers a second, more down-to-earth example of blockage, this one drawn from one of her patients. She tells of a young writer who became hypochondriac whenever she was "profoundly involved in a piece of creative writ-ing." Menaker says that this hypochondria "attests to guilt and antic-ipates illness or death as punishment for the autonomous act of cre-ation, an act which represents ultimate independence and therefore separation from parental introjects."[49] The anticipation of death al-luded to here grows out of fears engendered by the thought of sepa-ration—separation being a symbolic meaning in any act or assertion. These are fears of life as well as death, and they arise not only in anticipation of the completed work, "which has the value of an eter-nity symbol, but the particular creative process, [which] if it involves an exhaustive output, is by the same token a symbol of death, so that the artist is both driven on by the impulse to externalization and checked by the fear of death." Hence the writer's difficulty "both in beginning and in finishing his work";[50] instead of the creative will, fear and guilt pervert "the cosmic primal force" into counterwill or negative will, as in another of Menaker's patients, one who faced the threat of separation—in the form of both a finally completed disser-tation and the analyst's impending vacation—with a preemptive re-fusal or "leaving" of her own; an act, to be sure, but a negative or counter act, and one repeated in the refusals of many a blocked writer or artist.[51] In Rank's words, "the inhibitions, then, of which most artists complain, both during creation and in its intervals, are the ego's necessary protections"—against guilt and fear. The writer who is blocked and cannot overcome this block becomes a neurotic, because for Rank the sole difference between the two is that "in the neurotic the fear of life predominates and so checks all expression in life, while the artist-type *can* overcome this fear in his creation and is driven by the fear of death to immortalize himself."[52] Rank borrows a metaphor from Schopenhauer to make the point: Life is a loan, death a repayment.[53]

These theories of creativity and blockage may well have had a personal source. Alone among the inner circle of Freud's early followers, Rank lacked medical training. He came to psychoanalysis through literary and philosophical influences, especially those of Ibsen and Nietzsche, and his earliest literary ambitions, according to some, were never fully abandoned.[54] Throughout his life, according to this account, Rank felt guilty about the diversion of his energies into psychological research; hence his description of *Art and Artist* as "an organic growth rising out of an intensive struggle of many years' standing over a personal problem—a lived experience that ultimately took shape in the present work."[55] That this struggle was over what he saw as a personal failure of creative will is suggested in several passages of Nin's *Diary* in which Rank regrets what he sees as his own creatively confining or straightened circumstances as therapist and researcher and seems almost to envy his former patient's artistic resolve. The conflict may also have affected the style as well as the substance of his writings. Freud was quite open about Rank's style: "You will understand if I speak directly to what I perceive as the shortcomings of this paper," he declared at an early meeting of the Vienna Psychoanalytic Association, "You do not know how to stay within the limits of the subject and how to outline the topic clearly."[56] Rank's disappearance from the psychoanalytic mainstream derived only in part from his early death and the organized hostility of the psychoanalytic establishment from which he broke; the obscurity of his style also played a part. This obscurity was in large measure a product of his prolixity, as he himself was well aware. Coming to the point, he once admitted, left him indifferent—a reaction that may well have grown out of the very "life fear" that inhibits the artist. In like manner, the many florid or "cosmic" patches in his writing—Jones complains of "a hyperbolical vein more suitable for the announcement of a new religious gospel"[57]—attest to Rank's artistic ambitions, his hopes for the psychoanalyst as "a new kind of artist." For all his fluency, Rank seems to have thought of himself as a blocked artist. Although as a theorist Rank had "an iron diligence, the envy of many colleagues," and "finished effectively" what he began, as an artist he "lacked perseverance and focus on a small area" and "tasted too many fruits."[58] It is an important element of his real, if flawed, achievement to have offered a new and infinitely suggestive account of why this should be so.

Ego Psychology

Ego psychology complicates the orthodox Freudian view of writer's block by locating it in secondary or elaborational, as well as primary or inspirational, phases of creation—thus conforming to the actual experience of many blocked writers. It also places new stress on the controlling and organizing factors in creation, which the earliest and most orthodox theorists were rightly (and almost from the start) accused of ignoring or underplaying. In the process, a more thorough and systematic account of defenses is brought to bear upon discussion of a work's formal properties.

This shift of interest from primary to secondary processes was part of a larger shift in psychoanalysis in general, one that is usefully epitomized in the reception accorded a work of applied analysis by Bergler's old chief at the Psychoanalytic Freud Clinic, Eduard Hitschmann. Hitschmann's work, entitled *Great Men: Psychoanalytic Studies* (1956), was reviewed by Heinz Kohut, who began his career as something of an ego psychologist. Kohut saw Hitschmann's book as hopelessly dated, a product of "the early period of psychoanalysis which remained his home." When Hitschmann writes of the moral scrupulousness of Albert Schweitzer, for example, he posits "the existence of an unconscious guilt feeling which originated in early years and was renewed by regression." This, Kohut argues, is reductive. To a forward-looking ego psychologist (and here Kohut would include himself), "a keen awareness of the misery existing in the world and the determination to live a life devoted to the suffering are the autonomous attitudes of a mature ego. One might rather pose the question why this man was capable of maintaining his ideals beyond the temporary crisis of his early years and thus, during a period of unparalleled crisis of Western Christian civilization, could become by his very existence the spiritual support of so many."[59] Why not, in other words, consider Schweitzer's accomplishment an *accomplishment*, a product of control and compassion rather than conflict and unconscious psychic compromise? Are there not, in the words of Heinz Hartmann, the foremost theoretician of ego psychology, "moral motivations which have the full dynamic significance of independent forces in the mental economy"?[60]

To understand how so radical a shift in outlook came about, something must be said of the origins, as well as the basic assumptions, of ego psychology. Ego psychology is the name given to that line or branch of post-Freudian theory which stresses the mind's adaptive and integrative capacities.[61] It grew out of Freud's *The Ego and the Id* (1923), in which a tripartite structural theory of the psyche (id, ego, and superego) replaced the old topographical model of the conscious, preconscious, and unconscious. The theory was then elaborated in *Inhibitions, Symptoms, and Anxiety* (1926) and Anna Freud's *The Ego and the Mechanisms of Defence* (1936), and it received its definitive expression in Hartmann's *Ego Psychology and the Problem of Adaptation*, which was first published in 1939, but was not translated into English until 1958. In the postwar period, thanks in part to the joint publications of Hartmann, Kris, and Rudolf Lowenstein, ego psychology became the dominant trend in North American psychoanalytic theory. Its single most influential aesthetic application was Kris's *Psychoanalytic Explorations in Art* (1952), a compilation of essays stretching back to 1932.[62]

Ego psychology differs from classical Freudianism not only in its emphasis on adaptation but in its account of what adaptation is: the work, in part, of an agent. Ego psychology associates this agent with, or sees it as, an expression of the ego—that part of the ego, to be more precise, which is free from instinctual conflict. The ego is conceived of as having its own motives or interests: those of adaptation, including the need to be productive, to enjoy life, and to maintain equilibrium in the face of external threats or pressures. These motives or interests exist prior to the influence of frustration. "Motivation is thus derived from two independent sources," write the American object-relations theorists Jay R. Greenberg and Stephen A. Mitchell, "the (unchanged) drives which relate to reality only secondarily, and those adaptive capacities of the ego which are inherently related to the environment."[63]

The energy drawn upon by inherent ego interests—because all psychic or mental activity derives, by analogy with "the other natural sciences," from movements in energy[64]—is conceived of by ego psychology as neutralized or desexualized. Neutralized energy is what Freud calls "bound," as opposed to "free" or "mobile," energy. Free or mobile energy derives from the unconscious and is used in the primary process. "Its regulative principle," writes Roy Schafer, "is tension reduction (the pleasure principle)."[65] In the words of J. Laplanche and J.-B. Pontalis, "it flows towards discharge in the speediest and most direct fashion possible,"[66] as in the inspirational bolt from the blue. Bound energy, however, is associated with the secondary process, which Freud (but not always his ego-psychology followers) sees as the work of later and more advanced mechanisms in the psychical structure.

Bound energy, the energy of the secondary or elaborational processes, can be controlled and directed, harvested and measured out; the ego can also transform it into mobile energy. In like manner, according to Hartmann, the ego is capable of neutralizing free energy, transforming it into bound energy; and it is in part through this neutralization and diversion of free energy that the ego is able to adapt, to establish that reciprocal relation with the environment which constitutes maturity.[67] Thus, in Hartmann's system, the ego is no longer merely passive or dependent, Freud's "poor creature owing service to three masters" (19:56), the psychic eunuch scorned by early psychoanalytic apostles of the will, such as Rank and Alfred Adler.[68]

Hartmann's account of how the ego's autonomous organizing capacities develop in the "normal" person has been called the most important of his contributions to psychoanalytic theory.[69] What Hartmann offered was a model or standard against which to measure pathology, for "in order to fully grasp neurosis and its etiology, we have to understand the etiology of health too."[70] In Hartmann's theory, development is measured in two ways: by the degree of independence the ego or subject attains from the environment or object, and by the correlative stability of that object or environment in the subject's eye—the extent to which the subject is able to tolerate the object's otherness and independence. At this point, of course, ego psychology meets or becomes object relations.

As for the ultimately hypothetical nature of Hartmann's—or any—model of "normal" development, this is openly admitted: no person's ego functions follow exactly what the theorist conceives of as their innately programmed developmental course—even granted the "average expectable environment"[71] (an ego-psychology equivalent of Winnicott's "good-enough mother") that Hartmann postulates as a precondition of "normal" development. Although not originally or necessarily constituted by conflict, the so-called conflict-free or autonomous ego functions are inevitably affected by it. "The normal human being," writes Hartmann, "is free neither of problems nor of conflicts. Conflicts are part of the human condition."[72] As a consequence, development or adaptation always involves detours or regressions. These are necessary and protective, like the somatic "regressions" of sleep and orgasm. Hartmann's model of the ego and its development, claim its defenders, takes account of not only defensive and autonomous ego functions but also the influence of the former on the latter. And this model also, of course, involves a radical shift in attitudes toward defenses. No longer are defense mechanisms, such as fantasy or denial, treated as merely pathological, or regressive in a negative sense: they can also be seen more positively, as agents of adaptation, necessary and facilitating withdrawals from which both strength and new perspectives can be attained.

How, then, do the theories of ego psychology relate to the creation of works of art, or the failure to create them? They do so in three ways: first, by providing a much more thorough and elaborate range of defenses with which to identify the secondary or formative aspects of creation—thus shifting attention from the content of the work, the inaugurating or underlying fantasy, to the containing or taming mechanisms of defense or form, as in the elaborate taxonomies of the American literary theorist Norman Holland, in which different id impulses (oral, anal, phallic, and genital) call forth separate and corresponding defenses;[73] second, by their conception of the ego's role in the primary process, as in Kris's theory of "regression in the service of the ego"; and, third, by their matching of the vicissitudes of development—by which is meant the various stages and struggles on the road to ego autonomy or mature object relations rather than mere "substitute satisfactions"—with the problems the artist or writer encounters in giving form to his or her art.

By far the most influential of these applications is Kris's account of the primary process. The creation of a work of art, writes Kris in "Approaches to Art," the first of the essays in *Psychoanalytic Explorations in Art,* involves two stages or conditions: "inspiration and elaboration," the equivalents of Freud's primary and secondary processes. Inspiration is characterized "by the feeling of being driven, the experience of rapture, and the conviction that an outside agent acts through the creator." In elaboration, however, "the experience of purposeful organization, and the intent to solve a problem predominate. The first has many features in common with regressive processes: impulses and drives, otherwise hidden, emerge. The subjective experience is that of a flow of thoughts and images driving toward expression. The second has many features in common with what characterizes 'work'—dedication and concentration."[74] Elaboration is thus a species of what Kris calls "reality testing": an awareness and acceptance, for instance, of the independence and integrity of the medium, or of the historical state of the genre in which the artist or writer is working—an attentiveness, that is, to the needs and interests of the audience and its larger culture.[75] None of these ideas is particularly new, even in psychoanalysis. But the opposition between inspiration and elaboration is not as clear-cut as it first appears, because when Kris goes on to contrast inspiration with "the psychotic condition," the former is said to be a state in which "the ego controls the primary process and puts it into service," while in the latter "the ego is overwhelmed by the primary process."[76] The ego is thus given a role in both aspects or phases of creation, whereas in earlier psychoanalytic aesthetics its role was often marginalized, even in what would usually be thought of as secondary processes.

Hartmann explains how such a view of creation was new to psychoanalytic theory. "We are generagly accustomed," he writes in "The Concept of Health" (1939), "to think of regressive behavior as the antithesis of conduct adapted to reality."[77] It was Kris, in a paper of 1935, and Hartmann after him, who turned this view around, emphasizing that regression could be adaptive as well as escapist, what Crews calls a species of *reculer pour mieux sauter.*[78] Like the other defenses—for example, denial, projection, and intellectualization—regression has been rescued or rehabilitated by ego psychology and is now conceived of as potentially helpful or health-giving. Provided, of course, it does not go too far and is controlled. "The world is all the richer for having a devil in it," declares William James, "so long as we keep a foot upon his neck."[79] "When regression goes too far," writes Kris, "the symbols become private, perhaps unintelligible even to the reflective self; when, at the other extreme, content is preponderant, the result is described as cold, mechanical, uninspired."[80]

A strong ego makes possible this compromise between regression and control, so for Kris and his fellow ego psychologists the artist is conceived of as the exact opposite of the unstable neurotic frequently associated with the Freudian view. The writer's ego has to be especially strong because it must channel as well as withstand the flow of id energies. "Flexibility of repression" is a sign of strength rather than a symptom, just as writing or the creation of a work of art is to be clearly distinguished from symptom formation. Writing now becomes a communicative as well as a self-expressive phenomenon, and what it communicates—always in addition to what Freud calls its "manifest content"—is the sense that the repressed *can* be communicated, that the ego can let loose the id without being swamped or overcome by it. Art is thus always, in Crews's words, "the triumph of form over chaos, meaning over panic, mediated claims over naked conflict, purposeful action over sheer psychic spillage."[81] The sense of mastery, the excitation of and escape from danger entailed in creation, makes the process pleasurable. For Kris, this sense recalls "one of the earliest, and frequently neglected thoughts of Freud: the suggestion that under certain conditions man may attempt to gain pleasure from the very activity of the psychic mechanism"[82] (though opponents of ego psychology claim that it undervalues the role such activity plays "as corrective of social convention for Freud").[83] Creation is thus a form of catharsis for Kris: like Aristotelian purgation, it "enables the ego to re-establish the control which is threatened by damned up instinctual demands," and offers pleasure "in both discharge and control."[84] As for the successful reception of a work of art, when "the audience passes from passivity to activity and . . . the work of art is recreated . . . the process in the spectator has some semblance to that which the artist experienced."[85]

What, then, makes this process—one of productive regression, of "regression in the service of the ego"—possible? Roy Schafer offers six "overlapping factors" (there is a lot of this sort of scrupulous imprecision in psychoanalytic theory) favoring ego strength or productive regression.[86] These factors have been harvested from a variety of influential ego-psychology sources: Fenichel on the definition of ego strength; Erikson, Hartmann, Kris, and Rapaport on the neutralization of aggressive or libidinal energies—that is, free or mobile energies; Erikson again on the social and cultural forces involved in healthy development. The first factor that Schafer offers is knowledge of, and confidence in, one's feelings, so "when the regressive process . . . comes too close to drives, affects, and fantasies not assimilable in consciousness, [one knows that] opposite signals will trigger the search for defensive disguise of content or reversal of the entire process" (p. 129). The second factor is a secure sense of self, for it is precisely the lack of such a sense that makes affects and drives seem threatening, as in the schizophrenic's fear of intimacy, which, according to Schafer, "conspicuously involves a fear of disintegrating, exploding, being totally engulfed" (p. 129). The third factor is a history of having mastered early traumata, a history that frees the individual "to have subjective experiences which imply in certain respects how it was once to have been a child, and to have felt feminine, receptive, helpless, omnipotent, and generally fluid in internal state and object relations" (p. 129). The fourth factor is a moderate superego and "flexibility rather than rigidity or fluidity of defense and controls" (this is an especially tautologous factor because it is precisely this condition that Schafer's factors are meant to facilitate). The fifth factor is "a history of adequate trust and mutuality in inter-personal relations, particularly in the early mother-child relation," the result of which is a confidence that the world will accept what one produces rather than respond "with panic, withdrawal, or arbitrary punishment" (p. 130). The sixth factor is that the repressed material—be it disguised in the form of a joke, the solving of a problem, or a work of literature—be valued by the community.

What prevents or hampers regression in the service of the ego, and thus blocks the writer, are guilt and anxiety over the "unconscious significance" (p. 126) of release or relaxation. To those for whom, in Schafer's words, regression means "passivity, sinful and defiant transgression, and magically potent destructiveness towards authority and whatever persons and things are involved, be they external or internalized, real or phantasied" (p. 126), creation will be impossible, the primary process will be thwarted. Schafer reiterates Kris's point about the relation of inspiration to such guilt and anxiety: inspiration is a way for the potentially guilt-ridden to externalize responsibility, not so much for the product or content of the work as for the process that generates it. In sum, writing—or any process that calls for regression—is impossible for those who are overly concerned about "the ego's relative autonomy from the id, disturbances of the complex balance between active and passive ego functions, and the ego's greater vulnerability to superego condemnation" (p. 128). And this, of course, is pretty much what the classical Freudian has to say: that what inhibits the writer is fear of psychic dissolution, of surrender to the repressed, or of massive retaliation for such surrender on the part of the repressive mechanism.

The third and final effect or influence ego psychology has had on notions of blockage and creativity involves what Kris calls the "psychology of forms." The central tenet of this "psychology" (there is not much of it) is that the problems the artist faces in structuring and communicating his or her work are like those faced by the developing ego: both writer and individual seek a balance or accommodation between subject (or self) and object, as in "normal" development. The formal features of the text or work of art are thus determined by what Gilbert Rose calls "the dialectic between separation and fusion, control and ambiguity, tension and release, thought and feeling or action"[87]—or elsewhere, in specifically ego-psychology or economic terms, primary and secondary processes. As Rose traces this dialectic at work in a variety of literary forms, success—that is, true creation—is consistently depicted as an idealized vision of the working of the mind or the relation between perceiving subject and perceived object; this is the source of its appeal to both writer and reader. In like manner, the failure of an artist or art work is seen as analogous to a failure in adaptation or adjustment—a failure in object relations.

At which point, as I have suggested, ego psychology becomes object relations, as both Rose and Kohut admit (Kohut being the other theoretician from an ego-psychology orientation to attempt at least the beginnings of a "psychology of form").[88] Rose's aesthetic in particular is highly synthetic, as deeply indebted to English object-relations theorists—particularly Winnicott, Ehrenzweig, and Milner—as to their American ego-psychology counterparts. For this reason I shall turn from his and other ego-psychology accounts of the causes of failed adaptation or blockage to object relations itself, suggesting only that, for some time now, ego psychology has pointed to a relation between development or adaptation and the problems of form (without, until recently, specifying its nature) and that in doing so it has implied a connection between the causes of artistic success or failure and the construction of a "normal" or healthy individuality.

British
Object-Relations Theory

The theories of creativity and blockage I discuss in this chapter grew out of what is usually called the English School of Psychoanalysis. This school emerged as a distinct group just before World War II, its followers having been brought together by the teachings of Melanie Klein (1882–1960).[1] Among Klein's early followers were Joan Riviere and Susan Isaacs; later followers include Paula Heimann, Marion Milner, and Hanna Segal. Others less immediately or directly influenced by Klein's writing and teaching were D. W. Winnicott, W. R. D. Fairbairn, Michael Balint, and Harry Guntrip, all of whom had been working independently along related lines. Of this latter group, Fairbairn is perhaps the most innovative figure, though also the least influential, especially in the aesthetic realm (in large part because of his relative isolation in Edinburgh). The line of descent is from Klein, and its place of origin is London, where all the theorists I discuss in this chapter lived and worked. These theorists not only knew one another's work but were clear and explicit in acknowledging mutual influence. They also produced much of their most important writing at approximately the same period, in the 1950s and early 1960s. Although each has a distinct style or approach, the terrain they cover—their central understanding of what facilitates or inhibits creativity—is the same. Together, they constitute the single most interesting movement in psychoanalytic aesthetics, and their individual works are often clearer and more persuasive when looked at as versions of a larger theory.

Kleinian Object Relations

Kleinian theory begins with the insistence that the analyst look for the origins of neurosis behind or beneath the Oedipal stage, in earlier layers of personality development. What Klein claimed to have dis-

covered by focusing, at Sandor Ferenczi's suggestion, on earliest infancy, were preverbal fantasies of rage and aggression in children.
These fantasies she associated with Freud's late and incomplete
theory of the death instinct—a theory to which she gave central importance in her own writings. Access to preverbal fantasies in children could be attained, she argued, by watching and joining them in
play, particularly in games that involved assuming family roles or
parts. As Klein had already discovered in her work as a nursery-
school teacher, play was an infant equivalent of free association in an
adult patient. "In their play," she writes, "children represent symbol-
ically phantasies, wishes and experiences. Here they are employing
the same language, the same archaic, phylogentically acquired mode
of expression as we are familiar with from dream."[2]

Although Freud had published his case history of Little Hans in
1909 (a study based on indirect analysis conducted through instruc-
tions to the child's father), he never made a systematic survey of pre-
Oedipal neuroses. Nor did he base his accounts of children on direct
observation, but rather on extrapolations from adult fantasy and
memory. It was Klein, and Freud's daughter Anna, who opened the
field of child analysis, though the latter worked along lines suggested
by another Viennese analyst, Hermine von Hug-Hellmuth, the only
other analyst before 1919 to attempt to treat children (though only
children in the latency phase, just before puberty). The differences
between Klein and Anna Freud were, in the first instance, therapeutic: for Anna Freud, children of the pre-Oedipal period were still so
dependent upon their parents that they could not attain a full transference—that is, a negative as well as a positive one. In addition,
because both the superego and the Oedipus complex, according to
classical theory, are later developments, deep Oedipal analysis for
very young children is impossible. The analyst's role, therefore,
ought to be educational and supportive rather than analytic or neu-
trally interpretive, as in Klein's approach;[3] the aim ought to be to
strengthen the child's developing superego.

The differences between Klein and Anna Freud were deep and fundamental and came to a head early on,[4] though Klein's developed
theory was only brought to completion in a paper of 1946 entitled
"Notes on Some Schizoid Mechanisms." The key moment or element
in this theory—the line of demarcation between different levels or
phases of what Klein identifies as pre-Oedipal development—occurs
when the infant recognizes its mother, and then its father and others,
as real and separate. Earlier, the infant was aware not of people—
separate and whole individuals with their own rights, feelings, and
needs—but of objects. These objects are not so much "things," as in

conventional usage, as parts of people; what Klein, therefore, calls "part objects" (they are also called part objects because of the way the infant splits them into ideal and persecutory aspects).

In the stage before the infant connects these objects with real and whole human beings, its feelings toward them are projections of its own impulses. These impulses, argues Klein, are often aggressive or envious, irrespective of the infant's environment and the love of the mother. (Just how much importance Klein attached to the role of real people in infant development is a matter of dispute.)[5] They are pre-Oedipal manifestations of the death instinct—something Freud would deny because for him the death instinct is a later development. The impulses produce anxiety, a fear of annihilation, causing the infant to entertain defensive fantasies of attacking and destroying. This is because for Klein, extrapolating from what might be called Freud's "Jungian" strain, in *Totem and Taboo* (1913) and elsewhere, the death instinct stands not only for the destructive tendencies we turn outward in aggression but also for the fear of our own death, which underlies and animates them. "The fear of annihilation by the destructive force within us," she writes in "On Identification" (1955), "is the deepest fear of all."[6]

The "part object" toward which the infant's aggressive and envious impulses are in the first instance directed is the nurturing breast, by which is meant not only the literal breast of the mother but also the a priori image of the breast instilled by, or derived from, phylogenetic memory. When infants project their feelings onto the breast, particularly during moments of frustration during weaning, they both deny their own hostility and transfer it onto the breast, imagining the breast as retaliating and persecuting in a potentially annihilating counterattack. When this bad breast is then reintrojected, it forms the persecutory aspect of the superego.[7]

But the newborn infant also possesses life as well as death instincts, again as in Freud's later, speculative writings; and these contrary life instincts, including both sexual and self-preservative impulses, are at the same time projected onto what the infant fantasizes as a wholly good object or breast, which is itself introjected. The infant then identifies with the introjected good object, which becomes the infant's ideal self, "the core of both the ego and the superego."[8] What threatens the infant is the bad breast, the persecuting object, which the infant tries to protect itself against by recourse to defense mechanisms (such as denial), a process that only increases the split between good and bad objects. The good object becomes the ideal object/self, which is seen as invulnerable; the idealized self pretends or aspires to omnipotence. But when the infant becomes hungry, for example, the fiction of omnipotence is destroyed, because for an infant "frustration is felt as a persecution."[9] The infant again feels threatened by annihilation, which leads to further splitting, further paranoia.

The central irony of the initial deflection or projection of the death instinct is that it comes back to haunt—to persecute—the infant; the initial defense serves only to make matters worse. The infant defends himself or herself against the fantasized attack of the "bad" breast by launching a counterattack. This takes the form either of a greedily sadistic oral impulse—an impulse to devour the breast, to rip and tear it—or, even more surreally, of the impulse to despoil and damage the breast with the only other weapon the infant has: "the device of soiling with excrement." "In phantasy," writes Klein, in "The Importance of Symbol Formation in the Development of the Ego" (1930), "the excreta are transformed into dangerous weapons: wetting is regarded as cutting, stabbing, burning, drowning, while the faecal mass is equated with weapons and missiles."[10] Riviere offers a more precise and extended catalog:

> Loose motions, flatus and urine are all felt to be burning, corroding and poisoning agents. Not only the excretory but all other physical functions are pressed into the service of the need for aggressive (sadistic) discharge and projection in phantasy. Limbs shall trample, kick and hit; teeth shall bite, gnaw, mangle and cut; mouth shall devour, swallow and kill (annihilate); eyes kill by a look, pierce and penetrate; breath and mouth hurt by noise, as the child's own sensitive ears have experienced.[11]

At the same time, what the infant conceives as his or her good points are projected onto the idealized object, the good breast, and what were previously conceived of as acts or weapons of aggression become expressions of love: feeding is experienced as communion rather than depletion; urination and defecation are experienced as reciprocal offerings, infant equivalents of the mother's gift of milk.[12] The result of all these processes—splitting, projection, idealization— is the weakening of the ego. "Splitting," writes Klein in "On Identification," "is effective to the extent that it brings about a dispersal of anxiety and a cutting off of emotions. But it fails in another sense because it results in a feeling akin to death—that is what the accompanying disintegration and feeling of chaos amount to."[13] It is the primary task of infant development to work through this debilitating cycle.

Klein's term for this cycle, the first and grimmest stage in development, is the "paranoid-schizoid position," which combines Fairbairn's earlier term "schizoid position" (1941), used to identify the first stage in his own parallel account of pre-Oedipal development, with her own initial term, "the paranoid position." Klein first put the two terms together in 1942 to suggest the interconnectedness at this earliest stage of psychic development of splitting and persecuting anxiety. As for "position," rather than "phase" or "stage," this is Klein's way of suggesting not only that the infant is capable of experiencing object relationships—that is, relations with the same object—from different positions, different points of view, but also that the developing individual continues to fluctuate between such "positions," that "this interaction exists in some measure throughout life." [14] What is misleading about the term "paranoid-schizoid position" is that it implies illness, whereas Klein thinks of it as normal and healthy; it is only unhealthy when the infant is unable to outgrow or work through it. [15]

Sometime after the sixth month, when the infant begins to recognize the mother as a real and separate person, and itself as one also, it has reached what Klein calls the "depressive position." And at this point the complications and entanglements of Klein's theory take on an almost Gothic involution. At first, though, there is a deceptive glimmer of light, for the position "begins" or is inspired by the infant's recognition that the fantasied attacks on the mother's breast have not been fatal and that the mother is still loving. The mother as a loving whole is in turn loved, and a good image or object—a whole object, in the sense of a whole person, one who is neither totally good nor totally bad, as in the paranoid-schizoid position, but rather the source both of what the infant needs and wants *and* of its frustrations and pains—is taken into what Klein calls the infant's inner world or inner sense of the world. This inner world, the "site" of the introjected part objects of the paranoid-schizoid position, is a world we all carry around with us—a world formed on the pattern of what we first loved and hated in life. One of its most important features, as has been suggested, is to off-load guilt-inducing feelings and impulses. In the external world, what Freud calls the "presence of Necessity" forces one to acknowledge at least some imperfections or limitations; in the inner world, the need to be free of taint or failing, to have all one wants or thinks one needs, is more difficult to check.

In the paranoid-schizoid position, the infant projected aggressive feelings onto the part object and the difference between separate self and external object was blurred. Now a sense of separate or distinct inner and outer reality begins to develop. The old fears of attack and persecution from part objects recede. In their place comes another sort of anxiety: that the newly whole and loved mother—both the external one and the internal image of her—will be or has been lost. What creates this fear and makes it doubly upsetting for the infant are the still-powerful sadistic, greedy impulses—the still-living death instinct—within it. In other words, though the depressive position is marked by the weakening of these impulses, they have by no means disappeared. In the depressive position, depressive feelings merely predominate over paranoid-schizoid ones; separation from the object, ambivalence, guilt, and loss can at last be accepted, though the possibility of "regression" to the earlier position is always there. This is also the time (Freud would put it much later) at which the Oedipus complex develops, and Klein weaves the Oedipus conflict into the child's fantasied attacks on the mother in moments of regression.

In the paranoid-schizoid position, it was the subject—the infant— who was seen as threatened; in the depressive position, what causes anxiety is fear *for* the object, which the infant now sees as threatened by his or her own aggressive impulses. Such development—the shift from one position to another—can be seen in Klein's account of one of her patients, a hypochondriac whose fears of being poisoned or destroyed gradually gave way, over the course of analysis, to fears of another sort: not so much for himself as for "his poor, endangered organs." He sought to nurse and protect these organs "in a way which made clear that [they] represented the injured internal objects."[16] This shift, to Klein, represents progress, a development into or toward the depressive position, which is why Winnicott thinks the term "depressive position" as misleading as "paranoid-schizoid position." For Klein, after all, "being depressed is an achievement, and implies a high degree of personal integration."[17]

In "normal" development, according to Klein, the persecutory elements in the superego recede, and guilt becomes a source not of fantastical persecutors but of what Segal calls "a realistic concern for the fate of one's objects, external and internal."[18] In this concern, the physical reality of the object, the real parent, plays a crucial role—if only because he or she has obviously survived, for all the murderous fantasy of the infant. Projection, idealization, omnipotent fantasies, and all other forms of perceptual distortion fall away, and "a sense of psychic reality develops—acknowledging and assuming responsibility for one's own impulses and the state of one's own internal objects."[19] Instead of a false image of the object, a compound of the infant's fears and needs, which at the same time causes the infant to falsify his or her own sense of self by denying needs and objects, comes maturity: in object-relations terms, a sense of both independence and interdependence, as well as a consequent capacity to love.

The infant's concern for the safety and integrity of the loved object and fear that the loss of this object has been the fault of his or her attacks give rise to the wish to restore and re-create. This wish remains with one forever, whenever one experiences loss. Always, at some level, the loss is experienced as a retaliation for one's own destructiveness. And this feeling issues in acts of imaginative reparation, in which the subject finds a way of restoring the lost object. "The attempts to save the love object," writes Klein in "A Contribution to the Psychogenesis of Manic-Depressive States" (1935), "to repair and restore it, attempts which in the state of depression are coupled with despair, since the ego doubts its capacity to achieve this restoration, are determining factors for all sublimations and the whole of the ego development."[20]

Klein and her followers believe that the wish to repair is at the heart of creation. But Klein herself only partially developed the aesthetic dimension of this belief: like those of Freud and Jung, her essays on aesthetics and creativity were diversions or applications and in themselves were hardly an advance over orthodox psychoanalytic aesthetics.[21] The importance of Klein to the study of writer's block and of creativity in general lies in the use to which her theories have been put. The theories matter because they enable Klein's followers, and those influenced by her theories, to revise orthodox assumptions about artistic creation in three respects: to see the creative impulse as a way of confronting, rather than deflecting or evading, anxieties; to provide specifically psychoanalytic explanations for the origin and character of formal—secondary or cognitive—features of the creative process and work of art (and for the difficulties artists and writers have with those features); and to do justice to the role of the environment—by which is meant in part both the medium and the larger culture—in the creation of, or failure to create, works of art. These are also the lines, as we have seen, along which ego psychology seeks to revise orthodox psychoanalytic aesthetics, though the post-Kleinians have produced a much more detailed and interesting revision.

Hanna Segal (b. 1918)

Of the post-Kleinian theorists I discuss in this chapter, Hanna Segal is most clearly associated with Klein herself. This is not only because she was analyzed and trained by Klein but because she has done so much to give Klein's theories wider circulation, both in her *Introduction to the Work of Melanie Klein* (1964) and in her 1979 study of Klein for the Fontana Modern Masters series. Segal's most important work on artistic creativity is the 1955 essay "A Psycho-Analytical Approach to Aesthetics." Its central premise is that "the task of the artist lies in the creation of a world of his own," even when that artist is a realist, consciously intent upon the representation of external reality.[22] The impulse that underlies artistic creativity is the need to recover a lost past.

At which point Proust is invoked, not only because the recovery of a lost past is so clearly his subject but because of his insistence that such recovery is only possible after a full acceptance of loss. "It is only by renouncing," says one of his characters, the painter Elstir, "that one can re-create what one loves."[23] Proust has to give up the lost objects of his childhood in order to be able to restore them in his internal world and then in his fiction. Here is how Segal states the full theory: "All creation is really a re-creation of a once-loved and once whole, but now lost and ruined object, a ruined internal world and self. It is when the world within us is destroyed, when it is dead and loveless, when our loved ones are in fragments, and we ourselves in helpless despair—it is then that we must re-create our world anew, reassemble the pieces, infuse life into dead fragments, re-create life."[24] As for writer's block: "It would follow that the inability to acknowledge and overcome depressive anxiety must lead to inhibitions in artistic expression."[25]

Segal's interest in artistic creativity grows out of her clinical work. "Early in my practice," she writes in the preface to *The Work of Hanna Segal* (1981), a collection of her essays, "my attention was forcibly drawn to problems of symbolism. I was lucky in that among my first patients I had both psychotics and artists inhibited in their work. Both these categories of patients made necessary the understanding of the symbolic process . . . the artists because they were ever struggling for symbolic expression and any disturbance of the symbolic function was an interference with their work."[26]

By interference, Segal means the production of inferior work, as well as no work. In both cases, though, the cause is the same and familiar. If the painting of one of Segal's patients suffers from "the effect of superficiality and prettiness," this is because of the unusual strength of her sadistic impulses and the consequent despair into which they throw her; this despair in turn leads her to deny the existence of depressive feelings. What her work reflects in its chocolate-box simplicity is "a constant make-believe that all was well with the world."[27]

More interesting, perhaps, is Segal's account of another blocked artist, a writer who, for all her professional commitment to words, retained a childhood belief that using them broke, as Segal reports, "an endless unity into bits": "It was like 'chopping up,' like 'cutting things.' It was obviously felt by her as an aggressive act."[28] This case produces clear symbolic confirmation of Segal's sense that the foundation of writing, as of all artistic creation, is the subject's ability to tolerate separation from its objects, to know and accept the distinction between self and other. "To use words," writes Segal, "meant acknowledging the separateness of the world from herself, and gave her a feeling of loss." It also made her acknowledge her own aggression, her concept of writing as "chopping up," "cutting," "losing the object." And beneath this fear, of course, was the fear of her own death, of herself being alone and apart, cut up and cut off. By not writing, a manic defense of the rearoused paranoid-schizoid position, the patient hoped "magically to control and avoid death."[29] She simply could not muster the ego strength to face the fact of death, a fact that lay beneath the acknowledgement of loss. Segal's role, therefore, was to help her patient, through the transference, to work back into and through the depressive position, as well as to accept the loss of the internal figure, which the therapist came to stand for, to mourn its loss openly, and in the process to achieve ego strength or maturity. Only then could she re-create or restore, through her writing, a clearly separate object.

What, though, enabled this writer to make such an act of reparation? And why do some such acts, and not others, result in works of art? On one level, Segal's answer is disappointingly familiar and tautologous: the writer differs from the neurotic "in that he has a greater capacity for tolerating anxiety and depression."[30] However, a new and fruitful emphasis is placed on the writer's consciousness: the writer or artist knows what he or she is doing. Which raises the question of form. The artist differs not only from the neurotic or daydreamer but also from the well-adjusted individual, the individual who is able to work through the depressive position, in the clarity of his or her own sense of reality, by which is meant the reality of both the internal world and the external one, as embodied in the artistic medium. "The real artist, being aware of his internal world which he must express, and of the external materials with which he works, can in all consciousness use this material to express the phantasy."[31] The successful work of art must, therefore, contain the full force of persecutory and depressive fears, as well as a formal structure, a wholeness, which allays anxiety. Not only is there "no aesthetic pleasure without perfect form,"[32] there can be no successful artistic creation without it.

Wholeness, for Segal, is the beautiful. The work of art is said to have to contain both ugliness, by which is meant powerful persecutory and depressive material, and beauty, or the realized image of wholeness. This latter image represents or constitutes an acknowledgment of separation. "Restated in terms of instincts," Segal concludes, "ugliness—destruction—is the expression of the death instinct; beauty—the desire to unite into rhythms and wholes—is that of the life instinct. The achievement of the artist is in giving the fullest expression to the conflict and the union between these two. . . . [T]he death instinct is acknowledged, as fully as can be borne. It is expressed and curbed to the needs of the life instinct and creation."[33] In this theory, form plays the crucial role: form redeems the destructive impulses contained or expressed in the work's content; form weaves that content into an image of the whole and loving object.

Such a theory ensures that a clear line is drawn between the destructive or neurotic material contained in a work of art and both the work itself and the underlying impulse that created it. Segal makes this point with great force in a second, shorter essay, an account of William Golding's 1964 novel *The Spire*. This essay, "Delusion and Artistic Creativity" (1974), begins with the usual plot summary, so at first it seems that the novel is going to be treated simply as a case history of the central character's manic delusion and its collapse. But Segal then goes on to construct a more interesting and complicated account of not only this novel but all works of art. "As in any work of art," she argues, "the novel contains also the story of its own creation and it expresses the problems, conflicts and doubts about the author's own creativity. The agonizing question that the author poses himself is, 'Is my work a creation or a delusion?'"[34] This central artistic problem derives from the dual nature of the art work itself: its transmission or embodiment of the beautiful and the ugly. The specific interest of *The Spire* is that it poses this problem directly: it makes us ask why the central character's creation—the spire—is, ultimately, a delusion, rather than a great or even true work of art. The answer is that works of art must contain both reparative *and* destructive or aggressive impulses and that the latter must be acknowledged if they are to be overcome. The impulse behind the spire, though, is one of denial—denial of its creator's aggressive instincts. "Jocelin [the creator] does not aim, in his creation, at destroying any objects: what he is creating is an ideal picture of himself, including an omnipotent potency, at the expense of the parental figures. He seems to be serving God, but it is his spire, standing for a part of his own body, which is to reach heaven omnipotently."[35] The work of art must show the object as attacked and lost and *then* restore it; in doing so, it acknowledges the separateness of subject and object. Jocelin's spire is an idealization of the self; Jocelin *is* the spire. The true artist, though, acknowledges the symbolic nature of his or her creations; the artist confronts reality rather than distorting it, as does Jocelin. Segal concludes:

> Where Jocelin's spire will soon collapse, William Golding's cathedral and spire stand complete, continuing and bringing to life a whole new world in which we can become engrossed. But the theme itself which William Golding chose is significant: the collapse of the work is always a threat of which the artist is aware. And here Golding describes a particular threat which must be experienced by any artist. Artists are often accused of being narcissistic, which is a great misconception, but the particular kind of omnipotent narcissism represented by Jocelin must be a temptation that they probably have always to struggle with and to overcome.[36]

Marion Milner (b. 1900)

Marion Milner shares Segal's view of the art work as a product of both destructive and reparative impulses, though the terms she uses to describe the creative process, as well as her emphases, are different. She talks of the impulse to merge or fuse, in place of destructive or greedy-sadistic impulses; she substitutes the terms "separation" or "de-fusion" for reparative impulses. Milner first applies these terms directly to artistic creation in *On Not Being Able to Paint* (1950), though in *A Life of One's Own* (1934) and *An Experiment in Leisure* (1937) the importance of the distinction they represent is already clear. I would like to approach Milner's theories, though, by looking at a later essay, "The Role of Illusion in Symbol Formation." This essay first appeared in 1952 under another title and was given its present and better-known name in 1955, when presented at a symposium on the work of Melanie Klein.[37]

The starting point of Milner's essay is an account of current psychoanalytic theories of symbolism, including those of Rank, Sachs, Freud, Jones, and Klein. Milner's aim is to reconsider "the conditions under which the primary and secondary objects [in symbolism] are fused and felt as one and the same."[38] She suggests that these conditions need not always derive from dread, either of the original object itself or of loss of it. Nor need the power of symbols always derive, as she says in *An Experiment in Leisure*, from "some crude infantile desire that I ought to have left behind long ago."[39] The need for symbols might also be seen more positively, as a necessary and healthful "fusion of self and other." Symbols are ways of locating "the familiar in the unfamiliar," and their creation derives from or requires "an ability to tolerate a temporary loss of sense of self, a temporary giving-up of the discriminating ego which stands apart and tries to see things objectively and rationally and without emotional colouring."[40] This ability is something children possess in play. Only gradually do they lose it, discovering the boundaries between subject and object. It is also part of writing, as of other forms of creation, and of therapy as well. All of these activities are ways of allowing illusions into life. The artist, or spectator, or reader, or analysand, "allows himself to experience, within the enclosed space-time of the drama or the picture or the story or the analytic hour, a transcending of that common-sense perception which would see a picture as only an attempt at photography, or the analyst as only a present-day person."[41]

For Milner, development is marked by the ability to tolerate "the difference between the feeling of oneness, of being united with everything, and the feeling of twoness, of self and object."[42] One vital function of art is "to foster this growth, by providing conditions in which a recurrent partial return to the feeling of being one is possible."[43] What impairs the symbolic, and thus artistic, capacity is a too-early differentiation of self and other, as in the case of a child patient of Milner's for whom the domestic disruption and uncertainty of World War II meant a constant and premature distinction between internal and external reality, a forcing of the process. It was only in the analytic session that the child was able to overcome his fear of merger, "to find a bit of the external world that was malleable; he had found that it was safe to treat it as a bit of himself, and so had let it serve as a bridge between inner and outer." In such sessions, it is the job of the analyst to facilitate the symbolic process: in the early stages, "when he could not feel that he had 'made' me, that I was his lovely stuff, then I was the opposite, not only bad but also alien, and bad because alien."[44] However, once the child has been given sufficient opportunity to "regress" to the fused state, in which other is felt as self, he can then reach the stage of "de-fusion," which Klein and Segal identify with the depressive position, in which the object is recognized as whole and separate. When Milner's patient reached this stage, he felt tremendous relief, and "we were then able to reach his depression about injuries that he had felt he was responsible for, both internally and externally, in his family situation and in relation to me."[45]

Milner concludes the essay by relating the problem of her patient to that of the artist. The artist seeks a way to express, on the one hand, a fused or private vision of the world, which conforms to his or her needs and desires, and, on the other hand, a so-called objective or public vision, in which the distinction between subject and object, self and other, is acknowledged. The need to balance these two visions or impulses is at the heart of artistic creation. Both sides make claims, as in Segal's insistence on the beautiful or whole *and* the ugly or destructive. This is a point Milner brilliantly exemplifies in *On Not Being Able to Paint,* an account of her experiments with free drawing.

Milner's experiments with free drawing involved the reversal of much of what she had been taught in art school: they were, in the first instance, an attempt to let "hand and eye do exactly what pleased them without any conscious working to a preconceived intention."[46] The result, she felt, was "a form of visual reflection on the basic problems of living" (p. xvii). The first of these problems recalls the 1952 essay on symbolism. Painting "is concerned with the feelings conveyed by space," and these feelings are in turn "deeply concerned with ideas of distance and separation and having and losing" (p. 12). The successful painter, Milner speculates, does not fear a merging of identities, or melting of boundaries, between self and other—which is close to what she says about the successful symbol-maker. These were the fears that inhibited Milner's own initial artistic efforts: fears not only of losing oneself in a world without differentia· tion but also of investing that world with one's own internal life—with needs and impulses that might well prove ugly and destructive, greedy and infernal. The fantasies generated by such fears are of consuming everything, of eating up and destroying the outer world in the process of making it one's own. "To see life and action in inanimate things," she writes of her early difficulties in painting, "was a trick of the imagination which had better be fully repressed" (pp. 42–43).

Blockage, though, can also come from what might be called the opposite direction: as a product of fear of separation; separation or differentiation being no less vital to art and life than merger. It was only at the beginning of Milner's art studies or experiments that blockage seemed to derive solely from fear of merger, or "a denial of the basic fact of one's bodily life which does not transcend space" (p. 56). Later, Milner recognized another sort of fear:

At the moments of having to realize the limits of the body, when beginning to make marks on paper, all the anxieties about separation and losing what one loved could come flooding in. And then there could also come, with the anxieties, an attempt to ease them by calling on the imposed moral law, turning to rules for . . . control . . . yet by that very reliance on rules perhaps stultifying from the start the very thing one was seeking to achieve. (P. 57)

The blocked artist can be overcome by fears of separation as much as by fears of merger; these fears derive from "the inescapable discrepancy between subjective and objective, between the unlimited possibilities of one's dreams and what the real world actually offers us" (p. 68). Thus, the achievement of the successful artist or writer is "to be able to break down the barrier of space between self and other, yet at the same time to be able to maintain it, this seems to be the paradox of creativity." The successful artist

> seems to have an unyielding determination neither to deny his dream nor the claims of external reality. He does not, as the neurotic in us does, try to deny the conflict altogether. . . . In his practice he recognizes the real objective qualities of his medium but he manipulates these to fit his inner conception. . . . He does not try to deny or forget about illusion, instead he seeks to affirm it and take responsibility for it, even in its most primitive aspects. (P. 134)

The artist's inner conception must be reconciled to "the demands of that external reality which is society . . . some public artistic convention such as the outline or the musical scale or the grammar and vocabulary of a particular language, something that his particular time and place in history make available for him to use in conveying his private idea" (p. 134). The sort of drawing Milner had been taught in art school, though, "represented a monologue of thinking that would not listen to what action had to say," and the fear this training catered to was fear of chaos, so for Milner reciprocity would have to begin with "a willingness to accept chaos as a temporary stage" (pp. 74 and 76). Acceptance of this sort required an effort of will, an effort to "plan the gap into which the new thing was to fit" (p. 116). And Milner writes powerfully of the potentially inhibiting difficulty of such effort, as "when the scribbled free drawing did not begin to look like a recognizable object soon enough . . . [and] I would deliberately force it into something recognizable." This forcing, it could be argued, "blocked" creative potential, so the drawing "had an unpleasant quality for which the word 'meretricious' came to mind" (p. 117). Milner believes that the impediment here, the inhibiting factor, is an *absence* of will; she lacked the self-control to continue in an unplanned manner, "not knowing what was going to happen" (p. 104).

Milner's theories also help to account for the sort of blockage caused by George Eliot's "chilling ideal which crowd[s] . . . laborious uncreative hours." Milner noticed that several of her blocked patients revealed "an extremely idealized notion of what their products ought to be." They often associated this idealized notion with a sensation of total satisfaction, as in "the experience of orgasm whether genital or pregenital" (p. 149). Two fears were hidden in this association: not only that the actual work would fail to live up to the patient's orgasmic expectations but that if it did it would lead to madness, because the experience of orgasm, of a blissful letting go, was frightening as well as thrilling—frightening because it seemed to involve not only loss of distinction but "letting go of all voluntary control of the muscles," as in elimination, with its disillusioning consequences. For patients who make such associations, the analyst's role is not to deny the idealization—which, after all, reflects actual sensations— but to remind the patient that what is produced by such sensations has to be worked with: "The beautiful mess does not make a picture or poem all by itself" (pp. 150–51). Although it is not wrong to seek out such bliss, it is also not enough: the artist must face up to, "submit himself to," the real qualities of the medium, even while seeking to bend or mold it to internal needs. The problems that the artist faces in doing so are but a type of the problems we all face in coming to terms with the world; these problems "are first experienced, in all of us, if our experience has been normal, long before we have any words to tell of it or power to know . . . what is happening to us" (p. 146). The source of blockage, as of that of creativity, lies in patterns established in earliest infancy—patterns connected with our relation to objects.

D. W. Winnicott (1896–1971)

D. W. Winnicott came to psychoanalysis from pediatrics, in part because his treatment of children led him to conclude that they "showed difficulties in their emotional development in infancy, even as babies."[47] His first analyst was James Strachey, Freud's English translator, and at Strachey's suggestion he also began work with Klein, from 1936 to 1941, as well as undertaking a second analysis with Riviere, Klein's co-worker. What drew Winnicott to Klein was not only a shared belief in the pre-Oedipal origins of neurosis— though Winnicott always resisted Klein's claim that the paranoid-schizoid position "dates from the very beginning"[48]—but also his own observation of greed in infants and of their fascination with their own "insides" and those of the mother.[49]

Winnicott's most important departure from, or revision of, Kleinian tenets is his identification and account of a third factor in development, aside from what might be called external and internal realities. This third factor in the life of a human being, "a part that we cannot ignore," is an "intermediate area of *experiencing*, to which inner reality and external life both contribute." Its purpose is to "exist as a resting-place for the individual engaged in the perpetual task of keeping inner and outer reality separate yet inter-related."[50] Winnicott associates or identifies this intermediate area with what he calls "transitional objects" or "transitional phenomena," the sorts of childhood objects and patterns of behavior which occur "between the thumb and the teddy bear, between . . . oral eroticism and true object-relationship, between primary creative activity and projection of what has already been introjected, between primary unawareness of indebtedness, and the acknowledgement of indebtedness" (p. 90). Examples of transitional objects and phenomena are the child's blanket, or a bundle of wool, or an eiderdown, or an infant's mannerisms or babbling, or "the way an older child goes over a repertory of songs and tunes while preparing for sleep" (p. 90). When an infant uses a transitional object to go to sleep, to allay anxiety, the object "*is not an internal object* (which is a mental concept)—it is a possession. Yet it is not (for the infant) an external object either." This is because it is "never under magical control like the internal object, nor is it outside control as the real mother is" (p. 94). The transitional object also differs from what is conventionally thought of as a symbol because its actuality—as a blanket, say, rather than a breast—"is as important as the fact that it stands for the breast (or mother)." Although the infant "assumes rights over the object. . . . Nevertheless some abrogation of the omnipotence is a feature from the start" (p. 92). Were it not, according to some object-relations theorists (though not Winnicott), it would move from being a true transitional object into what Elizabeth Wright, via Phyllis Greenacre, calls "that permanent security prop, the fetish."[51]

Writing comes into all this when Winnicott turns to the parent's reaction to transitional phenomena. The parent colludes in the infant's illusions, allowing the infant gradually to "decathect" their power. The object, writes Winnicott, with characteristic insouciance, simply "loses meaning, and this is because the transitional phenomena have become diffused, have become spread out over the whole intermediate territory between 'inner psychic reality' and 'the external world as perceived by two persons in common,' that is to say, over the whole cultural field."[52] The purpose served by the infant's transitional objects or habits is replaced, in the first instance, by play, and then by a host not only of cultural phenomena, including artistic creativity and appreciation, and religious feeling, but of less public or publicly approved activities or phenomena, including "fetishism, lying and stealing, the origin and loss of affectionate feeling, drug addiction, the talisman of obsessional rituals, etc."[53]

Underlying Winnicott's account of this gradual dispersal or diffusion of transitional phenomena is his assumption "that the task of reality-acceptance is never completed, that no human being is free from the strain of relating inner and outer reality." Creative writing, like play or the transitional phenomena that precede play, offers relief or rest from this strain. And the adult world tolerates creative writing's fictional nature for the same reasons the parent protects the infant's illusions: because of "an intuitive recognition of the strain inherent in objective perception."[54] "It is a matter of agreement between us and the baby," writes Winnicott of the parent's intuitive response to transitional phenomena, "that we will never ask the question 'Did you conceive of this or was it presented to you from without?' The important point is that no decision on this point is expected. The question is not to be formulated."[55]

Implicit in Winnicott's stress here on adequate nurturing—what he elsewhere calls "the facilitating environment" or "the good-enough mother"—is a theory of blockage. If the child is to develop, or the writer to write, the precise nature, the phenomenological status, of the transitional object—be it a scrap of blanket or a novel—cannot and should not be anatomized, either by or to the child or writer. For doing so would violate its transitional nature, as both internal or subjective *and* external or objective. Art involves, in Coleridge's famous phrase, a "willing suspension of disbelief," as much for the writer as for the reader or spectator. Just as the transitional object "has to be protected from those who would force it into the open; force the process of development,"[56] so the writer, like the reader, has to maintain a balance between internal and external demands or realities, has to "will" the suspension of disbelief. Nor is the need for such balance restricted to children and artists. Winnicott's adolescent patients, for example, need to be defended against what he calls "being found, that is to say being found before being there to be found."[57] And something similar is true of adults, even "normally" adjusted ones. In his 1963 essay "Communicating and Not Communicating Leading to a Study of Certain Opposites," Winnicott concludes that the need for a subjective world outlives the perception of an objective one and that each of us possesses an inner or core self made up of interactions between this inner world and the adult self that meets the outside world. The analyst must be careful not to violate or force this "non-communicating central self, forever immune from the reality principle, and forever silent";[58] he or she must respect the patient's right not to communicate.

Writing, like other forms of culture, is a way of allowing for an interchange between the inviolate, subjective core self and the external world. But such interchange is only possible if the writer is confident enough to tolerate tension or paradox. Winnicott and the other theorists discussed in this chapter believe that adult confidence originates in earliest development. As Winnicott says in his late essay "The Location of Cultural Experience" (1966), "in order to study the play and then the cultural life of the individual one must study the fate of the potential space between any one baby and the human (and therefore fallible) mother-figure who is essentially adaptive because of love. . . . [T]he 'deprived child' is not only restless and unable to play, [he or she] has an impoverishment of capacity to experience in the cultural field."[59]

The opposition or tension between internal and external, union and separation, can take several forms in the course of artistic creation. The writer must strike a balance, for example, between originality and what Winnicott calls "the tradition"—a point also made by Milner and Segal. "In any cultural field," writes Winnicott, with a true and welcome sense of the complications of his subject, "it is not possible to be original except on a basis of tradition. Conversely, no one in the line of cultural contributors repeats except as a deliberate quotation, and the unforgivable sin in the cultural field is plagiarism."[60] That there is a connection between plagiarism and blockage is seen in Coleridge's career. Coleridge's childhood, at least in his own account of it, was not what Winnicott would call "facilitating," and this helps to explain, and not only to a Winnicottian, both Coleridge's lifelong lack of confidence and his obsession with originality—with a view of his creations as coming wholly from within, most famously in the account of the genesis of "Kubla Khan," a poem in which, as he says in its prose preface, "all the images rose up before him . . . without any sensation of consciousness of effort."

Coleridge's obsession with the ideal of originality, or the claims of subjectivity, is both fueled by and fuels fear: the danger, as so often in Coleridge's poems, of solipsism; of the creation of a world without distinctions, and so without bearings. Moreover, if, as Coleridge says in "Dejection: An Ode," "we receive but what we give, / And in our life alone does Nature live" (47–48), it may be that what we give—the internal needs we express in our writing—are the sorts of needs Klein identifies as greedy, sadistic, destructive, depressive, envious. Writers obsessed with originality find themselves not only isolated or unhoused but also subject to their own threatening projections. Hence, for instance, the vertiginous qualities of "Kubla Khan," its immense and shifting geography of the sublime; hence also the sense of evil—of a sinful or destructive impulse—hidden not only in the landscape but in poetic power, as in the last section's admonition to

"Beware! Beware!" the poet's "flashing eyes, his floating hair" (49–50). More often than not, Coleridge felt these fears so intensely that he either completely stopped writing, was blocked, or resorted to a borrowing so consistent and transparent as to earn the name of plagiarism. The claims to originality had still to be forwarded, but fear of originality left the poet—as well as the philosopher—no choice but unacknowledged borrowing. Or so it could be argued—and shall be, in part two, which discusses the literary dimensions of originality and writer's block.

Winnicott's own account of the relations between plagiarism, blockage, and the rival claims of internal and external realms centers around the case of a patient, an art teacher, whom he describes as living "from poem to poem (like cigarette to cigarette in chain smoking)."[61] The reason for this patient's obsessive quotation (the poems were by *other* people) was her inability to perceive herself: "I don't seem able quite to BE"; "It's as though there isn't really a ME."[62] According to Winnicott, the function of the quotation was not so much, or merely, a defense as a way of communicating a deep fear of communication; thus Winnicott is like Milner in emphasizing the adaptive potential of what others might see as evasive or distorting. The fear itself and the patient's consequent "blockage" and "plagiarism" (the obsessive quotation) have origins that are, in one sense, just the opposite of those of Coleridge. The patient clings to the external world not so much out of fear of engulfing it by giving free rein to subjective need, as of revealing the emptiness of her own internal life. Albert Hutter, in a discussion of Winnicott's essay, draws out the implications of this feeling: "It is through writing that we dare to externalize and 'objectify' ourselves—undoubtedly why writing is so difficult and so filled with what we loosely call 'writer's block.' Every time we face a blank page it is as though we face what this patient feels so exaggeratedly about herself but which all of us surely feel at one time or another: the page mirrors our own blankness, our emptiness."[63] What Winnicott's patient fears about her own "self expression," in this case verbal as well as written, is not criticism per se, but "a more fundamental fear that if the criticism goes far enough or long enough it will uncover a vacuum."[64]

The origins of this fear conform to Winnicott's theories of child care and are revealed through the workings of Winnicottian therapy. The analyst provides the patient with a "facilitating environment"; he or she enables the patient to start "by existing and not be reacting,"[65] which is the adult equivalent of allowing the child to play. The analyst does this not by interpreting the patient's material, but by affording a proper setting. In the words of Greenberg and Mitchell, "the person

of the analyst and the analytic setting 'hold' the patient; in the relia-
bility, attentiveness, responsiveness, memory, and durability of the
analyst the aborted self of the patient becomes unstuck and continues
to grow." This is quite different from orthodox therapy because
"whereas Freud's major emphasis in discussing the liberating value
of psychoanalysis is on the freedom *from* illusion, Winnicott empha-
sizes the increasing freedom to *create* illusion." [66] Winnicott chooses
this emphasis because he believes that the world can be apprehended
only after it has shown itself to be hospitable: illusions make reality
possible. It is, therefore, the analyst's job to take the role of "the good-
enough mother." The analyst must function as a mirror, allowing the
patient to be reflected in the person of an other. Only when that other
is acceptably personalized—a reflection of the child's or patient's desires—can it then grow into a genuine other. This is a view similar to
Lacan's theory of "Le Stade du Miroir," and Winnicott acknowledges
his debt to Lacan in *Playing and Reality* (1971). [67]

When Winnicott's poem-quoting patient at last feels secure in the
analytic environment, she produces a piece of her own writing: in
this case, suggestively, a card in black announcing her birthday,
which she calls her "deathday." At this point, Winnicott observes,
"the patient seemed to be in the room with me." A space had been
created in the analytic session in which the patient felt free to express
her subjective self to another, to bridge the gap between internal and
external realms. This interpretation is confirmed for Winnicott by the
patient's allusion to a poem by Gerard Manley Hopkins. This poem,
"Spring and Fall," is about death and the seasons, and in it an adult
speaker addresses a frightened and grieving child. Part of the poem's
appeal derives from the manner in which the speaker confirms the
child's growing sense of the painful truths of existence, of "the blight
man was born for." In Hutter's words, "we can experience in and
through this poem the capacity of the parent to reflect back to the
child that child's perceptions, even in things like death and loss; by
our capacity to accept loss and to mourn that acceptance, we are,
paradoxically, able to foster the reality and the growth of the child's
own identity." [68] What brought the patient to the Hopkins poem was
her achievement in the analytic session of a separate or distinct identity; an achievement experienced, as Klein would have it, as loss and
separation (hence "deathday"). The patient has moved from paranoid fears—of being engulfed and having no identity—to depressive
fears, a movement that Winnicott as well as Klein sees as a progres-
sion.

"Spring and Fall" is not the only poem by Hopkins discussed by
Winnicott and his patient, which is appropriate given Hopkins's own

problems both with his identity (as poet and priest) and with writing. Hopkins had great trouble reconciling his Jesuit vocation with his writing. Before becoming a Jesuit, he burned his finished poems, and for seven or eight years stopped writing completely. This period was not an easy one for Hopkins: "Time's eunuch," he called himself in "Thou Art Indeed Just, Lord," as well as in his letters. When he did resume writing, he produced only nineteen poems in nine years: "Every impulse and spring of art seems to have died in me," he wrote to his friend Robert Bridges three years before his own death. And yet as Hopkins's letters and poems suggest, the "organic" metaphor of desiccation brought him no peace: "it kills me to be time's eunuch," is what he wrote to Bridges.[69] All of which is reflected in the poems themselves, which are often torn or tensed in ways that call to mind Winnicott's account of the problems of individuation. In Hopkins's case, the tensions are expressed in terms of the rival claims of self and God, as in these lines from "To Seem the Stranger Lies My Lot, My Life":

> . . . Only what word
> Wisest my heart breeds dark heaven's baffling ban
> Bars or hell's spell thwarts. This to hoard unheard,
> Heard unheeded, leaves me a lonely began.
> (11–14)

Lines such as these help to explain the patient's allusion to a line from another Hopkins's poem, "Carrion Comfort." Winnicott tells the patient that he thinks she is waiting for him to say something positive: "She said: 'It was in my mind: "Don't make me wish to BE!"' That's a line of a poem by G.M. Hopkins.'"[70] In "Carrion Comfort," Hopkins, like George Herbert before him, seeks to establish his identity by defying God and by expressing anger at God's terrifying mysteries. In the end, though, Hopkins returns to God, who has not been destroyed by his anger. In Hutter's words, Hopkins "can find himself reflected in the continued (undamaged) existence and continued acceptance of another being."[71] That the patient herself sees the poem this way is clear from her likening of the function of God to the function of the analyst: "Someone to be there while you're playing."[72] Winnicott agrees with this, as indicated in "The Mirror Role of Mother and Father" in *Playing and Reality:* "Psychotherapy is not making clever and apt interpretations; by and large it is a long-term giving back what the patient brings. It is a complex derivative of the face that reflects what is there to be seen. I like to think of my work in this way, and to think that if I do this well enough the patient will find his or her own self, and will be able to exist and to feel real."[73]

The blocked writer, according to Winnicott's theory, needs just such an environment; its absence both accounts for blockage and keeps it in place.

Anton Ehrenzweig (1909–1966)

Anton Ehrenzweig's *The Hidden Order of Art* (1967) is probably the best-known work of British object-relations aesthetics—certainly in North America. Its influence, though, has been diffuse, in part because of the variety of disciplines it draws on, including aesthetics, psychology, philosophy, educational theory, and literary criticism. Ehrenzweig trained in the law (he was a magistrate in his native Austria, immigrating to Britain in the 1930s) before turning first to gestalt theory and then, in London, to the writings of the post-Kleinians, particularly those of Milner, Segal, and Adrian Stokes. Ehrenzweig's first book, *The Psychoanalysis of Artistic Vision and Hearing* (1953), laid the groundwork for the series of essays published in psychoanalytic and artistic journals in the 1950s and 1960s, which became *The Hidden Order of Art*, but its collective (rather than individual) perspective made it even harder to categorize than his later writings. From the first, though, Ehrenzweig had influential supporters, including Herbert Read and E. H. Gombrich, as well as a number of prominent artists, especially painters.[74]

Ehrenzweig's starting point in *The Hidden Order of Art* is what he calls the child's vision of the world. This vision, he argues, is the product of an unstructured or undifferentiated mode of perception which is syncretistic rather than analytic, an assumption that flatly contradicts gestalt notions of child perception—gestalt theory in general being attentive only to surface or conscious order.[75] As Ehrenzweig writes in *The Hidden Order of Art*, "the child does not break down the shape of some concrete object into smaller abstract elements and then match the elements of his drawings one by one. His vision is still global and takes in the entire world which remains undifferentiated as to its component details."[76] Such a vision need be neither confused nor imprecise; it can produce the most exact of discriminations, despite its obliviousness to abstract details—as in the case of caricature, for example, in which a total sense of the subject, rather than a more minute attention to particulars or abstract patterns, produces recognition, overcoming even the most extreme distortions. Hence the trouble Ehrenzweig takes to dissociate his theory of syncretistic or dedifferentiated perception from Kris's "regression in the service of the ego." What he rejects in Kris's formulation is its vision of id activity (though not the release of id activity) as uncontrolled and primitive, because for him the child's perception is an active faculty capable of molding images and making fine discriminations. Ehrenzweig's term for the broadening of focus involved in the child's vision of the world is "scanning," and it is his contention that scanning—or the cast of mind which makes it possible—plays an essential role in artistic creation.

What guides syncretistic or instinctual perception is libido. It is libido that leads the perceiver "straight [to] the total individual objects without awareness of their abstract elements." When analytic awareness of abstract pattern begins to dawn, around the eighth year of life, "'latency' has stunted the child's sexual drives" (p. 18). The onset of "mature" perception marks the beginning of a lifelong split between different orientations to reality. This split is between analysis and intuition, between abstract gestalt elements and the total object, between precise, detailed focus and scanning, between fragmentation and wholeness, differentiation and dedifferentiation—oppositions that recall Klein's two positions, as well as their subsequent modification in the aesthetics of Segal, Milner, and Winnicott. (Their origin probably derives from Ehrenzweig's early interest, everywhere apparent in the essays of the 1950s, in Nietzsche's distinction between Apollonian and Dionysian impulses.) What makes an artist, or a healthy individual, is the ability to move smoothly between the two states or, in Ehrenzweig's terms, forms of attention. Neither must be denied or slighted. "In this sense the artist's creative attitude towards his work is only a particular instance of a more general social adaptation" (p. 109).

Much of *The Hidden Order of Art* is taken up with an elaboration of this distinction. To begin with, all the arts are canvassed and shown to be especially hospitable to, or dependent upon, syncretistic powers. The visual artist, for example, needs a flexible, scattered consciousness in order to hold "all elements of the picture in a single individual act of attention. He cannot afford the fatal bisection into figure and ground imposed by the conscious gestalt principle" (p. 124). So also with the musician, who must "train himself to scatter his attention over the entire musical structure so that he can grasp the polyphonic fabric hidden in the accompaniment" (p. 125). It is only "laymen" who overvalue the focussed or vertical elements in music, allowing melody to become the sole object of attention. As for writers, again and again one encounters a comparable drive toward totality of vision, together with its consequent fear of uncharted waters. "Ideas rush in me," writes Virginia Woolf, "often though this is before I can control my mind or pen"; "I write variations of every sentence; compromises; bad shots; possibilities; till my writing book is like a lunatic's dream." Only if such a period of uncontrolled and seemingly unproductive expression can be tolerated will the work be completed. "My mind," Woolf realizes, as must every artist, according to Ehrenzweig, "moves in idleness. To do nothing is often my most profitable way."[77]

The necessity of a scattered or "empty" attention in creation—which feels like "doing nothing"—is a product of the extraordinary range, the surging chaos, of possibilities open to the artist; a range so wide that it defies any conscious weighing up. As a consequence, the creative person must master fears generated by lack of control, by not knowing—that is, knowing consciously—the end result of certain decisions; and this makes the role of the teacher (in art education, for example) analogous to that of the Winnicottian analyst. He or she makes space for the unconscious and gives the would-be artist the confidence to disrupt or lay aside overly rigid or precise visualizations. The art teacher becomes a surrogate "good-enough mother." In like manner, when Ehrenzweig makes the same point in terms of the will, of "a passive but acute watchfulness for subtle variations in the medium's response,"[78] his words recall those of Milner on the importance of the ground or medium. Again and again, Ehrenzweig insists that "the rigid student bent on complete conscious control of the working process will blind himself to the constant modulations of pictorial space while the structure of the work gradually unfolds."[79] On the other hand, dedifferentiation can itself go too far, becoming an exclusive and limiting goal.[80]

Although Ehrenzweig's theories begin with the distinction between analytic and synthetic, differentiated and dedifferentiated modes of perception, they also introduce a third component or term. The creative process is seen as a three-stage affair: it begins with what Ehrenzweig calls a "schizoid" phase, which is marked by fragmented projection, in which split-off parts of the self are projected onto the work, be it a canvas or story or sound. This stage is followed by "a 'manic' phase of unconscious scanning and integration when art's unconscious substructure is formed," a stage in which the multiple and hidden connections between fragmented projections are intuited, though they are not yet necessarily apparent on "the surface gestalt."[81] The precise nature of these connections is not clear in Ehrenzweig's writings, as one might expect, though presumably they are outside surface or gestalt distinctions between, for example, male and female, before and after, above and below, right and left, in front and behind (p. 182).

In the third stage, the conscious or analytic powers return and the work is made more intelligible, its unconscious substructure brought into relief or consciousness. The integrated structure uncovered in the second stage is now, in the third stage, taken back, or "re-introjected" (p. 102), into the artist's ego. In the first two stages, the artist's fears are those of the paranoid-schizoid position: a fear of persecution by split-off and projected elements; a fear of being cut off in a world without bearings, and a potentially hostile one at that. In the third stage, the fears are those of the depressive position, of loss and guilt, and they are made especially intense if the second stage, in which fragmentation is meant to be overcome, succeeds. "Who has not experienced the grey feeling of the 'morning after,'" writes Ehrenzweig, "when having to face the work done on the day before? Part of the creative capacity is the strength to resist an almost anal disgust that would make us sweep the whole mess into the waste-paper basket" (p. 103). By "morning after," here, Ehrenzweig means something like "the clear light of day," that daylight or Apollonian world of conscious vision which must translate a work's "hidden" order into waking or surface terms.

This three-stage process, Ehrenzweig believes, is the inevitable, though not the sole, subject matter or content of art. Like Segal, Milner, and Stokes, he believes that the creative process itself is always a work's "minimum content" (p. 171); that it always reflects the conflict or contrast between "containment (trapping) and expansion (liberation)" (p. 173) or differentiation and dedifferentiation; though "if we look more closely we find that all three phases of creativity including projection, fragmentation, dedifferentiation, integration and re-introjection are associated with the basic theme of trapping and liberation."[82]

This theme brings us to blockage, about which Ehrenzweig has quite a lot to say, though his references are for the most part to painting rather than writing. For Ehrenzweig, blockage is primarily a product of fear of dedifferentiation, of the inability to tolerate ambiguity or uncertainty. He has little to say about overreliance on the unconscious, which is surprising given his account of the dual or polar nature of the creative process. This makes Ehrenzweig's theory very much like that of Keats, for whom blockage occurs when the writer is incapable of "being in uncertainties, mysteries, doubts, without any irritable reaching after fact and reason." What Ehrenzweig calls "ego dissociation," the letting loose or surrendering of conscious faculties, with their sharp distinctions between self and other, is the psychoanalytic equivalent of Keats's "negative capability." And that Keats was talking as much of literal blockage as he was of value (of "what quality went to form a Man of Achievement especially in Literature") is clear from his immediate reference to Cole-

ridge as a type "incapable of remaining content with half knowledge." [83] What blocks, then, is fear of the unfocused, the half-known,
and Ehrenzweig weaves this fear into that of the classical or orthodox
Freudian account of blockage. "Once undifferentiated perceptions
have become inaccessible to consciousness," Ehrenzweig writes,
"they become invested with id phantasy. Then the unconscious fear
of id phantasy will reinforce the already existing split between the
different levels of vision and harden further the rigidity of the ego." [84]

Somehow the artist must come to feel that the suspension of surface faculties need not mean chaos, annihilation, and death; that instead it can be a way of uncovering order or coherence, the sort of
order in which "repressed and dedifferentiated images are safely contained, melted down and reshaped for re-entry into consciousness." [85] The art teacher, for example, must be like the psychoanalyst
who allows "the patient's fragmented material to sink into the containing womb of his own (the analyst's) unconscious without premature wish to rearticulate it and put it back into the patient at a fully
articulate level" [86]—a view of the therapist very much like that of
Winnicott. Among the literary examples Ehrenzweig points to in support of this view is that of Rilke, whose breakthrough as "a true poet"
came only after he allowed himself, through the encouragement of
Lou Andreas-Salomé, to surrender to or let loose fantasies of omnipotence and homosexuality. [87]

Creativity, then, is for Ehrenzweig but an instance of a larger or
more general process of development, one that involves a perpetual
conflict and accommodation between differing modes of perception.
And this, of course, is the view of all the theorists of this chapter.
"The child's creativity," writes Ehrenzweig, "accompanies and sus-
tains his developing human relationships."

> In order to enrich ourselves as individuals we have to reshape
> and change our human relationships without respite by projec-
> tion and introjection. A frequent failure in human relationships
> is due to the same ego rigidity that impedes creativity. . . . Crea-
> tivity, then, may be self-creation, but it is possible only through
> social intercourse, whether with other individuals as happens in
> social creativity in the narrower sense of the word, or through
> the medium of impersonal creative work. [88]

For all the theorists of post-Kleinian object relations, writing, like all
forms of artistic creation, is thus both a sign of and a means to health,
while blockage reflects a larger and pervasive failure in development.

Adrian Stokes (1902–1972)

Adrian Stokes was an art critic and aesthetician who developed an interest in psychoanalysis in the 1920s, after reading *The Interpretation of Dreams* and *The Psychopathology of Everyday Life*. This interest led eventually to a lengthy analysis with Melanie Klein in the 1930s and to a gradual adoption of Kleinian theory and terminology in his own writings. Crucial to Stokes's understanding of art was Klein's account of the two "positions" through which the developing infant works in the course of maturation. In his writings after the 1930s, Stokes set out to relate these positions to an opposition or distinction he had already identified in his earlier criticism: between what he called carving and modeling traditions. In Richard Wollheim's words, "the overall point to be made is that in each case, the mode or tradition of art is held to reflect or celebrate the kind of relation to the outer world that is typical of the corresponding position."[89]

The distinction between carving and modeling is introduced in Stokes's first book, *The Quattro Cento* (1932), an attempt to identify a mode of art especially associated with fifteenth-century Italy, but by no means confined to it (hence *Quattro Cento* rather than *Quattrocento*). As it developed in subsequent books, the distinction became more and more abstract: in Wollheim's words, "carving and modelling are now thought of as the two most general attitudes that the artist might adopt to his medium—attitudes derived from, but not confined to, the techniques or procedures after which they are named" (p. 18). In *The Quattro Cento*, the distinction grows out of a discussion of fifteenth-century attitudes toward stone; or, more specifically, the capacity of Renaissance sculptors "from the South" (Stokes means southern Italy) to make stone "bloom" (p. 35), thus overturning its conventional symbolic identity as barren. At no other time, writes Stokes of fifteenth-century Italy, "have the materials that artists use been so significant in themselves. The materials were the actual objects of inspiration, the stocks for the deeper fantasies" (p. 42). This was also true of the symbolic content of Quattro Cento art, which was directly related to the medium, so "the creative act itself, the turning of the subject into concrete and particular and individual form, *is* the symbol" (p. 44). "Form," writes Stokes in "Form in Art," his contribution to the 1952 Melanie Klein symposium, "has a content of its own. . . . Form in art *is* content."[90] In all his writing, Stokes stresses the importance of the medium, and not just in the visual or plastic arts. "The artist or would-be artist," he writes, "may be distinguished by the extent to which he cathects a medium. . . . For the poet, words, for the sculptor, stone, are pregnant materials with which they are in communion, through which they crystallize particular phantasies. In a sense the work of art is not new enactment but re-affirmation of a pre-existent entity [in the medium]. This medium is allowed once more a full and separate life: it is restored."[91]

Nowhere is the importance of the medium more clearly seen than in stone carving, particularly the carving of limestone; and nowhere is limestone carving more triumphant for Stokes than in the reliefs in the Tempio Malatestiano in Rimini. *The Stones of Rimini* (1934), Stokes's second book, begins with a distinction between sculptural or carving and plastic or modeling values: "As everyone knows," Stokes writes, "carving is a cutting away, while modelling or moulding is a building up."[92] But for Stokes, carving is also associated with farm labor, whereas modeling is associated with manufacturing and trade: "Just as the cultivator works the surface of the mother earth so the sculptor rubs his stone to elicit the shapes which his eye has sown in the matrix. The material, earth or stone, exists. Man makes it more significant. To wash, to polish, to sweep, are similar activities. But to weave or to make a shoe, indeed the processes of most trades, are pre-eminently manufacture, a making, a plastic activity, a moulding of things." Carving is indissolubly linked to "a particular substance"; modeling is abstract.[93] Today, as for some time, modeling or plastic values predominate.

Although *The Stones of Rimini* laments the death of the carving tradition—often in apocalyptic terms—in later works Stokes gives greater emphasis to the importance of the *interaction* of carving and modeling traditions. This is especially true of works in which the psychoanalytic implications of the two traditions are most explicit. In *Colour and Form* (1950), for example, it seems at first that carving is the desired artistic impulse or mode because it reveals "all the figures of the inner life . . . as a fixture, as one harmonious family, steadfast, completed as an open rose, open, revealed." The modeler, on the other hand, imbues spatial objects with "the animus and calculation of inner life,"[94] in part because initial differentiations are sharp. In modeling, the artist's impulse is that of the projected aggression of the paranoid-schizoid position: the work of art is molded, modeled, *made* to reflect an inner vision, and its meaning comes not from within the material itself, is not, as in carving, "an accumulation, an augmentation upon the surface, a mere outwardness."[95]

Yet as Stokes goes on to say, the modeling impulse is as essential to true creation—and as capable of inaugurating it—as the carving impulse; for though the artist in the modeling tradition "appropriates objects in terms of his subject-matter, controls them, reduces them, without much ado, to aspects of dominant ego trends," if the product is aesthetic (a qualification that seems rather to beg the question), "the artist will have made of himself an 'entity'. . . . Then, however summary and masterful his treatment, the affirmation of enduring otherness survives."[96] In other words, something of the carving or depressive impulse to repair and restore will be expressed. In like manner, the products of artists in the carving tradition must bear some marks, must contain, all that is implied of aggression and appropriation in the impulse of the modeler. For example, Cézanne, a painter in the carving tradition,[97] "applied a steel-bright knife to pattern and to distinctions." His art represents, in part, "an extraordinary attack upon his apples and upon the landscapes of his home."[98] And yet these attacks are gathered within, or contained by, paintings rich in love and respect. In all successful works of art, then, be they the products either of modeling or carving impulses, the effect created is not only of a whole and self-sufficient object but of one that seems also to reach out to, to "invite," the spectator or reader. "A poem, like a picture," writes Stokes in *The Invitation in Art* (1965), "properly appreciated, stands away from us as an object on its own, but the poetry that has gripped, the poetry of which it is composed, when read as an unfolding process, combines with corresponding processes by which we find ourselves to some extent carried away."[99] The creative impulses behind these effects are, of course, the ones identified not only by Klein but also by the other theorists of this chapter. As Stokes says in *Reflections on the Nude* (1967),

> the poem, the sum-total, has the articulateness of a physical object, whereas the incantatory element of poetry ranges beyond, ready to interpenetrate, to hypnotize. . . . There is, then, in art a firm alliance between generality and the obdurate otherness of objects, as if an alliance, in regard to the body, between the positive rhythmic experiences of the infant at the breast and the subsequent appreciation of the whole mother's separate existence (also internalized), complete to herself, uninjured by his aggressive or appropriating fantasies that had caused her disappearance (though it was for one moment) to be mourned as the occasion of irreparable loss.[100]

Stokes's sense of the importance—the necessity—of the modeling tradition was a relatively late development in his aesthetics, and Tony Pinckney, in a "Kleinian" account of the poetry of T. S. Eliot, has suggested an interesting connection between this development and the character and fortunes of literary modernism. In 1926, at the height of Stokes's interest in Italian carving, he met Ezra Pound in Rapallo. Pound shared Stokes's admiration for the reliefs of the Tempio Malatestiano, which he had already written about in the *Cantos* (17 and 20). After Stokes's accounts of the Tempio began appearing in the late 1920s, Pound encouraged him to work on a book exploring the purely historical background of the Tempio. Stokes never did so, and Pinckney conjectures that his disaffection with the personality of the Tempio's patron, Sigismondo Malatesta, "whose nearest contemporary equivalent was Benito Mussolini,"[101] coincided with a growing sense of the value of the modeling impulse. Pound, however, remained obsessed with the virtues of carving, which he associated in his own writings with the epithet "cut"; and both his poetry and his political thought, as well as that of his modernist allies, T. E. Hulme, Wyndham Lewis, and the early Eliot, reveal the dangers of such an obsession. For Pinckney, Pound's fascination with the carving tradition "entails a negation of paranoid-schizoid affects,"[102] a negation that helps to explain the modernist's habitual distrust of Romantic aspirations, of merging and subjectivity, for example. Pinckney connects the classicism of the modernists—their stress on limits and reserve, on the discrete and autonomous—with a limiting "cult of *machismo* . . . a virulent anti-feminism and an authoritarian politics."[103] That Stokes suspected such a connection is seen, for Pinckney, in his gradual disillusion not only with Sigismondo but also with the exclusive claims of the carving tradition. Pinckney argues that "Stokes's initial over-investment in the carving tradition in *The Quattro Cento* and *The Stones of Rimini*—the very works that brought him into close association with Pound—may itself constitute a defense against the dual aspects of the paranoid-schizoid."[104] Stokes, though, was able to overcome his anxieties in a way Pound never could, and the gradual emergence of a sense of the value of modeling in his writings is a sign of genuine development.

When Stokes discusses blockage, he does so in terms that recall the previous theorists of this chapter. For instance, in "The Luxury and Necessity of Painting," one of *Three Essays on the Painting of Our Time* (1961), he mentions "several great painters" who had trouble with their eyes. The source of this trouble, when psychosomatic, is identified in Kleinian terms as "an unconscious sense of guilt, usually strong, in connection with the greedy, prehensile, and controlling act of vision as it has appeared to the fantasy in early years."[105] When this guilt is sufficiently intense, an inhibiting or blocking perfectionism can result, what Stokes calls "the compulsion to 'get things right' issuing in part from the fear of deformity and aggressiveness."[106] "A painter," writes Stokes in *The Invitation in Art*, "to be so, must be capable of perpetrating defacement in order to add, create, transform, restore, the attack is defacement nonetheless."[107] The aggressive component in creation must be expressed if the work is to succeed, as Segal argues in her account of Golding's *The Spire.* In Stokes's words, "if attack be reduced below a certain minimum, art, creativeness, ceases; *equally, if sensibility over the fact of attack is entirely lulled, denied.*" No one can be a good artist "unless at one time he reckoned painfully with the conflicting emotions that underlie his transformations of material, the aggression, the power, the control, as well as his belief in his own goodness and reparative aim." And this is as true of the verbal as the visual arts, so "it is 'seconds out of the ring' for every writer as he opposes his first unblemished sheet, innocent of his *graffiti.*"[108] Blockage ensues, then, when the writer is overly anxious about his or her aggressive impulses. And it can occur either in the paranoid-schizoid position or later on, "as an inhibition of the depressive viewpoint itself by a major regression to earlier schizoid or paranoid phases (Klein, 1946), a state of affairs that rules out any question of aesthetic paramountcy owing to the inability to undergo depressive suffering."[109] This ought, by now, to be familiar: blockage can grow out of extremes both of paranoid-schizoid and depressive anxieties, as Klein would have it; room must be made for the ugly (the partial and aggressive) as well as the beautiful (or whole), as Segal would have it; for a feeling of oneness (union or merging) *and* twoness (or separation), in Milner's terms; or internal and external realms, in Winnicott's. In Stokes's account, as in Ehrenzweig's and those of all the other theorists of this chapter, the blocked writer is unable to negotiate rival claims or impulses, and this inability is a sign of a larger or more general problem of adaptation or object relations, the source of which, invariably, lies in the earliest experiences of infancy—the earliest attempts to sort out subject from object, self from other.

Of all the psychoanalytic accounts of blockage discussed so far, this one seems the most sophisticated and persuasive. It is also, as I hope to show in the chapters that follow, especially those on Wordsworth and Coleridge, most clearly supported by the language and experience of writers themselves.

PART TWO

Literary History

⌒5⌒

Theories of Origin

The Burden of the Past

The literary historian shares with the psychoanalyst a sense that the source of blockage derives from the past. But even when literary history makes direct or explicit use of psychoanalytic concepts, the past it looks to is literary, rather than personal or biographical. What burdens writers is less their relation with their parents, say, or their internal images of them, than their sense of what has already been written. This sense has always been with writers, but became particularly prominent, it has been argued, in the eighteenth century, the essential "crossroads" between the Renaissance and our modern world of acute literary self-consciousness. The most influential recent proponent of this view is W. J. Bate, who first voiced it in the Alexander Lectures at the University of Toronto in 1969, published a year later as *The Burden of the Past and the English Poet*.[1]

Bate chooses the eighteenth century for several reasons. To begin with, there is the existence of mass printing. Since the Renaissance, "the means of preserving and distributing the literature (and more recently the other arts) of the past have immeasurably increased, and to such a point that we now have confronting the artist . . . a vast array of varied achievement, existing and continually multiplying in an 'eternal present.'"[2] In earlier eras, according to Washington Irving, the difficulties of copying and dispersal prevented authors from being "inundated by the intellect of antiquity . . . drowned in the deluge." In Irving's time,

> the inventions of paper and the press . . . put an end to all these restraints. The stream of literature has swoln into a torrent— augmented into a river—expanded into a sea. A few centuries since, five or six hundred manuscripts constituted a great library; but what would you say to libraries, such as actually exist, containing three and four hundred thousand volumes; legions of authors at the same time busy; and the press going on with fearfully increasing activity, to double and quadruple the number?[3]

Those writers who first experienced this "inundation"—the "eternal present" of print—did so, moreover, just after the single most brilliant creative period in the language; what Dryden called the work of "the Gyant Race before the Flood."[4] All thematic, formal, social, and psychoanalytic problems pale before the consequences of this inheritance, before what Bate calls "the remorseless deepening of self-consciousness, before the rich and intimidating legacy of the past." Bate cites Eliot as a representatively burdened witness: "Not only every great poet, but every genuine, though lesser poet, fulfills once for all some possibility of the language, and so leaves one possibility less for his successors."[5]

Bate sees the symptoms of this new and basic blocking anxiety about the past in an extraordinarily rapid change in critical fashion in the eighteenth century. The developed neoclassicism of the early Augustans was no native-born and slow-maturing plant; rather, it was a new and sudden importation, a product, in large measure, of French influence on the newly restored Stuart court (though the classicizing tendencies of Jonson and his "sons" also played a part). This nonnative quality the writers themselves fully recognized, "from Dryden, Rhymer, and Temple down to Hazlitt and Francis Jeffrey a century and a half later."[6] Compare, suggests Bate, the rise of neoclassicism with that of Romanticism; the latter so slowly generated, so long in development, especially in verse and fiction, as opposed to critical theory; the former a sort of instant orthodoxy, with adaptive and transformative powers so strong and urgent that they seem the products of deepest need and anxiety. Neoclassicism, in short, is seen as a defensive strategy of post-Renaissance writers: hence, for example, its devaluation of "invention"; or its stress on "truth" rather than "originality," as though the two were somehow opposed values; or its emphasis on "decorum," a way to give space to writers who felt that everything had been done, so "pruning," "honing," "cutting down," became both answers (something *did* remain to be done) and symptoms—of limitation, of degeneration.

The irony of this last point was but a symptom of a more general irony of neoclassicism: the defense or escape it provided only reinforced those burdens under which the "enlightened" or eighteenth-century poet thought he labored. By the 1730s and 1740s, the neoclassicists even began to suspect, alarmingly, that the very best of the classical past—Homer and the Greek tragedians—belonged with the inhibiting Renaissance masters, what Bate calls "the excluded Renaissance past."[7] Although Alexander Pope published editions of Homer and Shakespeare, his own poetical practice rested on an ideal of refinement and decorum, what he called "one way left of excelling."[8] And that this was seen as a diminished way is suggested by the obsession of his age with how little it had achieved in the "greater genres," epic and tragic drama, a "fact," as one scholar of the eighteenth century has said, "as obvious to them as it is to us."[9] Poetry, it seemed, was cultivating progressively smaller plots; the writing of the period, in Matthew Arnold's famous phrase, was thought to lack "poetic largeness, freedom, insight, benignity."[10]

Hence the many works of the period lamenting lost power, including poems by William Collins, Thomas Gray, William Shenstone, and Joseph and Thomas Warton, poets of "sensibility," who occupy what Geoffrey Hartman calls "the interlunar moment," a poetical "liminal zone," in Jean-Pierre Mileur's words, separating "the full light of day from the coming darkness."[11] The tone of these poets, writes Mileur, "is more melancholy than sad, which is to say that there is a pleasurable element of new freedom mixed with the sadness—the freedom accompanying a defeat for which one cannot be blamed and against which no amount of genius can prevail."[12] In Gray's "Elegy in a Country Churchyard" (1750), for example, poetic powerlessness is famously figured not only in the limited status of the "rude forefathers of the Hamlet"—and the limited possibilities open to them— but also in the inert, passive manner in which their activities are detailed.[13] In "Stanzas to Mr Bentley" (1752), in which poetic limitation is openly acknowledged, Gray's tone is comparably enervated (the concluding words of the last three lines have been lost):

> . . . not to one in this benighted age
>   Is that diviner inspiration given,
> That burns in Shakespeare's or in Milton's page,
>   The pomp and prodigality of heaven
> As when, conspiring in the diamond's blaze,
>   The meaner gems, that singly charm the sight,
> Together dart their intermingled rays,
>   And dazzle with a luxury of light.
> Enough for me, if to some feeling breast
>   My lines a secret sympathy [   ]
> And as their pleasing influence [   ]
>   A sigh of soft reflection [   ]
>   (17–28)

The missing words here seem almost appropriate; the note is one not only of inertia but of pleasurable acceptance. Two years later, in "The Progress of Poesy" (1754), Gray sounds this note again. The poem traces the Muse's steps from the remotest and most barbarous-seeming nations to Greece, Italy, and the England first of Shakespeare ("Nature's darling," 84), then of Milton (who "rode sublime / Upon the seraph-wings of Ecstasy," 95–96), and then Dryden. Anxiety enters in with Dryden. Although driven by "Two Coursers of ethereal race" (105), Dryden's poetical chariot is a "less presumptuous car" (103) than Milton's, and this prepares us for the newly modest or lowered expectations of the concluding stanza:

> Hark, his hands the lyre explore!
> Bright-eyed Fancy hovering o'er
> Scatters from her pictured urn
> Thoughts that breathe and words that burn.
> But ah! 'tis heard no more—
> Oh! Lyre divine, what daring spirit
> Wakes thee now? Though he inherit
> Nor the pride nor ample pinion
> That the Theban Eagle bear
> Sailing with supreme dominion
> Though the azure deep of air:
> Yet oft before his infant eyes would run
> Such forms as glitter in the Muse's ray
> With orient hues, unborrowed of the sun:
> Yet shall he mount and keep his distant way
> Beyond the limits of a vulgar fate,
> Beneath the Good how far—but far above the Great.
>
> (107–23)

"The convoluted syntax of that last line," writes Mileur, "very nearly succeeds in obscuring Gray's conviction that the progress of poesy represents for moderns a permanent decline in greatness. This new Pindar anticipated by Gray, though soaring far above the merely good, is nevertheless doomed to remain far below the truly great."[14] Gray's reference to "the Theban Eagle" in line 115 even manages to imply a decline from Greece to Shakespeare.

Similarly explicit references to decline or loss occur in Collins: in "An Epistle: Addressed to Sir Thomas Hanmer, on his Edition of Shakespeare's Works" (1743), with its talk of "the Muse's happier days" (1); in the "Ode on the Poetical Character" (1746), in which the speaker "retreats" from the poetry of his age to that of Milton, but does so "In vain" (72) because

> . . . such Bliss to One alone
> Of all the sons of soul was known,
> And Heaven and Fancy, kindred powers,
> Have now o'erturned the inspiring bowers,
> Or curtained close such scene from every future View.
>
> (72–76)

Similarly, "The Manners. An Ode" (1746) begins by distinguishing past greatness, "that ampler range" (21), from the diminished measure of a present, cultivated harmony, "where Science sure is found, / From Nature as she lives around / . . . alluring from a safer Rule" (27–28, 33).

Over and above such instances—others of which could be quoted from the Wartons, Shenstone, or Mark Akenside—lies the evidence of the lives themselves (or what we have of them) and the relative slimness of the output. To Pat Rogers, the "sensibility" poets "are capable of wonderful short bursts; but they rarely sustain this quality for long. They compose splendid poetry, but rarely complete wholly satisfactory poems. . . . There is something disjointed about the output of these men."[15] Gray's poetry, for example, seems to have been written, as he admitted of "The Progress of Poetry," "by fits & starts at very distant intervals." "You will, I hope," he advised Horace Walpole of the "Elegy in a Country Churchyard," "look upon it in the light of a *thing with an end to it;* a merit which most of my writings have wanted, and are like to want."[16] When Gray returned to Cambridge at the age of twenty-six, he became, according to Rogers,

> the first "academic poet," in the sense that he was not merely a learned and bookish writer but also one who seemed to use intellectual inquiry as a surrogate for writing. At times, his extensive research into natural history, music, early literature and the rest appears to be a mode of escape. At other times, as in his Pindaric poems, the weight of knowledge is brought to bear frontally on his own creative practice. A term often applied to Gray is "fastidious." This may refer simply to the fact that he declined the public office of laureate on what seem rather frivolous grounds; or that he was given to revising copiously; or that he was never in a hurry to publish.[17]

This description sounds very much like writer's block, and it may help to account for the notorious vehemence Johnson brought to his *Life of Gray.* "What signifies so much knowledge," Johnson quotes an earlier biographer, "when it produced so little? Is it worth taking so much pains to leave no memorial but a few poems?" This, of course, is an accusation to which Johnson himself felt vulnerable; hence his impatience, notably with Gray's "unprofessional," proto-Romantic habits of composition. "As a writer he had this peculiarity, that he did not write his pieces first rudely, and then correct them, but laboured every line as it arose in the train of composition, and he had a notion not very peculiar, that he could not write but at certain times, or at happy moments: a fantastick foppery to which my kindness for a man of learning and of virtue wishes him to have been superior." [18]

Gray's relative silence, his blockage, was more calmly borne than that of Collins, who shared many of his qualities and standards. Collins's feelings of inadequacy, it has been argued, resulted in breakdown when he was thirty. "Irresolution," writes Rogers, "lies at the heart of [his work]—a vacillating bookish capacity to be over-impressed by his literary heroes, a tendency to revise too much, an inability to finish things." [19] "The latter part of his life," writes Johnson, "cannot be remembered but with pity and sadness. He languished some years under that depression of mind which enchains the faculties without destroying them, and leaves reason the power of right without the knowledge of pursuing it." [20]

The poetry of defeat was only one consequence of what Bate identifies as a new and crippling self-consciousness. Another was the age's violent oscillation between doctrinaire imitation, in which poets, to adapt James Sutherland's phrase, "wrote poems" rather than "poetry," [21] and what Voltaire calls "senseless eccentricity." [22] Collins and Gray also fit this description, shifting from strict adherence to classical models, on the one hand, to the forms and subject matter of exotic primitivism, either Northern European or Oriental, on the other. "In retrospect," writes Rogers of Gray's recourse to Old Welsh and Old Norse models in "The Bard" (1754) and other late poems, "it looks as if Gray was simply trying to replenish a sadly depleted imaginative store." [23] And much the same could be said of late Collins in a poem such as "An Ode on the Popular Superstitions of the Highlands of Scotland" (1750). "As with Gray," continues Rogers, "it is significant that Collins can only envy the minstrels of old— he cannot emulate them. There is something incestuous about the primitivist revival of the mid-century; again and again we find the poet writing *about* ancient bards, rather than investing his own work with bardic qualities. This ode contains rich romantic notions, but their appeal is their remoteness to Collins 'on the southern coast.'" [24] To Roger Lonsdale, "the poem displays at times a disabling rift between the poet whose imagination longs to shed its inhibitions and the sophisticated metropolitan intellectual" [25]—an accusation that applies equally to other forms of eighteenth-century extravagance, from the grisly excesses of the so-called Graveyard School of Robert Blair (1699–1746) and Edward Young (1683–1765) to the willful turbulence of the Gothic. Hence Wordsworth's complaint at the end of the century against "frantic novels, sickly and stupid German tragedies, and deluges of idle and extravagant stories in verse." [26] Roger Shattuck points to *Rameau's Nephew* (1761) as a dark parable of this eighteenth-century trend and notes its influence on Goethe's Faust, another figure, like the overreaching protagonist in Diderot's novella, of sense-less or compulsive originality, of "originality for originality's sake."[27]

In the eighteenth century, then, literature was thought of in "modern" terms: as in decline. And various reasons were adduced in explanation. To begin with, writing and art in general were felt to suffer from more hopeful developments in other spheres. The state, for example, was thought to be too well-ordered to provide the marvels needed for epic or heroic genres; literary power, in William Duff's words from the *Essay on Original Genius* (1767), "will seldom Appear in a Very Great Degree in Cultivated Life."[28] The language, newly exact and denotative, was believed to inhibit metaphoric richness, the sort of invention characteristic of unruly genius. So also with the thought of the new age, which was said to be altogether too precise and developed for the poet, because poetry, according to this argument, thrives best in transition between barbarism and what Richard Hurd, writing in 1759, calls "the refinements of reason and science."[29] Hence the growth of criticism in the eighteenth century, and with it Joseph Warton's complaint of 1756 that "in no polished nation, after criticism has been much studied, and the rules of writing established, has any very extraordinary work ever appeared."[30] In the face of suspicions such as these, the poet who did not give up completely felt himself reduced either to parody, or a poetry of tidying or convention, or wild and willful novelty—inartistic by its own standards because extraneous, and thus tinged with self-loathing.

As the eighteenth century progressed, therefore, so did a sense of the limitations of neoclassicism, and, gradually, the values it underplayed came to the fore. Originality and genius, in particular, became ideals, only accentuating, as in the case of Gray and Collins, the poet's feelings of uneasiness and inadequacy. Coleridge (born in 1772) is a later type or victim of this transformation; a poet blocked, so he himself proclaimed, by notions of genius. "I have too clearly before me the idea of a poet's genius to deem myself any other than a very humble poet," he wrote in a letter of 9 April 1814. By the age of forty-one, Coleridge had "for many years given [poetry] up in despair," a victim of his sense of the necessity and impossibility of being different.[31] Even those Romantic poets who triumphed over burdensome or blocking notions both of the past and of the poetical character shared those notions, and they sought out genuine avenues of originality in subject matter and style. It was not enough for Coleridge that Wordsworth "stands nearest of all modern writers to Shakespeare and Milton." Wordsworth had to do so "in a kind perfectly unborrowed and his own."[32] An anecdote recounted by Charles Lamb suggests that Wordsworth held similar views. Leafing through a new book by Godwin, Wordsworth came across the words "all modern poetry is nothing but the old genuine poetry, new vamped, and delivered to us at second, or twentieth hand." According to Lamb, who had just bought the book, Wordsworth seized a pencil and, "in great wrath," wrote in the margin: "This is false, William Godwin. Signed William Wordsworth."[33] As William Hazlitt said of the poetical ambitions of "the Lake School," "a thorough adept . . . is jealous of all excellence but his own. He does not even like to share his reputation with his subject; for he will have it all proceed from his own power and originality of mind."[34]

The Limits of Literary History

Bate's book never makes clear why some poets were able to lift the burden of the past and the inhibiting poetical ideals it generated, while others were not. Nor does he say much about the source or cause of periods of blockage within otherwise productive careers (why the past seems only sometimes to inhibit particular writers). In Keats, for example, the past can, on occasion, loom as the shaming standard it was to Gray and Collins. "Is there so small a range / In the present state of manhood," Keats asks in "Sleep and Poetry" (1817), "that the high / Imagination cannot freely fly / As she was wont of old?" (162–65). The answer, at moments, is yes. "My spirit is too weak," is how Keats responds "On Seeing the Elgin Marbles" (1817), "—mortality / Weighs heavily on me like unwilling sleep, / And each imagined pinnacle and steep / Of godlike hardship tells me I must die" (1–4). The effect of past greatness, in other words, inhibits, though Keats rather luxuriates in his sense of inferiority (even as he builds a sonnet out of it—a common response in the period). "Great Muse," cries a despondent Endymion, type of the artist and of Keats himself:

> . . . thou know'st what prison
> Of flesh and bone, curbs and confines, and frets
> Our spirit's wings. Despondency besets
> Our pillows, and the fresh tomorrow morn
> Seems to give forth its light in very scorn
> Of our dull, uninspired, snail-pacèd lives.
> Long have I said, how happy he who strives
> To thee! But then I thought on poets gone,
> And could not pray . . .
> (4.20–28)

This passage comes after a brief Gray- or Collins-like account of the progress of poetry from earliest times, when Hebrew, Greek, and Roman literature flourished, and England "was a wolfish den. / Before our forests heard the talk of men" (5–6), to a flowering of English verse with Chaucer and the Elizabethans, and finally to the pale present, in which "despondency besets / Our pillows" (22–23). But even when despondency is overcome, according to this pessimistic strain in Keats, the result is dispiriting, a literature of lesser forms and aspirations. "Modern poets differ from the Elizabethans in this," writes Keats to his friend J. H. Reynolds: "Each of the moderns like an Elector of Hanover governs his petty state, and knows how many straws are swept daily from the Causeways in all his dominions and has a continual itching that all the Housewives should have their coppers well scoured."[35] This is exactly the anxiety Bate identifies: the modern poet as self-consciously limited or burdened by the past, reduced to a poetry of mere correction, pruning, honing—in Keats's words, to "sweeping" and "scouring." Keats told his friend Richard Woodhouse that he sometimes felt "there was nothing original in poetry to be written; that its riches were already exhausted—and all its beauties forestalled."[36]

When Keats voices these anxieties, he does so not only in terms that recall Bate and the eighteenth-century sources he cites, but in larger, metaphysical terms. In the sonnet "When I Have Fears" (1818), Keats faces the possibility of an early death, "Before my pen has gleaned my teeming brain" (2). He looks out at the sky and beholds "upon the night's scarred face, / Huge cloudy symbols of a high romance" (5–6), the shadows of which "I may never live to trace / . . . with the magic hand of chance" (7–8). This last phrase, "the magic hand of chance," is noteworthy in two respects: to begin with, it suggests that poetic power is outside human or conscious control, a product of inspiration and spontaneity, an impulse that must come "as naturally as the leaves to the tree." Speaking as the aspiring poet in "Sleep and Poetry," Keats tells us that he must "kneel / Upon some mountain-top until I feel / A glowing splendour round about me hung, / And echo back the voice of thine own tongue" (49–52). At the same time, the phrase alludes to a larger destiny (and insecurity), one that governs all aspects of existence, including life and death. And because this destiny is blind and mysterious, Keats has nothing to quiet his fears, and the sonnet ends in unsettled and unsettling musing: "then on the shore / Of the wide world I stand alone and think / Till love and fame to nothingness do sink" (12–14). This ending neatly exemplifies a structural and musical ideal for Keats, as expressed in the "Epistle to Charles Cowden Clarke" (1816): "the sonnet swelling loudly / Up to its climax and then dying proudly" (60–61). To some, it recalls the ending to Milton's sonnet "When I Consider How My Light Is Spent" (1655), which discusses comparable fears. However, in Milton's poem the quiet of the final line, "They also serve who only stand and wait," is settled and settling, sustained by a faith no longer available to Keats and nowhere in evidence in his poem. Although Milton also is dependent on outside forces for his creative powers, those forces are known and, ultimately, trusted; and this has a special—if mixed—impact upon his ability to write.

Keats sees Milton's faith or surety as a limitation as well as a strength, which brings us back to Bate and the burden of the past. That Milton "appears to have been content" with what Keats characterizes, in a well-known letter of 3 May 1818 to Reynolds, as "Dogmas and superstition" only proves that "a mighty providence subdues the mightiest Minds to the service of the time." But times change, and Keats is enough a child of the nineteenth century to see them changing for the better. What he calls "the grand march of intellect" is a good thing (one thinks, for instance, of the striking plea for modernity in "Ode to Psyche," in which Keats writes of competing with the ancients, but in a new, autonomous, "psychological" manner), yet it also creates problems for the contemporary writer. Wordsworth, for example, may be a "deeper" poet than Milton, being unblinkered by dogma and superstition, but he also lacks "epic passion"—precisely because he has no faith. The present allows the poet to "see further," but robs him of strength, turning would-be poetical "emperors" into mere "electors," a view that recalls Hurd on "the refinements of reason and science" and helps to explain what might be called a "generic block" suffered by post-Miltonic poets of epic.[37] More importantly, the comparison of Milton and Wordsworth points to a crucial shift in belief: from faith in the essential texts and values of religious culture to faith in the power of poetry or secular letters, as well as in the visionary insights it affords. This new faith throws the poet back upon himself and increases the possibility of guilt and anxiety.

Keats's fears of blockage are instructive—and representative of his age—but also relatively rare: past greatness is as likely to inspire as to inhibit him. This is most famously the case in the sonnet "On Chapman's Homer" (1818), in which Keats's own powers, it has been argued, for the first time blossom in the full light of past greatness.[38] A similar impression can be derived from the letters, especially those written in the midst of the most ambitious projects. Here, for example, is Keats's account of his hopes for *Endymion*: "I must," he writes his friend Benjamin Bailey, on 8 October 1817, "make 4000 Lines of one bare circumstance and fill them with Poetry; and when I consider that this is a great task, and that when done it will take me but a dozen paces towards the Temple of Fame—it makes me say—God forbid that I should be without such a task!"[39] That is, in the words of a letter written almost exactly a year later, "I was never afraid of failure; for I would sooner fail than not be among the greatest."[40] The duality in these instances is characteristic: Keats is indeed self-conscious about his task—and about the achievements of past greatness—yet does not balk or block. "The Cliff of Poesy towers above me," he writes to Benjamin Haydon in May 1817, "I do begin arduously where I leave off, notwithstanding occasional depressions: and I hope for the support of a High Power while I climb this little eminence. . . . Is it too daring to fancy Shakespeare the Presider?"[41]

Statements such as these go hand in hand with calm and clear-sighted prescriptions for fallow periods: "Whenever I feel myself growing vapourish," Keats writes to his brother and sister in a journal letter of 17–27 September 1819, "I rouse myself, wash and put on a clean shirt brush my hair and clothes, tie my shoestrings neatly and in fact adonize as I were going out—then all clean and comfortable I sit down to write."[42] This is just like bluff, no-nonsense Kingsley Amis, who recommends a shower or shaving for moments of blockage.[43] For all his keen insight into the anxieties of influence and the blocking fears they generate, Keats is to be believed when he declares that "the only thing that can ever affect me personally for more than one short passing day, is any doubt about my powers for poetry—I seldom have any, and I look with hope to the nighing time when I shall have none."[44]

Why Keats should be relatively free from doubts—why he should doubt at one moment and not another—are questions Bate never really addresses, and his silence sends us back to personal, as opposed to what might be called literary historical, psychology, as well as to the theorists of part one. The closest Bate comes to dealing with the implications of an example such as Keats's occurs toward the end of *The Burden of the Past and the English Poet*, in which he sounds a brief and stirring note of optimism, an evocation of what Keats called the "immortal freemasonry" of great writers. "Always available to man, if he hopes to rise above 'cultural declines' and fatigues from whatever cause—or to rise above anything else that threatens to imprison or deflect him personally—is the companionship, the support to the heart and spirit, of a direct and frank turning to the great."[45] This turning, though, requires "boldness," which is not the "*soi-disant* boldness of negativism, of grudgingly withholding assent as we establish our identities, prate of our integrity, or reach into our pockets for our mite of 'originality.'"[46] Yet "boldness," of course, begs the very questions that matter: How do you get it? Of what does it consist? Why does it so often disappear? "The vision of greatness," Bate tells

125

us, "can operate suddenly as a release as well as an incentive to the creative initiative of the spirit";[47] some poets succeed, whereas others, comparably belated and self-conscious, lack "the boldness of spirit that seizes upon opportunities and creates new ones."[48] And that is it—which is why Bate's final paragraphs revert to the pessimism that has animated almost everything that has gone before. "In no other case," he writes of artistic creation, "are you enjoined to achieve and at the same time to try, at all costs, *not* to follow closely what you admire. . . . Yet here, in the arts, the split is widening." The consequence is neurosis, one symptom of which, for many writers, is blockage. Bate concludes: "When we face obviously conflicting demands, when the pressures (or what I imagine the pressures to be) are ones that enjoin us to move in two different—in fact, two opposing—directions at once, what do we do then? I think of the fable of the donkey that starved when he was confronted, on each side, with two equally distant bales of hay. The arts stutter, stagger, pull back into paralysis and indecision before such a conflict of demand."[49] Or blossom with the mysterious resourcefulness of a Keats.

Romantic Theory and Blockage

Influence anxiety, as has already been suggested, was but one of several burdens newly assumed—or felt to be newly assumed—by the post-Miltonic writer. A related or concomitant set of burdens derives from the rise of Romantic theories of creativity, which Bate sees as reactions against the "defensive strategy" of neoclassicism—a sort of return of the repressed. These theories—of natural genius, originality, spontaneity—are important to the study of writer's block in two respects. First, because they locate poetic power, as in Keats's "magic hand of chance," in nonrational or uncontrollable mental faculties, thus tending to consign the would-be writer to a passive position, "kneeling," as in Keats's phrase, "upon some mountain-top." Second, because their influence lives on, and is clearly the source of many of the assumptions about writers or artists made by psychoanalytic theory, the source of the term *writer's block*.

At the heart of what Bate refers to as "developed neoclassicism" is a mechanistic psychology derived from the principles of natural science and English empirical philosophy. This tradition conceives of writing, like all other complex mental functions, in terms analogous to those of the operations of the physical world. Thus David Hartley's theory of association, as expounded in *Observations on Man* (1749), which played a vital role in solidifying neoclassical accounts of literary creativity, is modeled on "the method of analysis and synthesis

recommended and followed by Sir Isaac Newton";[50] and Lord
Kames's *Elements of Criticism* (1762) aims "to draw the rules of criticism from human nature, their true source,"[51] by ascending "gradually to principles, from facts and experiments."[52]

The purely mechanical nature not only of physical but also of
psychical and literary explanation, though, raises as many questions
as it answers: to begin with, how is it that the result of these causal
or mechanical motions should be, say, a cosmos rather than a chaos—
or a poem rather than gibberish? The answer has unsettling implications. In the case of order or design in the physical realm, a designer
is posited: "This most beautiful system of the sun, planets, and com-
ets," admits Newton, following in the footsteps of Robert Boyle and
others, "could only proceed from the counsel and dominion of an
intelligent and powerful Being."[53] And the same is true in the literary
or psychological sphere, in which the designing deity is replaced by
a reigning mental power, variously labeled "judgement," "reason," or
"understanding." That the two sorts of design (or designer) are seen
as related is clear from the following lines from Dryden's "To My
Honoured Friend Sir Robert Howard" (1660):

> No atoms casually together hurl'd
> Could e'er produce so beautiful a world
> Nor dare I such a doctrine here admit,
> As would destroy the providence of wit.
>
> (31–34)

Hence recourse to God and to a reigning faculty such as judgment or
reason; hence, too, the suspicion that the true source of literary
achievement is unknowable, that beneath the assurance provided by
mechanical or scientific analogies lies a vital, distinguishing, subjective factor, what French neoclassicists such as Dominique Bouhours,
René Rapin, and Nicolas Boileau called the *je ne sais quoi*.[54]

For the most part, though, the importance of this subjective factor
was played down in the early decades of the century; the first generation of Augustans conceived of writing as a rational, orderly activity, something explicable, controllable, imitable. Poets, as the Greek
origin of the term suggested, were makers—of objects, poems. As a
consequence (Bate would call this its unconscious origin), the theory
was reassuring, the source of calm and commanding certainty. For
example, to Thomas Rhymer, arguing in support of William Davenant's attack on poetic inspiration, it is a wonder that any writer "enabled to speak from the principles of nature and his own meditation,
loves rather to be thought to speak by inspiration, like a Bagpipe"[55]—
as opposed to, say, an Aeolian harp. Although early-eighteenth-

century poets admitted the existence of inspiration, they did so in what M. H. Abrams calls "a brisk and business-like way," insisting "that it be subject to the control of judgement, decorum, and the rules."[56] This attitude recalls the assurance of ego psychology, as do several other neoclassical tenets. "Though his discourse," according to Rapin, "ought in some manner to resemble that of one inspired; yet his Mind must always be serene, that he may discover when to *let his muse run mad*, and when to govern his Transports."[57] Which is to say, the writer lets the Muse run mad—in psychoanalytic terms, regresses—in the service of "Mind" or ego. There is even an eighteenth-century equivalent of Hartmann's distinction between free and bound energies, with their differing speeds of discharge. To Alexander Gerard, in the *Essay on Genius* (1774), "when an ingenious track of thinking presents itself . . . to true genius . . . imagination darts alongst it with great rapidity; and by this rapidity its ardour is more inflamed. The velocity of its motion sets it on fire, like a chariot wheel which is kindled by the quickness of its revolution. . . . Its motions become still more impetuous, till the mind is enraptured by the subject, and exalted into an ecstasy."[58] In such a way, poetic transport is anatomized, as the release of what the ego psychologist would call free energy. In both cases, the unknowable is made known, domesticated by the authority of scientific terminology.

The resulting confidence is nowhere more clearly shown than in the first-generation Augustan writers, as in Jonathan Swift's easy ridicule of influence anxiety in *The Tale of the Tub* (1708). "It is reckoned," he writes in the famous "Digression in Praise of Digressions," "that there is not at this present a sufficient Quantity of new Matter left in Nature to furnish and adorn any one particular Subject to the Extent of a Volume. This I am told by a very skilful carpenter, who has given a full Demonstration of it from the Rules of Arithmetic."[59] This is hardly the voice of a worried man. Or take Pope's well-known account of literary invention in the *Essay on Criticism* (1709). Pope begins, as should any writer, with what is given:

> First follow Nature, and your judgement frame
> By her just standard, which is still the same;
> Unerring Nature, still divinely bright,
> One clear, unchanged, and universal light.
> Life, force, and beauty must to all impart,
> At once the source, and end, and test of art.
> Art from that fund each just supply provides,
> Works without show, and without pomp presides.
> (68–75)

Noteworthy here, aside from Pope's general air of calm good humour, are the words "standard," "source," and "fund," which suggest a starting point for the writer, one that guards him (Pope would not have been thinking of women writers) against potentially blocking fears. Nature, in the sense of material, is a given, and composition is but the shaping or ordering of material, the best way of presenting what is known. As for "ancient rules," they are but "Nature methodized" (89): "To copy Nature is to copy them" (140).

When Pope discusses what I have called the subjective factor in writing, the *je ne sais quoi*, he remains unruffled. Some beauties produced by great poets, he readily admits, "No precepts can declare, / For there's a happiness as well as care" (141–42), a species of "nameless graces which no methods can teach, / And which a master hand alone can reach" (144–45). That great poets such as Homer and Shakespeare

> From vulgar bounds with brave disorder part,
> And snatch a grace beyond the reach of art,
> Which without passing through the judgement, gains
> The heart, and all its end at once attains
> (152–55)

is cause neither for anxiety nor for the abrogation of rules. To begin with, the temptation to "transgress" (164) should be seldom heeded: "The winged courser, like a generous hawk, / Shows most true mettle when you check his course" (86–87). But even when it is heeded, says Pope, would-be Homers and Shakespeares, "have at least their precedent to plead" (166)—that is, remain within the realm of orderly procedure and judgment. Although genius operates according to no known rules, this does not mean it is ruleless; Johnson echoes this faith toward the end of the century when he declares, in the *Life of Congreve* (1781), that even "enthusiasm has its rules."[60]

By the end of the century, though, confidence such as this was on the wane, with what Abrams calls "momentous" consequences. Once writing ceased to be conceived of as "a supremely purposeful activity" and became instead "a spontaneous process independent of intention, precept, or even consciousness,"[61] the writer was newly isolated, thrown back on his own internal resources, with nothing "given." This isolation has logical and historical connections with Romantic individualism in general, and it allies the writer to such "Pensoroso" figures as Collins's "pilgrim" in "Ode to Evening" (1746) or the speaker in Gray's "Elegy in a Country Churchyard," as well as to later wanderers and outcasts not only in the poems of Wordsworth and Coleridge but also in those of Byron, Shelley, and Keats.

The particulars of this momentous change, even when drawn with the broadest of brushes, are complicated, involving German as well as English sources.[62] They begin with the growing prominence in England of the *je ne sais quoi*, particularly in Edward Young's influential *Conjectures on Original Composition* (1755) and the writings of the generation of young poets—Gray, Collins, and the other poets of "sensibility"—who emerged about the time of Pope's death in 1744; are then taken up in the last quarter of the eighteenth century by German idealist philosophy, from which Freud and the movement he built derived so much; and, finally, filter back to England, primarily through the influence of Coleridge and Wordsworth (or Coleridge *on* Wordsworth). Chief among the tenets of this new account of writing is a distinction between two types of ordering procedure, variously labeled fancy and imagination, intelligence and nature, conscious and unconscious. By fancy or intelligence is meant the associative and mechanical aspects of mental functioning. The higher faculties of imagination or nature are associated with grace or genius, the mysterious power of a Shakespeare or Homer. "An Original," writes Young, using a newly influential organic metaphor, "rises spontaneously from the vital root of genius; it *grows*, it is not *made*. Imitations* are often a sort of *manufacture* wrought by those *mechanics, art* and *labour,* out of pre-existent materials not their own."[63] This distinction recalls Freud's division between primary and secondary processes, or conscious and unconscious, as well as Jung's privileging of the "symbolic" or "visionary" poet. "Therefore dive deep into thy bosom," Young exhorts the poet, "contract full intimacy with the stranger within thee . . . let thy genius rise (if a genius thou hast) as the sun from chaos."[64] The frightening or pejorative implications of the metaphors used here ("stranger," "chaos") also recall Freud and Jung, perhaps because they were developed by later German writers important to psychoanalysis, in particular Novalis and E. T. A. Hoffman.

Although the twists and turns that brought such theories to Freud can be variously tracked, the path from Hoffman (1776–1822) is a clear one.[65] Hoffman thought of himself as a genius, an artistic messiah to a degraded present, a messenger from a higher, future realm, in which humanity would possess an "immediate perception of all being" and "an understanding of the fundamental pattern, the pure harmony of existence."[66] Hoffman's use of the double as a symbol of humanity's alienated condition clearly anticipates Freud's theories of the repressed contents of the unconscious, as does his depiction of the transcendent realm—the realm of the true artist—as amoral. For Hoffman, genius is demonic and often associated with sexual transgression, a sign of its distance from, and superiority to, the conventions of a degraded, bourgeois "many." Hence the prominence first of incest and then of homosexuality in his stories; hence also the connection between sexual "deviation" and art, both of which are said to transcend what Keats (in "Sleep and Poetry," line 158) called the "muddy stream" of conscious, everyday reality. The genius, though, is alienated in another sense as well: the larger division he marks between the one and the many, the transcendent and the mundane, is repeated within his own individuality. His higher or transcendent self is the part of him, in Robert Currie's words, "which is truly of the one, while his lower self is the part of him which is still of the philistine many."[67] And this division also recalls Freud and Jung on the artist.

The story of how these ideas—of genius, originality, spontaneity—found their way back from Germany to England at the beginning of the nineteenth century has been frequently told. All that needs to be noted here is how quickly and surely they took hold. If "the cultivated Briton of the Elizabethan age looked to Italy to improve his mind; and the cultivated Briton in Dryden's time and the Enlightenment looked to France; by Romantic and Victorian times he looked almost slavishly to Germany."[68] And what he found there, as Bate and others have argued, was an image that the neoclassical age had partially buried or repressed: that of the writer as elevated and apart, and of writing as an exalted mystery rather than a craft. Such ideas were in themselves inhibiting, even in pre-Miltonic days; in a newly secular age, one without religious sanctions, they were even more so. To assume the writer's role under these conditions was to risk transgression, to open oneself to guilt-inducing fears and temptations. Hence the prominence of blockage in the lives of Romantic writers and the rash of incompletions and fragments that marks their careers. And hence the prevailing mood of anxiety and inadequacy with which the writer takes up his task. "Oh! mystery of man," writes Wordsworth in book eleven of the 1805 *Prelude*,

> from what a depth
> Proceed thy honours. I am lost, but see
> In simple childhood something of the base
> On which thy greatness stands . . .
> . . . The days gone by
> Return upon me almost from the dawn
> Of life; the hiding-places of man's power
> Open; I would approach them but they close.
> I see by glimpses now; when age comes on,
> May scarcely see at all . . .
> (11.329–32, 334–39)

This is a characteristic moment in Wordsworth. But it is also characteristic of Romanticism in general. "The further I go in my story," writes Jean-Jacques Rousseau in the *Confessions* (1765–70), "the less order and sequence I can put into it. . . . Now the story can only proceed at haphazard,"[69] which is in part why it is never finished. The chief characteristic of the Romantic work, writes Friedrich Schlegel in 1811, is that it "can never be completed."[70] To the student of writer's block, the record is richly, if dispiritingly, suggestive: William Blake abandons *The Four Zoas*, which Jean Hagstrum calls "that spectacular literary ruin,"[71] Coleridge cannot finish "Christabel" and "Kubla Khan" (to name but the best known of his poetic incompletions), Keats gives up on the two "Hyperion" fragments, Shelley's "The Triumph of Life" is left unfinished, Byron's *Don Juan* simply stops, Wordsworth's *The Recluse* remains incomplete, Thomas De Quincey's autobiography keeps growing and growing and is never brought to a close. The list could easily be extended. Nor is the age without ample evidence of generic blockage. While unable or unwilling to complete longer works, the later Wordsworth wrote sonnet after sonnet. "In the course of the same afternoon," he writes in 1822, "I have filled up many a moment in writing sonnets, which might easily have been better employed."[72]

So familiar are incompletion and procrastination in the age that the "fragment" itself takes on the status of a literary type. Thomas McFarland, in whose rich catalogue of Romantic "diasparactions" I have been trawling, invites us to

> open the Oxford edition of Shelley's poetical works (one could do the same with the new Penguin edition of Wordsworth's poems), and in the table of contents observe such titles as "Prince Athanase: A Fragment"; "Fragment: Home"; "Fragment of a Ghost Story"; "Fragment: To One Singing"; "A Fragment: To Music." Or, to limit attention to poems written in 1819, one notes "Fragment: To the People of England"; "Fragment: 'When Men Gain Freely'"; "Fragment: 'follow to the deep wood's weeds'"; and then further down in the work of the same year, a veritable barrage of additional fragments—seventeen by actual count.[73]

What is noteworthy here is less the fact of incompletion than the age's implied acceptance of it, even its celebration of it. According to Mario Praz, the extreme Romantic "exalts the artist who does not give a material form to his dreams—the poet ecstatic in front of a forever blank page."[74] Blockage creates a new literary form in the Romantic era, just as inhibiting thoughts and fears, in a variety of ways, generate a new subject matter. One aspect of this subject matter—a new fascination with the sublime—shows just how paradoxical the Romantic account not only of blockage in general but of writer's block in particular can be. For it is the peculiar distinction of the sublime to conceive of moments of blockage and fragments of understanding as enabling as well as inhibiting, as ways through.

Writer's Block and the Romantic Sublime

As the Romantic image of the writer evolved, so did an interest in the sublime. This is in part because the sublime offered the eighteenth-century writer a way of taming and opening out for discussion the subjective factor in composition, the factor behind which crowded attractive but dangerous notions of genius, originality, and spontaneity. Because the sublime was sanctioned by classical authority, it was free from censure. Its effect, though, was to undermine authority, whether conceived of in terms of authors or of the rules they were thought to codify.

The eighteenth-century understanding of the sublime derives originally from a rhetorical treatise of the first or second century A.D. attributed to the Greek philosopher Longinus. The origins of this treatise, *Peri Hypsous,* were in a long tradition of ancient rhetoric. For Longinus, the sublime, or *hypsos,* is principally a rhetorical style, emotive in purpose, which "not only persuades but even throws an audience into transports *(ekstasis)."*[75] Beneath Longinus's concern with style, though, lies what Samuel Monk calls "an expression of a quality of mind and experience."[76] It is this quality, rather than the detailed prescriptions that compose most of Longinus's surviving manuscript, upon which eighteenth-century writers built. What mattered to such writers was Longinus's stress on "boldness and grandeur in the *Thoughts"* and "the *Pathetic,* or the power of raising the passions to a violent and even enthusiastic degree"—in part because, unlike subsequent features of the sublime listed by Longinus, these "are the gifts of nature, whereas the other sorts depend in some measure upon art."[77] By highlighting Longinus's initial stress on passion and thought (rather than expression), eighteenth-century theory made him a sanction for the psychological study of the creative writer and of the reader's response to his work, as well as for the claims of unruly genius.

Longinus did not become an influential figure in England until the 1670s, twenty or so years after the publication of the first English translation by John Hall in 1652. Although Milton, for instance, knew of Longinus, he seems not to have been much influenced by him, for all his subsequent identification in the eighteenth century with everything for which Longinus stood. Longinus only began to matter in England after Boileau's French translation of 1674 became known, and so closely was the sublime connected with French influence that Johnson referred to the term in his *Dictionary* (1755) as "a Gallicism, but now naturalized."

By 1711, however, Longinus had become a subject of eulogy in Pope's *Essay on Criticism* ("himself the great sublime he draws"),[78] as well as a medium for satire, again by Pope in *Peri Bathous, or the Art of Sinking in Poetry* (1728), which, in Monk's words, "presupposes a familiarity with the treatise on the part of the town, and bears out other pieces of evidence that Longinus had come into his own."[79]

That Longinus's popularity should have spread from Boileau, whose *L'Art poétique* (1674) was the fullest and most influential expression of the neoclassical code, is appropriately ironic. "Boileau," writes Monk, "unwittingly set at work in the world two forces that eventually became mutually hostile."[80] Not only had Boileau translated Longinus's treatise, but, in his preface to the translation and the later *Réflexions Critiques sur quelques Passages du Rheteur Longin* (1694), he brought out its aesthetic as well as rhetorical implications. These implications would further the subjective or psychological study of creativity. It was Boileau who stressed the importance to Longinus of strength of conception, or "grandeur in the *Thoughts*," as well as strong emotion. To Boileau, the Longinus who mattered was an aesthetician rather than a rhetorician, and the object of his study was inner or psychological, an experience of writer and reader. This was also the line taken by English writers who followed in Boileau's wake, including John Dennis, Joseph Addison, John Baillie, David Hume, Edmund Burke, Lord Kames (Henry Home), Thomas Reid, and Archibald Alison. Thus, when the sublime came eventually to be distinguished from the beautiful, its subversive effect on neoclassical tenets—tenets Boileau himself had done so much to establish—was already obvious.

Although the sublime played a crucial role in bringing the potentially inhibiting poetical ideals of Romanticism to the fore, its importance was more than merely literary. As Thomas Weiskel argues, "in the history of literary consciousness the sublime revives as God withdraws from an immediate participation in the experience of men. . . . The Romantic sublime was an attempt to revise the meaning of transcendence precisely when the traditional apparatus of sublimation—spiritual, ontological, and (one gathers) psychological, and even perceptual—was failing to be exercised or understood."[81] Thus the audience for Longinus, the source of his new popularity in the eighteenth century, was derived from a larger crisis of modernism, one of which literary anxieties, including those that block, were only a part. What Longinus offered was an experience of transcendence, in Weiskel's words, "without any conventional theology, a natural religion."[82]

Another, more direct link between writer's block and the sublime derives from the sublime experience itself, as we can see if we turn for a moment to Kant's *Critique of Aesthetic Judgement* (1790), which Monk believes is the fullest and richest account of the subject, one that "took the isolated discussions of earlier thinkers and welded their fragmentary aesthetic together so as to create a truly philosophical system."[83] At the heart of Kant's theory of the sublime lies the assumption, stated in the preface to the second edition of the *Critique of Pure Reason* (1781), that objects must conform to our cognitions, rather than cognitions to objects. The sublime is concerned with limitless and therefore formless objects, the sorts of objects which can only be conceived by what Kant, in the *Critique of Aesthetic Judgement*, calls a "super-thought" of totality. The experience of the sublime is thus one of discontinuity, of a lack of harmony or correspondence between the object and our attempts to represent it. If the object itself is "what is beyond all comprehension great," it cannot be natural because in nature all magnitudes are relative. Only our imagination can encompass the absolute magnitudes of sublime phenomena. Hence the sublime is "that, the mere capacity of thinking which evidences a faculty of mind transcending every standard of sense."[84]

What Kant is suggesting here is that sublimity involves us in the experience of blockage, which he calls "a momentary checking of the vital powers." This experience, though, turns out to be positive or propitious, resulting in a sudden influx of power. What makes it positive is the supra- or extra-analytic faculty—associated by Kant with "reason," as opposed to "understanding"—whereby the mind or imagination exalts in its ability to conceive the very totality that its senses have just failed to take in. This account of the sublime experience recalls comparable accounts of religious insight, moments in which the analytic powers recede before a higher order of meaning, an apprehension of divinity. Such moments are evident everywhere in Romantic writing, not only in the depiction of natural sublimity— whether in the form of what Kant calls the dynamic sublime (towering rocks and mountains, volcanoes, waterfalls, thunder, and lightning) or the mathematical sublime (numberless sequences or aggregates, as in Wordsworth's "multitudes of stars," the mazelike corridors of Gothic fiction, or the proliferating stairways of Piranesi)—but also in what might be called the sublime of composition. When Wordsworth is blocked, he is as likely to be blocked by the towering figures of Milton and Homer as by a vision of Snowdon; by proliferating literary options (plots, tropes, subjects, forms, tones) as by numberless stars. And just as the "checking" or blockage occasioned by natural sublimity proves a way through to something higher, something "sublimed" or elevated, so do comparable moments of blockage in the act of composition; so that fluency, mysteriously, issues out of analytic failure, and the blocked poet's subject ("which way to turn") suddenly appears.

Both the dynamic and the mathematical versions of the sublime, including the compositional sublime, can be viewed in psychoanalytic terms. To Weiskel, the moment of blockage in the dynamic sublime is specifically Oedipal: the threatening or inhibiting features of the father, either in the form of a giant literary predecessor or a natural phenomenon such as the peak that looms in front of Wordsworth as he rows his stolen "elfin pinnance" in book one of *The Prelude*, are what block. This makes the totality of the sublime experience a "sublimation"—or successful overcoming—of potentially inhibiting Oedipal fears. "The poet is uniquely vulnerable to the hypsos of past masters, but his counteroffensive of identification or mimesis can make the power of hypsos his own. In its Romantic transposition, this identification exhibits the precise features of an oedipal crisis." [85] The writers who succeed in "subliming" the fears they face build their experiences into an aesthetic theory; the very fears that doom their sensibilitous predecessors become the self-conscious material of their poems and of the transcendent moments around which they are so often built.

Weiskel's Freudian terms derive in part from Harold Bloom, but the sublime can also be explained in something very like the language of object relations. In a brilliantly suggestive essay of 1978, "The Notion of Blockage in the Literature of the Sublime," [86] Neil Hertz focuses on the mathematical as opposed to the dynamic sublime, seeing the threat it poses to the writer's identity in pre-Oedipal terms. To Hertz, the sublime is best understood as the attempt of the perceiving subject to reestablish boundaries between himself or herself and what is perceived—even while minimizing the differences between them. The revelatory metaphor in the literature of the sublime (by which Hertz means the secondary literature, including works by McFarland, Monk, and Weiskel, as well as primary sources, such as Longinus and Wordsworth) is that of deluge. The subject, whether poet or theorist of the sublime, is overwhelmed by sheer numbers—of stars or sublime theorists; multitudinousness threatens blockage. At the moment of blockage, though, the subject totalizes and thus contains the illimitable. Here is how Hertz describes the process in reference to the literary historian: "The scholar's *wish* is for the moment of blockage, when an indefinite and disarranged sequence is resolved (at whatever sacrifice) into a one-to-one confrontation [i.e., a single sense of what the sublime means], where numerical excess can be converted into that superogatory identification with the blocking agent that is the guarantor of the self's integrity as an agent."[87] These terms recall the vocabulary of object relations, of the opposition or tension between union and separation, the internal and the external. The sublime is a way of negotiating or balancing rival impulses, which are connected to larger or universal problems of adaptation, the source of which lies in the earliest, pre-Oedipal experiences of infancy, the earliest attempts to sort out subject from object, self from other. In the sublime, balance is restored, in part because blocking fears are neither denied nor unchecked. The writer not only faces and overcomes inhibiting fears but also looks to them as a way to greatness; he or she "wishes" for the moment of blockage. Such a wish, as in Keats's "God forbid that I should be without such a task," is a mark of the special and mysterious power attributed to the Romantic writer and of the importance to Romanticism of the experience of blockage.

Bloom and Blockage

The obvious Oedipal features of Bate's notion of the past as a source of blockage take center stage in Harold Bloom's influential theory of literary creation. This theory was first expounded in 1973 in *The Anxiety of Influence*, though much of it had been anticipated in Bloom's earlier, "nontheoretical" works on Shelley, Blake, Yeats, and Romanticism in general. The theory was soon expanded and complicated in a swift succession of publications, the outpourings of a burst of productivity which, in Elizabeth Bruss's words, "in many ways parallels the flood of activity—the new journals, the massive accumulation of books—in the academy at large."[88] These books include *A Map of Misreading* (1975), *Kabbalah and Criticism* (1975), *Poetry and Repression* (1976), and *Agon* (1982). At the heart of the theory they expound is Bloom's contention that literary history—that is, true poetic achievement—is the work of "strong poets," of whom there are very few, the major post-Renaissance sequence consisting of "Blake, Wordsworth, Shelley, Keats, Tennyson, Browning, Yeats, Whitman, Emerson, Stevens."[89]

Strong poets make literary history by misreading the work of their predecessors "so as to clear imaginative space for themselves."[90] Poetic influence thus involves two strong poets and proceeds "by a misreading of the prior poet, an act of creative correction that is actually and necessarily a misinterpretation."[91] Before this act of correction, though, the poet experiences a moment of what Bloom calls "flooded" apprenticeship or "oceanic bliss," such as that recorded by Keats in the "Chapman's Homer" sonnet. This moment involves the apprentice poet in a vertiginous loss of identity. So intense is the vision of past greatness that the apprentice begins to lose all sense of self or anchorage. The precursor is not only an image of all the apprentice poet desires but also a "numinous shadow," "ancestor-God," or "covering cherub"—"in short," in Geoffrey Hartman's words, "a blocking agent."[92] To overcome him, the apprentice poet, or "ephebe," must discover in his predecessor's work "a fault that is not there."[93] Strong poets, also called "figures of capable imagination" (after Stevens), "appropriate" their strong predecessors rather than identify with them, and they do so in an act of "poetic misprision,"[94] an act that can take one or several of six forms, which Bloom calls "revisionary ratios" (later, in response to the criticisms of Paul de Man, "tropes"). These forms or tropes, like Freudian defense mechanisms, are means of evading anxieties. Bloom calls them "revisionary" because they alter or revise the predecessor, and "ratios," in Blake's sense, because they are reductive. The esoteric names he gives them (clinamen, tessera, kenosis, daemonization, askesis, apophrades) are not only drawn from but create their own religious and philosophical heterodoxy, thus allying Bloom's project as literary historian with those of Greek and biblical revisionists.

Being a strong poet is no easy business. To begin with, only the strong poet fully appreciates and understands the achievements of his strong predecessors, the figures to whom he is drawn. And the pressure of these achievements is especially intense for post-Renaissance poets (here Bloom introduces a Bate-like historical dimension to his theory) because their predecessors are usually greater. Only in rare instances is the confrontation of strong poets a painless one; Shakespeare's example, as Bloom writes in *The Anxiety of Influence*, is "the largest instance in the language of a phenomenon that stands outside the concerns of this book: the absolute absorption of the precursor."[95] A second sort of influence that lies outside Bloom's theory derives from "a generosity of spirit, even a shared generosity." This is because "where generosity is involved, the poets involved are minor or weaker"[96]—an assertion that Keats's example, to go no further afield, hardly supports. "Poets-as-poets are not lovable,"[97] concludes Bloom (and, again, one thinks of Keats). The pleasure we take in a strong poet's work is in the bold resourcefulness of his narcissism, what Ann Wordsworth calls the "ferocious expression of defensive energy [required] to prevent his work being blocked by the past."[98] Strength in this sense, as Hartman says, "is chiefly cunning: more Jacob's strength than Esau's, more Odysseus than Achilles."[99]

What the strong poet expresses in his battles with a mighty precursor are "universal anxieties of indebtedness, for what strong poet desires the realization that he has failed to create himself."[100] Strong poets have a "desperate insistence upon priority."[101] A strong poet's denial of any influence upon him is a sign of both strength and anxiety; and the anxiety is inevitable, because Bloom seems, in Bruss's words, "to have ruled out from the start any possibility of growth or significant transformation." Literary change, for Bloom, "is only a redistribution (or an outright loss) of the same elements."[102] This is as true for pre- as for post-Romantic poets, and no truly strong poet believes otherwise, including, presumably, those poets, such as Horace or Pope, who claim an easy, collegial (rather than combative) relation to the past. This is why Bloom calls all poetical devices "figures of willed falsification rather than unwilled knowledge."[103] Only weak poets believe in, or are at peace with, a vision of poetry as craft rather than psychic battle. The dubiousness of this assertion is only partly a product of Bloom's insistence on strength. Also worth noting is the way Bloom's focus on a single precursor ignores what McFarland calls "minimal and dispersed influence": "not only strong poets and their juxtaposition, but philosophical systems, novels, journals, and other cultural formation," as well as other sorts of influential poems (McFarland cites Gottfried Bürger's *Lenore*) which were hardly what Bloom would call "strong."[104]

Bloom's debt to Freud is obvious: "the relations between poets," he writes, are reminiscent of what Freud called "the family romance," by which is meant that stage of fantasy life in which children think of themselves as changelings, deny that their parents are their parents, and "quest" for new ones[105]—a quest that often succeeds in life as it does not (for Bloom) in art, because in life mother can be exchanged for wife, or father for husband. That family or Oedipal relations are the underlying model of literary influence is suggested to Bloom by the observation that "for so many centuries, from the sons of Homer to the sons of Ben Jonson, poetic influence has been described as a filial relationship."[106] This relationship, moreover, constitutes the true subject matter of poetry, so that Bloom (again, like Freud) insists that poems are never really about their ostensible subjects. Strong poets may present themselves as looking for truth in the world, but what they are really concerned with is other poems: "The covert subject of most poetry for the last three centuries has been the anxiety of influence, each poet's fear that no proper work remains for him to perform."[107] Thus, "a poem is a response to a poem, as a poet is a response to a poet, or a person to his parent," or that "all interpretation depends upon an antithetical relation between meanings, and not on the supposed relation between a text and its meaning."[108] And to say that all poems are about other poems is also to say that they are about other poets: "To the poet-in-a-poet, a poem is always *the other man*, the precursor, and so a poem is always a person, always the father of one's Second Birth. To live, the poet must *misinterpret* the father by the crucial act of misprision which is the re-writing of the father."[109] Poetic creation "is reached only through trespass,"[110] and the evidence of such trespass is found in those moments in a poem when the rhetorical logic—the smooth surface fluidity—breaks down. Bloom calls these moments "crossings," "significant disjunctions in which meaning appears to be collected."[111]

Bloom's account of sublimation is also, though more complicatedly, Freudian. For Freud, sublimation lies at the root of all creation, and the fantasies sublimated are mostly erotic, even those that appear at first to be ambitious. For Bloom, however, the fantasies that matter concern death and immortality. "The fundamental human problem at the heart of all influence anxiety," he writes in *Kabbalah and Criticism*, "is the deep, hidden identity between all psychic defence and the fear of dying,"[112] a view that at first seems to have affinities with Rank and the object-relations theorists, though Bloom never mentions them. What *is* orthodoxly Freudian in Bloom is his view of writing as an escape or refusal of limitation. Hence his attraction to Giovanni Battista Vico's theories of the origins of poetry. For Vico (1668–1744), the poetic impulse originates in the earliest poets' attempts to ward off death and danger through interpreting auguries or divination. "Why do men write poems?" asks Bloom. "To rally everything that remains, and not to sanctify nor propound."[113] "A poetic 'text,'" he writes in *Poetry and Repression*, apparently with deconstructive colleagues in mind, "is not a gathering of signs on a page, but is a psychic battlefield upon which authentic forces struggle for . . . the divinating triumph over oblivion."[114] The type of the strong poet is Milton's Satan, "organizing chaos, imposing a discipline despite the visible darkness, calling his minions to emulate his refusal to mourn"[115]—and all in the service of an essential usurpation. For, in Mammon's words, "what place can be for us / Within Heaven's bound, unless Heaven's Lord supreme / We overpower?" (2.235–37).

The chief difference between this melancholy theory and Bate's comparably distressing views is Bloom's equivocal attitude to history. Like Bate, Bloom sees the "progress" of poetry as a decline: "The great poets of the English Renaissance are not matched by their Enlightened descendants, and the whole tradition of the post-Enlightenment, which is Romanticism, shows a further decline in its Modernistic and post-Modernist heirs."[116] Like Bate, Bloom dates consciousness of this decline from the Enlightenment, which inaugurates the age—our age—of "post-Miltonic" poetry and "post-Cartesian" philosophy, though Bloom also reminds us that "no poet since Adam and Satan speaks a language free of the one wrought by his predecessors."[117] Later, however, well into *A Map of Misreading*, Bloom recants, no longer accepting "my previous emphasis on the anxiety of influence as a post-Enlightenment phenomenon" and minimizing the difference as one of degree rather than kind. It matters that the poetry of the Romantics and their followers is "consciously late," that post-Miltonic poetry "deliberately reduces to the interplay of personalities," that fewer strong poets have emerged since the Romantics, and that our current "cultural situation" is "of such belatedness that literary survival itself seems fairly questionable."[118] Yet the larger process, of which this new consciousness is but a part, has been a continuous one, and, in the books that follow *The Anxiety of Influence*, what strikes one about the story Bloom has to tell is, as Bruss says, "the unbroken continuity, the utter simplicity of the decline, without gap or throwback or syncopation."[119] In the later works, Bloom more frequently refers to this larger picture, speculating not only on a decline within pre-Miltonic and post-Miltonic eras but also on earlier declines—within classical and biblical traditions, as in the shift from oral to written cultures in the Torah, in which the earlier, oral tradition is seen as less subject to blocking anxieties (because less bothered about its unrecorded origins). At the same time, though, in any given local context or argument, Bloom is as likely as Bate to privilege the break between pre- and post-Miltonic eras.

As Bloom's theory develops, its relation not only to history but to the ostensible object of its study—actual poets—recedes, and Bloom himself, as "poet-critic," takes center stage. In one sense, this development only confirms the theory; the inexorable decline that Bloom traces with increasing urgency and vagueness is mirrored in his own writing. *Agon* and *Poetry and Repression* paint the poet's dilemma with new darkness: "Whatever small or passing increments were possible in preceding versions of revisionism are eliminated here," writes Bruss of *Poetry and Repression*. "To revise is to subtract from glory, and troping can neither alter, undo, nor add to the true condition of the world, which is one of continual erosion and decay." As a consequence, "the strength needed for survival becomes progressively more cruel, violent, and deceitful,"[120] a process that Bloom traces in terms that are themselves newly violent and deceitful, as much as the operations he attributes to the works themselves or their creators. Whether what he says about a poem or poet is "true" ceases to matter (at least that is the impression); what matters is that the reader be aroused or astonished.[121] Just as the poet "lies" to keep poetic possibility alive, so Bloom's increasingly cavalier treatment of evidence aims to enhance "the fading potency of major poems that now seem threatened by continental scepticism, on the one hand, and canonical tedium, on the other."[122] To the charge that he is inconsistent or difficult to follow (in several senses), Bloom replies *de haut en bas:* "I hope I have made clear, by now, that in expounding my own critical theory and practice, I neither want nor urge any 'method' of criticism. It is of no concern of mine whether anybody else ever comes to share, or doesn't, my own vocabularies of revisionary ratios, of crossings, of whatever . . . I don't want to privilege any vocabularies, my own included. Autonomy and novelty are the goals of strong reading as they are of strong writing."[123] In other words, Bloom's theories apply as much to critics as to poets—actually, to all writers who want to matter. The gathering extremity of his own writings (or "readings") is performative, an obvious and self-conscious index of the very blocking anxieties that are his subject.

Thomas McFarland: Beyond the Freudian Model

Thomas McFarland's contribution to discussion of the literary past as blocking agent grows naturally out of an interest in Coleridge, the subject of his first book on Romantic writing, *Coleridge and the Pantheist Tradition* (1969). In a subsequent book, *Romanticism and the Forms of Ruin* (1981), he projects Coleridgean anxieties about blockage onto the period as a whole, identifying "incompleteness, fragmentation, and ruin"[124] as defining motifs in the life of the writer in general. And in the essays of a third book, *Originality and Imagination* (1985), he deals specifically with the problems of influence and tradition identified by Bate and Bloom. The first of these essays, "The Originality Paradox," begins by insisting, as do Bate and Bloom, that Romantic attitudes are by no means Romantic inventions, "that Childe Harold is no more egotistic than Almanzor; nor Almanzor than Tamberlaine";[125] or that Plato, in his attacks on "imitative" poets, is no less obsessed with originality and the claims of the individual than Shelley. McFarland quotes Eric Havelock in support of this view of Plato: "It was [Plato's] self-imposed task . . . to establish two main postulates: that of the personality which thinks and knows, and that of a body of knowledge that is thought about and known. To do this he had to destroy the immemorial habit of self-identification with the oral tradition. For this had merged the personality with the tradition, and made a self-conscious separation from it impossible."[126] In Mc-Farland's own words, "the attraction/rejection tension between Plato and Homer is the counterpart of the individual/tradition tension that constitutes the originality paradox, and is in fact the archetypal exemplification of the depth, unavoidability, and constancy of that paradox."[127]

From here, McFarland proceeds to trace anxieties about the past up to the present, along the way providing a context for the growing darkness and desperation of Bloom's own writing about influence anxiety. McFarland believes that the romantic insistence upon originality and genius culminates in the early twentieth century in dadaism, surrealism, and Italian futurism (or *antipassatismo*, which Renato Poggioli translates as "the down-with-the-past-movement")[128]—all of which attempt, "by hyper-emphasis on the conception of originality, to deny the relevance of the exponentially increasing deluge of culture" (p. 8). The extremism and violence of this denial, though, produced a countermovement or "classical" reaction, in the writings of Irving Babbitt, T. E. Hulme, and T. S. Eliot. McFarland compares Eliot's "Tradition and the Individual Talent" (1919) to Young's *Conjectures on Original Composition* and sees both, regardless of their actual influence, as attempts to restore a lost balance between culture and identity, a balance that McFarland insists is "a constant of all culture that is not pre-literate" (p. 22). However, Young and Eliot come to this equilibrium from opposite directions, with the former seeking to redress "an overwhelming existence of tradition," and the latter taking as given "the rampant stress on originality and seeking to restore the dignity of tradition" (p. 10). The actual effect of their works, though, was the opposite of what they intended. Young became a voice for the new dispensation, whereas the insistence of Eliot that "the emotion of art is impersonal" and that "the progress of an artist is a continual self-sacrifice, a continual extinction of personality,"[129] marked him as the preeminent anti-Romantic of his age. McFarland views Eliot as "purchasing his insistence upon tradition by sacrificing the paradox whose recognition he sought to renew" (p. 11).

The reaction Eliot represented was not to last, being in turn "swept away in the new tide of Romanticism that followed World War II," a tide that McFarland sees as having reached its "apex" in the 1960s, "when all the claims to uniqueness were assembled in grotesque and overwhelming duplication" (p. 11), and out of which, McFarland implies, the despairing theories of Bate and Bloom were born. The crisis that Bate and Bloom represent is not, as their rhetoric implies, apocalyptic, a staggering or stuttering into silence, but rather a stage—

though an extreme one—in an ongoing and ever-renewing conflict. The blocking fears that they identify are but "an intensification of elements permanently present, and not the historical appearance of new reality" (p. 14); what McFarland calls the "originality paradox" "cannot be resolved, although in differing historical epochs one aspect of it can be emphasized or partly repressed in favor of the other" (p. 22). That the very best of critics realize the permanence of the conflict is shown by McFarland's many quotations in support of tradition from those among their number we think of—and have quoted—as champions of originality. The great writer's relation to tradition, McFarland argues, is always double. Milton boasts in *Paradise Lost* of "things unattempted yet in verse and rhyme" (1.16), betraying an anxiety Bate and Bloom have encouraged us to see as post-Miltonic, but in doing so, as McFarland and others have pointed out, he is quoting someone else.[130] Presumably, we are at this very moment swinging back—if we have not done so already—to an age of tradition and convention, one in which the sorts of assumptions, psychoanalytic and literary, that generated the very term *writer's block* will fall—or continue to fall—into disfavor.

McFarland's theories, though, are not themselves without psychoanalytic analogues. If Freud looms as the model behind Bloom and Bate and the privileging of Romantic notions of creativity (just as ego psychology recalls neoclassicism, with its emphasis on tradition and on a vision of creation as purposeful, orderly, and mechanical), McFarland's notion of balance or permanent paradox recalls the aesthetics of British object relations. For there, too, the problems the writer faces are related to larger, universal questions of balance—between self and other, subject and object, inner and outer, individual and tradition. And blockage occurs only at the point at which one or other of the opposing claims is exclusively forwarded. Although no one is as thorough as McFarland in his search for evidence of tradition, he also insists on the importance of an autonomous factor in creation. "Though it may have been the reading of earlier poems that made Wordsworth write verse," concludes one of McFarland's essays in *Originality and Imagination,*

> it was his personal experience of the orange sky of evening that made him a great poet. . . . The full truth is a tension of opposites. There is tradition, and tradition is extraordinarily important; but there is also such a reality as individual talent. Even after all respect is paid to the power and ingenuity of Bloom's conception of poetry's genesis and development, a truer accounting of cultural process would seem to be that rendered by Her-

der, who observes that two principles underlie intellectual history. "They are *tradition* and *organic powers.* All education arises from imitation and exercise, by means of which the model passes into the copy. What better word is there for this transmission than *tradition?* But the imitator must have powers to receive and convert into his own nature what has been transmitted to him, just like the food he eats. Accordingly, what and how much he receives, where he derives it from, and how he applies it to his own use are determined by his own receptive powers." [131]

To those who lack either receptive powers or respect for and access to tradition, the way to great poetry—for both McFarland and the object-relations theorists—is blocked. To those who lack individual talent, the power that shapes internal or subjective need, the same is true. Nowhere is this clearer than in the life and works of the subjects of the chapters that follow, Wordsworth and Coleridge. For Wordsworth, though, the terms in which creativity and its inhibition are discussed are directly psychological—the "external" is less the tradition or a strong precursor than the parent. For Coleridge, the terms fit more easily into the sort of poetical influence anxiety examined in this chapter—though Coleridge's blockage is a particularly rich and various thing.

~6~

Wordsworth and Writer's Block

Wordsworth's great theme, it has been said, is loss, and loss for Wordsworth is always in part loss of poetical or "genial" power. He is our first great poet of writer's block, even when poetic incapacity is expressed in his verse in metaphors of emptiness or dearth. "I cannot paint what then I was," he declares in "Tintern Abbey," "That time is past." What is passed, here, is not only "What then I was" but the ability to paint it. The drama or conflict of the poem, as so often in Wordsworth's verse, is an internal one familiar to many a blocked writer: between fear of loss, which in its literary dimension is often experienced as loss of control as well as loss of power, and a refusal to acknowledge this fear, which itself blocks creation, stops the flow. Nor is this drama simply a matter of theme or statement; it is also embodied in a characteristic tension or rhythm in Wordsworth's verse, one usually identified as an alternation of expository and interpretative passages, an alternation that can be likened to what Arnold calls the "laboured, self-retarding" movement of Miltonic epic.[1] In Wordsworth, fear often shapes this movement: rising panic creates a rhythm or momentum, which is then slowed or silenced by a voice of questionable reassurance. As Wordsworth's anxieties proliferate, often in the form of a multiplication of choices (as in the initial stage of the Kantian mathematical sublime), the poet steps back or away, steadies himself, then starts again, returning with careful, willed calm to his poem, the source of his fears. Nowhere is this pattern of patient and precarious restartings more clearly seen than in *The Prelude*, the composition of which has been likened to "a continuous series of disintegrations and reintegrations."[2] The first 285 lines of book one not only establish the pattern but also are explicitly about not being able to write, employing what another critic calls "the paradoxical fiction that a poem can go on at length about its failure to get going at all."[3]

The Experience of Blockage:
The Prelude, 1.1–285

The Prelude opens with Wordsworth's return to the countryside, "coming from a house / Of bondage, from yon city's walls set free" (1.6–7). That city has been the site not only of breakdown but of blockage, of that "long-continued frost" (1.49) under which Wordsworth's creative powers have lain dormant. What Wordsworth feels now, after confinement in the city, is "free, enfranchised and at large" (1.9). His freedom, though, even in the "glad Preamble" of lines 1–54, is experienced as a problem as well as a promise, a problem such as faces any writer at the moment of composition:

> What dwelling shall receive me? in what vale
> Shall be my harbour? underneath what grove
> Shall I take up my home? and what sweet stream
> Shall with its murmurs lull me to its rest?
> The earth is all before me . . .
> (1.11–15)

The question, in other words, is where to begin, which way to turn not only for Wordsworth the wanderer but also for Wordsworth the writer. Here, in lines 11–15 of the poem, is the first, muted instance of what will be revealed as a familiar pattern: a range of possibilities—tropes, paths, patterns—looms before the poet and threatens to overwhelm him. The repetitions ("What dwelling," "underneath what grove," "what clear stream") do not yet, as they will in later and less composed contexts, betray panic, and it is not quite fair to associate the need to be "lulled" with a mind moving too fast or clutching. For the moment the poet seems unthreatened, though the lines that follow seed doubts.

These doubts begin with the allusion to book twelve of *Paradise Lost* ("The earth is all before me"), which suggests a possible literary dimension to Wordsworth's predicament, as if Wordsworth were asking: Could I be equal to *that* sort of achievement? Later on, this dimension is treated explicitly: as Wordsworth contemplates the poetical paths open to him, he canvasses a range of epic subjects from the past. Should he, perhaps, attempt "some British theme, some old / Romantic tale by Milton left unsung" (1.179–80), or a Spenserian song of knights and chivalry (one that, in the 1850 version, "winds / Through ever-changing scenes of votive quest," lines 180–81)? As the list of possible subjects multiplies (there are eight other items, including more obscure and then more personal ones, and the randomness with which they are set out reinforces the sense that the poem is moving without plan), the question Wordsworth seems to be asking is: "What subject shall receive me? thereby repeating 'What dwelling shall receive me?'"[4] The earlier questions were in part disguised versions of a greater and less composed question: What do I write about? And the obscurity of some of the topics Wordsworth canvasses (Gustavus I of Sweden, the transformation of Mithridates, the struggles of Sertorius) not only hints at belatedness as the first of several sources of anxiety but puts the lie to the opening assertions of total freedom of choice.

The allusion to Milton in line 15 brings the poem's first stoppage, with its immediate gesture of reassurance. Wordsworth turns to the world about him—the external world—for support: "The earth is all before me. With a heart / Joyous, nor scared of its own liberty, / I look about" (1.15–17). The profession of calm control recalls a comparable moment in "Tintern Abbey," just after the admission of loss ("That time is past") quoted at the beginning of this chapter:

> . . . Not for this
> Faint I, nor mourn nor murmur; other gifts
> Have followed; for such loss, I would believe,
> Abundant recompense . . .
>   (85–88)

The conjunction here of "I would believe" and "Abundant recompence" raises the same sorts of doubts as "nor scared of its own liberty." The suspicion in both passages is of something willed and uneasy in Wordsworth's assertions, an impression heightened in *The Prelude* by the lines that follow. "I breathe again!" (1.19), continues Wordsworth, in a phrase that points initially to the contrast between past bondage in "yon city's walls" and present liberty, but may also hint at gathering anxieties, which are occasioned by liberty itself and meant to be dispersed by reference to the past (as if Wordsworth were saying, "But after all, I *am* free"). Yet even as Wordsworth, in effect, collects himself, "Trances of thought and mountings of the mind / Come fast upon me" (1.20–21), and eight lines later his ambitions threaten to choke him and need to be tamped down again. One thinks of Lear: "O me, my heart, my rising heart! but down!" And of the Fool's reply: "Cry to it, nuncle, as the cockney did to the eels when she knapped 'em o' the coxcombs with a stick, and cried 'Down, wantons, down!'" (3.3.15–18). Neither Lear's nor Wordsworth's mounting thoughts will rest, for all their "knapping." In Wordsworth's case, their return is signaled by a proliferation of options such as occurs in lines 11–15:

> . . . whither shall I turn,
> By road or pathway, or through open field,
> Or shall a twig or any floating thing
> Upon the river point me out my course?
> Enough that I am free . . .
>   (1.29–33)

Or simply, "Enough": that is, calm down, breathe deeply (the sort of thing one says to someone hyperventilating), focus, get up and look about. (In the 1850 version, with the anxieties of composition well behind him, "Enough that I am free" becomes "Dear Liberty!")

That Wordsworth is indeed experiencing, beneath the calm surface assurance of the opening lines, the anxieties of what today we would call writer's block is clear from what follows. Once again, in lines 34–39, he turns to the external world for anchorage, to soothe and slow his gathering anxieties. But the external world only recalls the initial "sweet breath of heaven / . . . blowing on my body" (1.41–42), which sets in motion "a corresponding mild creative breeze" (1.43) within, the very breeze that "inspired" the preceding lines and that Wordsworth now fears may become, as the reader may already have sensed, "A tempest, a redundant energy, / Vexing its own creation" (1.45–47). The stepping back or "breathing space" that lines 33 and following were meant to constitute brings explicit recognition of the problem. Where do I turn? What should I write? One of the effects of this passage is to keep the present moment of composition before the reader, so that the reader is always aware that the subject of the poem is Wordsworth's difficulty in writing it, as the following lines make clear:

> Thus far, O Friend! did I, not used to make
> A present joy the matter of my song,
> Pour out that day my soul in measured strains
> Even in the very words which I have here
> Recorded . . .
>   (1.55–59)

Although Wordsworth talks here of "joy" and "measured strains," the larger phrase, "not used to make / A present joy the matter of my song," also registers. Wordsworth is improvising, and it makes him uneasy. With every burst of confidence comes a corresponding fearfulness, a pattern or precariousness that recalls the following well-known lines from "Resolution and Independence":

> But, as it sometimes chanceth, from the might
> Of joy in minds that can no further go,

As high as we have mounted in delight
In our dejection do we sink as low;
To me that morning did it happen so;
And fears and fancies thick upon me came.
(22–27)

These are much like the words of the opening of *The Prelude*, in which seemingly benign or welcome "Trances of thought and mountings of the mind / Come fast upon me" and need to be quickly tamped down with the reassurance of "I cannot miss my way. I breathe again!" In both cases, creative capacity is threatened not by dearth but by what Stephen Parrish calls "a superabundant flow of inspiration."[5]

When Wordsworth eventually, imperceptibly, begins to move out of this potentially debilitating cycle, the threat of blockage still looms. After walking for some time "with careless steps" (1.70), he sits down under an oak, and, in the midst of comparably careless musings ("Passing through many thoughts"),

. . . I made a choice
Of one sweet Vale, whither my steps should turn
And saw, methought, the very house and fields
Present before my eyes: nor did I fail
To add, meanwhile, assurance of some work
Of glory there forwith to be begun,
Perhaps too there performed . . .
(1.81–87)

This last phrase ("Perhaps too there performed") recalls the anxieties of previous lines, whereas the passage as a whole confirms the equivalence of literal and metaphoric "turnings," in which the path taken refers to the poem itself, as well as the poet's journeying. Yet something *has* happened—though, characteristically, Wordsworth does not immediately act upon it, rising only when "the sun / Had almost touched the horizon" (1.96–97). The change is marked by a new and startling vividness in the verse:

. . . Thus long I lay
Cheered by the genial pillow of the earth
Beneath my head, soothed by a sense of touch
From the warm ground, that balanced me, else lost
Entirely, seeing nought, nought hearing, save
When here and there, about the grove of oaks
Where was my bed, an acorn from the trees
Fell audibly, and with a startling sound.
(1.87–94)

What makes this moment of heightened perception possible for Wordsworth is the partial lifting, for the first time in the present of the poem, of anxieties about writing; these anxieties cloak or threaten to drown not only Wordsworth but also the world—the external or object world—he means to communicate and transfigure. At just the moment Wordsworth seems lost to the world, the world intrudes with a saving singularity, as in the sudden appearance of the leech-gatherer in "Resolution and Independence." The mysteriousness of this intrusion will, of course, lead to further anxieties because creative power is depicted as beyond conscious control, as visiting the poet—dropping in on him, like the falling acorns—unawares. Nevertheless, a potentially deadening subjectivity has begun to lift.

In previous lines, Wordsworth alternated between consuming self-absorption, in which subjective need—the need to begin "some work / Of glory"—guttered or choked off poetical flow, and a blank externality, in which Wordsworth turned to the outer world but never quite saw it or brought it alive because he needed so much from it. Here, though, there is no seeking: the external world—"the earth / Beneath my head," "a sense of touch / From the warm ground"— "balances" Wordsworth by bringing him out of himself, while at the same time quickening his quickening perceptions. The word "balanced" is telling, for it points to the conditions that prevail in true creation: that is, as Wordsworth puts it in book twelve of *The Prelude,*

> A balance, an enobling interchange
> Of action from within and from without;
> The excellence, pure spirit, and best power
> Both of the object seen, and eye that sees,
> (12.376–79)

or, in equally familiar words from "Tintern Abbey," a "mighty world / Of eye, and ear,—both what they half create, / And what perceive" (105–7). When Wordsworth's fears threaten to block, one or the other of these factors dominates: "action from within" swamps the object world, or the object world (full of proliferating choices or paths, of external powers "not to be withstood") threatens to overwhelm the poet.

This is the conclusion to which Wordsworth comes later in book one, about one hundred or so lines before the poem settles into its subject:

> When, as becomes a man who would prepare
> For such a glorious work, I through myself
> Make rigorous inquisition, the report

> Is often cheering; for I neither seem
> To lack that first great gift, the vital soul,
> Nor general Truths, which are themselves a sort
> Of Elements and Agents, Under-powers,
> Subordinate helpers of the living mind:
> Nor am I naked in external things,
> Forms, images, nor numerous other aids
> Of less regard, though won perhaps with toil
> And needful to build up a Poet's praise.
>   (1.157–68)

To write, Wordsworth implies, one must look to internal resources, to that "vital soul" which will bend and inspirit the material of the poem, as well as to the material itself, the necessary stuff of the world ("external things, / Forms, images") upon which the imagination works. This is precisely the duality or "balance" attained in the silence of the oak grove, where the impression made by the falling acorns seems to derive as much from the poet's receptiveness as from the startling clarity of the sounds themselves.

When Wordsworth at last rises and heads toward Grasmere, the vale of his "choice," the familiar pattern of stops and starts recurs, though now the voice of reassurance is more convincing:

> It was a splendid evening, and my soul
> Did once again make trial of the strength
> Restored to her afresh; nor did she want
> Aeolian visitations; but the harp
> Was soon defrauded, and the banded host
> Of harmony dispersed in straggling sounds,
> And lastly utter silence! "Be it so;
> It is an injury," said I, "to this day
> To think of any thing but present joy."
> So, like a peasant I pursued my road
> Beneath the evening sun, nor had one wish
> Again to bend the Sabbath of that time
> To a servile yoke. What need of many words?
>   (1.101–13)

What is new here is the gently ironic self-knowledge of Wordsworth's depiction of himself as "a peasant" (previously he had likened himself to a knight, a prophet, and a priest) and of his talk of "the Sabbath of that time" and of writing as a "servile yoke." Wordsworth knows just what he is doing—just how much reassurance he is seeking—when he asks, at the beginning of an epic venture, "What need of many words?" This self-knowledge distinguishes him from an earlier poet such as Gray, who also sought reassurance in the analogy of poet and homely peasant.

In the lines that follow, Wordsworth claims that the rest of his two-day journey was untroubled by thoughts of writing. When such thoughts return, once he reaches Dove Cottage, his account is distanced, which reinforces the impression of a new level of understanding or self-knowledge. Gone is the characteristic agitation—the proliferation of options, the need to reign in. "But speedily a longing in me rose / To brace myself to some determined aim" (1.123–24) declares Wordsworth,

> But I have been discouraged; gleams of light
> Flash often from the east, then disappear
> And mock me with a sky that ripens not
> Into a steady morning . . .
> (1.134–37)

The control with which the metaphor of creative light unfolds here precludes mimetic or performative agitation. Wordsworth has reached a new level—has made progress—in his journey toward poetic health and, though still checked or blocked, is able to view his false starts *ab extra*. Hence the degree of generalization in the passage that follows, which does not in this case feel like a protective regrouping, but rather a genuinely disinterested inquiry:

> The poet, gentle creature as he is,
> Hath, like the Lover, his unruly times;
> His fits when he is neither sick nor well,
> Though no distress be near him but his own
> Unmanageable thoughts . . .
> (1.146–50)

Such times are to be distinguished from a more productive indolence, when the mind, in a Miltonic allusion that likens the poet to the Creator of Genesis, "duteous as the mother dove / Sits brooding" (1.151–52). What Wordsworth is now expressing is a much less settled inactivity, a time of "less quiet instincts, goadings on / That drive [the mind] as in trouble through the groves" (1.153–54). Such moments are inevitable in creative endeavour and only become blocks if protracted. "With me is now such passion," admits Wordsworth, "which I blame / No otherwise than as it lasts too long" (1.155–56).

What exactly it feels like to experience this "passion" is the subject of the lines that follow. To begin with, the poet mistakes "Proud spring-tide swellings for a regular sea" (1.178) and is seduced into canvassing possible epic subjects. These subjects immediately prompt a host of "deadening admonitions," in which in each case

> . . . the whole beauteous fabric seems to lack
> Foundation, and, withal, appears throughout
> Shadowy and unsubstantial . . .
> (1.226–28)

All the poet can do at such moments is step back, calm himself. At which point, when things are bad, the stepping back is itself seen as symptomatic rather than therapeutic. "From this awful burden," writes Wordsworth in a passage of Kafkaesque involution and self-doubt,

> . . . I full soon
> Take refuge and beguile myself with trust
> That mellower years will bring a riper mind
> And clearer insight. Thus from day to day
> I live, a mockery of the brotherhood
> Of vice and virtue, with no skill to part
> Vague longing that is bred by want of power
> From paramount impulse not to be withstood,
> A timorous capacity from prudence,
> From circumspection, infinite delay.
> Humility and modest awe themselves
> Betray me, serving often for a cloak
> To a more subtle selfishness; that now
> Doth lock my functions up in blank reserve,
> Now dupes me by an over-anxious eye
> That with a false activity beats off
> Simplicity and self-presented truth.
> (1.235–51)

What is immediately noteworthy here is the poet's helplessness in the face of characteristically Romantic notions of creativity. The poet is dependent upon a "paramount impulse not to be withstood" and powerless to distinguish such an impulse from "Vague longing that is bred by want of power." At any moment, the impulse to write can be false, a chimera, and analytic powers ("skill to part") are useless to determine which is which, at least at the beginning. When "prudence" dictates skepticism or resistance, the immediate and opposite suspicion arises: that the impulse is real and delay is "timorous" and likely to be "infinite," "a cloak / To a more subtle selfishness."

"More subtle selfishness" indirectly suggests a second source—

aside from fears of inadequacy—of Wordsworth's inhibition: it implies that the impulse itself might be "selfish" (it is, after all, "paramount," "not to be withstood"). This suspicion recalls Milner and Ehrenzweig, both of whom see blockage as a result, in part, of a fear that art or creative perception is a way of investing the world with one's own deepest and most fearful (because fearsome) longings—with needs or drives that are ultimately greedy or aggressive (i.e, "selfish"). Resisting the "paramount impulse" is selfish, but the impulse itself might also be. In any event, Wordsworth is now thoroughly "locked up" or blocked by a tangle of self-doubtings, and this makes him desperate. He begins to grab or clutch at the world, to force material onto the page, falling victim to "an over-anxious eye / That with a false activity beats off / Simplicity and self-presented truth." In Keats's famous phrase, Wordsworth is "incapable of being in uncertainties, mysteries, doubts" and is blocked by an "irritable reaching after fact and reason." To Coleridge (the occasion of these remarks), just such a reaching out, "an *anxiety* of explanation and retrospect," was a "characteristic defect" of Wordsworth's verse.[6] The irony of this defect—with its resulting "selfish" deformation of "self-presented truth"—is that it grows out of the poet's very attempts to escape from the self.

At this point Wordsworth reaches a nadir, what Hartman calls "an experience of aphasia"[7]—that is, blockage. Wordsworth is

> . . . baffled by a mind that every hour
> Turns recreant to her task; takes heart again,
> Then feels immediately some hollow thought
> Hang like an interdict upon her hopes.
> This is my lot; for either still I find
> Some imperfection in the chosen theme,
> Or see of absolute accomplishment
> Much wanting, so much wanting, in myself,
> That I recoil and droop, and seek repose
> In indolence from vain perplexity,
> Unprofitably travelling towards the grave,
> Like a false steward who hath much received
> And renders nothing back.
> (1.259–71)

Here again, Wordsworth's condition is conceived in terms that recall object relations: "either still I find / Some imperfection in the chosen theme": that is, in the material, external world, the world of the other (conceived of in this instance as the poem's subject matter or "material"); "Or see of absolute accomplishment much wanting": that is, much wanting in the internal realm, in Wordsworth's own powers (though here it is the sense of the internal as inadequate, rather than soiled or selfish, that predominates). Only the closing reference to receiving but not giving back sounds a new and potentially saving note—the first stirrings of a reparative impulse. In his despair, Wordsworth has somehow managed actually to see the other, and to see that it has needs; to look beyond his own dilemma to the separate claims of the object world, from which, in earlier, healthier times, he had gained so much.

At this point in the poem, in lines 271 and following, a way through is found and, as in the sublime, it is initially experienced as something inexplicable, outside rational control. Wordsworth's subject matter, his theme, literally flows forth out of cognitive exhaustion:

> Was it for this
> That one, the fairest of all rivers, loved
> To blend his murmurs with my nurse's song,
> And, from his alder shades and rocky falls,
> And from his fords and shallows, sent a voice
> That flowed along my dreams? For this, didst thou,
> O Derwent! travelling over the green plains
> Near my "sweet Birthplace", didst thou, beauteous stream,
> Make ceaseless music through the night and day
> Which with its steady cadence, tempering
> Our human waywardness, composed my thoughts
> To more than infant softness, giving me
> Among the fretful dwellings of mankind
> A knowledge, a dim earnest, of the calm
> That Nature breathes among the hills and groves.
>   (1.271–85)

The River Derwent flows along the far side of the garden wall of the house in Cockermouth where Wordsworth was born. He identifies it with the nurse who soothed him in infancy: it "loved / To blend [its] murmurs with my nurse's song." The nurse, of course, is a figure of the mother, and the music she and the river offered Wordsworth, with its "ceaseless" (or seamless) "steady cadence," "composed" his thoughts and calmed him. By turning to it now, re-creating it in memory, Wordsworth is, in object-relations terms, repaying a debt, "repairing" a reality that "selfishness"—projection, idealization, omnipotent fantasies, and, in fact, all forms of perceptual distortion such as are suggested by the phrase "an over-anxious eye"—has been felt to injure. Having reached a position in which all seems lost, a position of the most extreme subjectivity and isolation, and having acknowledged and given himself up to that loss, Wordsworth is at last able to make an act of reparation. One recalls Hanna Segal, for whom "all creation is really a re-creation of a once-loved and once whole, but now lost and ruined object, a ruined internal world and self. It is when the world within us is destroyed, when it is dead and loveless, when our loved ones are in fragments, and we ourselves in helpless despair—it is then that we must re-create our world anew, reassemble the pieces, infuse life into dead fragments, re-create life."[8] For Wordsworth, "helpless despair" means creative despair or blockage—so that blockage, as so often for writers of his age, becomes almost a precondition of creativity, the necessary darkness before revelation. It is the poet's reason for writing, as well as his subject matter.

Such a reading raises an interesting interpretative possibility. What is the meaning of the puzzling phrase "Was it for this," which finally introduces the poem's true autobiographical subject? In the words of Simon Stuart, a follower of Segal and other post-Kleinian theorists,

> the question has now become a pregnant ambiguity: "was it in vain, all for nothing, for this negative state, that the Derwent flowed along my dreams?" Or "was it in preparation for this un-creative state, so that I have the basic resilience to face it, to verbalize it, and by this means to accept it, and snatch victory from the abyss of failure?". . . . The question "was it for this?" is kept open and intentionally unformulated since the answer can only be formulated in *la recherche du temps perdu*. If the past can be enshrined in verbal symbols the question answers itself.[9]

Subsequent passages support this conclusion. At the moment of blockage, Wordsworth seeks to re-create in memory the object world he has lost. Without quite knowing why, he returns to earliest childhood, as much out of love for the thing itself—the thing he has lost—as out of a need to bring it alive again, to regain poetic health and personal joy. The two go together, and they constitute the terms of creative power: acknowledgment of loss is acknowledgment of the other or object in its independence; only when this acknowledgment is made can it be defied by subjective need, in an act of re-creation which is also an act of reparation.

Infancy and the Origins of Creative Power: The Prelude, *2.237–395*

The "Blest Babe" passage from book two of *The Prelude* concerns itself as much with the sources of blockage as with those of poetic power,

but it begins with an account of power, as well as of the origins in
infancy of a healthy, enabling relation to objects:

> Blest the infant Babe,
> (For with my best conjectures I would trace
> The progress of our being,) blest the Babe,
> Nursed in his Mother's arms, the Babe who sleeps
> Upon his Mother's breast; who, when his soul
> Claims manifest kindred with an earthly soul,
> Doth gather passion from his Mother's eye!
> Such feelings pass into his torpid life
> Like an awakening breeze, and hence his mind
> Even [in the first trial of its powers]
> Is prompt and watchful, eager to combine
> In one appearance, all the elements
> And parts of the same object, else detached
> And Loath to coalesce . . .
> (2.237–50)

The first point to note here is how Wordsworth likens the strength
that the child receives from his mother as he reaches out to the world
to "an awakening breeze," the very breeze of inspiration which acti-
vates the poet in the opening lines of book one. A link is established
between nature, mother, and inspiration, and the power this link
conveys is both integrative and discriminating. The infant's mind is
made "prompt and watchful, eager to combine / In one appearance,
all the elements / And parts of the same object, else detached." This
is not the wholly undifferentiated state of infant omniscience—what
Freud calls "infant narcissism"—in which all objects are interrelated
because they are projections; rather, it is a later state in which the
distinct or individual properties of the other are acknowledged. The
mother's protection, the calm and serenity of her arms and nourishing breast, frees the child and awakens him to the outside world, to
a "prompt and watchful" attentiveness. Integrative power helps to
create objects that are discrete, whole, external.

> . . . Thus, day by day,
> Subjected to the discipline of love,
> His organs and recipient faculties
> Are quickened, are more vigorous, his mind spreads,
> Tenacious of the forms which it receives.
> (2.250–54)

Here, too, the claims of inner and outer are registered: the mind
"spreads," suggesting its active, formative power, yet it does so in

order to acknowledge and hold "the forms which it receives." As in a later passage, the "universal power / And fitness in the latent qualities / And essences of things" (2.344–46) is joined to an internal, subjective power, "strengthened with a superadded soul, / A virtue not its own" (2.347–48). That this reciprocal relation in simple perception also obtains in the creation of works of art is explicitly stated in lines 258–76; and again (or still), what makes it possible is the nurturing "Presence" of the mother:

> From this beloved Presence, there exists
> A virtue which irradiates and exalts
> All objects through all intercourse of sense.
> No outcast he, bewildered and depressed:
> Along his infant veins are interfused
> The gravitation and the filial bond
> Of Nature that connect him with the world.
> Emphatically such a Being lives,
> An inmate of this *active* universe;
> From nature largely he receives; nor so
> Is satisfied, but largely gives again,
> For feeling has to him imparted strength,
> And powerful in all sentiments of grief,
> Of exultation, fear, and joy, his mind,
> Even as an agent of the one great Mind,
> Creates, creator and receiver both,
> Working but in alliance with the works
> Which it beholds.—Such, verily, is the first
> Poetic Spirit of our human life.
>   (2.237–48)

The infant, like the poet, is connected to the world, which makes both the world and the self come alive. He lives "an inmate of this *active* universe." The world is not lost, but "received"; the mind works "in alliance with the works / which it beholds." Creativity involves not only a shaping of the world to one's needs but also a recognition of the world's immutable otherness.

The inevitable loss of the beloved and enabling "Presence" of the mother—a literal loss, in Wordsworth's case—is the first threat to incipient poetic power, and the ability to overcome this loss depends upon symbolic transference. In Kleinian theory, this transference is viewed ambivalently: on the one hand, if aggressive and destructive tendencies have not been worked through in infancy, symbolization opens the way to fearful projections and omnipotent delusions; on the other, if the infant has successfully overcome early anxiety situations, if his or her earliest environment has been stable and nourishing, what Winnicott calls "facilitating," symbolization becomes a way of confronting rather than evading fears. "Diversity of strength / Attends us," writes Wordsworth in book eleven, "if but once we have been strong" (11.327–28).

For Wordsworth, earliest infancy was indeed a time of strength. Symbol formation was neither inhibited nor inhibiting, and as a consequence the mother's loss was faced rather than evaded by symbolic transference. Here is Wordsworth's description of the process:

> For now a trouble came into my mind
> From unknown causes. I was left alone
> Seeking the visible world, not knowing why.
> The props of my affections were removed,
> And yet the building stood, as if sustained
> By its own spirit! All that I beheld
> Was dear to me, and from this cause it came,
> That now to Nature's finer influxes
> My mind lay open, to that more exact
> And intimate communion which our hearts
> Maintain with the minuter properties
> Of objects which already are beloved,
> And of those only . . .
> (2.291–303)

The mother disappears, and the son is "left alone / Seeking the visible world." This he does (not knowing why) because he has come to associate the mother with nature, with a world that is both other and benevolent (or "filial"). What makes his search "mature" or "adult"—the terms Segal uses to describe healthy or nonevasive symbolic transference—is his recognition of the separateness and individuality of the object (or object world) onto which he has transferred his feelings of love for the mother. What Wordsworth beholds, he beholds in its discrete particularity: the "finer influxes" of objects are noted, their "minuter properties" are registered in a communion that is both "exact" and "intimate." Nature or "the world" both is and is not the mother in these lines, a duality maintained in later lines in which Wordsworth speaks of how

> . . . the soul,
> Remembering how she felt, but what she felt
> Remembering not, retains an obscure sense
> Of possible sublimity . . .
> (2.334–37)

Sublimity, here, is associated with the triumphant feelings, the "visionary power" (2.330), of the Blest Babe: Wordsworth is able to recapture some of that power after the mother's death. But at the same time, he recognizes the fact of loss, the fact that he can remember only "how," not "what," his soul felt. The present state is invested with symbolic significance, but it is carefully distinguished from the original state and is recognized as an object or state in itself. As Segal says of the "fully formed" symbol or "symbol proper" (as opposed to more primitive and evasive or distorting symbols), "its own properties are recognized, respected, and used, because no confusion with the original object blurs the characteristics of the new object used as a symbol."[10] A balance is maintained between subjective need—the desire for complete power and satisfaction, for a world of total responsiveness—and objective reality.

That the balance between internal and external is difficult to attain is only gradually apparent to the growing boy. Here is how Wordsworth describes the boy's situation after his mother's loss and his first wondering recognition of her continued presence—and his survival—in nature:

> . . . I still retained
> My first creative sensibility;
> That by the regular action of the world
> My soul was unsubdued. A plastic power
> Abode with me; a forming hand, at times
> Rebellious, acting in a devious mood;
> A local spirit of its own, at war
> With general tendency, but, for the most,
> Subservient strictly to the external things
> With which it communed. An auxiliar light
> Came from my mind, which on the setting sun
> Bestowed new splendour; the melodious birds,
> The gentle breezes, fountains that ran on
> Murmuring so sweetly in themselves, obeyed
> A like dominion, and the midnight storm
> Grew darker in the presence of my eye:
> Hence my obeisance, my devotion hence,
> And hence my transport.
> (2.378–95)

The opening lines of this passage suggest that, initially, "creative sensibility" is threatened from outside, from "the regular action of the world," a world that "subdues." But immediately an opposite threat is suggested, a product of internal need, "plastic power" itself, which can at times be "rebellious, acting in a devious mood." When Wordsworth's "creative sensibility" is at work, this power is "for the most / Subservient strictly to the external things / With which it communed." It is "an auxiliar light"—that is, both an ally and a subordinate—ennobling and enriching what is itself already rich, as in "fountains that ran on / Murmuring so sweetly in themselves." Yet this power is also described as domineering, in that sun, birds, breezes, fountains, storms have "obeyed / A like dominion." Perhaps in compensation, Wordsworth declares his own "obeisance" and "devotion" (to nature or the external realm, presumably) two lines later. The tensions here—between internal "plastic power" and "external things," objects "in themselves"—are obvious: as soon as the claims of one are sounded, the other pushes forward, not in balance or reciprocity, but in potential conflict, as is suggested by words such as "dominion" and "obeisance." The passage as a whole is meant to express creative health, but potentially blocking tensions are everywhere apparent.

Throughout his life, Wordsworth battled to keep these tensions in check, in his relation to both objects (or nature) and people. The same doubleness or ambiguity with which he views the power and glory of nature characterizes his relation to society. McFarland sees him as "impelled toward but at the same time retreating from both isolation and community . . . as it were suspended in an emotional force-field between them."[11] On the one hand, isolation (or relative isolation) was for Wordsworth a precondition of productive effort; on the other, it was a danger, as for the solitary of "Lines Left upon a Seat in a Yew-tree," who "many an hour / A morbid pleasure nourished, tracing here / An emblem of his own unfruitful life" (27–29), or Vaudracour in book nine of *The Prelude*, who, cut off "from all intelligence with man" (9.928), in "solitary shades / His days . . . wasted,—an imbecile mind" (9.933–34). The creative life requires a balance between such extremes, but in different poems one or other of the rival claims of subjective and objective need predominates, threatening to block. This is true even though Wordsworth's early infancy was "strong," and his adult life was productive, because the relief that art affords us from what Winnicott calls "the strain inherent in objective perception"[12] is no less dependent upon a comparably straining negotiation of inner and outer.

Blockage and Subjective Need: The Prelude, 10.806–930

In some poems or passages, the source of blockage is principally internal, as in book ten of *The Prelude*, in which Wordsworth describes the intellectual crisis from which his sister, Dorothy, finally rescued him in the mid–1790s. The crisis was brought about by the collapse of Wordsworth's hopes for France and the French Revolution, the first stage of which began with his reaction to England's entry into the war. Ultimately, like so many others, Wordsworth was forced to turn to more personal, as opposed to directly political, sources of renovation. The manner in which he describes his eventual break-down when these also failed him recalls the opening account of lit-erary blockage in book one, as well as the object-relations terminol-ogy of balance, projection, and reparation in the "Blest Babe" passage from book two.

"This was the time," begins Wordsworth, of the period after Eng-land's joining of the "confederated host" in 1793,

> . . . when, all things tending fast
> To depravation, the philosophy
> That promised to abstract the hopes of man
> Out of his feelings, to be fixed thenceforth
> For ever in a purer element
> Found ready welcome . . .
> (10.806–11)

The opposition established here and in the lines that follow is be-tween "philosophy" (or reason) and "feelings" (or nature). These terms mask a familiar tension, because in the very next line philoso-phy is associated with enthusiasm, the "purer element" being a "Tempting region . . . / For Zeal to enter and refresh herself, / Where passions had the privilege to work" (10.811–13). Philosophy is thus, paradoxically, the instrument of subjective need and idealization, of a realm in which "the dream" (10.815) holds sway; what opposes it is a world of "nature, time, and place" (10.823)—that is, the objective world. The freedom subjective impulse seeks in this case is "The free-dom of the independent mind" (10.825), "an independent intellect" (10.830) (phrases lifted from *The Borderers*, in which they are put in the mouth of a villain whose "master passions are pride and the love of distinction");[13] these are precisely the freedoms that the French Revolution itself released. In both cases, the aim is an earthly para-dise, a realm of total subjective power such as that associated with infant omnipotence. In the French Revolution,

> . . . The inert
> Were roused, and lively natures rapt away!
> They who had fed their childhood upon dreams,
> The play-fellows of fancy, who had made
> All powers of swiftness, subtlety, and strength

Their ministers,—used to stir in lordly wise
Among the grandest objects of the sense,
And deal with whatsoever they found there
As if they had within some lurking right
To wield it;—they, too, who of gentle mood
Had watched all gentle motions, and to these
Had fitted their own thoughts, schemers more mild,
And in the region of their peaceful selves,
Did now find helpers to their hearts' desire,
And stuff at hand, plastic as they could wish,—
Were called upon to exercise their skill.
                                        (10.708–23)

Although these lines are complicated, the underlying impression
they convey is of a world becoming for its inhabitants (whether
"gentle" or otherwise) "plastic as they could wish"; that is, one in
which the intellect could operate freely, independently, and to a purpose. The association of such a world with childhood is made not
only in this passage but also in Wordsworth's earlier account of the
French Revolution's phases. When liberty gives way to terror, infancy's unrestrained energies and appetites are revealed:

. . . all perished, all—
Friends, enemies, of all parties, ages, ranks,
Head after head, and never heads enough
For those that bade them fall. They found their joy,
They made it, ever thirsty as a child,
(If light desires of innocent little ones
May with such heinous appetites be matched),
Having a toy, a wind-mill, though the air
Do of itself blow fresh, and make the vane
Spin in his eyesight, he is not content,
But, with the plaything at arm's length, he sets
His front against the blast, and runs amain,
To make it whirl the faster.
                                        (10.334–46)

The dangers here—of a world without bearings and restraints, of naked and heedless energy—are precisely those feared in moments of
blockage. The French Revolution gave impetus to subjective need, to
a desire for personal autonomy, which is the political and social
equivalent of the poet's "plastic power." Its aim, like that of the political theory Wordsworth turned to after 1793, was eventually seen by
him as the denial or defiance of "The limits of experience and of

truth" (849), whether conceived of as naturally imposed limits (natural feelings and failings) or tradition, in the form of either conventions or institutions.

In the years preceding Wordsworth's breakdown, the balance between the subjective and the objective all but disappeared: "my mind was both let loose, / Let loose and goaded" (10.863–64). As a consequence, Wordsworth was

> . . . drawn
> Out of a heart which had been turned aside
> From Nature by external accidents
> And which was thus confounded more and more,
> Misguiding and misguided . . .
> (10.885–89)

The propulsive force here is subjective need, as opposed to a "heart" instinctively responsive to, and compounded of, a fixed and limiting nature. "Heart" as objective or external is, I realize, confusing, but the larger drift is clear: once one side of the opposition between inner and outer dominates, the result is blockage (being "confounded more and more"). As Wordsworth persists in his search for "independent intellect," for a world conforming wholly to a dream of total freedom, he hurries anxiously from scheme to scheme, blocked at every moment by the sorts of fears which paralyzed him in book one:

> . . . Thus I fared,
> Dragging all passions, notions, shapes of faith,
> Like culprits to the bar; suspiciously
> Calling the mind to establish in plain day
> Her titles and her honours; now believing,
> Now disbelieving; endlessly perplexed
> With impulse, motive, right and wrong, the ground
> Of moral obligation, what the rule
> And what the sanction; till, demanding *proof*,
> And seeing it in every thing, I lost
> All feeling of conviction, and, in fine,
> Sick, wearied out with contrarieties,
> Yielded up moral questions in despair.
> (10.889–901)

Here are the accelerating rhythms, the familiar accumulation of clauses, the desperate turning from one scheme to another, the sense of all ballast or anchorage gone. The result is anxious clutching, in this case "towards mathematics and their clear / And solid evidence" (10.904–5), a "turn" that seeks to establish the mind's dominion, attempting to exclude everything that is not the mind (all those "accidents of nature, time, and place").

It is from this state that Dorothy rescues Wordsworth, in an intervention that in several respects anticipates the appearance of the leech-gatherer in "Resolution and Independence":

> . . . then it was
> That the beloved Woman in whose sight
> Those days were passed, now speaking in a voice
> Of sudden admonition—like a brook
> That does but *cross* a lonely road, and now
> Seen, heard and felt, and caught at every turn,
> Companion never lost through many a league—
> Maintained for me a saving intercourse
> With my true self; for, though impaired and changed
> Much, as it seemed, I was no further changed
> Than as a clouded, not a waning moon:
> She in the midst of all, preserved me still
> A Poet, made me seek beneath that name
> My office upon earth, and nowhere else;
> And, lastly, Nature's self, by human love
> Assisted, through the weary labyrinth
> Conducted me again to open day,
> Revived the feelings of my earlier life,
> Gave me that strength and knowledge full of peace,
> Enlarged, and never more to be disturbed,
> Which through the steps of our degeneracy,
> All degradation of this age, hath still
> Upheld me, and upholds me at this day.
>   (10.907–30)

Dorothy's "sudden admonition" resembles the "peculiar grace" of the leech-gatherer's appearance, which is also sudden ("unawares"), bringing with it "apt admonishment." Dorothy's voice, moreover, is likened to a "brook," which recalls not only the "stream" into which the old man's talk is transformed by Wordsworth but also the rescuing Derwent at the end of the initial passage of book one of *The Prelude*, which "loved / To blend his murmurs with my nurse's song." These passages describe a way back to health, one that moves from a state of blockage occasioned by subjective need to a saving intervention from the external realm. This realm, paradoxically and magically, returns the poet to contact with internal sources of strength (which is why its appearance here is associated with the sublime, for all the vital importance of Dorothy's this-worldliness). Contact with the ex-

ternal, in other words, is the only way back to the strengths of childhood or subjectivity, to "a saving intercourse / With my true self"
(10.915–16). Once rescued, Wordsworth is able to see that the condition from which he was rescued was but temporary: "I was no further
changed / Than as a clouded, not a waning moon" (10.917–18). That
is, he was blocked both as a person and, as the next line makes clear,
as an artist; Dorothy's intervention "preserved me still / A Poet"
(10.919–20). Here also, though, the rescue is only temporary because, at the very end of the passage, the potential recurrence of
blocking fears is subtly hinted at in the overemphatic "never more to
be disturbed" (10.927).

"Resolution and Independence"

A second and more directly literary example of the blocking power
of subjective need is afforded by "Resolution and Independence," in
which the source of creative inhibition takes the form of "plastic
power," rather than "philosophy." That blocked literary creativity is
the poem's subject is clear not only from internal evidence but from
our knowledge of its genesis. Wordsworth wrote "Resolution and Independence" with Coleridge and the first version of "Dejection: An
Ode" particularly in mind. Wordsworth first read this ode in April
1802 and, as Dorothy's journals and William and Dorothy's letters attest, was much affected by what McFarland calls Coleridge's "entire
symphony" of unhappiness and creative debility.[14] "Resolution and
Independence" was composed in May, after receipt of another deeply
troubled missive from Coleridge. The poem is an answer to a poet
whose deep unhappiness arises out of blockage.

The poem begins at a moment of wholeness and interaction, of
"creative sensibility," but by stanzas 4 and 5 Wordsworth is inexplicably cut off from both the scene itself and the poet's necessary balance between subjective and objective claims. What cut him off are
self-generated "fears and fancies" (27) that cloud the morning's richness with "blind thoughts" (28). Instead of experiencing the present
moment, Wordsworth is lost in thoughts of future "solitude, pain of
heart, distress, and poverty" (35). At which point—a point of potential blockage—the appearance of the leech-gatherer provides a breakthrough:

> Now, whether it were by peculiar grace,
> A leading from above, a something given,
> Yet it befell, that, in this lonely place,
> When I with these untoward thoughts had striven,

Beside a pool bare to the eye of heaven
I saw a Man before me unawares:
The oldest man he seemed that ever wore gray hairs.
(50–56)

The sudden appearance of the leech-gatherer is presented, as was
Dorothy's appearance in book ten of *The Prelude,* in sublime or transcendent terms. However, it is characteristic of Wordsworth that this
quasi-divine apparition is also, emphatically, earthbound and that it
never quite solves the dilemma or impasse that seems to have called
it forth. This is as it should be, as Geoffrey Hartman suggests, because for Wordsworth to see "heaven in a leech-gatherer and infinity
in a handful of leeches,"[15] he would have to lose touch with the very
otherness or solidity that makes the old man a saving figure. Here is
how Wordsworth describes the leech-gatherer's importance in a letter
of 14 June 1802 to Sara Hutchinson (some of the lines he refers to are
from an earlier version of the poem):

A young Poet in the midst of the happiness of Nature is described as overwhelmed by the thought of the innumerable re-
verses which have befallen the happiest of all men, viz. Poets. I
think of this till I am so deeply impressed by it, that I consider
the manner in which I was rescued from my dejection and despair almost as an interposition of Providence. "Now whether it
was by a peculiar grace, A leading from above." A person reading this poem with feelings like mine will have been awed and
controuled, expecting something spiritual or supernatural—
What is brought forward? "A lonely place, a Pond" "by which an
old man *was,* far from all house and home"—not stood, nor sat,
but *was*—the figure presented in the most naked simplicity possible.[16]

What matters to Wordsworth is the unadorned objective *fact* of the
leech-gatherer's existence: it is the object itself which has rescued
him.

This view of the old man's meaning and dramatic function finds
support in the stanza that originally followed, which Wordsworth deleted in 1820, probably because Coleridge had criticized it in the *Biographia Literaria* as an example of "inconstancy" of style:

My course I stopped as soon as I espyed
The Old Man in that naked wilderness:
Close by a Pond, upon the further side,
He stood alone: a minute's space I guess
I watched him, he continued motionless:

> To the pool's further margin then I drew;
> He being all the while before me full in view.[17]

Wordsworth's care here about location ("close by," "further side," "further margin"), together with the absolute stillness or fixity of the old man, helps to communicate the saving "objectivity" of the moment. "I watched him, he continued motionless." The line establishes precisely the bearings Wordsworth had lost. Hence the pedantic thoroughness of "He being all the time before me full in view," which makes simple perception seem to be what it was for Wordsworth in this context—an achievement. It is important to Wordsworth that the old man, as he says in stanza 8, appears before him "unawares" (55), because it suggests what the deleted stanza makes so much of: the unmediated nature of the apparition, the saving power of the object to break through subjectivity and occluding panic.[18]

The specific lesson Wordsworth takes from the old man is not only patient endurance but a persistent connection with the external, the very means by which the leech-gatherer lives, as the opening lines of stanza 12 suggest:

> At length, himself unsettling, he the pond
> Stirred with his staff, and fixedly did look
> Upon the muddy water, which he conned,
> As if he had been reading in a book.
>
> (38–41)

What at first seems a traditional image of narcissism, as well as another of the poet's projections, turns out to be something quite different, an example of scrupulous attentiveness. Wordsworth is seeing something actually there: the unsettling of the water is the leech-gatherer's way of getting *past* his own image ("himself unsettling"), for it is only by disturbing the pond's surface that he can get to its bottom and "read" it, discovering there the leeches that provide him with a livelihood. A comparable connection to the external world is no less vital to the true poet, whose livelihood also depends in part upon a disruption of subjectivity, a reaching past the self and its projections.

As in *The Prelude* passages, this moment of breakthrough is nothing permanent. In the stanzas that follow, "plastic power" reasserts itself and the figure of the old man is clothed in metaphor.[19] Wordsworth loses sight of the leech-gatherer, and what he says becomes undifferentiated "matter." But he is not entirely cut off, though, and his meaning as a symbol of endurance is firmly registered. Still, what is not registered or resolved by the speaker is the question of the importance of his independence, and of the claims of the other. There is a headlong quality about the poem's concluding lines, something willed as in "Tintern Abbey." The power of subjective need continues to crowd and threaten what is given and, thus, to bring Wordsworth again to a standstill. This dilemma was recurring: what made Wordsworth a great poet was in part the power to "forget / That I had bodily eyes, [so that] what I saw / Appeared like something in myself, a dream, / A prospect in my mind" (*The Prelude*, 2.366–71); but this power always also represented a threat. "I was often unable to think of external things as having external existence," he says in one of the Fenwick notes, "and I communed with all that I saw as something not apart from, but inherent in, my own instinctual nature. Many times while going to school I grasped at a wall or tree to recall myself from the abyss of idealism to the reality. At the time I was afraid of such processes." [20] As "Resolution and Independence" suggests, fear of the abyss—of unbridled subjectivity—was long in dying. When it could not be quieted, the result was paralysis. At the same time, though, Wordsworth seems to have needed or been inspired by his fears; overcoming them, it could be argued, brought out his strength as a poet.

Blockage and Externality: "Ode: Intimations of Immortality"

When Wordsworth complains in stanza 1 of "Ode: Intimations of Immortality" that "The things which I have seen I now can see no more" (9), he has in mind things seen through the poet's mediating vision. What is lost is not so much the world as the poetical power that "apparalled" it "in celestial light" (4). Wordsworth's habitual search for this light affected him physically. When Hazlitt first met him, he was struck by "a severe, worn pressure of thought about his temples, a fire in his eyes (as if he saw something in objects more than the actual appearance)." [21] What Wordsworth seemed to Hazlitt to be seeing was something the object itself might block; which is to say, attention to "outward appearance" or the external world was not only a precondition of poetic achievement, as in "Resolution and Independence," but a potential impediment. In "Ode: Intimations," the external is viewed in this latter sense, as something that must be seen through or got over.

Here is how Wordsworth describes his relation to the object world in the poem's opening stanzas:

I

There was a time when meadow, grove, and stream,
The earth, and every common sight,

To me did seem
  Apparelled in celestial light,
The glory and the freshness of a dream.
It is not now as it hath been of yore;—
  Turn wheresoe'er I may,
    By night or day,
The things which I have seen I now can see no more.

II

The rainbow comes and goes,
  And lovely is the Rose;
  The Moon doth with delight
Look round her when the heavens are bare;
  Waters on a starry night
  Are beautiful and fair;
  The sunshine is a glorious birth;
  But yet I know, where'er I go,
That there hath past away a glory from the earth.
(1–18)

The flatness here is a species of blockage, just as is a comparable flatness in stanza 5 of "Resolution and Independence," in which the bliss of the opening stanzas is reduced to distant and distracted summary ("I bethought me of the playful hare"). In the earlier poem, creative achievement was blocked by "fears and fancies [which] thick upon me came." And, at first, the same seems true in "Ode: Intimations," in which Wordsworth tells us in stanza 3 that "To me alone there came a thought of grief" (22). This thought, though, does not cut him off from the outside world for more than a line; in the rest of stanza 3, thanks to an unspecified "timely utterance" (23), Wordsworth is returned to the glories that surround him. In this case what "throngs" are mountain echoes, the trumpeting of cataracts; "And I again am strong" (24).

When in stanza 4 the sense of lost vision recurs, presaged by a too strenuous profession of sympathetic identification ("The fulness of your bliss, I feel—I feel it all" [41], "I hear, I hear, with joy I hear" [51]), loss is associated with natural particulars:

  —But there's a Tree, of many, one,
A single Field which I have looked upon,
Both of them speak of something that is gone:
  The Pansy at my feet
  Doth the same tale repeat:

171

Whither is fled the visionary gleam?
Where is it now, the glory and the dream?
(51–57)

What is gone here is not what is given—Tree, Field, and Pansy still speak to Wordsworth—but what he in turn would give, the "visionary gleam" that brings them to life, in poetry preeminently. This "gleam" is not, I agree with Trilling, synonymous with "poetic power," but it *is* essential to it, being the subjective or shaping component in the creation of art. And in "Ode: Intimations" its diminution is hardly viewed, in Trilling's words, as "right and inevitable."[22] On the contrary, it is viewed as disastrous and contingent.[23]

In the stanzas that follow, the fading of poetic powers, of the "visionary gleam," is described in several ways. To begin with, "Shades of the prison-house begin to close / Upon the growing boy" (66–67). What is external, symbolized by the prison house, closes off or darkens vision, and a natural process (aging) is conceived of as something imposed or external, part of the object world Wordsworth had lost sight of in "Resolution and Independence." "The Youth, who daily farther from the east / Must travel" (72–73) in search of the visionary gleam, until "At length the Man perceived it die away, / And fade into the light of common day" (76–77), is urged on by something quite different from subjective need. Even in those stanzas (5–8) in which the condition of infant blessedness is recalled, nature's brute or imperious power intrudes. As the child takes up one or other "fragment from his dream of human life" (92), he becomes a "little Actor" (103), "filling from time to time his 'humourous stage' / With all the Persons, down to palsied Age, / That Life brings with her in her equipage" (104–6). Again, obviously, it is "Life" that paralyzes ("palsies"). Later on, the child is explicitly distinguished from the adult (from "us") by knowing intuitively the light ("visionary gleam") "Which we are toiling all our lives to find, / In darkness lost, the darkness of the grave" (117–18). The source of this darkness is not internal but external: it derives from our circumstances—from the fact that we are toiling toward (in?) the grave. It may seem as though the fault is our own—it is we who cannot find a light that is there—but this is because nature or "Life" has plunged us in darkness. If our faculties are restricted, it is because we labor under an "inevitable yoke" (125), one externally imposed. If we are blocked, it is for the same reason the child will be: because "Full soon thy Soul will have her earthly freight / And custom lie upon thee with a weight, / Heavy as frost, and deep almost as life" (127–29); that is, poetic power will be buried, snowed up, frozen.

All that remains to the adult poet are glimmers, "embers" (130), and Wordsworth describes them in terms that clearly attribute blame to the object world. What the poet must kindle or keep alive are "those obstinate questionings / Of sense and outward things, / Fallings from us, vanishings; / Blank misgivings of a Creature / Moving about in worlds not realized" (143–47). By "realized," Wordsworth means something like brought to life, inspirited, "realized" in the sense of fulfilled. It is the poet's job to battle outward things, then, not only by questioning them but by refusing to let them batten on to and occlude internal power. To do so, he must overcome the "listlessness" and "mad endeavour" (158) that they have already, as they close about him from infancy, induced.

At this point, a crucial dimension of the poem needs to be examined, for it is this dimension that leads on to what in chapter one I identified as a species of qualitative blockage in Wordsworth's later poetry. The sort of thing I have in mind is the anxiety that underlies the strenuous and not altogether convincing affirmations noted previously (as in "for such loss, I would believe, / Abundant recompense," from "Tintern Abbey"; "with a heart / Joyous, nor scared at its own liberty," from book one of *The Prelude*; the willed and unresolved assertiveness of the concluding lines of "Resolution and Independence"; and "I feel—I feel it all" and "I hear, I hear, with joy I hear," from "Ode: Intimations"). What these lines point to is an internal, psychological drama or conflict, one in which a surface faith in the benevolent power of nature or the object world is confronted by what Bloom calls a "dark undersong," that of nature as a "hidden antagonist"[24]—rather than anchor, nurse, guide, guardian. This sense becomes progressively stronger from "Tintern Abbey" to "Resolution and Independence" to "Ode: Intimations," and in the latter poem it breaks into the open as something more than an undersong. As it becomes more prominent, it is also subject to more violent denials, moments of repression—of willed or extraneous optimism—which break up and confuse the logical and metrical flow of the verse.[25]

The only sense that can be made of such moments is dramatic sense, so that when McFarland echoes Coleridge by asking "What does all this mean?" of the optimism of the poem's concluding lines—lines that constitute "a kind of absolute in their disconnectedness and incoherence"[26]—the obvious answer is that Wordsworth is trying desperately to cling on to hope and to deny what he has earlier presented as a brute fact of existence. "This poem," writes Wordsworth of "Ode: Intimations," "rests entirely upon two recollections of childhood, one that of a splendour in the objects of sense which is passed away, and the other an indisposition to bend to the law of death as applying to our own particular case."[27] What the poem is "about" is Wordsworth's inability or unwillingness to give up these recollected states.

At which point the oddness of Wordsworth's theme needs to be recalled. Writers are not like chess players or mathematicians; there is nothing inevitable about the sort of decline in poetical power Wordsworth is here describing. At the very least, there is nothing to prevent a thirty-two-year-old poet (Wordsworth's age at the time of writing "Ode: Intimations") from producing poetry that matters. When Wordsworth tells us in *The Prelude* that he can only "see by glimpses now, when age comes on / May scarcely see at all," he is still a relatively young man, no older than thirty-five. The anxiety his poetry expresses is no product of inevitably fading powers; rather, it grows out of neurosis, which is why it makes sense to think of his later falling off as a form of writer's block. Wordsworth is suffering from the reassertion of fears about his own identity or integrity: these fears issue in a defensive embrace of nature, which is a form of denial. In "Ode: Intimations," the consequence is confusion (or dramatic conflict). In the poems that follow, it is disabling rigidity.

Qualitative Blockage: *"Elegiac Stanzas" and the Anticlimax*

In the poetry written before 1807, Wordsworth makes blocking fears, whether conceived of as the product of internal or external forces, his subject. In most of the poetry that follows, of which there is a great deal, these fears are so powerful that they cannot be faced. What this means is that a sharp line is drawn between the self and the other, the subject and the object, and the difficult but enabling interchange between them, which is earlier identified as the true source of poetic power, is lost. The result, in H. W. Garrod's words, is "the most dismal anti-climax of which the history of literature holds record."[28] Instead of simply giving up in the face of blocking fears, Wordsworth turned to his task with grim deliberation, producing either deadened and distant echoes of earlier work, or retreating into rigid and often clumsy orthodoxy. Only for brief moments at the beginning of the decline were the fears themselves given open expression, at last shorn of protective qualifications. One such moment occurs in "Elegiac Stanzas," the poem Wordsworth composed during a period when he was at work on *The Recluse* and *The Excursion*, in the year after his brother's death by drowning in 1805. "Elegiac Stanzas" provides vital clues to qualitative blockage in the later work.

The poem opens with a memory of Peele Castle, which stands on an island near the coast of Lancashire. What occasions the memory is a painting of the castle in a turbulent storm, the work of Sir George Beaumont, Wordsworth's friend and patron. In Wordsworth's memory, which is the product of "four summer weeks I dwelt in sight of thee" (2), the scene surrounding the castle was calm: "Thy Form was sleeping on a glassy sea" (4). This calm, he felt, was something deep and lasting, "no sleep; / No mood, which season takes away, or brings" (10–11). Now, though, as he tells us in stanza 2, he sees the calm as delusion:

> Ah! THEN, if mine had been the Painter's hand,
> To express what then I saw; and add the gleam,
> The light that never was, on sea or land,
> The consecration, and the Poet's dream.
>
> (13–16)

Here Wordsworth attacks the very "plastic power" whose loss he lamented in "Ode: Intimations." The "gleam" is a "light that never was," a falsification or "Poet's dream." All that heightens and makes blessed ("consecrates") the world is delusion, which suggests that the external realm is both dark and disinherited, if not damned.

What Wordsworth would have painted, he tells us in line 32, was "A steadfast peace that might not be betrayed"—a line that recalls the famous "Nature never did betray the heart that loved her" from "Tintern Abbey." The line might mean several things: not only that nature itself is essentially benevolent and will not betray the poet by diminishing or overwhelming him but that it can withstand betrayals (not itself be betrayed) from within—the betrayals of an "over-anxious eye."

Now, though, Wordsworth believes something quite different, which he has only hinted at in earlier poems such as "Tintern Abbey" and "Ode: Intimations":

> So once it would have been,—'tis so no more;
> I have submitted to a new control:
> A power is gone, which nothing can restore;
> A deep distress hath humanized my Soul.
>
> (33–36)

"Submitted" and "control" are the telling words here because they alert us to the source of Wordsworth's anxiety in the period before his present disillusion. He implies that he gave himself up to nature in the past; nothing here, in the poem itself, justifies Bloom's annotation of "new control" as "not the reciprocal relation with Nature."[29] The power that is now "gone" could mean the power Wordsworth himself possessed as a poet—"plastic power"—which might therefore suggest that nature had "betrayed" him by taking it away, as is implied in "Ode: Intimations," or it could mean that nature's own "radiance" (line 177 of "Ode: Intimations") is gone, which fits more happily with the rest of the line, a line that seems to regret its passing. The "deep distress" that has brought this change about is, of course, the loss of the brother, and "humanized" suggests that there had been something wrong—something less than human—about Wordsworth's previous relation to nature, a suggestion that supports my view that what was "no more" was not the reciprocal relation of true creativity, but that defensive assertiveness identified earlier as a denial of doubts about nature. Although the cruel and senseless loss of the brother is more than enough to justify a sense of betrayal, there is also (especially as the poem was written a year after the event) room for feelings of guilt and shame to add to Wordsworth's emotion—feelings induced by the sort of blind clutching that refused to acknowledge imbalance in his sense of the relation between subject and object, self and other. There is a real impulse of self-wounding, a masochistic relish, in the lines that follow, especially when Wordsworth says of Beaumont's painting, "This work of thine I blame not, but commend; / This sea in anger, and that dismal shore" (43–44).

What is so distressing about the poem is that nothing has been learned. One sort of imbalance—the defensive embrace of nature as anchor, nurse, and guide—has been replaced by an opposite extreme. Wordsworth now identifies with an isolated and impregnable self, as figured in Peele Castle itself:

> And this huge Castle, standing here sublime,
> I love to see the look with which it braves,
> Cased in the unfeeling armour of old time,
> The lightning, the fierce wind, and trampling waves.
>
> (49–52)

Here is the perfect image of rigid denial, of a self locked up against the world, "Cased in unfeeling armour." The fears that in "Ode: Intimations" sent Wordsworth into a desperate embrace of the external realm have finally broken through the defensive embrace that gesture constituted: Wordsworth has at last cut himself off from harm.[30]

What complicates this reading of "Elegiac Stanzas" is Wordsworth's association of his earlier relation to nature with isolation of a different kind—the sort that his withdrawal to the Lake District seemed to imply. In the past, Wordsworth looked to his removal from London as a way of establishing contact with the external realm—even when

those around him tempted him to see it as a withdrawal. Now he
accepts the reading of his life that the younger Romantic poets gave
it. Hence the poem's penultimate stanza:

> Farewell, farewell the heart that lives alone,
> Housed in a dream, at distance from the kind!
> Such happiness, wherever it be known,
> Is to be pitied; for 'tis surely blind.
>
> (53–56)

The irony and futility of Wordsworth's position are pointed up by the
juxtaposition of the new creed with the image of a self "Cased in the
unfeeling armour of old time." His new expression of social concern
is another defensive gesture, an evasion or denial of a deeper subjective impulse of self-protection. Wordsworth is not insincere in his
profession of a newly "humanized" resolve, but the preceding metaphors reveal a deep, unconscious confusion. Hence the familiar unsatisfactoriness of the poem's concluding assertions:

> But welcome fortitude, and patient cheer,
> And frequent sights of what is to be borne!
> Such sights, or worse, as are before me here.—
> Not without hope we suffer and we mourn.
>
> (57–60)

Welcome such sights? Here is a confusion as pronounced in its way as
that in the concluding lines of "Ode: Intimations"; and here also its
source is a defensive or clutching denial, though in this case what is
being denied is the importance—the saving importance, for all its
capacity to disappoint and wound—of the object world.

What follows in the years to come is a poetry of blockage: a poetry
of fortitude (if not patient cheer), but one locked up. McFarland
points to a "trifling" but telling anecdote from the last decade of
Wordsworth's life to suggest what became of him once he cut himself
off so: "Nothing however said or done to me for some time has in
relation to myself given me so much pleasure as a casual word of
Anna's that the expression of my face was ever varying. I had begun
to feel that it had lately been much otherwise."[31] That it *had* been
otherwise is the impression most readers have taken from the later
poetry, the poetry of Wordsworth's decline, whether judged to have
begun in 1810, 1808, 1806, or even 1805. For though the later poetry
is not without moments of imaginative power, or the virtues of a
new—that is, older—ceremoniousness (John Jones's view),[32] it is also
ever on the alert against the earlier enabling—and ennobling—interchange of self and other, subject and object, hurrying much more

damagingly than in earlier poems into denial or the blank (because unmediated) certitudes of faith.

Hartman points to a telling instance of this new blankness in the late "progress poem" entitled "Processions. Suggested on a Sabbath Morning in the Vale of Chamouny," from *Memorials of a Tour on the Continent* (1820). At the very moment Wordsworth recognizes a vivifying power within himself, he pulls back:

> Trembling, I look upon the secret springs
> Of that licentious craving in the mind
> To act the God among external things,
> To bind, on apt suggestion, or unbind;
> And marvel not that antique faith inclined
> To crowd the world with metamorphosis,
> Vouchsafed in pity or in wrath assigned;
> Such insolent temptations wouldst thou miss,
> Avoid these sights; nor brood o'er Fable's dark abyss!
>
> (64–72)

Advice such as this, in which both the external world and the fabling powers that vivify it are rejected, really does close matters up for the poet. "Licentious cravings" and "insolent temptations" are to be resisted not simply because they violate a dark and frightening truth, as in "Elegiac Stanzas," or lead one into the "dark abyss" of subjectivity, but because they threaten Wordsworth's protective orthodoxy. Imaginative activity is transgression as well as delusion, of a piece with the creation of false gods.[33] "Nature," here and elsewhere in late Wordsworth, is thus something both new and deadened, for it excludes all aspects alien to the Christian vision, aspects such as Wordsworth admonishes the reader to "avoid" in "Processions," lest they give rise to "insolent temptations."

The poetry of the decline is as full of such "avoidances" as it is of imaginative restriction. In the following passage from *The Excursion* (1814), for example, revelation depends as much on blindness as it does on imaginative orthodoxy:

> This little Vale, a dwelling place of Man,
> Lay low beneath my feet; 'twas visible—
> I saw not, but I felt that it was there.
> That which I *saw* was the revealed abode
> Of Spirits in beatitude . . .
>
> (2.870–74)

"Revelation" here comes from neither imaginative power nor nature itself (Wordsworth cannot even see the Vale). It comes from blind faith, bred of defensive fear and denial. Such passages, in Shelley's words from a note to *Peter Bell the Third,* provide "curious evidence of a gradual hardening of a strong but uncircumscribed sensibility, of the perversion of a penetrating but panic-stricken understanding."[34] The result, in poems such as the *Ecclesiastical Sonnets* (1822), the *Evening Voluntaries* (1835), and the *Sonnets upon the Punishment of Death* (1841), is a poetry *of* rather than *about* blockage. These poems, in F. W. Bateson's extreme formulation, are "empty, pretentious, humourless, clumsily expressed, often without any human feeling in them at all. They deserve all the abuse and ridicule they have had poured upon them."[35]

Although Wordsworth's decline was neither as complete nor as calamitous as Bateson claims (even in the poems he singles out), rigidity and its consequences are everywhere apparent. There is a new emphasis on "the stern word" as a fit "theme for praise and admonition high" (*Sonnets upon the Punishment of Death,* 3.42); passions invariably "spread like plagues" ("Translation of the Bible," in *Ecclesiastical Sonnets,* 29.12); both the literal Duddon River and the figurative "stream of liberty" are replaced by "a HOLY RIVER, on whose banks are found / Sweet pastoral flowers, and laurels that have crowned / Full oft the unworthy brows of lawless force" ("Introduction," in *Ecclesiastical Sonnets,* 26.9–12). Even when Wordsworth returns to his central "project" or theme—that of "How exquisitely the individual Mind / (And the progressive powers perhaps no less / Of the whole species) to the external world / Is fitted" (*Home at Grasmere,* 63–67)—the treatment is often flat or deadened, as in "Ejaculation," in *Ecclesiastical Sonnets:*

> Earth prompts—Heaven urges; let us seek the light,
> Studious of that pure intercourse begun
> When first our infant brows their lustre wore.
>
> (56.9–11)

Elsewhere, the treatment is not so much flat and deadened as elegiac and incomplete, or antique in its ceremoniousness, as in the *Vernal Ode* (1820), with its opening reference to an April "When all the fields with freshest green were dight" (2), or "Ode: Composed upon an Evening of Extraordinary Splendor and Beauty" (1820), in which "An intermingling of Heaven's pomp is spread / On ground which British shepherds tread" (39–40). Stephen Gill notes comparable features in the earlier odes of 1816—"Thanksgiving Ode," "Ode Composed in January 1816," and the "Ode" ("Who rises on the banks of Seine")—describing them as "empty of human beings, unanchored in specific place or event. Echoes of earlier poems . . . sadly remind readers how far Wordsworth is from his own poetic terrain."[36] When Wordsworth is faced in these later poems with what in 1808 he calls the "gulf" that "renders nothing back" ("The Tuft of Primroses," 214–15), or the "un-approachable abyss" ("To the Clouds," 30)—analogues to the "dark abyss" of the "Processions" poem—his only recourse is a blank (because unmediable) assertion of faith—faith in an undying deity beneath the surface mutability.[37] In the best of the later poems, a vulnerable, "liminal" quality recalls the meditative melancholy of Gray—even as the poems echo Gray-like formal properties (of diction, imagery, and rhythm). Later Wordsworth at his best grows to resemble the defeated or blocked poets of "sensibility." At his worst, he is all "unfeeling armour."

Generic Blockage:
Wordsworth and The Recluse

The great irony of Wordsworth's most productive years, those between 1798 and the variously dated decline, is that throughout them he seems to have thought of himself as laboring under the pressure of a great task deferred. That task was *The Recluse*, the epic poem to which he had dedicated himself as early as spring 1798, six or so months before he began work on *The Prelude*. Even when most productive, in other words, Wordsworth felt blocked, inadequate to the sort of writing he most valued.

The idea for *The Recluse* seems to have originated with Coleridge, with whom Wordsworth had been in close contact the previous summer. According to Coleridge's recollections in *Table Talk* (1832), the poem was to take the following form: "Wordsworth should assume the station of a man in mental repose, one whose principles were made up, and so prepared to deliver upon authority a system of philosophy." By the end of the poem, this philosophy would disclose "a redemptive process in operation . . . [which] reconciled all the anomolies, and promised future glories and restoration."[38]

At the heart of this "redemptive process," as Coleridge wrote to Wordsworth in a letter of 30 May 1815, was the philosophical project of "removing the sandy sophisms of Locke, and the mechanic dogmatists and demonstrating that the senses were living growths and developments of the mind and spirit in a much juster as well as higher sense, than the mind can be said to be formed by the senses."[39] That is, *The Recluse* was to provide a philosophical justification for precisely that interaction Wordsworth had celebrated as the true and renovating relation between man and nature, as well as the source of all true poetic achievement. And this project, of course, was also Coleridge's—and one that would defeat him as well.

In the winter of 1799 Wordsworth and Coleridge were in Germany, in part to collect the philosophical materials that both hoped to incorporate into their major projects. This was also the time when Wordsworth began to draft the first pages of autobiographical verse which would become *The Prelude*. When Wordsworth returned to England the following summer, he still felt inadequate to the task of *The Recluse* and decided instead to expand and complete the autobiographical fragments of *The Prelude* begun in Germany. Coleridge, upon hearing of this plan, voiced the first of a series of worries about Wordsworth's resolve in a letter of 12 October 1799: "I long to see what you have been doing," he writes of Wordsworth's work on *The Prelude*, "O let it be the tail-piece of 'The Recluse'! for of nothing but 'The Recluse' can I hear patiently. That it [*The Prelude*] is to be addressed to me makes me more desirous that it should not be a poem of itself."[40] Four years later, Coleridge wrote to Thomas Poole, revealing that Wordsworth

> has at length yielded to my urgent and repeated—almost unremitting—requests and remonstrances—and will go on with the Recluse exclusively.—A Great Work, in which he will sail; on an open Ocean, and a steady wind; unfretted by short tacks, reefing, and hawling and disentangling the ropes—great work necessarily comprehending his attention and feelings within the circle of great objects and elevated Conceptions—this is his natural Element—the having been out of it has been his disease. . . . I really consider it as a misfortune that Wordsworth ever deserted his former mountain Track to wander in Lanes and allies.[41]

Already then, by autumn 1799, Wordsworth's closest poetical ally conceives of him, in the midst of other great "achievements," as "diseased," off-track.

When the two-part *Prelude* was completed in 1799 and put aside, not to be published except as a sort of preface to *The Recluse*, Wordsworth began his first serious attempt to write the central philosophical section of his epic. These were the lines that he was later to call *Home at Grasmere*, and they show that though Wordsworth "is writing dutifully, often with great beauty and tenderness . . . he [has] no system to offer."[42] *Home at Grasmere* is then left off, and by April 1800 Wordsworth is at work on a second volume of *Lyrical Ballads*. He did not resume writing *Home at Grasmere* until 1806, at which point its title was still *The Recluse. Part First. Book First. Home at Grasmere*.

There is much evidence that the fate of the unfinished poem

weighed heavily upon Wordsworth from 1800 to 1806. "I am very anxious," he writes to Coleridge on 6 March 1804, the time at which he was producing the most important philosophical passages of *The Prelude*, "to have your notes for the Recluse. I cannot say how much importance I attach to this; if it should please God that I survive you, I should reproach myself forever in writing the work if I had neglected to procure this help." And three weeks later, after news of Coleridge's illness while waiting to set sail to Malta, Wordsworth confesses that "Your last letter but one informing us of your late attack was the severest shock to me, I think, I have ever received. . . . I cannot help saying that I would gladly have given 3 fourths of my possessions for your letter on The Recluse at that time. . . . Do for heaven's sake, put this out of the reach of accident immediately." [43] What Wordsworth is after from Coleridge is a way to begin—and he does not get it. Yet in letters to friends and patrons, Wordsworth continues to outline his plans for the poem and reasserts his determination to devote to it "the Prime of my life, and the chief force of my mind." [44] When he finally completes the expanded version of *The Prelude*, he writes on 25 December 1804 to Beaumont, "then I propose to fall with all my might on [*The Recluse*], which is the chief object upon which my thoughts have been fixed these many years." [45]

Blockage of another sort occurs when *The Prelude* is finished in May 1805. Instead of feeling free and happy, Wordsworth is depressed. "I finished my Poem about a fortnight ago," he writes to Beaumont on 3 June 1805. "I had looked forward to the day as a most happy one . . . but it was not a happy day for me I was dejected on many accounts; when I looked back upon the performance it seemed to have a dead weight about it, the reality so far short of the expectation; it was the first long labour that I had finished, and the doubt whether I should ever live to write the Recluse, and the sense that I had of this Poem being so far below what I seemed capable of executing, depressed me much." [46] Six months later, Dorothy is writing of her brother as "very anxious to get forward" and "reading for the nourishment of his mind, preparatory to beginning"; [47] that is, no doubt, trying for himself (in Coleridge's absence) to find appropriate philosophical terms for the central section of *The Recluse*, which as yet consisted only of the incomplete first part of book one. When Wordsworth at last returned to *Home at Grasmere* sometime in the late spring or early summer of 1806, he revised what he had already written in 1800, added a bit more, as well as the title "Book First, *The Recluse*," and moved the lines originally conceived of as the poem's "Prospectus" to the end. This last move completed "Book First," but it turned *Home at Grasmere* into another preface or deferral, as opposed to the thing itself. Once again, Wordsworth had evaded the task at hand, even as he was performing it.

At which point, still unable to face the central section of *The Recluse*, he turned back to *The Excursion*, the narrative poem he had earlier, in an 1804 letter to De Quincey, described as a quite separate project ("I have also [in addition to *The Prelude* and *The Recluse*] arranged the plan of a narrative poem").[48] A year later, though, Wordsworth spoke of this poem as part of *The Recluse* itself, and, when it was finally finished in 1814, that is how it was advertised. For Wordsworth prefaces *The Excursion* with the lines originally intended for the "Prospectus" to *Home at Grasmere*, thus keeping the longer poem alive to the public and identifying *The Excursion* as a sort of relief or respite from the as-yet-unwritten philosophical speculations of the central section.

Between 1806 and 1814, while busying himself with *The Excursion* and revisions to *The Prelude*, Wordsworth made one other attempt at book two of the main body of *The Recluse*. This was the 594-line fragment "The Tuft of Primroses," composed in 1808. It is clear from this fragment that Wordsworth has begun to lose hope. Instead of using philosophy to move beyond the personal or biographical and to reveal "future glories and restoration," as had been his original intention (and also Coleridge's), he turns to history.[49] What history suggests, though, throughout "The Tuft of Primroses," is that human endeavor is always "sullied and disguised" and that no lasting achievement—which is what Wordsworth hoped *The Recluse* would be—is possible. At the same time, solitude is no longer viewed as a way forward, but as evasion—the longing for rest or quietude, a life in which "hope and meaning are as one" (292).[50]

After the publication of *The Excursion* in 1814, Wordsworth turned immediately not to *The Recluse*, which it so grandiloquently advertised, but to the readying of a two-volume collected *Poems*, to be published in 1815.[51] At the same time, he began to revise *The Prelude*, and, just as expansion of *The Prelude* was a way of evading *The Recluse* in previous years, revision of it served a comparable defensive function in the years that remained. These defensive maneuvers resemble the movements of the river at the beginning of book nine of *The Prelude*, which serves as a recurrent symbol of the poet's mind and of the form of the poem as it traces that mind's development. Like the river, Wordsworth is frightened to death of the "onward road" (9.3), seeing it as leading "direct to the devouring sea" (9.4). Hence his evasive "motions retrograde" (9.8), as if *The Recluse* itself, like the river's "way direct," in the 1850 version, "would engulph him" (9.3, 4).

Of these fears, Wordsworth's family and closest friends were fully aware. When in 1824 it seemed that Wordsworth might get back to work on the poem, his wife hid her hopes "lest he should be scared by the prospect."[52] Dorothy told Crabb Robinson that her brother felt "the task so weighty that he shrinks from beginning it."[53] Yet neither she nor Wordsworth's wife could remain silent. "After fifty years of age there is no time to spare," writes Dorothy in 1821, "and unfinished works should not, if it be possible, be left behind."[54] In 1828 Wordsworth's daughter Dora writes to her future husband, Edward Quillinan, of *The Power of Sound* that though "we all think that there is a grandeur in this poem . . . it ought to have been in *The Recluse*, and Mother on that account but half enjoys it." A month later, she writes of how "every day he finds something to alter, or new stanzas to add, or a fresh sonnet—or a fresh poem growing out of one just finished, which he always promises will be his last."[55] In 1831 he returns at last to *The Recluse*, but manages only a further revision of *Home at Grasmere*, before turning again to more revisions of *The Prelude*. In 1832 Dora writes that though her mother is still complaining about Wordsworth's "tiresome small poems" and is "vexed that she cannot get him down to his long work," she herself does not "believe that *The Recluse* will ever be finished."[56] In 1836, when a new edition of *The Excursion* was published, the words "Being a Portion of *The Recluse*" were removed from the title page. Finally, two years later in May 1838, the American George Ticknor visited the Wordsworths and recorded the following observation in his *Journal:*

> Mrs Wordsworth asked me to talk to him about finishing . . . *The Recluse;* saying that she could not bear to have him occupied constantly in writing sonnets and other trifles, while this great work lay by him untouched, but that she had ceased to urge him on the subject, because she had done it so much in vain. I asked him about it, therefore. He said that the Introduction, which is a sort of autobiography, is completed. This I knew, for he read me large portions of it twenty years ago. . . . On my asking him why he does not finish it he turned to me very decidedly, and said, "Why did not Gray finish the long poem he began on a similar subject? Because he found he had undertaken something beyond his powers to accomplish. And that is my case." We controverted his position, of course; but I am not certain the event will not prove that he has acted upon his belief. At any rate, I have no hope it will ever by completed.[57]

In one sense, this melancholy history is hardly one of blockage because with each evasion came new work, and it could well be argued, in the manner of Kenneth Johnston, that the "creative fiction" of *The Recluse* was subconsciously useful to Wordsworth and that his "dutiful commitment to his large public project freed his imagination to create shorter poems of more enduring value." [58] In another sense, though, this new work was but a way of putting off the work that mattered, and Wordsworth himself felt thwarted, for all his productivity. This is part of the pressure under which he is laboring at the beginning of *The Prelude*. The resourcefulness with which he made the experience of blockage his subject seems never to have removed from Wordsworth the sense that he was blocked.

The Case of Coleridge

The evidence that Coleridge suffered from writer's block is of several sorts. To begin with, there is the simple fact of how little he produced. If Wordsworth's "golden prime" as a poet was limited to the work of a decade, Coleridge's, according to E. K. Chambers, amounted to a mere "handful of golden poems."[1] Coleridge wrote twice as many lines between the ages of eighteen and twenty-six as in all the following thirty-six years of his life. And the lines that live—the handful of golden ones—are those written in the early period. Most of the important poems were produced between 1795 and 1798, except for what Norman Fruman calls the "Indian summer"[2] of Coleridge's poetic creativity in 1802, the year in which he composed not only "Dejection: An Ode" but also "The Picture" and "Hymn Before Sunrise, in the Vale of Chamouni." Thereafter, only "The Blossoming of the Solitary Date Tree" (1805), "To William Wordsworth" (1806), and a scattering of short, despairing lyrics—"The Pains of Sleep" (1803), "Human Life" (1815), "Limbo" (1817), "Ne Plus Ultra" (1817), "Work Without Hope" (1825), and "Coeli Enarrant" (1830)—have commanded serious attention.[3] Between 1801 and 1806, from his twenty-ninth to his thirty-fourth year, Coleridge published almost nothing. "No major writer whose life we know well," comments W. J. Bate, "has been so reduced, for so long a period or at so crucial a time in his life."[4]

Even when in his prime, though, Coleridge's poetry betrays signs of blockage. Two of his three most important poems, "Kubla Khan" (1798) and "Christabel" (1797), are incomplete, while the third, "The Ancient Mariner" (1798), is "in its author's own testimony, unsatisfactory in its completion."[5] The so-called conversation poems are neurotically hedged with apologies and disclaimers, as if for Coleridge their very appearance depended upon an admission of inadequacy. As for the *Biographia Literaria* (1817), the most important of Coleridge's prose works, structurally it is a mess, an "immethodical miscellany,"[6] aptly subtitled a collection of biographical "Sketches,"

full of distracting stops and starts, lost or unfollowed arguments, ex-
cuses and deferrals, with internal subheadings such as "A chapter of
digressions and anecdotes" and "A Chapter of requests and premonitions concerning the perusal or omission of the chapter that follows."
Crucial conclusions are "reserved for a further publication" or are
simply abandoned with a row of asterisks.[7] "Of all the books that
have been influential in modern times," writes Walter Pater of Coleridge's three most important prose works, *Biographia Literaria, Aids to
Reflection* (1825), and *The Friend* (1809–10), "they are furthest from
artistic form—bundles of notes; the original matter inseparably
mixed up with that borrowed from others; the whole just that mere
preparation for an artistic effect which the finished literary artist
would be careful one day to destroy." *The Friend,* according to Hazlitt,
was "an enormous title-page; the longest and most tiresome prospectus that ever was written; an endless preface to an imaginary work."[8]
Its last number typically ends: "To be continued in the next number."

Coleridge's career is littered with half-finished projects, partially
written theses, tracts, epic poems, philosophical and theological treatises, promised but unwritten letters and articles. McFarland quotes
Charles Lamb, joking in 1815: "Coleridge is just dead. . . . Poor Coleridge, but two days before he died he wrote to a bookseller proposing
an epic poem on the 'Wanderings of Cain,' in twenty-four books. It is
said he has left behind him forty-thousand treatises in criticism and
metaphysics, but few of them in a state of completion."[9] Nowhere is
this dispiriting pattern of projection and deferral clearer than in the
case of the "Opus Maximum," a vast philosophical synthesis first
mentioned as early as 1796, and publicly advertised in 1814, and
again in 1817 in the *Biographia Literaria.* In 1814 Coleridge wrote a
letter claiming that he was in the process of printing the work in
Bristol. But he did not get down to writing any of it until he took up
residence with James Gillman in 1816. The work itself was never finished, its products dispersed in a variety of lesser publications and
unfinished projects, though several hundred manuscript pages of it
exist.

Coleridge was fully aware of the reputation his unfulfilled promises were earning him. As he writes in the "Prospectus" of *The Friend,*
"the number of my unrealized schemes, and the mss. of my miscellaneous fragments, have often furnished my friends with a subject of
Raillery, and sometimes of Regret and Reproof."[10] "I became a prov-
erb to the University for Idleness," he writes of his Cambridge days,
"—the time, which I should have bestowed on the academic studies,
I employed in dreaming schemes."[11] The problem, he continues in
the "Prospectus" of *The Friend,* was "overactivity of thought, modi-

fied by a constitutional Indolence, which made it more pleasant to me to continue acquiring, than to reduce what I had acquired to a regular form. . . . In Order fully to comprehend and develop any one Subject, it was necessary that I should make myself Master of some other, which again as regularly involved a third, and so on, with an ever-widening Horizen."[12] Here, as elsewhere, the problem is conceived of not as dearth or desiccation but as excess. As Coleridge says in a Notebook entry of 1804, his mind (like that of Eliot's Casaubon) is jammed with "large Stores of . . . unwrought materials; scarcely a day passes but something new in fact or in illustration . . . rises up in me, like Herbs or Flowers in a Garden in early Spring; but the combining Power, the power to do, the manly effective *Will*, that is dead or slumbers most diseasedly."[13] Throughout the Notebooks and letters, lack of productivity is experienced, in the words of Kristine Dugas, "as a deadening or blank void and as an internal storm, a Wordsworthian formulation of a mind 'vexed by its own creation'. . . . [P]owers felt to be frozen or suspended exist simultaneously with a vital creativity which persists but which has no outlet except to rage destructively about itself."[14]

Coleridge adduces several sources to explain his difficulties. In 1800 he complains that "my taste in judging is far, far more perfect than my power to execute."[15] Elsewhere, but in a similar vein, he is convinced that he "never had the essentials of poetic genius, and . . . mistook a strong desire for original power."[16] At other times, though, the picture is less clear, which makes his inactivity a source of mystery and guilt. "All this evening," he writes in an 1804 Notebook entry, "indeed all this day . . . I ought to have [been] reading and filling the margins of Malthus—I had begun and found it pleasant / Why did I neglect it?. . . . Surely this is well worth a serious Analysis, that understanding I may attempt to heal / For it is a deep and wide disease in my personal nature."[17] As this passage suggests, Coleridge by no means accepted inherent incapacity as an explanation for his failure to produce. It is not really that he lacks power, rather that he is "weak—apt to faint away inwardly, self-deserted and bereft of the confidence of my own powers."[18] The psychological nature of his difficulties is clear from the manner in which they manifest themselves. In 1814 he writes of being driven by "an indefinite indescribable Terror," one in which "the worst was, that in *exact proportion* to the *importance* and *urgency* of any Duty was it, as a fated necessity, sure to be neglected."[19] "My case is a species of madness, only that it is a derangement, an utter impotence of the *Volition*, and not of the intellectual faculties—you bid me rouse myself—go, bid a man paralytic in both arms rub them briskly together, and that will cure him. Alas!

(he would reply) that I cannot move my arms is my complaint and my misery."[20] This comment recalls De Quincey's account of Coleridge's appearance during the course of one of the few lectures he managed to deliver in 1808, at the very height of his blockage. His appearance "was generally that of a person struggling with pain and overmastering illness. His lips were baked with feverish heat, and often black in colour; and, in spite of the water which he continued drinking through the whole course of his lecture, he often seemed to labour under an almost paralytic inability to raise the upper jaw from the lower."[21]

That Coleridge never came to terms with his "paralysis"—but continued to struggle against it—is part of the reason why it makes sense to think of him as suffering from writer's block. In McFarland's words, "he did not bear his troubles with the stoic dignity of Wordsworth; rather he lived a life of deception made unquiet by interminable self-justifications and hypochondriac fancies. . . . He plagiarized; he procrastinated; he spent a dismaying amount of effort, as Dorothy Wordsworth said, 'in deceiving himself and seeking to deceive others.'"[22] Writing was a torment for Coleridge: "all the hell of an Author. I wish, I had been a tanner," he declares in a typical letter of 1800.[23] "I torture the poem, and myself, with corrections," he writes of his attempts in 1797 to finish "The Force of Destiny" (1817), "and what I wrote in an hour, I sometimes take two or three days in correcting."[24] Of "Christabel," he confesses in another letter that "every line has been produced by me with labour pangs."[25] Yet he never ceased trying to write, and his lack of productivity remained a continuing source of shame and self-reproach. "Yesterday was my Birth Day," he writes in a Notebook entry of 1804, "so completely has a whole year passed, with scarcely the fruits of a *month*.—O Sorrow and Shame! I am not worthy to live—Two and Thirty Years.—and this last year above all others!—I have done nothing!"[26] As this despairing entry suggests, strength of mind and breadth of learning were never in themselves enough for Coleridge. As he wrote of Hamlet, in words that have long been understood autobiographically, "action is the great end of all. No intellect, however grand, is valuable if it draws us from action and lead us to think and think till the time of action is passed by and we can do nothing."[27]

Coleridge's Psychology

Coleridge usually spoke of his troubles as psychological in nature. "I am a Starling self-encaged," he tells William Godwin, "and always in the Moult, and my whole Note is, Tomorrow, and tomorrow, and tomorrow."[28] "I have never loved Evil for its own sake," he writes of his addiction to opium, "nor . . . ever sought pleasure for its own sake, but only as a means of escaping from pains that coiled round my mental powers."[29] As Sara Coleridge wrote after her husband's death, in words that corroborate the psychological account of his addiction, "nothing was observed which could be ascribed to Laudanum, and the internal pain and uneasiness which he had suffered from all his life, and which my mother remembers his complaining of before he had ever recourse to opium, is supposed to have been some sympathetic nervous affliction."[30] That Coleridge's physical symptoms were worse when he was alone also supports the psychological account and relates directly to the inhibition of his creative powers. "The stimulus of conversation suspends the terror that haunts my mind; but whenever I am alone, the horrors . . . almost overwhelm me."[31] And writing, because a solitary occupation, is therefore dangerous. Hence Coleridge's lifelong "addiction" to conversation. A friend remembers him at Cambridge "ready at any time to unbend in conversation," his rooms in college being "a constant rendezvous of conversation-loving friends."[32] Even in the midst of Coleridge's darkest decade, in conversation, notes a contemporary, he was "the image of power and activity. His eloquence is unimpaired."[33] Yet when, in Hazlitt's sneering words, "he lays down his pen to make sure of an auditor [he] mortgages the admiration of posterity for the stare of an idler."[34]

Many of the most revealing accounts of Coleridge's neurosis occur in the Notebooks, as in the following entry of 1805:

> that I have been always preyed on by some Dread, and perhaps all my faulty actions have been the consequence of some Dread or other on my mind /—so in my childhood and Boyhood the horror of being detected with a sorehead . . . then a short-lived Fit of Fears from sex . . . then came Rob. Southey's alienation / my marriage—constant dread in my mind respecting Mrs. Coleridge's Temper . . . and finally stimulants in the fear and prevention of violent Bowel-attacks from mental agitation / then ⟨almost epileptic⟩ night-horrors in my sleep / . . . all this interwoven with its minor consequences, that fill up the interspaces—the cherry juice running in between the cherries in a cherry pie / procrast. in dread of this—and something else in consequence of that procrastination and etc.[35]

The importance of this passage lies in its refusal to locate the source of dread in any single external factor or physical ailment, but to see it as deeper—and present from the earliest days. Blockage, here, is but a symptom, "the cherry juice running in between the cherries."

Coleridge's childhood circumstances provide the first clue to his difficulties: they perfectly evidence what Winnicott would call a "nonfacilitating environment." Coleridge was the youngest of ten children, nine of whom were brothers, and though youngest children are often the objects of special affection, this is not always felt as an advantage in a large family. "My Father was very fond of me," recalls Coleridge, "and I was mother's darling—in consequence, I was very miserable."[36] In McFarland's words, "the likelihood of fragmentation of attention and relation on the part of the parents, and of the damaging aggressiveness from the jealously competing brothers, would inevitably be very high in such a situation."[37] McFarland supports this likelihood with the odd scarcity of Coleridge's references to his mother and with the coldness of a number of the references that do exist (in contrast to Wordsworth, Coleridge left almost no poetical accounts of his childhood, except for a couple of brief passages in the conversation poems). For instance, in the series of autobiographical letters Coleridge wrote to Thomas Poole in 1797, the only comment he manages to make about his mother is that she "was an admirable Economist, and managed exclusively."[38] In the nine unhappy years Coleridge spent at school at Christ's Hospital, he was never once visited by his mother, and only very rarely by other members of his family. He himself seems to have paid only three or possibly four short trips back to his home over the years, presumably because he was allowed no more. James Dykes Campbell called the mother "unemotional" and "comparatively uneducated." Gillman called her "a very good woman . . . over careful in many things, very ambitious for the advancement of her sons in life, but wanting perhaps that flow of heart which her husband possessed so largely." Richard Holmes, Coleridge's most recent biographer, describes her as having "all the ambition and drive of a perfect headmaster's wife."[39]

Coleridge deeply felt this lack of maternal love. At sixteen, he said of a school friend's mother that "she taught me what it was to have a mother"; at twenty-nine, he told Poole that Mrs. Poole "was the only being whom I ever *felt* in the relation of Mother."[40] He was equally open about the importance of maternal love to a child's development. In a letter of 1807 to his son Derwent, on the occasion of a separation from his wife, he greatly stresses the need for respect from son to mother: "She gave *you* nourishment out of her own Breasts . . . and she brought you into the world with shocking pains. . . . So it must needs be a horribly wicked Thing ever to forget, or wilfully to vex, a father or a mother: especially a mother."[41] This was from a man who in adult life rarely returned to visit his own mother and pointedly failed to attend her funeral.

That Coleridge felt abandoned by his family, his mother in particular, seems not, as the above passage suggests, to have alleviated a sense of guilt about her and a sense of her as wronged or injured—perhaps as a result of what Kleinian and post-Kleinian analysts would identify as aggressive projections. If in childhood one is "depressed, moping, friendless, [a] poor orphan, half starved," and as a consequence feels that "no one on earth has ever *Loved* me,"[42] one is likely to react angrily as well as needily. In Coleridge's case, aggression can be detected in terrifying images of the injured and avenging—as well as loveless and unreliable—mother. "Beneath the foulest mother's curse," he writes of the effect of such images in "The Three Graves" (1798), "No child could ever thrive: / A mother is a mother still; / The holiest thing alive" (256–59). This duality finds its complement in a letter of 1794: "Alas! my poor Mother! What an intolerable weight of guilt is suspended over my head by a hair on one hand—and if I endure to live—the look ever downward—insult—pity—and hell."[43]

The radical sense of insecurity that resulted from Coleridge's feelings of alienation from his mother accounts in part for the prominence of the themes of isolation and abandonment in his verse. The experience of loneliness pervades Coleridge's poetry: it lies at the heart of "The Ancient Mariner," is an important strand of "Christabel"—in which the absence of a protecting mother figures prominently—and is the starting point for almost all the conversation poems. "The Outcast," "The Hour when we shall meet again. *(Composed during Illness and in Absence),*" "Fears in Solitude," "The Wanderings of Cain," "An Exile," "The Blossoming of the Solitary Date Tree," "Separation," "Homeless," "Not at Home"—poem after poem presents us with images of abandonment and isolation, which is also why so much importance is attached to the themes of fellowship and hospitality, of the need for communion with both nature and other people.

His family background also helps to account for the frequency with which Coleridge, in his life as well as in his work, seeks to place himself in a position of dependence—seeks to be cared for and comforted as in childhood. Holmes points to the frequency of nursing and sickroom incidents in Coleridge's life and work, "in which the distinction between the adult and child could be magically suspended, responsibilities waived, and physical tenderness be freely exchanged without sexual guilt."[44] At the age of thirty-two, having been married for ten years and having fathered three children, Coleridge reveals in his Notebook that he has for the first time experienced "the melancholy, dreadful feeling of finding myself to be *Man,* by a distinct division from Boyhood, Youth, and 'Young Man.'—

Dreadful was the feeling—before that Life had flown on so that I had always been *a Boy*, as it were." [45] Only when Coleridge was able to re-create a position for himself as child—first in 1790–91 with the Evans family (three daughters and a mother who doted on Coleridge) in London, then, immediately afterward, with Robert Southey and the Fricker family (five daughters and a widowed mother) in Bristol, then with Wordsworth and Dorothy, then with the Gillman family in Highgate—did the more extreme and painful manifestations of his dread subside, so he was able to work and to finish what he began. "Ensconced benignly on the top floor of the hard-working Gillman's house in Highgate," writes McFarland, "Coleridge seems to us, by his obliviousness to many elements of adult responsibility, to be something like a pink, friendly infant of enormous mental powers." [46] However, the consequent spurt of creative activity at Highgate did not last long: Coleridge's childlike need for immediate gratification and his lifelong aversion to profitable labor soon reasserted themselves.

Coleridge and Object Relations

Coleridge was plagued not only with a pervading sense of isolation and abandonment but by fears of the world's instability, its unreliability. Here also we can attribute his difficulties to childhood experience, as in what probably seemed to him, for example, a capricious and bewildering removal from family to school, a removal that followed immediately, at the age of nine, upon his father's wholly unexpected death in 1781. "Me at the spot where first I sprang to light," recalls Coleridge in 1797, at the age of twenty-five, "Too soon transplanted, ere my soul had fix'd / Its first domestic loves; and hence through life / Chasing chance-started friendships" ("To the Rev. George Coleridge," 17–20). Whereas Wordsworth was able to project onto nature the sustaining and anchoring comforts of mother love, Coleridge could do so only briefly, under Wordsworth's influence. For Coleridge, the object world was marked, above all, by radical instability, as the deep divisions in the worlds of even his most famous poems attest. In "The Ancient Mariner," for example, a Wordsworthian vision of the essential unity and benevolence of nature, of the value of even its foulest and most insignificant-seeming creatures, is flatly and inexplicably contradicted by the poem's supernatural machinery, especially the memorable image of Death and Death-in-Life (two mother figures?) *gaming* for the mariner's soul. Similarly, though "The Eolian Harp" sings of a harmonious nature, of "the one life within us and abroad," its song is also, somehow, "wild," "various," "random," with intimations of sin and abandon, of "coy maids," "lovers," and "wooings," of the "unregenerate" and "sinful." A comparably disquieting note is struck by the eerily unstable moral identities of the characters in "Christabel," in which victim is also perpetrator ("Sure I have sinn'd," Christabel confesses in line 381), and the evil agent, Geraldine, the "worker of these harms" (298), looks like a victim "still and mild" (300). Such instabilities are of a piece with the mysterious, contingent nature of the many crimes that litter Coleridge's poems. In "Cain" (1798), *Osorio* (1797, but not performed until 1813, in a rewritten version entitled *Remorse*), "The Ancient Mariner," "The Three Graves," "Christabel," and "Kubla Khan," terrible crimes are committed (or suspected) against nature and man, and in each case the relation between motive and causation is shadowy and obscure. The world is changeable, unreliable.

In the 1790s, under the influence of Wordsworth, Coleridge produced a number of poems celebrating the healing and enlightening powers of nature. In "This Lime-tree Bower my Prison" (1797), "The Nightingale" (1798), and "Frost at Midnight" (1798), for example, nature is clearly benevolent and anchoring; "Influxes from without," as Coleridge says in his Notebook, "counteracting the Impulses from within, and *poising* the Thought."[47] But this period of faith in outward forms was short-lived, and, in subsequent poems, letters, and Notebook entries, nature not only figures less prominently but also is often inadequate and unstable. The fleeting "superficies of objects," Coleridge writes in 1803, only weaken "the Health and manhood of Intellect." "Of all men I ever knew," he writes in 1804, "I have the faintest pleasure in things contingent and transitory."[48] "I can *at times* feel strongly the beauties you describe," he writes to John Thelwall, "but more frequently all things appear little . . . the universe itself— what but an immense heap of *little* things? . . . My mind feels as if it ached to behold and know something *great*—something *one and individual*."[49]

This sense of nature as bewilderingly various (a "heap") and insignificant ("little") is characteristic of many later passages of natural description in the Notebook entries, entries that fall into a recurring pattern: though they begin with a vision of unity and harmony, one that seems to awaken creative powers, this initial stimulus is quickly followed by a moment of self-consciousness and disillusion, and then by a reaction in which nature itself is turned on, as untrustworthy and delusional.[50] For the most part, when nature disappoints in these passages it does so not because it is barren, but because it is overwhelming; its richness and amplitude, among other things, seem to mock Coleridge's own creative debility.[51]

Coleridge's view of the unreliability of outward forms is a prominent theme in a number of his poems. In "Lines Written in the Album at Elbingerode" (1799) a mountaintop vision of "Woods crowding upon woods, hills over hills,/ A surging scene" (2–3) leads to the conclusion that "outward forms" per se—that is, forms untouched by "the Life within"—are "Fair cyphers . . . of import vague / Or unconcerning" (17–20). In "Apologia pro Vita sua" (1800), the true poet "emancipates his eyes / From the black shapeless accidents of size" (3–4). In "The Keepsake" (1800), a lovingly detailed initial passage of natural description offers little sustenance to the lovelorn speaker— is all transience and loss—in contrast to "the flowers which Emmeline / With delicate fingers on the snow-white silk / Has worked" (14–16). In "A Stranger Minstrel" (1800), the glories of Mount Skiddaw only underline the absence of the speaker-minstrel's beloved, a symbol of inspiration; we and the minstrel realize he was mistaken to look for her in nature, because she, in the mountain's own words, "scorns a mount" that is "bleak and bare" (33). In "The Picture" (1802,) nature is again delusional, its protagonist, another "love-lorn man" who "would be something that he knows not of, / In winds or waters, or among the rocks" (24–25), being labeled a "Gentle lunatic" (21), and its narrator, who attempts to commune with a more "objective" reality, one unadulterated by projections of love, being no less misguided.[52] Hence the poem's closing invocation of Homer, the blind poet, the poet of "inward light" (12).

At this point, though, matters become darker and more complicated, for in other of Coleridge's poems the inadequacy of the outer world is matched by a sense of the unreliability of personal or internal resources; and again we can conjecture psychological or infant origins for such unreliability and also a direct link to creative inhibition. To begin with, there are the many motiveless crimes mentioned earlier, as well as correspondingly inexplicable moments of personal redemption, as when "a spring of love" (284) gushes from the heart of the mariner and he blesses the water snakes "unawares" (285). If every Christabel can be a Geraldine, or vice versa, how can the self be trusted? How, moreover, can it be trusted to speak, as it must do in art?[53] Hence the several poems in which Coleridge's speakers are unable to speak, as in the 1796 sonnet beginning "When they did greet me father," in which Coleridge—understandably, given his feelings about adulthood—fails to respond appropriately to the news of his son's birth. On receiving the news, Coleridge "retired and knelt / Seeking the throne of grace, but inly felt / No heavenly visitation upwards draw / My feeble mind, nor cheering ray impart" (2–5).[54] Coleridge's prayers are thwarted by "Th'unquiet silence of confused thought / And shapeless feelings" (7–8): he is blocked by an ominous inner disharmony that recalls the mariner's inability to pray when alone on "a wide wide sea" (233). "I looked to heaven," the mariner tells us, "and tried to pray; / But or ever a prayer had gusht, / A wicked whisper came, and made / My heart as dry as dust" (244–47). These lines recall a comparable moment in "The Pains of Sleep" (1803), in which the speaker's "Thirst of revenge" is blocked by a "powerless will / Still baffled, and yet burning still! / Desire with loathing strangely mixed / On wild or hateful subjects fixed" (21–24).

It is "Christabel," though, that provides the most telling examples of inner instability as a source of blocked utterance, particularly when Christabel loses the power of speech in part two, "the moment that dominates the narrative, the moment for which everything else seems only a preparation."[55] When roused from the trance that has produced her terrifying transformation, the maid falls at her father's feet and can only ask that Geraldine be sent away: "and more she could not say: / For what she knew she could not tell / O'er-mastered by the mighty spell" (618–20). The significance of this moment is hinted at in the enigmatic conclusion that follows, which is less a conclusion than a veiled or symbolic account of why the poem is abandoned.[56] The conclusion introduces a mysterious "limber elf" or "fairy thing," whose father loves it deeply. Yet when the father "at last / Must needs express his love's excess," all that issues from him are "words of unmeant bitterness" (663–65). The father's irrational violence prompts a general reflection from the narrator, one that sadly acknowledges the frequency—the typicality—of such discordant responses:

> . . . in a world of sin
> (O sorrow and shame should this be true!)
> Such giddiness of heart and brain
> Comes seldom save from rage and pain,
> So talks as it's most used to do.
> (673–77)

The father, like Coleridge in the sonnet on his son's birth, and like many of the speakers in others of his poems, cannot be trusted to utter his thoughts, so deeply unstable or "giddy" are they. The bitterness the speakers express is spontaneous or inadvertent, but it accurately reflects a deep emotional instability, which grows out of "rage and pain"; in Coleridge's case, emotions that originate from intense childhood experiences. Instances such as these suggest that Coleridge's blockage as a writer is as likely to derive from distrust of the inner self as of the objects that make up the material or outer world.

The narrator of "Christabel" is as volatile and undependable as the world and the characters he would communicate. Under such circumstances, art or utterance is dangerous, and it is better to say nothing, to simply break off in midpoem.

Coleridge's Plagiarisms

Coleridge's distrust of personal utterance and his acute sense of abandonment or isolation result not only in blockage but also in plagiarism. Of the several theories McFarland advances in explanation and mitigation of Coleridge's notorious "borrowings," the most interesting—in part because it is explanatory rather than exculpatory—relates to the complex of psychological issues discussed earlier in this chapter. McFarland begins by quoting two passages from the Notebooks:

> [The] first lesson that innocent childhood affords me, is—that it is an instinct of my Nature to pass out of myself, and to exist in the form of others.

> My nature requires another nature for its support, and reposes only in another form from the necessary indigence of its Being.

To these passages, one might add two others: Coleridge's plea of 1805 to Wordsworth, "that my Spirit purged by Death of its Weaknesses, which are alas! my *identity* might flow into *thine*, and live and act in thee, and be Thou"; and a comparable plea to Poole in 1796 to be "*near you*, to see you daily, to tell you all my thoughts in their first birth, and to hear your's, to be mingling identities with you, as it were."[57]

Each of these passages reveals Coleridge's deep need to identify with others, which McFarland relates not only to his troubled feelings about his mother but also to his relation to his brothers. "It seems that Coleridge developed an extreme anxiety from his relation to his brothers, and that this, as another form of the infantile sense of object loss, operated in conjunction with the more basic anxiety connected with his mother."[58] The poem that matters most in this context is "The Ancient Mariner," in which the protagonist's isolation is prefigured in the initial reaction of his shipmates to the disastrous consequences of his shooting of the albatross. As the gloss puts it, "The shipmates would fain throw the whole guilt on the Ancient Mariner," an unkindness that can be seen as symbolic of Coleridge's sense of the treatment his brothers had visited upon him throughout his life. "By poor Frank's dislike of me when a little Child," Coleridge writes of the brother from whom he claims to have suffered most, "I was ever from Infancy forced to be by myself."[59] The consequence of this sense of fraternal hostility and isolation was what McFarland calls "not merely a single but a double dependency, that is, he seems to have replaced the threatening brother and cold mother with an accepting brother and warm mother."[60] Hence, in part, the strength of his initial devotion to Southey and the Frickers, to Dorothy and William Wordsworth, and to the Gillman family.

That the brother was for Coleridge in some sense a figure of the father ("God bless you—my Brother—My Father!"[61] is how Coleridge closes a letter to his brother George in 1794) accounts in part for the doomed nature of the surrogate relations he formed, in particular those with the Wordsworths. Coleridge sought strength in Wordsworth and hoped to gain solidity and security as poet and man by contact with him. Yet Coleridge was also threatened by such contact because of the dependent or childlike relation it entailed, which was suffused with Oedipal anxiety.[62] On the one hand, Coleridge sought out brother figures to protect him against the father; on the other hand, these figures were themselves symbolic fathers. As a consequence, defense and transgression were indissolubly linked; one form of "stealing"—that is, stealing the father's place by writing words of one's own—gave way to another: plagiarism. The impulse to merge, to identify with the strength of an accepting brother, was also an attack, a literal theft of his words.

McFarland associates the plagiarisms with another of Coleridge's neurotic habits: compulsive annotation, a "lifelong fondness for joining marginalia to the books he read, a form of composition that, in terms of the number and variety of the books so adorned . . . has no real counterpart in either English or continental literature."[63] Such a habit or compulsion was, at the most, merely wasteful (of time and mental energy); the plagiarisms were something worse and became themselves sources, as well as symptoms, of blocking anxiety.[64] What Coleridge's contemporaries would have thought of McFarland's gloomy and convoluted psychoanalytic account of the plagiarisms is unknowable; it is clear, however, that they shared his sense of their guilt-inducing and inhibiting effect on Coleridge and that they refused to attribute them to anything as simple as a lack of ideas or inspiration. In De Quincey's words, Coleridge "spun daily, and at all hours, for mere amusement . . . theories more gorgeous by far, and supported by a pomp and luxury of images such as neither Schelling—no, nor any German that ever breathed, not John Paul—could have emulated in his dreams."[65]

Coleridge's Poetry of Blockage:
"Dejection: An Ode"

Chief among the texts that document Coleridge's struggles with blockage is "Dejection: An Ode," a poem especially interesting to the student of writer's block not only for the explicitness with which it discusses creative inhibition but for the light it sheds on two of the more frequently mentioned reasons for Coleridge's abandonment of poetry: his relations with Wordsworth and his turn to metaphysics or "abstruse research." The poem originated in a 340-line verse letter of 4 April 1802, which Coleridge wrote the night after hearing Wordsworth recite the recently composed initial 4 stanzas of "Ode: Intimations of Immortality," stanzas in which doubt seems, at least on the surface, to be overcome by a philosophy of joy in nature.[66]

The finished "Dejection: An Ode" begins with an epigraph from the medieval "Ballad of Patrick Spence," one that hints at the coming of storm and the end of an old dispensation. Coleridge uses the epigraph to introduce his own premonitions of a change in psychological as well as literal "weather," the present being a period of dull tranquility. Coleridge's dullness or deadness is associated, as in Wordsworth's poem, with poetic deadness, for it is a state marked by feeble words, the "dull sobbing draft, that moans and rakes / Upon the strings of this Aeolian lute" (6–7). What is coming promises to rouse Coleridge both as poet and as man: he seeks a "gust" (15) of inspiration, of the sort whose sounds "oft have raised me, whilst they awed, / And sent my soul abroad" (17–18). Such vivifying breezes "Might now perhaps their wonted impulse give, / Might startle this dull pain, and make it move and live!" (19–20). But if one recalls the original context of the ballad, one knows that the breezes might also prove fatal, because in the ballad the change in weather portends "harm" or shipwreck.

That Coleridge is here blocked, as well as depressed, is admitted explicitly in stanza 2. His dreariness is of a sort "which finds no relief / In word, or sigh, or tear" (24)—as if he had tried to utter it but could not. The beauty of the night sky is infected with the poet's deadness. As in the opening stanzas of "Ode: Intimations," natural glories are detailed with a flat and despairing matter-of-factness: "I see them all so excellently fair, / I see, not feel, how beautiful they are" (37–38). The problem, in other words, is conceived of as internal. The outer world is recognized as beautiful, but something within Coleridge prevents him from experiencing and expressing its beauty. That something Coleridge associates with his "genial spirits" (39), a term Wordsworth also uses to describe the poetical faculty. Coleridge does not feel empty; rather, he is a victim of some "smothering weight" (41). This weight deadens or occludes nature, for as Coleridge says in the poem's most famous lines, "O Lady! we receive but what we give, / And in our life alone does Nature live" (47–48). These lines, though, discredit the outer world, as well as the inner one, because without the addition of the soul's "sweet and potent voice" (57) all we are left with is an "inanimate cold world" (51)—a claim that seems to contradict stanza 2's sense of innate glory in the outer world. Coleridge has moved from the suggestion that something is wrong with himself, to the suggestion that there is no beauty or worth, nothing to rely on, independent of the self, which is the very movement detectable in his accounts of natural beauty in the later Notebooks.

In stanza 5, Coleridge explains to the Lady the nature and origins of that "sweet and potent voice" he has lost. What he lacks, he tells her, is "Joy," by which he seems to mean something like "vitality"; and its absence he attributes to a lack of moral worth. "Joy," he tells the "virtuous Lady," is available only "to the pure, and in their purest hour" (65). Joy opens "a new Earth and new Heaven, / Undreamt of by the sensual and the proud" (69–70). Although at first we are tempted to see this claim as an acknowledgement of buried guilt and aggression—the emotions that make all utterance dangerous for Coleridge—in stanza 6 blame is shifted to external circumstances. Early on in his life Coleridge possessed joy, which was strong enough to allow him to "dally" with "distress" (77), to make misfortunes "but as the stuff / Whence Fancy made me dreams of happiness" (78–79); "But now afflictions bow me down to earth" (82), and each "visitation" (84) of misfortune "suspends what nature gave me at my birth, / My shaping spirit of Imagination" (85–86).

In these lines, it is the outer world that has robbed Coleridge of creative joy. Joy is not missing, but is clouded over, or, as Coleridge says in a letter of 1793, one that anticipates the imagery of "Dejection: An Ode," he is "so closely blocked up by an army of misfortunes, that really there is no passage left open for Mirth or anything else."[67] Immediately, though, the loss of joy makes matters worse and sets off an internal process of inhibition, which keeps Coleridge in despair. His only recourse once the accidents of the external world rob him of joy is to emulate Wordsworthian calm or stoicism ("not to think of what I needs must feel, / But to be still and patient, all I can," 87–88), and then, in quite un-Wordsworthian fashion, to turn *from* nature—that is, in this context, to turn from poetry to metaphysics, "And happly by abstruse research to steal / From my own nature all the natural man—/ This was my sole resource, my only plan: / Till that which suits a part infects the whole, / And now is almost grown the habit of my soul" (89–93). Blockage leads Coleridge into yet more blocking habits. The embrace of philosophy is a form of denial, which only locks or tangles him up yet further.

At this point, one of extreme self-consciousness and debility, Coleridge turns yet again, as Wordsworth does so frequently in *The Prelude* and elsewhere, to the outer world. But Coleridge does so with a phrase that neatly captures the doubleness of his dilemma: "Hence, viper thoughts, that coil around my mind, / Reality's dark dream" (94–95). The phrase "Reality's dark dream" suggests that what he has been experiencing is just a "dark dream" of reality and thus the problem is one of subjectivity. But the phrase also suggests that reality itself is a dark dream, so the outer world, the world of externally imposed "misfortunes," is at fault. Thus, when Coleridge attends once more to the wind, he discovers that, though it is no longer "dull" and "sobbing" but wild and energetic (the lute no longer "moans" but sounds instead "a scream / Of agony by torture lengthened out," 97–98), he is still a victim of extreme subjectivity, of the solipsism of the previous stanzas. All of nature's energy is now conceived of in images of extreme horror and terror, and as these images accumulate we realize that the awakened breeze was no external visitation, but a gathering of internal fears and anxieties to something worse than desperation, a move beyond what in "Limbo" Coleridge calls "growthless dull Privation" (35) to "a fear far worse" (37): that "positive Negation" (38) which is the "Ne Plus Ultra" of nightmare. In this state, the "wind" sings of a barren and blasted landscape, of loneliness, of witches, of "all tragic sounds" (108), "of the rushing of a host in rout / With groans, of trampled men, with smarting wounds" (111–12), and, finally and tellingly, of infant isolation:

> . . . of a little child
>   Upon a lonesome wild,
> Not far from home, but she hath lost her way:
> And now moans low in bitter grief and fear,
> And now screams loud, and hopes to make her mother hear.
>   (121–25)

The horrors of Coleridge's projected internal world culminate in a vision of object loss, of the inability to make the mother hear: it is this that is, ultimately, all that Coleridge has to utter, and it is this that he *does not want to hear.*[68]

The poem ends on a somewhat positive note, though what is positive, characteristically, is envisioned as for another. The Lady will be visited by a healthful sleep and by a vision of a beautiful and benevolent night sky, in which "all the stars hang bright above her dwelling, / Silent as though they watched the sleeping Earth!" (130–31)— like a protector or mother. The lines recall the night sky of a crucial marginal gloss to "The Ancient Mariner," in which "everywhere the blue sky belongs to [the stars], and is their appointed rest, and their native country and their own natural homes." For the Lady, joy will not only "lift her spirit" but also "attune her voice" (134). This recuperative moment is importantly different from comparable moments in Wordsworth or in others of Coleridge's poems, for it offers little in the way of compensation for Coleridge himself. Although "Tintern Abbey" ends with Wordsworth's hopes for another (Dorothy), they form part of his own "abundant recompense," a recompense Coleridge is denied. At the end of "This Lime-tree Bower my Prison," Coleridge is able to "contemplate / With lively joy the joys we cannot share" (66–67). Here, though, there is no such communion. The positive note is more muted and poignant.

The poignancy is especially marked when one considers the circumstances of the poem's publication. "Dejection: An Ode" was published on Wordsworth's wedding day, and McFarland sees its concluding affirmation (at least for the Lady) as "a kind of wedding gift and affectionate acquiescence in the philosophy of joy once more."[69] Even here, then, in the most potent and unsparing of Coleridge's admissions of blockage and defeat, of the inability either to assert faith in the Wordsworthian philosophy or to find some other poetical creed to replace it, he capitulates. Although the main burden of "Dejection: An Ode" is a denial of the enabling link between communion with natural objects and poetic power, the message is muddied at the poem's conclusion. Coleridge still cannot get out from under Wordsworth's influence, which in part explains his turn from poetry to metaphysics or "abstruse research." It is as if, having lost faith in the Wordsworthian vision, Coleridge was unable to conceive of poetry as a means of communicating either his despair or his search for truth and security. Hence the turn to "abstruse research."[70]

When Coleridge turns to metaphysics, then, he does so partly out of a sense of poetic inadequacy, out of blockage. Yet the "turn" itself, as "Dejection: An Ode" suggests, begins to feel like the problem, especially because Coleridge never really gives up the wish to write poetry. Hence the several Notebook entries and letters in which a "loss" of poetic power is attributed to "my long and exceedingly severe Metaphysical Investigations," and what little he does produce seems "crowded and sweats beneath a heavy burden of Ideas and Imagery."[71] Whenever he wished to write verse, Coleridge complains in 1802, he "beat up Game of far other kind—instead of a covey of poetic Partridges with whirring wings of music . . . up came a Meta-physical Bustard, urging its slow, heavy, laborious, earth-skimming flight over dreary and level Wastes."[72] Although this metaphysical or speculative "Bustard" had always been with Coleridge ("I never re-garded *my senses* in any way as the criteria of my belief," he writes to Poole in 1797, "I regulated all my creeds by my conceptions not by my *sight* . . . I know of no other way of giving the mind a love of 'the Great', and 'the Whole'"),[73] what ensured its ultimate triumph was Coleridge's inability to sustain the Wordsworthian vision or to con-ceive of poetic statement in other than Wordsworthian terms.

Wordsworth, Coleridge, Genius

Part of the reason Coleridge could not break free of Wordsworth's alternately inspiring and inhibiting example was Wordsworth's con-tinued productivity. As Coleridge's last great poem, "To William Wordsworth" (1806), attests, his disillusion with the Wordsworthian vision was not disillusion with Wordsworth the poet or with the power of his verse. The strength of the poem derives in part from an essential goodness of heart, which allows Coleridge to admit Words-worth's continuing greatness. Its occasion was Wordsworth's reading of *The Prelude* to Coleridge soon after Coleridge's return from Malta in 1807, when he was both ill and deeply depressed. Coleridge wrote his own poem immediately after the reading concluded (it was the only work he published all year), and the generosity and seriousness of his praise for Wordsworth are especially noteworthy given Words-worth's own habitual public reserve in response to Coleridge's work. Although Coleridge listens "with a heart forlorn" (61), he is able to view Wordsworth "in the choir / Of ever-enduring men" (49–50). At the same time, he also reflects on his own comparative failures:

> Ah! as I listened with a heart forlorn,
> The pulses of my being beat anew:
> And even as Life returns upon the drowned,
> Life's joy rekindling roused a throng of pains—
> Keen pangs of Love, awakening as a babe
> Turbulent, with an outcry in the heart;
> And fears self-willed, that shunned the eye of Hope;
> And Hope that scarce would know itself from Fear;
> Sense of past Youth, and Manhood come in vain,
> And all which I had culled in wood-walks wild,
> And all which patient toil had reared, and all,
> Commune with thee had opened out—but flowers

> Strewed on my corse, and borne upon my bier
> In the same coffin, for the self-same grave!
>
> (61–75)

Coleridge likens his existence here to the mariner's death-in-life. He sees himself as roused by Wordsworth's verse, but only to a consciousness of all that he has lost and squandered. This consciousness awakens cries in him—this is what he has to utter—like those of a "babe / Turbulent" (65–66), one for whom all problems and dangers are projections. The familiar complex of self-doubtings and self-crossings, of "fears self-willed, that shunned the eye of Hope; / And Hope that scarce would know itself from Fear" (67–68) recalls Wordsworth's comparable desperation in book one of *The Prelude*, in which "Humility and modest awe themselves / Betray me, serving often for a cloak / To a more subtle selfishness" (245–47). Yet at the poem's conclusion Coleridge reveals a still-vital urge to write:

> Scarce conscious, and yet conscious of its close
> I sate, my being blended in one thought
> (Thought was it? or aspiration? or resolve?)
> Absorbed, yet hanging still upon the sound—
> And when I rose, I found myself in prayer.
>
> (108–12)

Here, the power of utterance is awakened. Under Wordsworth's influence, Coleridge is able to pray, which, as we have seen from his other poems, is a metaphor for poetic creation. But so tentative and unsure are the final lines that it is difficult to conceive of the breakthrough they constitute lasting much longer than the period of the poem's composition.

Part of Coleridge's problem in his relations with Wordsworth—and hence part of his problem with writing in general—derives from conscious as well as unconscious pressures, in particular those imposed by notions of poetic power. One such notion is expressed in "To William Wordsworth" itself, when Coleridge praises Wordsworth's poem for being "not learnt, but native, her own natural notes!" (60). Throughout his life, Coleridge suffered from a sense that his own poetry was the product not of spontaneity, of native wit, but of learning and labor. He also subscribed wholeheartedly to the doctrine of the true poet as genius. Although at times he would admit, as in "To William Wordsworth," that he was not without poetical gifts, for the most part he doubted that he had poetical genius. "As to myself," he writes in a letter of 1802 to Southey, "all my poetic Genius, if ever I really possessed any *Genius*, and it was not rather a more general *aptitude* of Talent, and quickness in Imitation / is gone."[74]

Coleridge's sense that he lacked poetical genius derived partly from the "Bustardlike" nature of the content of his poems, a content that drove him, McFarland writes, "to erect a verbal structure adequate to support and to display the monumental mass of theological philosophy that he intended to convey."[75] It was not a structure easily arrived at, or one that gave the impression of spontaneity. What lay behind it was learning, books; yet when Coleridge thought of true creation, "again and again," in Fruman's words, "his mind ran to the distinction between the self-originating artist and the one who works from books." When Coleridge felt himself increasingly thwarted or blocked, moreover, he turned more frequently to books. Fruman even sees Coleridge's notions of true creativity as the source of his plagiarisms, as well as his blockage: "If only he had been able to seize with a strong hand what he needed for his own purposes, boldly and openly, and had justified his borrowings by improving on them! Instead, he disguised his sources, denied influences, pretended to spontaneous composition even when he had worked desperately hard—in short, he acted like a man unsure that any credit would remain to himself if he openly acknowledged his obligations."[76]

"Kubla Khan"

Of all Coleridge's defensively introductory disclaimers, none is so artful and revealing as the preface to "Kubla Khan," written in 1816, almost twenty years after the poem itself. The preface begins with the admission not only that the poem is a "fragment" (something we might otherwise not have realized) but that it is only being published "at the request of a poet [Byron] of great and deserved celebrity." Coleridge himself thinks the verse of interest "rather as a psychological curiosity, than on the ground of any supposed poetic merits."

Once this initial disclaimer has been registered, Coleridge proceeds to tell the famous story of the poem's genesis: how he fell asleep in a lonely farmhouse in Somerset, under the influence of opium, having just read of the "Khan Kubla" in *Purchas his Pilgrimage* (1626); how in his sleep he composed "two to three hundred" lines of verse, "if that indeed can be called composition in which all the images rose up before him as *things*, with a parallel production of the correspondent expressions, without any sensation or consciousness of effort." This is Romantic creation with a vengeance (though Coleridge does question whether such creation can indeed "be called composition"): all conscious effort banished, poetic power confined wholly to the primary process, an exclusive product of genius, the imagination, spontaneity. When Coleridge awakens, he retains the whole of the dream composition, but, as he begins to write it down,

> at this moment he was unfortunately called out by a person on business from Porlock, and detained by him above an hour, and on his return to his room, found, to his no small surprise and mortification, that though he still retained some vague and dim recollection of the general purport of the vision, yet, with the exception of some eight or ten scattered lines and images, all the rest had passed away like the images on the surface of a stream into which a stone has been cast, but, alas! without the after restoration of the latter!

One effect of this passage, as of the preface as a whole, is to turn the poem that follows into a meditation on writing or the poetic process—like so many other poems of the period. The imagery of the preface helps to introduce the meditation by establishing a distinction between the world of poetic power and an unpoetical, matter-of-fact world of Porlock businessmen, between "vision" and "business"—a contrast underlined by the concluding simile of the person from Porlock as a "stone" scattering (i.e., shattering) images on the surface of a stream.[77]

In the preface, then, the outer world, one of "stone," shatters an internal poetic world, a world for which Coleridge does not strain but which is "given to him." Poetry's source is conceived of as outside conscious control and manifested in mysterious and evanescent moods or insights. It is also conceived of not as a "marriage" of inner and outer, but as deriving exclusively from inner sources. And this is true of the poem as well, in which nature is described, in the words of one commentator, "as externalizing herself both by flinging up the sacred river . . . and also by forcing great fragments, 'dancing rocks' into the air. In each case the objects made begin their existence by being 'flung forth' or externalized: they were not always there but are products of another inner world. Not only works of art, but various objects are here presented as erupting from a subterranean world."[78]

The irony of this vision of internal or unconscious creation is that it is introduced by a piece of prose so obviously "worked" or "concocted." Bate is devastatingly down-to-earth about the likely truth of the "Porlock" episode: "How could Coleridge be carrying with him, on his long walk from Nether Stowey, the huge folio of Purchas? He was certainly not likely to find it in the lonely farmhouse. . . . As for the man on business from Porlock: why should he be seeking out Coleridge, who had so few business dealings, and how, even so, would he have known that Coleridge, who had been seeking seclu-

sion, was staying at this particular place?"[79] The manner of the preface is as contrived as its matter: it also is consciously crafted, literary,
replete with stylistic "inventions" of a sort that its content would
deny as true creation, because only what is given, according to the
content, is art.

The extreme Romanticism of the matter or content of the preface—
a Romanticism in which primary processes are all that count in creation—is complicated by the poem itself. The poem can be divided
into two sections. It opens with a 36-line description of the Kahn and
his domains, from "stately pleasure dome" to "lifeless ocean." It then
breaks off, in a switch as abrupt and puzzling as any in Coleridge's
works (though one that resembles the "Conclusion" of part two of
"Christabel"), and presents us with a second vision, of "a damsel
with a dulcimar" singing "of Mount Abora." In this second vision,
Coleridge the narrator steps out more directly than in the first 36
lines; and he does so to lament his inability to "revive within me /
Her symphony and song" (42–43), a revival that would enable him
to "build that dome in air, / That sunny dome! those caves of ice" (46–
47). The first part of the poem is about successful creation; the second, about blockage.[80]

The second part of the poem also offers a new suggestion as to
what prevents Coleridge from writing—including what prevents him
from completing "Kubla Khan." Were Coleridge to regain the power
to sing the damsel's song,

> . . . all should cry, Beware! Beware!
> His flashing eyes, his floating hair!
> Weave a circle round him thrice,
> And close your eyes with holy dread,
> For he on honeydew hath fed,
> And drunk the milk of Paradise.
> (47–53)

Two points are noteworthy here. The first is that Coleridge associates
poetic capacity with danger. In full imaginative flow, Coleridge—or
"the poet"—is conceived of as wild and powerful, a figure to "Beware." He takes on some of the exotic abandon of the damsel herself,
as well as that of the Khan, whose mere "decree" or utterance produced the "stately pleasure dome." Coleridge's song, moreover, is not
only of Mount Abora (in the Crewe manuscript, Mount *Amora*, the
alternative seat of Paradise cited by Milton in book four of *Paradise
Lost*, and thus a type of false Eden) but of the paradoxical power that
combines a "*sunny* pleasure dome with caves of ice." The impression
of total freedom and omnipotence created in these lines clearly

threatened, as well as enticed, Coleridge. True poets can do anything they want: like the Khan, they can construct "miracle[s] of rare device." But what if their wants are those of a greedy child, a "poor orphan, half starved"? Is it safe for such figures to exercise poetic power?

The second noteworthy feature of the depiction of the poet in the poem's concluding lines—aside from a nice note of self-teasing in the description of the damsel's transformation—is its identification of poetic power with the imagined bliss and omnipotence of infancy, a state in which one drinks "the milk of Paradise" at will. David Beres, in a pioneering psychoanalytic account of Coleridge, connects the lost "pleasure dome" with the breast and sees the concluding image of "the milk of Paradise" as a reference to the child's buried wish for maternal security and gratification. (Beres also sees the mariner's ocean quest in psychoanalytic terms, quoting Fenichel on the "symbolic way . . . pursuit of rest and of protection at the mother's breast is expressed in the frequent yearning for the ocean.")[81] If poetic power is conceived of as deriving exclusively from internal sources, then the sense of oneself as starved by the mother, estranged from her milk and love, and even thwarted by her (she being the repository of all one's projected anger and greed), makes poetry seem impossible. In addition to which, of course, there is an Oedipal dimension to the fantasy: if the poet *does* manage to capture the damsel's power of song, he will be viewed as demonically possessed, as a figure of transgressive powers.[82] Even those who resist this sort of Freudianism are unlikely to miss the poem's ambivalent attitude toward creative achievement. In the more general terms of Jungian psychology (those of Maud Bodkin), "the image of the watered garden and the mountain height show some persistent affinity with the desire and imaginative enjoyment of supreme well-being, or divine bliss, while the cavern depth appears as the objectification of an imaginative fear."[83]

Such interpretations suggest that Coleridge's conscious conviction that poetic power derives from unconscious sources locks into—and is likely also to derive from—psychological needs. To be a poet, for Coleridge, is to give in to, or to be mastered by, "the streamy nature of association" and, without "the rudder of reason" to steer the mind, "the dangerous currents of association sweep it headlong into evil thoughts."[84] The River Alph in the poem has just such a seductive and headlong character, its power being at once "sacred" (3) and "savage" (14), alternately slanting down a green hill "as holy and enchanted / As e'er beneath a waning moon was haunted / By woman wailing for her demon-lover" (13–15), or meandering "with a mazy motion" (25) until sunk "in tumult to a lifeless ocean" (28). Images such as these reinforce one's sense of Coleridge's deeply divided attitude toward the sources of creative power.

Blockage and the Biographia Literaria

Coleridge's attraction to blockage as a literary topos or device is as prominent a feature of his prose as his verse, and nowhere more so than in the second most famous instance of creative inhibition in his writing, the fictitious "letter from a friend," which interrupts chapter thirteen of the *Biographia Literaria*. Coleridge's aim in the *Biographia* was voiced as early as 1803: "to write my metaphysical works as *my Life, and in* my Life—intermixed with all the other events or history of the mind and fortune of S.T. Coleridge."[85] This odd format for a work of philosophy may already be, in the words of one of the *Biographia*'s editors, a sort of "acknowledgement of failure, of some private incapacity ever to write a work of formal logical design however often he may have aspired to do so."[86] But at the same time, *out of* incapacity came a work of enormous influence and originality—in formal terms at the very least. Coleridge's admission of his "failure" to produce genuine or unadulterated philosophy provided a way through—though the work was not begun until another twelve years had passed, and only then under the pressure of real desperation (hence the speed with which it was produced; all but the last two chapters were drafted between June and September 1815).

The actual writing of the *Biographia* only began once Coleridge put himself in the hands of an old friend, John Morgan, in a final attempt both to cut down his consumption of opium and to pay off his debts. His initial intent was to *dictate* to Morgan what was originally meant to be a brief "Preface" of a new collection of verse, *Sybiline Leaves*. "Freed from the terror of seeing before him the blank page waiting to be filled," writes Bate, "reassured by the daily presence and help of so selfless a friend and dreading to disappoint him, Coleridge went on from paragraph to paragraph."[87] The result was a work that reproduced in its content the pattern of breakthrough following on the heels of blockage detectable in its origins.

The *Biographia* begins as biography, and it is not until chapter five that Coleridge turns in earnest to metaphysics, tracing the history of "the laws of association" from Aristotle to Hartley. By chapter eight, Coleridge has reached the "system of dualism" of Descartes and his "followers," including Spinoza and Leibnitz; in chapter nine he treats the rival "Idealist" tradition in both its mystical and Kantian strands. Chapter ten ought to bring to a head the book's intended philosophical purpose, that of reconciling the truths of nature, mind and Christian belief. This project, according to Bate, was at the heart of Coleridge's philosophical intentions throughout his life, for it promised a way of sanctioning the Wordsworthian (and, in some respects, Kantian) "organic or dynamic philosophy of nature—the conception of nature as a unifying process, to which he was so deeply drawn but which, to his distress, was so often discerned by the religiously orthodox as 'pantheism.'"[88] Chapter ten was to effect the resolution of philosophy and religion through its account of the imagination. In the event, though, Coleridge balked, offering instead "a chapter of digressions and anecdotes, as an interlude preceding that on the nature and genesis of the imagination or plastic power."

The "interlude" that is chapter ten is so long and rambling that by the time we get to chapter eleven, "An affectionate exhortation to those who in early life feel themselves disposed to become authors," we almost forget that it also was meant to be about the imagination— and is thus another instance of evasion or procrastination. Only in chapter twelve does Coleridge at last return to the crucial metaphysical issues he left off in chapter ten. And here, too, he finds a way to defer the central issue, offering instead "a chapter of requests and premonitions concerning the perusal or omission of the chapter that follows."

The evasions of chapter twelve are especially pathetic. On the very brink of committing himself and at last presenting his own ideas, Coleridge digresses on "the anxiety of authorship," disingenuously requesting his readers to "either pass on the following chapter [in which the imagination is at last discussed] or read the whole connectedly," even insisting, in the midst of this most heterogeneous of works, that "the fairest part of the most beautiful body will appear deformed and monstrous if dissevered from its place in the organic whole."[89] The rest of chapter twelve is taken up with a lengthy restatement of the problems he faces and the crucial role the imagination will play (if ever he gets to it) in reconciling a host of related dichotomies, including reason and understanding, self and nature, subject and object, organicism and Christianity. It is in these pages of uneasy reiteration and procrastination, moreover, that Coleridge most transparently plagiarizes, lifting untransmuted paragraph after paragraph from Schelling.

Chapter thirteen, "On the imagination, or esemplastic power," begins with several pages of highly technical philosophical summary restating the need for a *"tertium aliquid . . . no other than an inter-penetration of the counteracting powers, partaking of both."* This *tertium aliquid* is, of course, the imagination. Then the chapter breaks off with a line of asterisks. What follows, in a complete shift of register, is a bizarre admission: "Thus far had the work been transcribed for the press, when I received the following letter from a friend," a friend whom Coleridge praises for his "practical judgement," "taste" and "sensibility."[90] This friend, as Coleridge subsequently explained in a letter to his publisher,[91] was fictional, and the "letter" he wrote, which Coleridge then "quotes" in its entirety, is full of businesslike common sense—the product, one might almost guess, of another person from Porlock. How much abstraction, asks the friend, can the public stand? Doesn't a full-fledged philosophical treatment of the imagination merit a hundred-page chapter, one that would inevitably increase the cost of the book? "As for the public," the friend concludes,

> I do not hesitate a moment in advising and urging you to with-draw the Chapter from the present work, and to reserve it for your announced treatise on the Logos or communicative intellect in Man and Deity. . . . In that greater work to which you have devoted so many years, and study so intense and various, it will be in its proper place. Your prospectus will have described and announced both its contents and their nature; and if any persons purchase it who feel no interest in the subjects of which it treats, they will have themselves only to blame.[92]

The "letter from a friend" resembles the preface of "Kubla Khan" in several respects. As in the preface, the blocking agent is external: the friend's advice is sensible and practical, of the sort to which Coleridge must "reluctantly" accede. In this respect, it is a way of evading personal responsibility. At the same time, however, its effect is liberating, for though Coleridge responds by acceding to his friend's "very judicious letter," he does not entirely drop the discussion of imagination. "I shall content myself for the present with stating the main result of the chapter, which I have reserved for that future publication, a detailed prospectus of which the reader will find at the close of the second volume."[93]

Although this prospectus never appears, what follows immediately is the famous two-paragraph distinction between primary and secondary imagination, on the one hand, and imagination and fancy, on the other. The fame and controversy surrounding these distinctions can be looked at in two ways: as a product of the casual and elusive manner of their presentation—the distinctions simply are not as clearly or as fully drawn as they need to be—or as a product of the freedom the letter confers, the distinctions being memorable precisely *because* of their dramatic and unsystematic presentation. When looked at in this second way, the "letter from a friend" becomes an instance of breakthrough through blockage.[94]

McFarland makes a similar point about the *Biographia* as a whole: everything about it that bears evidence of blocking anxieties—anxieties that, in one sense, disfigure the work and leave it in fragments—accounts for its unique and compelling character. "This wild grab-bag," McFarland reminds us, "is the most important single work of critical theory and practice in all of English literature. The only conclusion to be drawn is that its provisional nature, or, if one wishes, its near-hackwork status, does not block the revelation of Coleridge's insights but is in fact the necessary condition under which they can be expressed." Without the blocked "Opus Maximum," there would have been no *Biographia:* "By displacing the hope of classical status onto the conception of *magnum opus*, he was enabled to produce casual and *ad hoc* writing that . . . is nevertheless among the treasures of our language."[95] In this respect, the *Biographia* is to the "Opus Maximum" as *The Prelude* was to *The Recluse*, a sort of "antechamber" to the projected "cathedral" itself, whereas the lesser prose works—the lectures, *The Friend*, the tracts, even the Notebooks—are like the lyrics and shorter narrative poems that Wordsworth in his "Preface" to *The Excursion* calls "cells" and "oratories" surrounding the cathedral-like bulk of *The Recluse*. For both Coleridge and Wordsworth, productivity was made possible by the deflection of inhibiting fears of authorship onto some greater and unaccomplishable work. Whereas Hazlitt, in contrast, reacted to blockage (ten "barren" years as a philosopher) by giving up, devoting himself wholeheartedly to a life of "letters"—journalism, occasional prose, controversy—Coleridge seems to have needed to keep his formal philosophical ambitions alive in order to produce the "lesser" work that resulted from their continuing blockage.

Coleridge and Language

Coleridge's incompletions may well derive, it has been argued, neither from psychological nor what I have called literary-historical sources, but from a series of startlingly "modern" (but also quite "ancient") attitudes to speech and writing, as well as to language in general. Throughout his career, Coleridge was reluctant to let his texts speak for themselves. Hence his many revisions and contextualizing prefaces and deferrals—marginal glosses, proliferating epigraphs, explanatory or propitiary digressions and delays. These various resistances express, to several scholars at least, the suspicion that all forms of finished utterance are both inadequate and duplicitous. According to this view, the function of the preface of "Kubla Khan," the glosses to "The Ancient Mariner," and the "Conclusion" of part two of "Christabel"—all of which, in different ways, establish as well as mark the incomplete character of the poems they accompany—is to expose an untruth, to disrupt the illusion of figuration or representation and keep the "constructed" and "willed" nature of utterance before the reader's mind.[96] Such incompletions are of a piece with "antipoetical" remarks scattered throughout the Notebooks; for example, warnings about the danger of "the understanding of Metaphor for Reality,"[97] or admonitions about the need to create "a form that all informs against / itself,"[98] that obeys "passions or universal logic," rather than "the logic of grammar."[99]

Another way to make sense of Coleridge's distrust of finished utterance is to consider the subject or creator of the utterance rather than the world or objects from which it is drawn. From this perspective, Coleridge's incompletions—the impulses that thwart his attempts to write—serve a truth about the self, as well as the other or outer world: the finished work is a lie about not only the object but also the subject. Edward Kessler, in his book *Coleridge's Metaphors of Being*, takes this view of Coleridge. To Kessler, "what at first may appear as the inability to conclude can be viewed as a deliberate (if not fully acknowledged) act of registering the limitations of what the poet called 'confining form.'"[100] These limitations apply principally to the self as revealed in writing, and they originate in a theory of Being which is rooted in process. "A completed life or a completed poem was disturbing to him," writes Kessler, "he viewed Being as a perpetual joining together of what we are and what we can be."[101] Hence the following remark from a letter of 1798 to his brother George: "Excuse my desultory style and illegible scrawl: for I have written you a long letter, you see—and am, in truth, too weary to write a fair copy, or re-arrange my ideas—and I am anxious that you should know me as I am."[102]

Finished works, like all things *written*, have a self-contained or autonomous, and hence falsifying, character. Coleridge's distrust of writing, his congenital reluctance or inability to commit himself in print, may derive from just this sense of its falsifying nature, from a sense that "Form is factitious *Being*."[103] Such a view of his writer's block places it in a long and venerable tradition of distrust of the written, one that stretches back to Plato and is still very much alive. This view also helps us to understand Coleridge's recourse to a variety of nonwritten or unfixed forms of communication—not only oral forms, such as the lecture and conversation, but also a variety of unofficial "writings," such as the letter, the marginal comment, the

Notebook entry. "His energy was not diverted from poetry," writes Kessler, "but was spent in bringing poetry into the service of Being, in making it follow the 'working of the mind,' regardless of whether the result was made visible as a conventional poetic form, a finished product."[104] Coleridge's refusal to call his works "poems" fits into this pattern ("Besides 'thoughts punctuated by rhymes' and 'that which affects not to be poetry,' Coleridge's list of substitutes for 'poem' includes . . . effusions, vision, epistles, fragments, improvisation, translation, imitation, 'a Desultory poem,' and 'a poem it ought to be'").[105] In instance after instance, according to this view, distrust of the falsifying fixity of the written word, rather than a lack of ideas or literary powers, helps to explain Coleridge's blocked productivity. After all, the terrible decade of inactivity which began for him at the turn of the century also produced the richest of unofficial utterances: the bulging volumes of letters and Notebooks. "Freed from the burden of feeling he had to write," notes Bate of Coleridge's period in Malta, "he spontaneously turned to his notebooks (some of his finest observations there date from the Malta period)."[106] Fear of utterance played its part in Coleridge's blockage—the Notebooks themselves make this very clear—but so also, at least to some extent, did a principled aversion to writing per se, to the falsifications writing entails.

Such an aversion may help to explain the characteristic difficulty of the late despairing lyrics, many of which are themselves fragments. What makes these poems difficult to follow is Coleridge's insistence that truth lies in some ineffable realm beyond or between the fixed particulars of existence and a realm of pure ideality, or mere image and mere abstraction. In "Phantom or Fact" (1803), for instance, we are offered "A Dialogue in Verse," which both formally and conceptually refuses to be settled or complete:

FRIEND

This riddling tale, to what does it belong?
Is't history? vision? or an idle song?
Or rather say at once, within what space
Of time this wild disastrous change took place?

AUTHOR

Call it a moment's work (and such it seems)
The tale's a fragment from the life of dreams;
But say, that years matur'd the silent strife,
And 'tis a record from the dream of life.
(13–20)

The Author's "answer" applies to all the late Notebook lyrics: again and again in these poems, words are inadequate to communicate or settle the truth Coleridge is seeking. What he required throughout his life, but more desperately in the later "inactive" years, was "a more perfect language than that of words—the language of God himself, as uttered by nature,"[107] or, as he says in a Notebook entry of 1808, "energy divinely languageless."[108]

At the same time, though, Coleridge persisted in writing, never allowing himself to lapse into mystical silence. This contradiction energizes the dense abstraction of the late lyrics and makes them different in character from the rote abstractions of the early lyrics. "To believe," writes Kessler, "that the 'powerful feelings' that Wordsworth expected from a poet weakened in Coleridge as he grew older is to accept an unfounded legend."[109] Coleridge's blockage, especially in his later years, may in part have been the expression not of neurosis or fear, but rather of a principled aversion to words, especially to words in their most restricted and restricting form—words in print. "Words," declares Coleridge in a Notebook entry, "what are they but a subtle *matter*? And the meanness of Matter must they have, and the Soul must pine in them, even as the lover who can press kisses only . . . [on] the garment of one indeed beloved."[110]

Such doubts—about the possibility of ever establishing the self as independent or autonomous—may underlie Coleridge's plagiarisms, as well as his incompletions. This is not to say that Coleridge's plagiarisms were somehow "principled" or "honest," only that they throw into relief the larger question of what might be called an inevitable belatedness, which language itself necessarily involves us in. Coleridge's borrowings might well be seen as extreme manifestations of a habitual distrust—and despair—of any assertion of independent selfhood. He knew plagiarism to be a lie, but he may have seen it (if not quite consciously) as the admission of a dispiriting truth about all claims to autonomy. The next chapter examines this possibility more fully and also introduces other sorts of "nonpsychological" aversion to writing. It is a mark of the rich complexity of Coleridge's inhibitions that he provides as important an example of the theories I shall introduce as of those that have come before; his failures and incompletions are quite as various and instructive as his successes.

PART THREE

External Prohibition

Writing, Speech, and Culture

This chapter canvasses a range of blocking factors which lies outside exclusively psychoanalytic and literary-historical explanation. It begins—with the example of Coleridge fresh in mind—by recalling that many blocked writers are also fluent speakers. What, aside from the obvious differences, are the qualities that distinguish written from spoken communication? Could there not be something about writing per se, as opposed to other forms of communication, that inhibits? These questions call to mind a long history of mistrust of the written word, one that relates clearly to the sorts of attitudes Coleridge expresses about writing and language in many of his later poems and Notebook entries. The origins of this mistrust can be traced to the gradual evolution of literacy in the West, to the shift from a predominantly oral culture, such as that represented by the Homeric or preclassical Greek world, to a predominantly written one. The shift took place when simple semiotic markings, or "shapes," as the Greeks called them[1]—that is, mere pictures or representations of things—were replaced by representations of *utterance*; in Walter J. Ong's words, "a coded system of visible marks . . . whereby a writer could determine the exact words that the reader would generate from the text."[2]

In Ong's sense, writing involves alphabetic skills, the earliest evidence of which in Greece occurs in documents produced no later than 700–650 B.C., though such skills had been developed by the Sumerians in Mesopotamia around 3500 B.C.[3] By the last third of the fifth century B.C., the teaching of letters had become standard practice in Attic primary schools, thus making possible the achievement of general literacy by the end of the Peloponnesian War in 405 B.C. (Aristophanes mockingly and suspiciously calls attention to this achievement in *The Frogs*).[4] In the previous three hundred years, it has been argued, Athens lived under a condition of semiliteracy or craft-literacy, "in which writing skills were gradually but rather pain-fully being spread through the population without any correspond-ing increase in fluent reading."[5] The consequent tension between the new alphabetic technology and older oral communicative habits be-came increasingly apparent as writing was diffused throughout the culture. It is Plato, writing in the early decades of the fourth century B.C., who not only expresses this tension most clearly but also lays out the implications of the transformation from speech to writing and of the differences between the two.

Plato's objections to writing are stated most forcefully in the *Phae-drus* (c. 370 B.C.), generally considered the last of the great central group of dialogues to which both the *Symposium* and the *Republic* be-long. The dramatic occasion of the *Phaedrus* is a walk in the country-side, along the banks of the River Ilissus. During this walk, Socrates' young friend Phaedrus tells him about a speech he has listened to that morning. The speech was delivered by Lysias, one of the most famous of the Attic orators, as well as a professional speech writer for the law courts. Phaedrus calls him "the ablest writer of our day."[6] The subject of Lysias's speech was love, and its ironic aim was to prove "that surrender should be to one who is not in love rather than to one who is" (p. 476). Phaedrus agrees to read Socrates a copy of the speech, and, after Socrates criticizes it, Phaedrus challenges him to produce a better one. Socrates' mock-modest reluctance to do so suggests his identification with a nonwriting culture: "My dear good Phaedrus, it will be courting ridicule for an amateur like myself to improvise on the same theme as an accomplished writer" (p. 484).

What follows are two speeches by Socrates and a series of dialecti-cal exchanges between Socrates and Phaedrus, over the course of which emerges one of the most powerful and memorable of Plato's accounts of love and the soul. This account is especially distin-guished among Plato's writings by its recourse to poetical effects, and to some readers it appears that "the poet in him has got the better of the philosopher."[7] When, therefore, toward the end of the dialogue as a whole, Socrates argues for the inferiority of the written to the spoken word, some part of the motive force for his denigration of the written may well lie in the unusual character of the dialogue itself, its highly metaphorical and lyrical—or nondialectical—manner. Hence Socrates' eagerness to reiterate the essentially philosophical nature of his task, to make absolutely clear the difference between philosophy and rhetoric or mere writing.

Socrates' attack on writing begins with an Egyptian myth of ori-gins. This myth tells of the god Theuth (alias Hermes), the inventor, among other things, of number, calculation, geometry, astronomy, "and, above all, writing" (p. 520). When Theuth offered writing as a gift to King Thamus or Ammon, the Egyptian Zeus, he claimed that it would "make the people of Egypt wiser and improve their memories" (p. 520). Thamus's reply constitutes Plato's first objection. The real effect of Theuth's invention will be the opposite of what he claims:

> If men learn this, it will implant forgetfulness in their souls; they will cease to exercise memory because they rely on that which is written, calling things to remembrance no longer from within themselves, but by means of external marks. What you have discovered is a recipe not for memory, but for reminder. And it is no true wisdom that you offer your disciples, but only its semblance, for by telling them of many things without teaching them you will make them seem to know much, while for the most part they know nothing, and as men filled, not with wisdom, but with the conceit of wisdom, they will be a burden to their fellows. (P. 520)

The first point to note here is that writing is associated with deceit. Just before this passage, Theuth used the word *pharmakon*, which is translated as "recipe," to describe writing. Writing is a "recipe for memory and wisdom" (p. 520). But *pharmakon* can also mean "drug," and this is clearly Thamus's view of writing. To Thamus, writing allows others to confuse true memory with recollection, the "conceit of wisdom" with real wisdom. Plato's concern is with the truth of what is written, as well as with the audience's proper reception. Writing is to be faulted not only because it can deceive the reader, who has no way of determining whether the writer *really* knows what he or she is writing about, but because it has no way of ensuring that its reception by the reader is accurate. This is part of what makes writing so much more difficult than speech: that the writer's audience—and the context of his or her communication—has to be invented and is uncertain.

If you ask written words to explain themselves, Socrates continues,

> they go on telling you just the same thing forever. And once a thing is put in writing, the composition, whatever it may be, drifts all over the place, getting into the hands not only of those who understand it, but equally of those who have no business with it; it doesn't know how to address the right people, and not address the wrong. And when it is ill-treated and unfairly abused it always needs its parent to come to its help, being unable to defend or help itself. (P. 521)

The anxieties that Plato expresses here are relatively common. Once you put something in writing, you run the risk of being misunderstood, and you cannot explain or defend yourself as you can in argument or conversation. If, like Coleridge, you distrust utterance per se—partly because you distrust what lies within you—how much better it is to be able to correct and interpret, as in conversation. Perhaps this sort of distrust underlies Coleridge's habitual effort to overcome the fixed and limited nature of the written word (as in his poetry) by transforming it into conversation, either by labeling it as such, or by surrounding the actual "text" with glosses and prefatory qualifications that approximate the explanatory or dialectical features of spoken interchange.

The sense of exposure and vulnerability with which Plato associates the written word—the sense of writing as unable to defend or help itself—finds expression not only in Coleridge but in other later writers. Iris Murdoch, for instance, relates Plato's arguments here to the writing resistances of contemporary philosophers such as Kierkegaard and Wittgenstein. Wittgenstein "wrote with reluctance because he feared that his books would fall into the hands of fools. He too thought there was little danger of forgetting what had once been properly understood. Criticizing some of his own work he is reported as saying in conversation: 'No. If this were philosophy you could learn it by heart.'"[8] Plato's other charge against writing—that it is inhuman or thinglike, unresponsive and inanimate—may connect to a comparably long-lived tradition that associates writing or print with death, as in the biblical assertion that "the Letter Killeth," or the poetic commonplace that books are "monuments." The great paradox of such a view, writes Ong, is that the very "deadness of the text, its removal from the living human lifeworld, its rigid visual fixity, assures its endurance,"[9] allowing the writer's ideas to live on. Although Plato, in one sense, wrote to keep philosophy alive (in Murdoch's words, "it was necessary for Plato, as it was for the evangelists, to write if the Word was not to be sterile"),[10] doing so ran the risk of freezing or rigidifying—killing with the Letter—a truth that was only a genuine truth when it lived in the soul.

Phaedrus readily accedes to Socrates' strictures against writing and, in the course of doing so, describes speech and writing in a manner that calls to mind a third sort of objection. There is, says Socrates, "another sort of discourse that is brother to the written speech, but of unquestioned legitimacy" (p. 521). "You mean," Phaedrus eventually responds, "no dead discourse, but the living speech, the original of which the written discourse may fairly be called a kind of image" (p. 521). Phaedrus's guess here is the correct one: the spoken per se is somehow closer to truth than the written, which is only "a kind of image," like the inferior imitations of the artist—imitations themselves of imitations, of the phenomenal world, as opposed to a world of fixed Truths or Forms.

The belief that speech is closer to reality than writing is what Jacques Derrida calls "phonocentrism." In the world view expressed by Plato, the spoken word is assumed to be a transparent medium; a one-to-one relation obtains between word and extramental referent. Derrida in turn calls this belief "logocentrism," which he thinks a myth, part of that "metaphysics of presence" which perpetuates the illusion not only that words *can* reflect something out there but that there *is* an out there—independent of language—to be reflected.[11] Writing suggests, much more damagingly than speech, that language, in whatever form it is technologized (i.e., orally or chirographically), has a structure that is independent of the external world or thought it is meant to communicate. Plato deplores this suggestion, which is why he disparages writing; Derrida accepts it. The fear that underlies Plato's distrust of writing is thus a fear of ever attaining truth through language. Such a fear may well play some part in the hostility to writing discernible in the aforementioned biblical injunction about the "Letter" killing, a tradition in which the Word, or second person of the Godhead, is not the human written word but the human spoken word; in which God the Father "speaks" his Son rather than writing him; in which Jesus, the Word of God, leaves nothing in writing, though we know he could read (Luke 4:16); and in which "faith comes through hearing" (Rom. 10:17).

Why writing should point up the deficiencies of language more clearly than speech is hinted at later in the *Phaedrus*. If the writer produces words "that can't either speak in their own defense or present the truth adequately" (p. 522), then why write? Socrates' answer reveals the essential artificiality and formality—the manufactured and factitious quality—of the written: "He [the writer] will sow his seed in literary gardens, I take it, and write when he does write by way of pastime, collecting a store of refreshment both for his own memory, against the day 'when age oblivious comes,' and for all such as tread in his footsteps, and he will take pleasure in watching the tender plants grow up" (p. 522). The gardens that Plato is talking of here are enclosed: a world of self-involved and self-generating structure without any way through to a wider and more important world, the sort of world opened by dialectic. Here Plato shows affinities with Freud, who also sees art—if not writing per se (the two are conflated in this passage from the *Phaedrus*)—as separated from "reality" and in the service of pleasure. Dialectic is to be distinguished from writ-

223

ing and art, though, in that it "plants and sows . . . words founded on knowledge" (p. 522); that is, in a real, rather than an artificial, garden.

As the habit of writing grows, moreover, the love of the real atrophies, and mere pleasure and power—the power to persuade, however unworthily—take precedence. Writing is thus connected in Plato's mind with the Sophists and a merely rhetorical power that can entertain, as in the forwarding of frivolous notions such as "that surrender ought to be to one who is not in love rather than one who is." The truly wise man "ought not to be designated by a name [for wisdom] drawn from [his] writings, but by one drawn from his serious pursuits" (p. 524). Far from being "serious," writing is the work of someone "on whose phrases he spends hours, twisting them this way and that, pasting them together and pulling them apart" (p. 524), activities that Plato conceives of as purely mechanical, without any connection with a content that matters.[12]

These strictures against writing are reiterated in another of Plato's works, or at least another work generally attributed to Plato, the *Seventh Letter*. The *Seventh Letter* is ostensibly a reply to a request for help made by the followers and relations of the murdered king of Syracuse, Dion, whom Plato had at one time tutored, and who earlier had occasioned his single, disastrous venture into practical politics. In this letter Plato tells of having himself experienced one of the dangerous consequences of writing. Dion's rival Dionysius was also an admirer of Plato and had written a book on Plato's philosophy. Plato's disapproval of this book is couched in terms of a denunciation not only of writing but of words per se, and it thus reveals an underlying anxiety about the illusory nature of what Derrida calls "logocentrism":

One statement at any rate I can make in regard to all who have written or who may write with a claim to knowledge of the subjects to which I devote myself—no matter how they pretend to have acquired it, whether from my instruction or from others or by their own discovery. Such writers can in my opinion have no real acquaintance with the subject. I certainly have composed no work in regard to it, nor shall I ever do so in future, for there is no way of putting it in words like other studies. Acquaintance with it must come rather after a long period of attendance on instruction in the subject itself and of close companionship, when, suddenly, like a blaze kindled by a leaping spark, it is generated in the soul and at once becomes self-sustaining. . . . If I thought it possible to deal adequately with the subject in a treatise or a lecture for the general public, what finer achievement would there have been in my life than to write a work of great benefit to mankind and to bring the nature of things to light for all men? I do not, however, think the attempt to tell mankind of these matters a good thing. (Pp. 1588–89)

By "treatise" or "lecture," Socrates means the kind of speech Lysias might deliver. Socrates is not quite saying that speech as well as writing inhibits truth—that truth is ineffable—only that fixed and formal speech, which approximates writing, as opposed to the speech of dialectic, does so.

The reason Plato gives for distrusting writing and formal speech is the essential inadequacy of language, in particular the metaphorical quality Coleridge distrusted in it. "Because of the inadequacy of language," Plato writes, our attempts to name, define, represent, and then know an object "do as much to illustrate the particular quality of [that] object as they do to illustrate its essential reality. . . . Hence no intelligent man will ever be so bold as to put into language those things which his reason has contemplated, especially into a form that is unalterable—which must be the case with what is expressed in written symbols" (p. 1590). The trouble with language is that it can only tell us what a thing is "like"; the thing itself, though, *is* itself and not infected with that which it is like. It is in the very nature of language to contaminate the thing that it seeks to communicate with that which it is not. This is the point, of course, around which Derrida has built his melancholy theory of deconstruction, which is why he makes so much of the following passage from the *Seventh Letter.* Plato is distinguishing between the essence of the "circle" and any human attempt to represent it:

Every circle that is drawn or turned on a lathe in actual operations abounds in the opposite of [the reality of circle], for it everywhere touches the straight, while the real circle, I maintain, contains in itself neither much nor little of the opposite character. Names, I maintain, are in no case stable. Nothing prevents the things that are now called round from being called straight and the straight round, and those who have transposed the names and use them in the opposite way will find them no less stable than they are now. The same thing for that matter is true of a description, since it consists of nouns and of verbal expressions, so that in a description there is nowhere any sure ground that is sure enough. (P. 1590)

Essential truth, Plato is here suggesting, lies beyond not only words but also all representation, including that which the phenomenal world itself constitutes. To discover the truth of "circle," one must move beyond words and representations, or use them in their freest form, to get beyond them, as in dialectic:

> Hardly after practicing detailed comparisons of names and definitions and visual and other sense perceptions, after scrutinizing them in benevolent disputation by the use of question and answer without jealousy, at last in a flash understanding of each blazes up, and the mind, as it exerts all its powers to the limit of human capacity, is flooded with light.
>
> For this reason no serious man will ever think of writing about serious realities for the general public so as to make them a prey to envy and perplexity. In a word, it is an inevitable conclusion from this that when anyone sees anywhere the written work of anyone, whether that of a law-giver in his laws, or whatever it may be in some other form, the subject treated cannot have been his most serious concern—that is, if he himself is a serious man. His most serious interests have their abode somewhere in the noblest region of the field of his activity. (P. 1591)

Here Plato comes very close indeed to admitting the inadequacy of language. If even the spoken word is to be distrusted, because it involves symbolization and approximation, how much more so writing and mimetic art, for, in Murdoch's words, "the introduction of further symbols and discursive *logoi* or quasi-*logoi* . . . naturally make a poor situation even worse and lead the mind away in the wrong direction." [13]

What is especially paradoxical about Plato's attack on writing is not only that it occurs in written form but that without writing philosophy itself would have been impossible. This is something Plato's attack on "creative" writing or poetry, in the *Republic* and elsewhere, makes clear—while also highlighting as-yet-unmentioned differences between speech and writing. Plato's attack on poetry is an attack not only on bad or immoral poetry but on poetry *as* poetry. In Eric Havelock's words, "Plato attacks the very form and substance of the poetical statement, its images, its rhythms, its choice of poetic language." [14] He does so for two reasons. First, because poetry as he understands it—that is, oral poetry or poetry that grows out of the oral tradition (there being no other kind in his age)—represents a massive repository of traditional wisdom, a "kind of social encyclopedia." [15] Poetry in this sense fits Hesiod's description, in the *Theogony,* of the content of the Muses' songs as "custom-laws of all and folk-ways of the immortals." [16] Second, Plato attacks poetry because it relies upon and helps to create what Havelock calls "the oral state of mind" (p. 41). In preliterate societies, "the only possible verbal technology available to guarantee the preservation and fixity of transmission [of culture] was that of the rhythmic word organized cunningly in verbal and metrical patterns which were unique enough to retain their shape. . . . Poetry is first and last a didactic instrument for transmitting the tradition" (pp. 42–43).

Plato, though, objected to both the tradition itself and the metrical habits its transmission called for and fostered. Chief among these habits is what Havelock calls "a state of total personal involvement and therefore of emotional identification with the substance of the poeticised statement" (p. 44). The audience for a Homeric recital had to identify with the performance "as an actor does with his lines," an identification attained "only at the cost of total loss of objectivity" (pp. 44–45). The acceptance and retention of tradition involved self-surrender or self-identification, a process bound to meet with Plato's disapproval. At the same time, what the audience was called on to identify with was itself wholly accepting—or at least so it could be argued. Homer's "encyclopedic vision," according to Havelock, expresses "a total acceptance of the mores of society, and a familiarity with and an affection for its thought-forms. . . . He profoundly accepts this society, not by personal choice but because of his functional role as its preserver and recorder" (p. 89). And the nature or character of the content preserved was itself essentially nonconceptual: a series of events rather than relations, categories, or topics, because, as Havelock argues, "only a language of event is amenable to the rhythmic-mnemonic process" (p. 173).

The need for preservation was especially intense in preclassical Greece because of the history of dispersal that followed the disintegration of the Mycenaean culture—the culture of the Homeric heroes themselves—sometime around 1200 B.C. Poetry was the answer to diaspora and decentralization: "The essential vehicle of continuity was supplied by a fresh and elaborate development of the oral style, whereby a whole way of life, and not simply the deeds of heroes, was to be held together and so rendered transmissible between the generations" (p. 119). Yet analysis and understanding, the very goals of Plato's philosophy, impeded this process. In attacking poetry, Plato is thus, again in Havelock's words, "entering the lists against centuries of habituation in rhythmic memorized experience. He asks of men that they should examine this experience and rearrange it, that they should think about what they say, instead of just saying it. And they should separate themselves from it instead of identifying with it" (p. 24).

Plato's objections to the oral culture help us to understand why, though he attacks writing in the *Phaedrus* and *Seventh Letter*, the *Republic* shows him unconsciously clearing the way for a method of understanding made possible only by writing. Plato's attack on the poets is in the service of a new kind of nonpoetic or conceptual discourse. His object is not only to ban pleasure or entertainment but also to seek a new—that is, rational or reflective—basis for cultural stability and formation. In preliterate societies, "you did not learn your ethics and politics, skills and directions, by having them presented to you as a corpus for silent study, reflection and absorption. You were not asked to grasp their principles through rational analysis. You were not invited to so much as think of them. Instead you submitted to the paideutic spell. You allowed yourself to become 'musical' in the functional sense of that Greek term" (p. 159). True knowledge, though, involves the creation of an autonomous self, a "me," in Havelock's words, "which is self-governing and which discovers the reason for action in itself rather than in imitation of the poetic experience" (p. 200). Poetry, as Plato understood it, was the enemy of such a self, and therefore of all genuine truth, because the aim of the good person is to move beyond any uncritical acceptance of both sense experience and convention, and the soul is the only agent of such a movement.

Thus it is only with writing that the soul or self Plato seeks, and the genuine truth that is its object, is attainable, for only with writing comes the psychic release that leaves room and energy for review and rearrangement. With writing, the strain on the psyche caused by original, or at least intellectual, thought is alleviated. This is, in part, suggests Ong, "because handwriting is physically such a slow process—typically about one tenth of the speed of oral speech. . . . With writing, the mind is forced into a slowed-down pattern that affords it the opportunity to interfere with and reorganize its more normal, redundant processes."[17] Plato's attack on writing in the *Phaedrus* is therefore something of an anomaly, an example of historical lag. In attacking writing, Plato was in the tradition of his teacher, Socrates, but he was not in the oral tradition. Although Socrates, as Havelock says, "remains fully embedded in oral methodology, never writing a word so far as we know, and exploiting the give and take of the market place," at the same time, through the dialectic, "he was committing himself to a technique which, even if he did not know it, could only achieve itself completely in the written word and had indeed been brought to the edge of possibility by the existence of the written word."[18] The same is true of the Plato of *Phaedrus*.

The relevance of Plato's attack on poetry to writer's block lies in its account of the distinctions between oral and written cultures. It is

228

possible, for instance, to find individual, contemporary examples of a mentality for which oral habits are especially suited, one that resembles, on a personal level, the mentality of the dispossessed communities of preclassical Greece, communities desperately in search of stability and continuity, and of the conserving rituals of oral expression. Coleridge's fluency in conversation, for instance, may well derive from his prominent sense of loneliness and isolation and from his deep need for identification and absorption. Writing, for him, only reinforced fears of isolation, of the separable soul. In like manner, the relation of Coleridge to the tradition—his plagiarisms—may partly be explained by a deep-seated need, for all his addiction to the Romantic cult of originality, for solidarity, which the preceding account of the shape of oral communities might elevate beyond a merely psychological interpretation such as McFarland's. "Writing and reading," as Ong reminds us, "are solitary activities that throw the psyche back on itself."[19] Hence, he adds, the absence for writers of any collective vision or concept of their readership corresponding to the performer's or oral poet's sense of "audience."[20] At the same time, writing increasingly separates poetry, in Havelock's words, "from the mainstream of cultural record and custom . . . [poetry] is converted into an exercise in . . . private insight. In parallel, the intellectual man tends to be recognised as a type participating in the body politic but not of it."[21] Coleridge's habitual need for collaboration, his sense of the communality of intellectual effort, may well be a personalized expression of the sorts of habits which characterize an oral culture.

What Coleridge needed, Ong and his mentor Marshall McLuhan might argue, was a word processor, which at least offers the illusion of an audience. If ours is indeed, as Ong would have it, an "age of secondary orality," if we all have become inhabitants of McLuhan's "global village," the characteristic isolation of the composing process may well be overcome. I once asked a blocked writer who is also a fluent speaker and lecturer (one of this book's rare forays "into the field") if he had ever tried taping and then transcribing his lectures. "Yes," he replied, but his reaction when presented with the typed transcript was not encouraging: "I know this," is what he thought; as if to say, "so it can't be very good," or "so what?" This answer seemed to imply that tape recorders are merely more efficient versions of the sort of shorthand available to Coleridge; the problem itself is unaffected. But is this true of other forms of technology? The same blocked writer was less pessimistic about word processors; he felt that their screens resembled human faces, were more responsive and animated than written or typed pages. Might they not serve as electronic equivalents of the faces in which, or on which, the lecturer sees his thoughts reflected? If so, they might help to overcome the inhibiting narcissistic component that he sensed at the heart of many a blocked writer, a component that the presence of an audience dissolves for the lecturer. Even those with little sympathy for psychoanalytic convolution have noted how human and companionable word processors can seem. "It's alive. It's a companion. With its big TV screen it looks like a head," comments a novelist interviewed in the *New York Times*. To another writer, "it seems as if the outside world has arrived and put itself at my command for a change. But then the drag is that I have to perform, which is a sense that writers didn't use to have when working on first or second drafts."[22] This last speaker is no blocked writer, but what he says—about performance and about the word processor as perfect audience—is relevant. Others have noted how word processors are often exempt from the hostility and paranoia evoked by the sight and sound of, say, typewriters. The speed and flexibility of the machines suggest a transparent medium; the word processor is loved, it could be argued, because it not only offers the writer an endlessly malleable sentence but is both an other or audience and a projection of one's own mind—which brings us back to the blocked lecturer and his theory of narcissism.

Even leaving aside this narcissistic element, though, it is clear that the impression of companionableness communicated by the new technology, as well as the ease of revision and correction it affords— the sense of being involved in a dialogue with the screen—returns the composing process to something like the conditions of oral communication. It is worth noting that many of Plato's objections to writing are identical to those leveled against the new technology. Like writing, computer systems such as word processors have been accused of weakening memory, of not being *truly* intelligent, of not being able to argue back, of being thinglike and dead. At the same time, word processors, no less than typewriters or pens, produce scripts or texts; and it is the text that creates a sense of private ownership or entitlement where words are concerned. In primary oral cultures, such a sense "is rare and ordinarily enfeebled by the common share of lore, formulas, and themes on which everyone draws."[23] It is only with writing, whether with pen or on a typewriter or a word processor, that accusations of plagiarism arise.

Finally, the inability to finish works, as in Coleridge's catalogue of fragments, can be connected to a bias toward what Havelock calls oral culture. This is because it is only with texts that closure becomes a defining characteristic of communication. "By isolating thought on a written surface, detached from any interlocutor, making utterance in this sense autonomous and indifferent to attack, writing presents utterance and thought as uninvolved with all else, somehow self-contained, complete."[24] Print culture not only creates the sense that a work must be closed, a unit in itself, but also, Ong argues, is the source of inhibiting Romantic notions such as "originality" and "creativity," "which set apart an individual work from other works even more, seeing its origins and meaning as independent of outside influence, at least ideally."[25] Hence those who resist the assumptions of a now-dominant writing culture run the risk of blockage—of seeing themselves as blocked, as did Coleridge. At the same time, the inability to conform to conventional notions of writing can also act as a way through. Browning, for example, could be thought to have achieved the unfixed, dialoguelike verse that Coleridge was groping toward in his later poems; open-endedness and incompletion became for Browning a *way* of writing. His poetry resists the closure and fixity of the written in a variety of ways, even as it presents closure—or the drive toward fixity—as blockage's source. One need only recall "Andrea del Sarto," a poem that treats control (perfection, wholeness, enclosure) as a source of creative inhibition, to see how fruitful a principled reaction against fixity can be and how Browning's own fears of blockage can be built into a poetry of freedom.

Plato's objections to writing are no more likely to explain blockage—Coleridge's or anyone else's—than the theories examined in earlier chapters. But they provide another, older, and more general context in which to place examples of internal resistance or creative inhibition. Some people cannot write, even though they wish to, because they carry within them the sorts of suspicions about the written which Plato so powerfully expresses. These suspicions may be unarticulated, and fueled by psychological need, but they connect to a long tradition of principled distrust not only of writing but also of language itself.

9

Blockage and Externality:
The Woman as Writer

I now turn to what might be called the social dimension of writer's block. Writing—whether "creative" or otherwise—is an obvious source of power, and access to it is inevitably restricted according to changing power relations, which create "mind-forged" as well as literal manacles. These manacles can make writers feel as much like "state prisoners, pen and ink denied,"[1] as real ones. And when they do, it makes sense to think of them as blocked. Such a reflection calls into question a crucial common-sense assumption: that writer's block is an internal rather than an external impediment, a psychological condition. The person who is shackled, or denied access to paper, pen, or ink, according to common sense, does not have writer's block. But what of the unshackled sixteenth-century woman (or working-class man) who does not write? Are the forces restricting such a person always or exclusively external? At what point do institutionalized prohibitions—for example, of class, sex, and race—become internalized? This is a question considered by the best of the psychoanalysts (and paid lip service to by most of the rest); their association with the rather flat image of the unconscious sometimes presented in part one is not altogether fair. The question has also, of course, been considered by thinkers in a long tradition of common-sense and quite other objections to, or reservations about, simple internal/external distinctions. Such reservations imply that our sense of what is internal—conventionally thought of as the distinguishing attribute of a genuine block—may well prove as problematic, as constructed, as our sense of the natural.

For example, let us return to the question of the would-be woman writer of the sixteenth century. Virginia Woolf, in a famous passage from *A Room of One's Own* (1929), asks us to consider the possibility that Shakespeare had a sister:

232

What would have happened had Shakespeare had a wonderfully gifted sister, called Judith, let us say. Shakespeare himself went, very probably,—his mother was an heiress—to the grammar school, where he may have learnt Latin—Ovid, Virgil and Horace—and the elements of grammar and logic. He was, it is well known, a wild boy who poached rabbits, perhaps shot a deer, and had, rather sooner than he should have done, to marry a woman in the neighborhood, who bore him a child rather quicker than was right. That escapade sent him to seek his fortune in London. He had, it seemed, a taste for the theatre; he began by holding horses at the stage door. Very soon he got work in the theatre, became a successful actor, and lived at the hub of the universe, meeting everybody, knowing everybody, practising his art on the boards, exercising his wits in the streets, and even getting access to the palace of the queen. Meanwhile his extraordinarily gifted sister, let us suppose, remained at home. She was as adventurous, as imaginative, as agog to see the world as he was. But she was not sent to school. She had no chance of learning grammar and logic, let alone of reading Horace and Virgil. She picked up a book now and then, one of her brother's perhaps, and read a few pages. But then her parents came in and told her to mend the stockings or mind the stew and not moon about with books and papers.[2]

Even if Judith were in a position to resist these external restrictions or impediments, what would have happened had she tried to follow in her brother's footsteps? Woolf imagines her in London:

She was not seventeen. The birds that sang in the hedge were not more musical than she was. She had the quickest fancy, a gift like her brother's, for the tune of words. Like him, she had a taste for the theatre. She stood at the stage door; she wanted to act, she said. Men laughed in her face. . . . She could get no training in her craft. Could she even seek her dinner in a tavern or roam the streets at midnight? Yet her genius was for fiction and lusted to feed abundantly upon the lives of men and women and the study of their ways. At last . . . Nick Greene the actor-manager took pity on her; she found herself with child by that gentleman and so—who shall measure the heat and violence of the poet's heart when caught and tangled in a woman's body?—killed herself one winter's night and lies buried at some cross-roads where the omnibuses now stop outside the Elephant and Castle.[3]

In one sense, this story hardly counts as an instance of writer's block, if only because Judith never actually wrote anything (and so could not technically be called a writer). What stops her from writing, moreover, are just those external forces that impede other sorts of what Woolf calls "labouring, uneducated, servile people."[4] But Woolf might well have imagined Judith differently, as a figure who herself believed, or came to believe, the prejudices ranged against her and who internalized them. This is a possibility hinted at in Judith's story, but only explicitly voiced later on in the book, when Woolf talks of the woman poet being not only "thwarted and hindered by other people . . . but tortured and pulled asunder by her own contrary instincts," by "a nervous stress and dilemma which might well have killed her."[5]

Such a movement—from "other people" to "contrary instincts," from external to internal—is reproduced in the larger structure of *A Room of One's Own*. Although the book begins with a series of obviously external blocking figures—the Oxbridge beadle who barks Woolf off his "turf," the black-gowned librarian who waves her out of the college library—it ends with an appeal to "the habit of freedom and the courage to write exactly what we think,"[6] as if to suggest that doing so is a matter of internal resolve, that the difficulties women face are within their power to remedy. This is a conclusion that might also be drawn about other "oppressed" groups—for instance, African-Americans, as in Mary Ellmann's comparison of "Negro apathy" with feminine passivity. "In both cases," writes Ellmann, "having restricted the participation of the group, the observer finds that inactivity is an innate group characteristic"[7]—which means that the resulting silence (or impairment) could in part be described as blockage, though its ultimate origins are external.

The conclusion to which such speculation leads is this: the woman who withdraws from authorship out of a sense, in Ann Bradstreet's words, of being "obnoxious to each carping tongue / Who says my hand a needle better fits,"[8] is only blocked if she believes the charge —believes, that is, in her intellectual or physical inferiority. To the seventeenth-century poet and essayist Margaret Cavendish, Duchess of Newcastle, writers are like blackbirds: "The hen can never sing with so strong and loud a voice, nor so clear and perfect notes as the cock; her breast is not made with the strength to strain so high."[9] Such a belief is bound to inhibit the woman writer, and the Duchess of Newcastle is not alone in voicing it. While compiling an anthology of women's poetry, the feminist critic Cora Kaplan was struck by a recurring note of apology. This note, she came to recognize, was as much an "unwitting acceptance of the law which limits [women's] speech" as "an anticipatory response to male prejudice."[10] To the extent that a woman writer accepts such a law, she can be said to suffer from an internal impediment or block, though one whose origins are neither strictly "psychological" (as in Oedipal or object-relations scenarios) nor strictly literary-historical (as in influence anxiety).

Chief among the pressures or prejudices the woman writer must resist are those of "biology," as in the Duchess of Newcastle's remarks about chest or breast size. From at least the time of Aristotle, "science" has been summoned to prove the incompatibility of womanhood and intellect, as well as the dire consequences of their combination. Aristotle's belief in the inferiority of women derived in part from a theory of the generative power of heat. Heat is active and necessary for growth; males are hot and dry, females are cold and moist. As Aristotle says in *On the Generation of Animals*, "there must needs be that which generates and that from which it generates. . . . [T]he male stands for the effective and active, and the female, considered as female, for the passive." From this "biological" differentiation, there follow comparable political and intellectual differentiations. "The courage of a man is shown in commanding," we are told in the *Politics*, "of a woman in obeying." And later on: "as the poet says of women, 'Silence is a woman's glory.'" [11]

Although subsequent Greco-Roman "scientists" modified these views, they were hardly less restrictive in their attitudes toward women. For example, Galen, the most influential of Greco-Roman medical writers, granted women a more active role in reproduction, but still described them as "imperfect, and, as it were, *mutilated*." Christine Battersby offers a range of early Christian and Renaissance modifications of views such as Galen's and then traces their continuing presence right through to the twentieth century. [12] Among examples gathered by other scholars, Wendy Martin quotes John Winthrop, governor of the Massachusetts Bay Colony, writing in 1645 about a female colonist, Anne Hopkins, who "has fallen into a sad infirmity, the loss of her understanding, which had been growing upon her divers years, by occasion of her giving herself wholly to reading and writing, and had written many books." [13] In the Victorian period, according to Elaine Showalter, women were thought to have "smaller and less efficient brains, less complex nervous development, and more susceptibility to certain diseases, than did men. Any expenditure of mental energy by women would divert the supply of blood and phosphates from the reproductive system to the brain. . . . Physicians estimated that 'maternal functions diverted nearly twenty per cent of women's vital energies from potential brain activity.'" [14] No wonder Elizabeth Barrett described doctors, in a letter to Robert Browning, as "the faculty" who "set themselves against the exercise of other people's faculties." [15]

According to Sandra M. Gilbert and Susan Gubar, views such as those described by Showalter help to explain the prominence of disease and illness in the lives of many pre-twentieth-century women writers. But even when women retained the health to write—that is, overcame the physically debilitating effects of false biology—their writing betrayed a diseaselike dis-ease. When the "poetical itch" of the eighteenth-century poet Anne Finch, Countess of Winchilsea, was caricatured by Pope, Gay, and Arbuthnot in the stage comedy *Three Hours After Marriage* (1711), the mockery "took"—not in this case in the form of blockage, but of an all-but-disabling insecurity. Although the countess sometimes saw women as "Education's, more than Nature's fools," in her Pindaric ode "The Spleen" (1701), she seems genuinely to believe in the afflictions and inadequacies to which women poets were meant to be subject. "O'er me alas," she writes of "Spleen,"

> . . . thou dost too much prevail.
> I feel thy Force, whilst I against thee rail;
> I feel my Verse decay, and my Crampt Numbers fail.
> Thro' thy black Jaundice I all Objects see,
>   As Dark and Terrible as Thee,
> My lines decry'd, and my Employment thought
> An useless Folly, or presumptuous fault.[16]
>   (74–80)

Noteworthy here, in respect to writer's block, is the poet's sense both of her own infection and of writing as unnatural and disease-breeding for women. Although words still flow, "I feel my Verse decay, and my Crampt Numbers fail"—under the pressure of a "biologically" determined anxiety, an anxiety, as Robert Southey said (to Charlotte Brontë), that "literature is not the business of a woman's life, and it cannot be."[17]

Another source of potentially inhibiting anxiety for women writers is the allegedly patriarchal character of most metaphors of authorship. According to this view, when a woman seeks to write, what she feels she must cultivate, as Aphra Benn puts it, is "my Masculine Part the Poet in my."[18] Gilbert and Gubar draw on a range of instances to establish not only the masculine associations of authorship in Western culture but the phallic associations of the pen. They cite Gerard Manley Hopkins on "the male quality [as] the creative gift"; Anthony Burgess on "the strong male thrust"; William Gass on "that blood-congested genital drive which energizes every great style." Battersby's comparable list of examples stretches from the Middle Ages, in which Jean de Meun, in his continuation of Guilliame de Loris's allegory *La Roman de la Rose* (c. 1237–77), anathematizes those males—priests included—"who with their stylets scorn to write / Upon the precious tablets delicate / By means of which all materials come to life," to the American novelist James Jones, for whom the author is "like one of those guys who has a compulsion to take his thing out and show it on the street."[19] My favorite instance, though, is that of Roland Barthes on the Marquis de Sade. When de Sade was imprisoned, he was denied "any use of pencil, ink, pen and paper." The result, declares Barthes, was a form of emasculation, for "the scriptural sperm" could flow no longer, and "without exercise, without a pen, Sade became *bloated,* a eunuch."[20] Metaphors such as these, Gilbert and Gubar argue, leave women writers out in the cold, for "if the pen is a metaphorical penis, from what organ can women generate texts?"[21]

This argument has hardly gone unchallenged. To Nina Auerbach, the metaphor of literary paternity ignores "an equally timeless and, for me, even more oppressive metaphorical equation between literary creativity and childbirth."[22] And if, as Elaine Showalter wryly retorts, "to write is metaphorically to give birth, from what organ can males generate texts?"[23] If anything, according to one critic of Gilbert and Gubar, literary production is "gender ambiguous," which accounts for the vehemence of male attacks on women's writing; such attacks are a product of writing's "taint of feminine identification."[24]

Gilbert and Gubar make a stronger case when they turn to the inhibiting effects of metaphors of a different kind. "Like the metaphor of literary paternity itself," they write, the "corollary notion that the chief creation man has generated is woman has a long and complex history. From Eve, Minerva, Sophia, and Galatea onward, after all, patriarchal mythology defines women as created by, from, and for men."[25] And created penless, so before the woman can write she must escape not only the male stereotypes that would deny her free expression but also the larger sense of herself as *written,* as object or blank page rather than subject or creator. In *Middlemarch,* for example, Dorothea is advised (by Will Ladislaw) to content herself with *being* a poem rather than writing one. Ezra Pound tells the poet H.D.: "You are a poem, though your poem's naught." As Robert Graves would have it, *Man Does, Woman Is.* After all, if writing requires what Barthes calls "scriptural sperm," then the text, the written, is female, as in another of Barthes's books, *The Pleasures of the Text* (1975), which reminds us that the critic's function is to "know" the written, the "corpus" or "body" of the text, including its most intimate "passages." If the pen is the penis, moreover, does that not, as Barthes's poststructuralist confrere Jacques Derrida argues, make the blank page a hymen; or, in his female translator's paraphrase, "the always folded . . . space in which the pen writes its dissemination"? To Gubar—from whom I have taken these examples—once literary production is likened to biological creativity, "the terror of inspiration for women is experienced quite literally as the terror of being entered, deflowered, possessed, taken, had, broken, ravished."[26]

The specific stereotypes into which women are written take two comparably inhibiting forms. The first is that identified by Woolf in "Professions for Women" (1931) as "the Angel in the House," and what is especially interesting about Woolf's account of her own struggle with this Angel is the admission that the prejudices she faced had been thoroughly internalized. "I discovered that if I were going to review books I should need to do battle with a certain phantasm. And the phantasm was a woman, and when I came to know her better I called her after the heroine of a famous poem, The Angel in the House. It was she who came between me and my paper when I was writing reviews. It was she who bothered me and wasted my time and so tormented me that I at last killed her."[27] The Angel had to be killed because she was constantly urging Woolf to accept a traditional role of submission, deferral, and service, "to be levelled," in Mary Wollstonecraft's words, "by meakness and docility, into one character of yielding softness and gentle compliance."[28] In such a role, according to John Ruskin, "power is not for rule, is not for battle, and . . . intellect is not for invention or creation, but for sweet orderings of domesticity."[29] "Be sympathetic," the Angel would whisper when Woolf was about to be critical, "be tender; flatter; deceive; use all the arts and wiles of our sex. Never let anybody guess that you have a mind of your own. Above all, be pure."[30]

This last injunction was also deeply inhibiting to Woolf the novelist. "Figure to yourselves a girl sitting with a pen in her hand, which for minutes, and indeed for hours, she never dips into the inkpot." What is blocking this girl, putting her "in a state of most acute and difficult distress," is that she "had thought of something, something about the body, about the passions which it was unfitting for her as a woman to say." The consciousness that men would be shocked by the expression of an unangelic female sexuality was a rock against which female novelists—girls such as this—consistently foundered, according to Woolf. Nor were such instances derived wholly from fear of male censure. At the end of the essay, Woolf explicitly admits as much: "Outwardly, what is simpler than to write books? Outwardly what obstacles are there for a woman rather than a man? Inwardly, I think, the case is very different; she has still many ghosts to fight, many prejudices to overcome. Indeed, it will be a long time still, I think, before a woman can sit down to write a book without finding a phantom to be slain, a rock to be dashed against"[31]

One of the dangers of attacking the Angelic stereotype is that such an attack calls forth the Angel's antitype, a monstrous figure of uncontrollable appetite, anger, and deceit. This is Gilbert and Gubar's "Madwoman in the Attic," the author as Charlotte Brontë's Bertha Mason. If the Angel is all spirit, the Madwoman is all flesh. If the Angel is selfless and dependent, the Madwoman is intransigent and autonomous. "Such figures," claim Gilbert and Gubar, "have drastically affected the self-images of women writers, negatively reinforcing those messages of submissiveness conveyed by their angelic sisters."[32] They also incarnate male fears of a limiting or imprisoning corporeality, which is why so much is made of the sexually frustrated character of the female writer, as well as of her grossly comical physicality. In *The Dunciad*, for instance, first prize for poetical dullness takes the form of the female novelist Eliza Haywood:

> Who best can send on high
> The salient spout, far-streaming to the sky
> His be yon Juno of majestic size,
> With cow-like udders, and with ox-like eyes.
>
> (2.153–56)

Second prize is the contents of a piss pot (2.157–58). The woman who wanted to write, or to write in an unladylike or unangelic fashion, ran the risk of becoming this sort of grotesque figure in her own eyes, as well as in those of the world. Some feminists claim that this risk is not gone. "Where is the ebullient, infinite woman," writes the French feminist Hélène Cixous, "who . . . hasn't been ashamed of her strength . . . surprised and horrified by the fantastic tumult of her drives (for she was made to believe that a well-adjusted normal woman has a . . . divine composure), hasn't accused herself of being a monster? Who, feeling a funny desire stirring inside her (to sing, to write, to dare to speak, in short, to bring out something new), hasn't thought she was sick?"[33]

Catherine Gallagher points to another stereotype inhibiting women's writing, one at least as old as those of patriarchy and matriarchy. This is the image of the writer as Whore, a metaphor with obvious connections to the monstrous propensities of the writer as Madwoman. Gallagher traces the metaphor to classical Greece, where "the associations of writing with femaleness in general and prostitutes in particular spread with increases in literacy itself."[34] The reasons for these associations ought in part to be clear from the previous section: writing obscures and devalues truth, as Plato would have it, and is especially associated with the Sophists, intellectual charlatans whose false wisdom, like the Whore's false passion, is "for sale." But Gallagher points to other reasons as well, such as Aristotle's uncertainty about whether writing

> most resembled the natural generativity of plants and animals or the unnatural generation of money, which, in usury, proliferates through mere circulation but brings nothing qualitatively new into being. At times Aristotle speaks of poetic making as a method of natural reproduction; at other times he speaks of the written word as an arbitrary and conventional sign multiplying unnaturally in the mere process of exchange. The former idea of language promotes the metaphor of literary paternity; the latter of literary usury and, ultimately, literary prostitution. (P. 40)

The examples Gallagher points to in support of the continuing life of this distinction, as well as of the metaphors that mark it, come from the Victorian period and have their origins in changed means of production, including the development of cheap serial publication and the massive growth of the reading public in the 1880s and 1890s, a growth that "made it impossible for any professional writer to claim independence of the marketplace" (p. 43). Yet, from at least the early Victorian period, "the identity of text and self begins to be strongly associated . . . putting the writer in the marketplace in the position of selling himself, like a whore" (p. 43). Women writers, for obvious reasons, were especially vulnerable to such associations: Gallagher cites George Eliot's essay "Silly Novels by Lady Novelists" (1856) and W. R. Gregg's essay "The False Morality of Lady Novelists" (1859) as examples of texts that stress the false, imitative, or merely conventional nature of women's writing. In each essay, a distinction is made between productive literary labors and mere "scribbling." As Eliot points out, "'in all labour there is profit.' But ladies' silly novels, we imagine, are less the result of labour than of busy idleness" (p. 44). Although such novelists are prolific, they produce nothing new or of value. Like the literal prostitute, the literary prostitute is "at it" all the time, counterfeiting passion and providing no offspring—that is, no *real* art. Gallagher sees this complex of associations at the heart of Eliot's own writing anxieties and points to the distinction she draws, in her note on "Authorship," written sometime in the 1870s, but not published until 1884 in *Leaves from a Note-Book*, between the writer and the author as a crucial one. Authorship, for Eliot, is "a breadwinning profession," whereas merely "to write prose or verse as a private exercise and satisfaction is not social activity." The dangers of authorship are those of the market; the author is tempted "to do over again what has already been done, either by himself or others" (p. 45). This is why Eliot likens his (really "her") works to an inflated currency or to the prostitute's false passion.

Also noteworthy in this regard is Gallagher's reminder that, for many nineteenth-century women writers, Eliot among them, authorship meant freedom from "patriarchal authority": "The woman in the marketplace is presumably free from the patriarch both in the sense that she needs the permission and approval of no single man and in the sense that finding her determination in the nexus of relationships with clients or public enables her to escape the identity imposed by a father" (p. 46). But such freedom, of course, is likely to seem threatening, as much to the author herself as to the patriarchal forces in her life, be they husbands or fathers. It is easy to imagine how, under such circumstances, a woman could associate the desire to write and publish with the bold illicitness of prostitution. Such were the fears, Gallagher argues, that hindered Eliot herself (though they hardly blocked her). Gallagher dryly adds that these fears had little to do "with a fear of writing or any anxiety about handling pens" (p. 59).

The metaphor of writer as Whore raises interesting questions about women and speech. In her autobiographical essay "Speaking/Writing/Feminism," Kaplan connects a lifelong anxiety about writing with a comparably long-lived attraction to speaking out. From her earliest school days, Kaplan found writing either fearful or boring: "My own written efforts were usually accompanied by a kind of terror that they would be derivative, cliché, inauthentic. . . . Every fragment of imaginative prose or verse from the age of six onwards has given me that stale ghosted felling *as I wrote it.*"[35] At first, this sounds like simple influence anxiety, of a sort Gilbert and Gubar believe women are unlikely to experience (so busy are they with more immediate and elementary questions of female identity, as well as with a search *for* predecessors and models). But as Kaplan explains, what unsettled her almost as much as a sense of the "givenness" of the written was a sense of its difference from speech, as well as of its greater value in the eyes of the culture: "To write was to do what my father did and what my mother valued. Talking, or more accurately, talking back got me into endless trouble. . . . In writing, the family morality seemed to say, the suspect personal gratifications of self-expression were reduced to an acceptable, ethical level through the displacement of words from mouth to printed page."[36]

Although in one sense this view of the differences between speech and writing seems to contradict Gallagher's point about writing (or publication) as "brazen"—the sort of thing a whore does—it also confirms the association of brazenness with female self-expression.

"Acting, speaking, showing off my adolescent body, most of all touching it," writes Kaplan, "were, I was convinced, tainted in my parents' eyes with egotism in general and female narcissism in particular."[37] For Eliot and many of her contemporaries, writing had these associations, which is why it was often identified with acting, as the figure of the Alcharisi in *Daniel Deronda* suggests. Today, though, Kaplan resists writing *because* it seems to exclude what she calls "the suspect personal gratifications of self-expression"—gratifications found in what she sees as the typically feminine spheres of speech and acting. "While I understand as an abstraction, that my wilfully raised voice usurps 'the place and tone of a man,' for me speaking out is also deeply entwined with femininity, with, for example, a conventional desire to be looked at."[38] What is interesting here is Kaplan's sense that—even given the larger and still-vital suspicion of *any* form of female self-expression—speech is viewed as more appropriately female than male, precisely because it has been superseded, as Plato feared it would be, by writing. Whereas in Plato's time writing was associated with women—an association that Gallagher still sees at work in the metaphor of writer as Whore—today, when writing is the discourse of power, it is speech that is seen as the woman's realm; or, rather, writing is conceived of as too elevated an activity to be contaminated by any merely contingent (i.e., female) associations. Hence the popular suspicion that "mere" talk—idle gossip, chatter—is the woman's province.

One final source of potential conflict between writing and women has to do with the common conception of the writer as autonomous and controlling, as in theories of ego psychology or certain strands of Romantic ideology. Because women have traditionally been dependent and oppressed, it would be difficult for them to think of themselves, given such notions, as writers. This point is made by several feminist critics who draw upon the theories of the French psychoanalyst Jacques Lacan. Lacan believes that the child achieves maturity when he or she becomes, at the Oedipal stage, a speaking subject, by which is meant a participating member of the language community—in Lacan's words, "the symbolic order."[39] Lacan claims that without this community or order, neither society nor the individual can survive. The inability to symbolize experience through language leads to psychosis. At the same time, though, the symbolic order inscribes sexual and social relations, which center around the value of the patriarch and the phallus—for Lacan, the symbols of fixed meaning and truth. Hence Derrida's clever coinage "phallogocentric," which signals the double tyranny of "phallocentric" *and* "logocentric" viewpoints.[40]

"Phallogocentrism" doubly excludes women. Lacan and Freud believe that the Oedipal stage is, for the female child, one of resignation
to a life of restricted speech.[41] Girls must align themselves with their
mothers, becoming what Juliet Mitchell calls "the representative of
'nature' and 'sexuality,' a chaos of spontaneous, intuitive creativity."[42]
"The female," writes Ezra Pound, "Is an element, the female / Is a
chaos / An octopus / A biological process."[43] Such views of the female
and of the development of female psychology help to account for "the
significant but statistically small presence of women as makers of
high culture . . . [as well as] their anxiety about their precarious position, about their difficulties (which are often made into strengths)
when using what is clearly in many ways a 'common' language."[44]
The examples of such anxiety which Kaplan points to are poetical, in
part because poetry—symbolic language at its most "controlled"—as
a genre is more closely identified with high culture than is prose fiction. The best-known and most vivid of the instances she cites comes
from Emily Dickinson:

> They shut me up in Prose
> As when a little Girl
> They put me in the Closet—
> Because they liked me "still."[45]

Dickinson's complaint raises the larger question of generic blockage
in women's writing. By the mid-eighteenth century, it has been estimated, the majority of the novels published in England were by
women.[46] Why, exactly, *are* women more prominent in the field of
prose fiction than in that of verse? Is this prominence solely a matter
of the novel's relative lack of status in high culture? Alternative answers are of several sorts. To begin with, the novel's rise (and poetry's
consequent decline) coincides with a gradual lifting of external restrictions on women. Moreover, fiction is—and has always been—a
more "practical" (i.e., lucrative) genre than verse: a woman could
support herself writing fiction. Fiction also owes less to classical tradition than does verse, and women traditionally have been denied a
classical education. Fiction's subject matter, moreover, is often said to
be that of the domestic scene, the life of the feelings, "trivial" observation—"all those things supposedly close to women's experience."[47]
Over and above these factors, though, Kaplan cites the role of the
speaking subject in verse, particularly in lyric. In her view, the single
coherent and individual speaker is a crucial and defining presence in
Romantic and post-Romantic verse. This speaker, as Coleridge implies in the *Biographia Literaria*, stands in the same relation to his
poem as God the Father stands in relation to his creation. The

speaker is the finite or human equivalent of what Coleridge calls "the infinite I AM."[48] And because women, for the reasons suggested earlier, have difficulty constructing themselves as speaking subjects, finite "I AM"s, they are more likely to turn to fiction than verse: for fiction, "whether Gothic, sentimental or realistic has a narrative structure and gendered characters in which the author can locate and distance her own speech. One might say that the narrative discourse itself provides a sort of third term for the woman author by locating (even, and perhaps especially, in a first person narrative) the loss or absence of power anywhere but in her own voice."[49] Yet it is also suggested (by women as well as men) that in fiction females resist or write against controlling conventions such as plot. When Arnold Bennett describes Eliot's style as "feminine in its lack of restraint, its wordiness, and the utter absence of feeling for form,"[50] he is voicing more than a merely masculine view. According to Cixous, for example, "a feminine textual body can be recognized by the fact that it is always without end."[51] "To put it at its simplest," asks Gillian Beer, "can the female self be expressed through plot or must it be conceived in resistance to plot? Must it lodge 'between the acts'? Virginia Woolf said that she could not make up plots and George Eliot that conclusions are at best negotiations."[52] When such views are combined with the image of the writer as controlling and autonomous— a shaper of plot and form—the result might well be inhibiting, to the woman novelist as well as the woman poet. And not every writer is strong enough to resist such conventions, as did Eliot and Woolf.

These suspicions underlie recent feminist attempts to discover or forge a way of writing that challenges the symbolic order. Woolf herself is often cited as a prototype of such writing, as are other male as well as female "modernists"; however, as Kaplan and others have suggested, nineteenth-century examples can also be found, including the "dream-form" poems of Christina Rossetti and Emily Dickinson, with their surreal distortions and weird jumps in logic, imagery, and theme. Literature of this sort belongs to what the French feminist theoretician Julia Kristeva calls "the semiotic," by which she means a way of writing that draws upon pre-Oedipal—that is, presymbolic— discourse. The semiotic, says Ann Rosalind Jones, is "an incestuous challenge to the symbolic order, asserting as it does the writer's return to the pleasures of his preverbal identification with his mother and his refusal to identify with his father and the logic of paternal discourse"[53] ("his," here, of course, referring to female as well as male writers). The semiotic, Kristeva argues, is the fluid, plural, prereferential, rhythmic, excessive language of Joyce, Mallarmé, Artaud, a language that delights in the pleasurable disruption of fixed or symbolic meanings and is thus especially appropriate to women's experience and needs. It is a language to be embraced rather than embarrassed by, encouraging the woman writer to see herself, in Barthes's terms, as *"la mère qui jouit"* rather than *"la mère qui souffrit."*[54] Nor is it only women writers who need to reconceive and to loosen up their notions of authorship. When Mary Ellmann wryly champions Norman Mailer's anarchic, anti-authoritarian prose style over the prose style of Simone de Beauvoir, for example, she is hardly being, in contemporary theoretical terms, antifeminist.[55]

Theories such as Kristeva's are the feminist equivalent of a phenomenon—or tactic—found in many instances of blockage: the impediment itself, in this case an inhibiting notion of femaleness, is viewed as a source of strength. Hence Kaplan's talk of female identity's "potentially hopeful incoherence," which "can and ought to lead to a politics that will no longer overvalue control, rationality and individual power." Instead of seeing women's exclusion from conventional notions of authorly authority as

a question of barred access to some durable psychic state to which all humans should and can aspire, we might instead see [women's] experience as foregrounding the inherently unstable and split character of all human subjectivity. . . . The instability of "femininity" as female identity is a specific instability, an eccentric relation to the constitution of sexual difference, but it also points to the fractured and fluctuant condition of all consciously held identity, the impossibility of a will-ful, unified and cohered subject.[56]

Whatever one thinks of the assumptions that underlie views such as these, their immediate function is clear: to transform inhibiting fears into virtues, blockage into breakthrough. In this respect, "the semiotic" is to the woman writer what "the sublime" was to the Romantic poet.

Other ways of overcoming exclusion, or an internalized sense of exclusion, are more modest and often involve painful compromise. To begin with, there are the early or "feminine" accommodations, in which women writers simply refused to publish, or turned to less threatening, because less elevated, genres, or protected their works by constantly apologizing for or disguising their true nature (for example, in the manner of Coleridge). This last tactic was a frequent resort of the Duchess of Newcastle, as even her autobiography— hardly a genre of self-deprecation (hardly a genre at all in the seventeenth century)—attests. The duchess presents herself in the autobiography as a model of female virtue. She is forever deferring—to

245

father, husband, children. Her writing is permissible only because she refuses to think of herself as a writer. Her *husband* is the writer; she merely scribbles: "He creates himself with his pen, writing what his wit dictates to him, but I pass my time rather with scribbling than with writing, with words than wit."[57] Those who accuse the Duchess of being vain for attempting to write an autobiography ("since none cares to know whose daughter she was or whose wife she is or how she was bred, or how she lived, or what humour or disposition she was of") are answered, unconvincingly, by the claim that her writing is of "no purpose to the readers, but it is to the authoress, because I write it for my own sake, not theirs."[58] The obvious illogicality of this *published* rationale suggests how strong the pressures were for the duchess to disguise her identity as writer. Nor were these pressures much weakened by the time the Countess of Winchilsea was writing, a generation or so later. As the countess admits at the end of an unpublished "Introduction" (1689?) to her poems, "So strong th'opposing faction still appears, / The hope to thrive, can ne'er outweigh the fears." As a consequence, her Muse is "contracted," and her audience is restricted to herself and a few friends.[59]

The earliest British woman novelists were more successful in their compromises. According to Showalter, they either "exploited a stereotype of helpless femininity to win chivalrous protection from male reviewers and to minimize their unwomanly self-assertion,"[60] or they published their works anonymously. Mary Brunton (1778–1816), a novelist who influenced Jane Austen, was quite explicit about the advantages of anonymity: "I would rather, as you well know, glide through the world unknown, than have (I will not call it *enjoy*) fame, however brilliant, to be pointed at,—to be noticed and commented upon—to be suspected of literary airs—to be shunned, as literary women are, by the more unpretending of my own sex; and abhorred as literary women are, by the pretending of the other!—my dear, I would sooner exhibit as a rope-dancer."[61]

If the novelists of Brunton's generation sought to disguise or underplay the fact that they were novelists, those of the next generation often sought to disguise their identity as women, most obviously through the use of male pseudonyms. The women writers of this generation, including the Brontës, Elizabeth Gaskell, Harriet Martineau, and Elizabeth Barrett Browning, belong to what Showalter identifies as the first of three phases, or periods, of women's writing in the nineteenth century, phases that can be found in all "literary subcultures, such as Black, Jewish, Canadian, Anglo-Indian, or even American." Showalter calls these phases in women's writing the Feminine, the Feminist, and the Female, and she describes the first of them as a prolonged period "of *imitation* of the prevailing modes of the dominant tradition, and *internalization* of its standards of art and its views on social roles."[62] Hence the novelists of the Feminine phase frequently undermine the aspirations of their heroines, by consigning them to either physical suffering or a happy marriage. At such moments, in Woolf's words about Charlotte Brontë's novels, "we feel the influence of fear . . . just as we constantly feel an acidity which is the result of oppression . . . a rancour which contracts those books, splendid as they are, with a spasm of pain."[63] Even so liberated and self-conscious a figure as Eliot, for example, insists as much upon the "Dodo"-like quality of her aspiring heroine Dorothea as upon her resemblance to Saint Teresa.

In the next generation, that of the so-called sensationalist novelists who precede the second, or Feminist, stage of nineteenth-century women's fiction, the fate of the heroine is no less gloomy. Although the novelists of this generation were equal to what Showalter calls "the commercial, competitive, self-promoting aspects of the literary life," they also felt obliged—that is, internally pressured—to tailor their plots to conventional prejudice. "Typically," writes Showalter of the three-decker novels of such "sensationalists" as Mary Braddon and Mrs. Henry Wood, "the first volume . . . is a gripping and sardonic analysis of a woman in conflict with male authority. By the second volume guilt has set in. In the third volume we see the heroine punished, repentant, and drained of all energy."[64] Here, too, as in the novels of their more respectable forebears, the hidden subject matter is the author's own troubled condition, a result of internalized prejudice. As Woolf says about an earlier generation, "one has only to skim those old forgotten novels and listen to the tone of voice in which they are written to divine that the writer was meeting criticism; she was saying this by way of aggression, or that by way of conciliation. She was admitting that she was 'only a woman,' or protesting that she was 'as good as a man.'"[65]

Submission within the work itself was matched in the first, or Feminine, generation of novelists by a scrupulous personal adherence to social and sexual norms. Showalter associates the majority of Feminine novelists with "a persistent self-deprecation of themselves as women, sometimes expressed as humility, sometimes as coy assurance-seeking, and sometimes as the purest self-hatred. . . . By working in the home, by preaching submission and self-sacrifice, and by denouncing female self-assertiveness, they worked to atone for their own will to write."[66] It is hardly difficult, given such pressures, to imagine women writers unable either to defame themselves in these ways or to withstand the accusations, internal as well as external, that their defamation meant to evade. One thinks of Alice James, for example, whose internalized convictions of weakness and narcissism resulted in literal, as well as figurative or literary, paralysis. Such a figure could well be thought of as blocked, even in the absence of any specifically psychological "condition." And, again, whether the blocking factor is internal or external is no easy question.

The fate of what Showalter identifies as the second stage of women novelists, those who published between 1880 and 1920, raises comparably problematic questions. The defining characteristic of this stage was overt protest, an open refusal of stereotype and accommodation; in prominent instances, the result could be described as blockage. The best known of the Feminist novelists—Sarah Grand, Olive Schreiner, George Egerton, Mary Coleridge, Elizabeth Robins—"often seem neurotic and divided in their roles, less productive than earlier generations, and subject to paralyzing psychosomatic illnesses, so that their fiction seems to break down in its form." Many, Showalter continues, "found it difficult to finish their books or to write more than one."[67] Olive Schreiner (1855–1920), probably the best known of this group, was a compulsive rewriter and could be said never to have completed any book upon which she worked. She was always frantically composing, yet was neither productive nor self-disciplined: "Her manuscripts disappeared mysteriously or were discarded; they waxed and waned over the years, pieced together out of fragments, endless revision, loving reconsiderations, accretions, patches." Although her first book, *Story of an African Farm* (1883), was a huge popular success, the effect of that success, in Showalter's words, was "writer's block": "For years Schreiner published only 'dreams,' sentimental allegories in the most nauseating *fin de siècle* style. . . . Anything longer than half-a-dozen pages triggered her anxieties."[68]

Schreiner was a troubled woman, and her blockage can be viewed in several ways. Like many prominent women writers of the first phase, she had an especially intense relationship with her father, in a family in which the mother had a secondary and passive role (in the case of the Brontës and Elizabeth Barrett, the mother was gone completely). The Oedipal overtones of such closeness might well explain both the daughter's creative urge and the transgressive anxieties it could generate. At the same time, Schreiner subscribed to the most exalted and potentially inhibiting notions of authorship, including the extremest Romantic theories of inspiration (she often said she needed to be possessed to write). Such notions can block because they put the writer at the mercy of impulses over which he or she has no control. Finally, it is possible to connect Schreiner's obsession with obesity in her fiction to the neurotic compulsion that prevented her from finishing anything—or, rather, that allowed her works to grow and grow. Her monumentally fat heroines can be seen, in object-relations terms, as symbolizing the very fears—of lack of nourishment on the one hand, and raging appetite and aggression on the other—so common in post-Kleinian accounts of creativity and inhibition. For Showalter, though, Schreiner's obsession with obesity and her disdain for the secondary features of composition are best viewed as symptoms of a conflict of female identity. The obese heroines suggest "a femaleness grown monstrous in confinement—a world full of Bertha Masons,"[69] whereas impatience with analytic or rational elements of composition suggests unconscious conformity to the Angelic stereotype. In short, despite Schreiner's overt feminism, she also was deeply affected by traditional sexual and authorial stereotypes—which accounts for her notorious refusal or inability to finish or publish her writing.

Similarly dispiriting conclusions can be drawn from the career of Dorothy Richardson (1873–1957), an important transitional figure between feminist and Female phases of British women's fiction. Richardson's main claim as a novelist, believes Virginia Woolf, was the invention of what she calls "a woman's sentence," "the psychological sentence of the feminine gender." This sentence was "of a more elastic fibre than the old, capable of stretching to the extreme, of suspending the frailest particles, of enveloping the vaguest shapes."[70] To Showalter, though, it was a sign of blockage, of being "afraid of an ending."[71] Although at first Richardson's style seems a principled protest against phallogocentrism, "a statement in itself, a response to the apocalyptic vision of Welles and Lawrence," in the light of her career as a whole, it begins to look symptomatic rather than consciously chosen or controlled. From 1939 until 1951, Richardson was at work on the last section of the unfinished novel sequence *Pilgrimage*. During this period, her relationship to the novel became even "more obviously possessive and anxious."[72] For Showalter, Richardson's defense of the novel as "a continuous process" was merely rationalization, a "myth" that enabled her to publish (because what she published was only an installment, it could not finally be judged). "Without such a sustaining illusion," Showalter writes, "Olive Schreiner, a novelist of very similar temperament, found herself endlessly writing and rewriting the same unfinished book."[73]

Richardson's "blockage," like that of the women writers discussed earlier, derives from the same internalized prohibitions as those that inhibited Woolf's Judith Shakespeare. The power of these prohibitions has diminished over the years—Richardson's lot, or rather her sense of her lot, was hardly as constricting as that of her nineteenth-century predecessors, let alone such pioneering figures as the Countess of Winchilsea or the Duchess of Newcastle—but it has by no means disappeared. The stereotypes live on, and their continuing power is evidenced not only in the works of Woolf and her followers in the third, or Female, generation (the rhythms of blockage are everywhere apparent in *A Room of One's Own,* a work full of stops and starts, as well as a vertiginous sense of proliferating possibilities) but also in the eloquent urgency of so much contemporary feminist scholarship, notably the work of those literary scholars (Kaplan, Showalter, Gilbert, and Gubar) to whom this chapter is so indebted. Although problems of female identity are not always the sole or determining source of inhibition in cases of blockage in women's writing, no account of the subject of writer's block which omitted them, or failed to discuss the larger issue of internalized social and cultural prejudice, would be of much use. Writing is a difficult and complicated business, one that involves all that a person is. The forces that define or deform a writer's sense of self reach far beyond any merely—or purely—psychological or literary-historical determinants. These may be commonplaces, but they are also true.

Postscript

By now it should be clear that summarizing my topic is not easy. Nevertheless, a few recurring themes from the previous pages might profitably be recalled in order to help focus the book's shape and purpose. For all its air of dubious or unearned authority, *writer's block* is a term that has certain advantages over its predecessors. The phenomenon it means to designate is not always an illusion; it is not always a term of rationalization or evasion of responsibility—though, like all terms, it has certain designs on us, as well as certain pretensions. Although often misused, it has its uses—as long as it is carefully restricted, to begin with, to genuine writers (no Joseph Grands or cognitively deficient college freshmen). When such writers find themselves unable to write because of obstructing internal factors— or internalized "external" factors, be they prejudices or taboos (as in, for example, the case of some would-be women writers) or principles (as in, for example, Coleridge's principled, if unconscious, distrust of the written word)—they are blocked.

The origins of such blocks have been variously tracked, but their workings often fit a common pattern: blocked writers fail to negotiate rival or opposing claims, variously associated with pairings such as inner and outer, primary and secondary processes, emergence and embeddedness, independence and incorporation, inspiration and elaboration, defusion and merger, subject and object, written and oral, "male" and "female." These oppositions reflect a deep and basic conflict, one that the psychoanalysts argue is rooted in our earliest relations with the world, whether that world is conceived of in terms of Kleinian "objects" or of people. Writing asks of writers, even those who feel most alienated, that they be at home in the world, by which is meant using and shaping it, as well as recognizing its otherness and integrity. This is a major theme of the book and one toward which each of the book's parts works, but its clearest theoretical expression is found in the writings of the post-Kleinians, which is

251

why part one builds toward post-Kleinian theory, and parts two and three revert to post-Kleinian terms and models.

A second major theme of the book is that there is a historical dimension to the problem: writer's block, as it is understood today, derives only in part from psychoanalytic theory; behind that theory lies a tradition of Romantic self-consciousness, a newly acute attentiveness to the claims of the inner world and to the dangers of those claims. This tradition signals a breakdown in the "truth" of received notions of self and other, one that Bate associates with a single originating shift in consciousness in the mid-eighteenth century, and that McFarland sees as part of a recurring oscillation, a sort of cultural psychohistory in which the mid-eighteenth-century marks only a stage. Which of these accounts of the historical origins of writer's block one accepts depends on one's perspective. On the one hand, the *accidie* from which medieval writers suffer, or the standard invocations of the Muse that appear in the work of their Renaissance successors, can be seen as evidence of the perennial nature of writerly difficulties; on the other, the formal character of their complaints marks them as different in kind from the more anxious and agitated complaints we associate with genuine blockage.

A third and final theme of the book is that blockage itself can bring insight, and with it the power to write. This is because the experience of blockage forces writers to rearrange their relations to the world and the self, inner and outer; to approach life—and not just the life of writing—anew. According to such a view, the obstructing factors in composition—the blocking agents—are not so much dissolved, as in the action of chemotherapeutic drugs, as sublimed, by being seen from a higher perspective; and the knowledge gained from this new perspective is knowledge of something more than just writing. The major Romantic lyrics of blockage are poems about the world and the way we know and shape it, as well as about writing. They reveal the great paradox of creative impairment: that it can be a necessary precursor to health, that blockage and breakthrough often go together.

Notes

1. Introduction

1. Alexander Grinstein, ed., *The Index of Psychoanalytic Writings*, 14 vols. (New York: International Universities Press, 1960–75), which covers the years 1900–1969, contains only four citations under the headings "writer's block" and "writing block." Two of these citations are to articles by Edmund Bergler, a third is to a review of *The Writer and Psychoanalysis*, and the fourth is to an article by Paul Goodman. *Psychological Abstracts*, which covers succeeding years, contains no citations. In the *Social Sciences Citation Index*, from 1972 to 1982, there are seven references, two of which are to reviews on a quite different subject, and one of which is a joke—of sorts. Mike Rose, *Writer's Block: The Cognitive Dimension* (Carbondale: Southern Illinois University Press, 1984), p. 11 (henceforth cited in the Notes as *WB*), ran computer searches of *Dissertation Abstracts* and *Educational Resources Information Center (ERIC)* and "found no formal social science/educational investigations." I ran computer searches of the *MLA Bibliography* (1963–89), *Dissertation Abstracts* (1861–1990), *Arts and Humanities Search* (1980–90), *Social Science Search* (1972–90), and *ERIC* (1966–90) and found little of use—fewer than a dozen articles—among the thirty or so references cited. Most of these references discuss problems in student composition and were written within the last five years.

2. Examples of such manuals or handbooks are Karin Mack and Eric Skjei, *Overcoming Writer's Blocks* (Los Angeles: J. P. Tarcher, 1979); Joan Mininger, *Free Yourself to Write* (San Francisco: Workshops for Innovative Teaching, 1980); Bill Downey, *Right Brain—Write On! Overcoming Writer's Block and Achieving Your Creative Potential* (Englewood Cliffs, N.J.: Prentice-Hall, 1984); and Victoria Nelson, *Writer's Block and How to Use it* (Cincinnati: Writer's Digest Press, 1985). The earliest of these handbooks is probably Dorothea Brande, *Becoming a Writer* (1934), which discusses the topic but never actually uses the term *writer's block*. A paperback reprint (Los Angeles: J. P. Tarcher, 1981) contains a "Preface" by John Gardner and an "Index," in which the term *writer's block* appears.

3. See Rose, *WB*, and Mike Rose, ed., *When a Writer Can't Write: Studies in Writer's Block and Other Composing-Process Problems* (New York: Guildford Press, 1985). Several of the contributors to *When a Writer Can't Write* figure in post–1985 *ERIC* and *Social Science Search* citations.

4. The claim is made in "Does 'Writer's Block' Exist?" *American Imago* 7, no. 1 (March 1950):1. In this article, Edmund Bergler refers to *writer's block* as "a term coined and genetically explained (as far as I know) by myself in a dozen studies on writers conducted over a period of nearly twenty years, and expounded in my recent book, *The Writer and Psychoanalysis.*" The earliest of these studies in English was published in 1944; the earliest in German, in 1935. Although writer's block is the subject—at least in part—of both articles, the actual term does not appear until an article of 1947. In the 1944 article "On a Clinical Approach to the Psychoanalysis of Writers," *Psychoanalytic Review* 31, no. 1 (January 1944):40–70, the term used is *work inhibitions*. Much of the material in this article has been included in *The Writer and Psychoanalysis*, with the term *writer's block* substituted. The first use of the term I can find is in "Further Contributions to the Psychoanalysis of Writers," *Psychoanalytic Review* 34, no. 4 (October 1947):455, in which the term appears once, without quotation marks. In the continuation of the essay, in *Psychoanalytic Review* 35, no. 1 (January 1948):33–50, the final section is "Psychoanalytic Curability of Writers with 'Writer's Block.'"

5. J. A. Simpson, senior editor (general) of the Oxford Dictionaries, letter to the author, 15 March 1984.

6. Listed unalphabetically as Eidelberg, L., and Bergler, E., "Der Mammakomplex des Mannes," Z 19, no. 4 (1933):547–83. Z is the common abbreviation for *International Zeitschrift für Psychoanalyse*. See Ludwig Eidelberg, ed., *Encyclopedia of Psychoanalysis* (New York: Free Press; London: Collier Macmillan, 1968), p. 232.

7. Among these is Eidelberg, in the *Encyclopedia of Psychoanalysis* and in an earlier article, "The Genesis of Agoraphobia and Writer's Cramp," Z 22, no. 4 (1936):571–94. Grinstein, *Index of Psychoanalytic Writings*, also lists Robert H. Jokl, "On the Psychogenesis of Writer's Cramp," Z 8, no. 1 (1922):168–90, and the Jungian therapist Jolande Jacobi, "A Case of Writer's Cramp," in *Case Studies in Counselling and Psychotherapy*, ed. A. Burton (Englewood Cliffs, N.J.: Prentice-Hall, 1959). For more recent references, see Robert Boice, "Psychotherapies for Writer's Block," in *When a Writer Can't Write*, ed. Rose, pp. 195–96.

8. The 1931 citation from the *O.E.D.* cross-references a noteworthy 1890 citation for "blocking": "W. James Princ. Psychol. II xxvi 527. We shall study anon the blocking and its release. Our higher thought is full of it."

9. These and other bibliographical and biographical details come from Dr. Melvyn Iscove's "Introduction" to the 1982 reprinting of the second enlarged edition of Edmund Bergler's *Counterfeit-Sex: Homosexuality, Impotence, Frigidity* (1951; reprint, New York: Grune and Stratton, 1982), pp. i–xii. Rose J. Orente, a trustee, like Iscove, of the Edmund and Marianne Bergler Psychiatric Foundation in New York, has also supplied me with a brief biographical note.

10. Edmund Bergler, *The Basic Neurosis: Oral Regression and Psychic Masochism* (New York: Grune and Stratton, 1949), contains Bergler's fullest, if most technical, exposition of "psychic masochism."

11. Bergler, *Counterfeit-Sex*, p. xi.

12. Bergler, "Does 'Writer's Block' Exist?" 13.

13. Bergler, *Counterfeit-Sex*, p. xi.

14. Lionel Trilling, "Art and Neurosis," in *The Liberal Imagination: Essays on Literature and Society* (Harmondsworth, Middlesex: Penguin, 1970), p. 175; Christopher Ricks, *Keats and Embarrassment* (Oxford: Oxford University Press, 1974), p. 88; and Norman Holland, *Psychoanalysis and Shakespeare* (1964; reprint, New York: Farrar Straus and Giroux, 1979), p. 148. The disciple to whom Holland refers is Arthur Wormhoudt, who applies Bergler's theories to the Romantic poets in *The Demon Lover* (New York: Exposition Press, 1949), and to Shakespeare in *Hamlet's Mouse Trap* (New York: Philosophical Library, 1956).

15. Edmund Bergler, *The Writer and Psychoanalysis* (Garden City, N.Y.: Doubleday, 1950), p. xiii.

16. The effect of the phrase "professional critics" on the reader's confidence is like that of the abrupt shifts of register found in even the best of psychoanalytic aestheticians. Here, for example, is the admirable D. W. Winnicott, from the "Introduction" to *Playing and Reality* (Harmondsworth, Middlesex: Penguin, 1974), p. xi:

> It is, of course, possible to see that this which may be described as an intermediate area has found recognition in the work of philosophers. In theology it takes special shape in the eternal controversy over transubstantiation. It appears in full force in the work characteristic of the so-called metaphysical poets (Donne, etc.). My own approach derives from my study of babies and children, and considering the place of these phenomena in the life of the child one must recognize the central position of Winnie the Pooh; I gladly add a reference to the Peanuts cartoon by Schulz.

Winnicott may well be aware of what this sounds like: the naïve clarity and simplicity of his writing, if not precisely *faux naif,* are surely studied. But for anyone who knows the literature of psychoanalytic aesthetics, the shift from metaphysical poetry to Winnie the Pooh has a familiar ring. It is like, for example, Hanns Sachs, the early Freudian, turning from Schopenhauer to other matters: "Shall we go on to discuss the case of classic music versus swing?" (*The Creative Unconscious* [Cambridge, Mass.: Sci-Art Publications, 1942], p. 174).

17. Alfred Kazin, "The Language of Pundits," in *Freud: A Collection of Critical Essays,* ed. Perry Meisel (Englewood Cliffs, N.J.: Prentice-Hall, 1981), p. 112.

18. Bergler, *Writer and Psychoanalysis,* p. 81.

19. A. A. Brill, "Poetry as an Oral Outlet," *Psychoanalytic Review* 18, no. 4 (October 1931):357 and 378.

20. Philip Roth, *My Life as a Man* (London: Jonathan Cape, 1974), pp. 239–40.

21. Edmund Bergler, "Can the Writer 'Resign' from His Calling?" *International Journal of Psycho-Analysis* 34, no. 1 (1953):42.

22. Quoted in David Timms, *Philip Larkin* (Edinburgh: Oliver and Boyd, 1973), p. 3.

23. *Schreibkrampf* and *Schreibmotorik* refer to "writer's cramp." *Der Schreiblock* is "a writing pad." *Die unfahigkeit zuschreiben* and *die Schreibunfahigkeit* refer to a variety of unspecified writing difficulties and are not necessarily psychological. *Block* and *blockieren* refer to psychological impediments, but are not compounded with *schreiben* or *schriften*. *Schreibstörung* means the inability to write manually—to exercise the proper muscles involved in writing—but includes not only emotional or psychological causes but also physical ones. French has *bloc* and *blocage* as psychological impediments, as well as related metaphorical expressions, such as *terreur la page blanc* or *horreur la page blanc*.

24. Philip Larkin, "An Interview with *Paris Review*," in *Required Writing: Miscellaneous Pieces, 1955–1982* (London: Faber and Faber, 1984), p. 71.

25. The poem was reprinted in *Observer*, 8 December 1985, and in Philip Larkin, *Collected Poems*, ed. Anthony Thwaite (London and Boston: Marvell Press and Faber and Faber, 1988), p. 202.

26. Quoted in Justin Kaplan, *Mr. Clemens and Mark Twain: A Biography* (1966; reprint, New York: Simon and Schuster, 1983), p. 71.

27. John Keats to J. H. Reynolds, 19 February 1818, in *The Letters of John Keats*, ed. Hyder Edward Rollins, 2 vols. (Cambridge, Mass.: Harvard University Press, 1958), 1:231.

28. Quoted in R.E.M. Harding, *An Anatomy of Inspiration* (Cambridge: Heffers, 1942), p. 15.

29. Quoted in P. N. Furbank, *E. M. Forster: A Life*, 2 vols. (New York: Harcourt Brace Jovanovich, 1977–78), 1:199.

30. Ibid., 1:249, 192.

31. Ibid., 1:204.

32. Ibid., 2:64.

33. Mark Twain to Monroe Conway, 1 August 1876, quoted in Walter Blair, *Mark Twain and Huck Finn* (Berkeley and Los Angeles: University of California Press, 1960), p. 99.

34. Mark Twain, *The Adventures of Huckleberry Finn*, in *Mark Twain: Mississippi Writings* (New York: Library of America, 1982), p. 710.

35. Ibid., p. 716.

36. Ibid.

37. Ibid., p. 717.

38. Quoted in Kaplan, *Mr. Clemens and Mark Twain*, p. 251.

39. "Introduction" to the Riverside edition, edited by Henry Nash Smith (Cambridge, Mass.: Riverside Press, 1958), p. xi.

40. But note Twain's comment: "I confined myself to boy-life out on the Mississippi not because I was not familiar with other phases of life . . . [but because] I lack the other essential: interest in handling the men and experiences of later times." Quoted in Bernard De Voto, ed., *The Portable Mark Twain* (New York: Viking Press, 1946), pp. 773–74.

41. At times, Twain associates writing with floating and letting loose: "Since there is no plot to the thing," he writes to Howells, while at work on *Tom Sawyer*, "it is likely to follow its own drift, and so is as likely to drift into manhood as anywhere—I won't interpose" (Letter of 21 June 1875, quoted in Kaplan, *Mr. Clemens*, p. 180).

42. Twain, *Huck Finn*, p. 739.

43. Twain, *Huck Finn* (Riverside edition), p. x.

44. Blair, *Mark Twain and Huck Finn*, p. 151. Bernard De Voto, for example, calls the work of this period, including *A Tramp Abroad* (1880), *The Prince and the Pauper* (1882), and *Life on the Mississippi* (1883), "essentially uncreative," in *Mark Twain at Work* (Cambridge, Mass.: Harvard University Press, 1942), p. 56.

45. Joseph Conrad to Edward Garnett, 29 March 1898, in *The Collected Letters of Joseph Conrad*, ed. Frederick R. Karl, 3 vols. (Cambridge: Cambridge University Press, 1988), 2:49.

46. Anthony Burgess, "Father of the Private Eye" (review of *Dashiell Hammett: A Life*, by Diane Johnson), *Observer*, 22 January 1984.

47. Recorded in James Boswell, *Journal of a Tour to the Hebrides with Samuel Johnson, LL.D.* (1785), ed. R. Chapman (London: Oxford University Press, 1970), p. 184.

48. Joseph Conrad to John Galsworthy, 22 December 1909, quoted in Jocelyn Baines, *Joseph Conrad: A Critical Biography* (New York: McGraw-Hill, 1960), pp. 259–60.

49. W. J. Bate, *Samuel Johnson* (New York: Harcourt Brace Jovanovich, 1975), pp. 378–79.

50. See, for example, Roland Barthes, "What Is Writing?" in *Writing Degree Zero*, trans. Annette Lavers and Colin Smith (New York: Hill and Wang, 1977), pp. 359–60.

51. George Miller, "A Model Science" (review of *Mental Models: Towards a Cognitive Science of Language, Inference and Consciousness*, by P. N. Johnson-Laird), *London Review of Books* 5, no. 20 (3–16 November 1983):18.

52. *WB*, p. xvi.

53. For a short, clear account of the early history of creativity as a field of academic study, see John Beloff, "Creative Thinking in Art and Science," in *British Journal of Aesthetics* 10, no. 1 (January 1970):59–67.

54. See Rose, *WB*, pp. 7–11 and 124, for accounts of earlier models of the composing process based on cognitive psychology.

55. Bergler, "Does 'Writer's Block' Exist?" 51–52.

56. "The Claims of Psycho-Analysis to Scientific Interest" (1913), in *The Standard Edition of the Complete Psychological Works of Sigmund Freud*, ed. and trans. James Strachey et al., 24 vols. (London: Hogarth Press, 1953–73), 13:186. Subsequent references to Freud's writings are to volume and page of the *Standard Edition*.

57. Quoted in Ernest Jones, *The Life and Work of Sigmund Freud*, 3 vols. (New York: Basic Books, 1953–57), 3:412.

58. Fry's criticisms are discussed in ibid., 3:410–12.

59. W. H. Auden, "Psychology and Art Today," in *Freud: A Collection of Critical Essays*, ed. Perry Meisel (Englewood Cliffs, N.J.: Prentice-Hall, 1981), p. 66. The essay originally appeared in *The Arts Today*, ed. Geoffrey Grigson (London: John Lane, 1935), pp. 1–21.

60. William Empson, *Seven Types of Ambiguity* (London: Chatto and Windus, 1930), p. 286. See also Ernst Kris and Abraham Kaplan, "Aesthetic Am-

biguity," in Ernst Kris, *Psychoanalytic Explorations in Art* (New York: International Universities Press, 1952), pp. 243–64.

61. Marie Bonaparte, *The Life and Works of Edgar Allan Poe: A Psycho-Analytic Interpretation*, trans. John Rodker (London: Imago, 1949), p. 664.

62. Hanna Segal, "A Psycho-Analytical Approach to Aesthetics," in *New Directions in Psycho-Analysis*, ed. Melanie Klein, Paula Heimann, and R. E. Money-Kyrle (London: Tavistock Publications, 1955), p. 392.

63. Ibid., pp. 390–91.

64. Paul Federn, "The Neurotic Style," *Psychiatric Quarterly* 31, no. 4 (October 1957):681–89. See also Lawrence Kubie, *Neurotic Distortions of the Creative Process* (New York: Noonday Press, 1973).

65. Franz Kafka to Felice Bauer, 29 November 1912, in Franz Kafka, *Letters to Felice*, ed. E. Heller and J. Born (Harmondsworth, Middlesex: Penguin, 1976), p. 185.

66. George Gissing, *New Grub Street* (Harmondsworth, Middlesex: Penguin, 1968), p. 154.

67. See Stephen J. Gould, "Darwin's Delay," in *Ever since Darwin: Reflections on Natural History* (New York: W. W. Norton, 1977), pp. 21–27.

68. Kris, *Psychoanalytic Explorations in Art*, pp. 72–73.

69. Rudolf Arnheim, *The Genesis of a Painting: Picasso's Guernica* (Berkeley and Los Angeles: University of California Press, 1962), p. 3. For the cognitive and *mimetic* character of the plastic arts in Greek culture of the classical period, see Wladyslaw Tartarkiewicz, *A History of Six Ideas: An Essay in Aesthetics*, trans. C. Kasparak (The Hague and Boston: Nijhoff, 1980), pp. 92ff.

70. Edith Hamilton and Huntington Cairns, eds., *The Collected Dialogues of Plato* (New York: Pantheon Books, 1961), p. 492.

71. Kris, *Psychoanalytic Explorations in Art*, p. 42.

72. Marion Milner, *On Not Being Able to Paint* (1950; reprint, London: Heinemann Educational Books, 1981), p. 134.

73. Ibid.

74. Ibid., p. 123.

75. Ibid., p. 124.

76. Paul Goodman, "On Writer's Block," in *Nature Heals: The Psychological Essays of Paul Goodman*, ed. Taylor Stoehr (New York: Free Life Editions, 1977), pp. 95–96.

77. The first quote comes from John Keats's letter of 3 February 1818 to J. H. Reynolds, the second from his letter of 8 October 1817 to Benjamin Bailey, in *Letters of John Keats*, ed. Rollins, 1:224 and 170.

78. Samuel Taylor Coleridge to Thomas Poole, [21 March] 1800, in *The Collected Letters of Samuel Taylor Coleridge*, ed. Earl L. Griggs, 6 vols. (Oxford: Clarendon Press, 1956–71),1:583.

79. Marilyn Butler, *Romantics, Rebels and Reactionaries: English Literature and Its Background, 1760–1830* (Oxford: Oxford University Press, 1981), pp. 69–71. To Coleridge's journalistic contemporaries, his fluency as a man of letters was undoubted. Daniel Stuart, editor of the *Morning Post*, preferred Coleridge "to Mackintosh, Burke, or any man I ever heard of," when it came to the writing of lead articles; "but when Coleridge wrote in his study without being

pressed, he wandered and lost himself" (quoted in Samuel Taylor Coleridge, *Essays on His Times*, ed. D. V. Erdman, 3 vols. [Princeton: Princeton University Press, 1978], 1:lxvii).

80. Richard Holmes, *Coleridge* (Oxford: Oxford University Press, 1982), p. 20. In his recent biography, *Coleridge: Early Visions* (London: Hodder and Stoughton, 1989), Holmes talks of Coleridge's unpublished writings—his letters and Notebook entries—in ways that obscure their difference from published work. To call the series of autobiographical letters he wrote to Thomas Poole in 1797 the "first fruits" (p. 135) of Coleridge's spiritual self-examination makes sense only if one remembers that they may not have *felt* like fruits—or accomplishments—to Coleridge because they were unpublished, merely letters.

81. George Eliot, *Middlemarch* (1871–72; Cambridge, Mass.: Riverside Press, 1956), p. 148.

82. Albert Camus, *The Plague*, trans. Stuart Gilbert (New York: Random House, 1948), p. 95.

83. Patrick McCarthy, *Camus* (New York: Random House, 1982), p. 226.

84. Herbert R. Lottman, *Albert Camus: A Biography* (Garden City, N.J.: Doubleday, 1979), pp. 530–31. The French edition is simply *Albert Camus* (Paris: Editions du Seuil, 1978), p. 571: "Après une longue periode de blocage où il avait sustitue à sa vrai vocation divers travaux d'adaptation."

85. Camus, *The Plague*, p. 239.

86. Ibid., p. 276.

87. Eliot, *Middlemarch*, p. 63.

88. Ibid., p. 207.

89. Diane Johnson, *Dashiell Hammett: A Life* (New York: Random House, 1983), p. 42.

90. Ibid., p. 154.

91. Ibid., p. 155.

92. Ibid.

93. Furbank, *E. M. Forster: A Life*, 2:132–33.

94. Quoted in John Updike, "Melville's Withdrawal," in *Hugging the Shore* (New York: Alfred A. Knopf, 1983), p. 98.

95. Ibid.

96. Ibid., pp. 105–6.

97. John Updike, *Bech: A Book* (New York: Alfred A. Knopf, 1970), p. v. For more on blocked Bech, see *Bech Is Back* (New York: Alfred A. Knopf, 1982).

98. Anne Tyler, "Still Just Writing," in *First Person Singular: Writers on Their Craft*, ed. Joyce Carol Oates (Princeton: Ontario Review Press, 1983), p. 172.

2. The Freudian Account

1. Freud treated H.D. in Vienna in 1933–34, but for a larger or nonliterary malaise: "I, like most of the people I knew in England, America, and on the continent was drifting," she writes in *Tribute to Freud* (1956; reprint, South Hinksey and Oxford: Carcanet Press, 1971), p. 6. See also "The Psychogene-

sis of a Case of Homosexuality in a Woman" (1920), in *The Standard Edition of the Complete Psychological Works of Sigmund Freud*, ed. and trans. James Strachey et al., 24 vols. (London: Hogarth Press, 1953–73), 18:147–72. Subsequent references to Freud's writings are to volume and page of the *Standard Edition*.

2. Reuben Fine, *A History of Psychoanalysis* (New York: Columbia University Press, 1979), pp. 275–76 and 534–68.

3. Quoted in Ernest Jones, *The Life and Work of Sigmund Freud*, 3 vols. (New York: Basic Books, 1953–57), 2:442–43. For complaints about the inadequacies of language in dream interpretation, see *The Interpretation of Dreams* (4:118 and 5:403 and 537); also "Fragment of an Analysis of a Case of Hysteria" (1905 [1901]), the so-called Dora case (7:9–10, 12–13, 59–60, and 112), in which Freud admits to the necessity of altering and shaping his material. "How bungled our reproductions are," Freud told Jung, apropos his account of the Rat Man case, "how wretchedly we dissect the great works of nature" (letter of 30 June 1909, in *The Freud/Jung Letters*, ed. W. McGuire [Princeton: Princeton University Press, 1974], p. 238). For an intelligent and informative account of Freud's own writing practice, see Patrick Mahoney, *Freud as a Writer* (New York: International Universities Press, 1982), which includes a discussion of French poststructuralist accounts of Freud and writing.

4. Sigmund Freud to Wilhelm Fliess, 31 May 1897, in *The Origins of Psychoanalysis: Letters to Wilhelm Fliess, Drafts and Notes: 1887–1902*, ed. Marie Bonaparte, Anna Freud, and Ernst Kris (New York: Basic Books, 1954), p. 208.

5. John Updike, "Why I Write," in *Picked-up Pieces* (London: André Deutsch, 1976), pp. 35–37.

6. Frederic Jameson, "Imaginary and Symbolic in Lacan: Marxism, Psychoanalytic Criticism, and the Problem of the Subject," in *Literature and Psychoanalysis: The Question of Reading: Otherwise*, ed. Shoshana Felman (Baltimore: Johns Hopkins University Press, 1982), p. 352.

7. Ernest Jones, *Papers on Psycho-Analysis* (London: Ballière, Tindall and Cox, 1948), p. 116.

8. Norman Holland, *Psychoanalysis and Shakespeare* (New York: McGraw-Hill, 1964), p. 18.

9. Frederick Crews, *Out of My System: Psychoanalysis, Ideology and Critical Method* (New York: Oxford University Press, 1975), p. 5.

10. J. Laplanche and J.-B. Pontalis, *The Language of Psychoanalysis*, trans. Donald Nicholson-Smith (New York: W. W. Norton, 1973), pp. 285–86.

11. Kurt Eissler calls "The Theme of the Three Caskets" "the first paper of Freud's in which death is assigned a central place," in "The Relation of Explaining and Understanding in Psychoanalysis: Demonstrated by One Aspect of Freud's Approach to Literature," in *The Psychoanalytic Study of the Child*, vol. 23 (New York: International Universities Press, 1968), p. 152. For Lacan's quite different account of the development of the theory of the *Todestrieb*, see "The Function of Language in Psychoanalysis" (1956), in *The Language of the Self: The Function of Language in Psychoanalysis*, trans. Anthony Wilden (Baltimore: John Hopkins University Press, 1968), pp. 81–85. See also, from a Derridean perspective, Sarah Kofman, *The Childhood of Art*, trans.

Winifred Woodhull (New York: Columbia University Press, 1988). Kofman's book, originally published in France in 1970, discusses, interestingly, not only Lacan's theory of the origins of the death drive but also other poststructuralist theories of writing discussed in chap. 8.

12. Holland, *Psychoanalysis and Shakespeare,* tries to explain this silence by distinguishing between a "psychological" and a "mythical" meaning in Freud's account of *Lear:* "His final union with Cordelia ('Have I caught thee?') represents on the mythical level a mature acceptance of death; psychologically, it is a further regressive attempt to 'have' his daughter" (p. 66). Holland's license for such a distinction is a remark Freud made in a letter of 25 March 1934 to J.S.H. Bransom about the latter's *The Tragedy of King Lear* (1934). In that letter, Freud characterizes "The Theme of the Three Caskets" as having dealt with "the mythological content of the material," whereas what he now sees as "the secret meaning of the tragedy" is Lear's "repressed incestuous claims on the daughter's love"—a "new" interpretation that is a reversion to the standard line. Nothing more clearly illustrates the piecemeal nature of Freud's aesthetics than his failure, even at this point, either to bring the earlier essay into line with his new account of the instincts (something that his sense of the latter's vulnerably literary or nonempirical character might have encouraged), or to account for its exceptional nature. But the discrepancy may also be simply a manifestation of Freud's larger difficulties with the death instinct: his unwillingness or inability to integrate it into earlier accounts of defensive conflict; his sense, for instance, that it was, on the one hand, "beyond" the pleasure principle, and, on the other, an expression of it, so "the pleasure principle seems actually to serve the death instincts" (*Beyond the Pleasure Principle,* 17:63).

This contradiction, as Laplanche and Pontalis point out, "led Freud subsequently to differentiate the Nirvana principle from the pleasure principle," with the former signifying the death instincts—the instincts that work toward death or the abolition of tension—and the latter signifying the demands of the libido (*The Language of Psychoanalysis,* p. 102). The death instincts, according to the new formulation, were to be contrasted with what Freud calls "life instincts" or "Eros," by which he means the two sorts of categories or instincts delineated in earlier writings. These are the sexual instincts and the ego instincts or instincts of self-preservation. Nowhere in Freud's writing about art and literature is the unallayed wish buried in a work of art or piece of writing identified with the ego instincts. See "The Economic Problem of Masochism" (1924), 19:155–72.

13. There is one other occasion, in "The Moses of Michelangelo" (1914), in which Freud identifies a sense of the real—of what is given and limits—with a work's purpose, underplaying the importance of the supposedly motivating wish. According to the traditional interpretation, Michelangelo had represented Moses at the moment of seeing his disobedient followers worshipping the golden calf: he is about to hurl the tablets to the ground. To Freud, though, the statue depicts Moses *after* the initial burst of anger, an interpretation based on a famously detailed "reading"—in the manner of dream interpretation—of the figure's position and hands, and of the way he holds the

tablets. Michelangelo "does not let Moses break them in his wrath, but makes him be influenced by the danger that they will be broken and makes him calm that wrath, or at any rate prevent it from becoming an act. In this way he has added something new and more than human to the figure of Moses; so that the giant frame with its tremendous physical power becomes only a concrete expression of the highest mental achievement that is possible in a man, that of struggling successfully against an inward passion for the sake of a cause to which he has devoted himself" (12:233).

On the one hand, this interpretation is perfectly consonant with Freud's view of art as a means of allaying ungratified wishes; the ungratified wish in this case is self-mastery, with Moses a "character-type, embodying an inexhaustible inner force which tames the recalcitrant world" (13:221). On the other hand, this is not the view Freud chooses to emphasize at the essay's conclusion, where the reason he gives for Michelangelo's choice of such a subject is connected with his sense of Pope Julius II, who commissioned the sculpture as one of a group of figures to adorn his tomb, and of Michelangelo's identification with him. "The artist felt the same violent force of will in himself," writes Freud of Michelangelo's sense of Pope Julius II, "and, as the more introspective thinker, may have had a premonition of the failure to which they were both doomed. And so he carved his Moses on the Pope's tomb, not without a reproach against the dead pontiff, as a warning to himself, thus, in self-criticism, rising superior to his own nature" (13:234).

What Freud stresses here are the warning and the reproach: the sense of the real all but eclipses the gratified wish. Michelangelo's Moses looks like the fulfillment of a wish—to maintain total control; in reality, it is a warning of the impossibility of such a wish—a warning critics have seen as applicable to Freud himself, as well as to Michelangelo and his patron. Any number of factors might inhibit the expression of such a truth, and fear of the father (or what stands for him) need not be one of them. "The Moses of Michelangelo," though, is a rare instance; on the whole, Freud saw chastening truths and warnings as part of a work's manifest content, like the "thought" that lends respectability to or protects a joke. Freud usually treats admonition in a work as a form of disguise, another way of diverting attention from the work's repressed wishes.

14. Lionel Trilling, *The Liberal Imagination: Essays on Literature and Society* (Harmondsworth, Middlesex: Penguin, 1970), p. 167.

15. Marion Milner, "The Role of Illusion in Symbol Formation," in *New Directions in Psycho-Analysis*, ed. Melanie Klein, Paula Heimann, and R. E. Money-Kyrle (London: Tavistock Press, 1955), p. 83.

16. Excerpts from the untranslated version of this essay, "Die Bedeutung der Psychoanalyze fur die Geisteswissenschaften" (1913), are cited and translated in Jones, *Papers on Psycho-Analysis*, pp. 95–97, 103–4, and 108–9. The essay was first translated in 1915 by C. R. Payne as no. 23 in the *Nervous and Mental Disease Monograph Series* (New York: Journal of Nervous and Mental Disease Publishing Co., 1915), and reprinted in installments over two years in the *Psychoanalytic Review* 2, no. 3 (July 1915):297–326; 2, no. 4 (October 1915):428–57; 3, no. 1 (January 1916):68–89; 3, no. 2 (April 1916):189–214; and 3, no. 3 (July 1916):318–35.

17. Doris Lessing, *The Golden Notebook* (1962; New York: Bantam Books, 1981), p. 62.

18. Ernest Jones, *Hamlet and Oedipus* (New York: Anchor Books, 1957), p. 100.

19. Hanns Sachs, *Freud: Master and Friend* (Cambridge, Mass.: Harvard University Press, 1944), p. 103.

20. Marie Bonaparte, *The Life and Works of Edgar Allan Poe: A Psycho-Analytic Interpretation*, trans. John Rodker (London: Imago, 1949), p. 663.

21. Richard Wollheim, "Freud and the Understanding of Art," *British Journal of Aesthetics* 10, no. 3 (July 1970):222.

22. The concept of forepleasure also appears in another work of 1905, the *Three Essays on the Theory of Sexuality*. In these essays, Freud distinguishes between "pleasure due to the excitation of erogenous zones," which is, of course, forepleasure, and the "end-pleasure" it generates, "due to the discharge of the sexual substances" (7:210). What is noteworthy here is Freud's association of extended sexual foreplay, or undue emphasis upon it, with perversion. For example, scopophilia (pleasure in looking) becomes voyeurism, or a perversion, when "instead of being *preparatory* to the normal sexual aim, it supplants it" (7:157). Perhaps a comparable distrust of aesthetic forepleasure plays some part in his ambivalence about art and artists. In "Psychopathic Characters on the Stage," for example, written at approximately the same time as "Creative Writers and Day-Dreaming," Freud talks of the dramatist's skill "in avoiding resistances and offering fore-pleasures" (7:310) and of the tragedian's need to "know how to compensate, by means of the possible satisfactions involved, for the sympathetic suffering that is involved" (7:305). In *An Autobiographical Study* (1925), Freud repeats an earlier reference to the artist's use "of the perceptual pleasure of formal beauty as what I have called an 'incentive bonus'" (20:65). That there is something belittling or superior—and ultimately limited—about this conception of what is aesthetic is neatly (if unconsciously?) suggested in E. H. Gombrich's rococo paraphrase: "A thought which perhaps it would be rude or indecorous to utter plain is dropped as it were into the magic spring of the primary process, as one can dip a flower or twig into the calcine waters of Karlsbad" ("Freud's Aesthetics," in *Literature and Psychoanalysis*, ed. E. Kurzwill and W. Phillips [New York: Columbia University Press, 1983], p. 134). The aesthetic bonus in this sense is decoration or surface, like the spun-sugar façades of Viennese rococo.

23. Hanns Sachs, *The Creative Unconscious* (Cambridge, Mass.: Sci-Art Publications, 1942), pp. 168–69 and 176.

24. The connection Freudians draw between beauty and sexual excitation has a perfectly respectable philosophic and scientific ancestry—and was fashionable in Freud's day. According to Jack Spector, it "approaches theories developed by Darwin concerning the origins of the sense of beauty in the 'artistic' display of decorative finery in order to attract a mate" (*The Aesthetics of Freud: A Study in Psychoanalysis and Art* [New York: McGraw-Hill, 1972], p. 104).

25. Holland, *Psychoanalysis and Shakespeare*, p. 40.

26. Ibid., p. 41.

27. Ibid.

28. Ibid. That this is a common view is suggested by a similar assumption made by the contemporary American screenwriter William Goldman: "Sure, we want our secondary roles to be as distinctive as we can make them," writes Goldman in defense of the old Hollywood practice of giving all the best lines to the star, "But, movies are not Chekhov. There are not nine people we root for" (*Adventures in the Screen Trade* [New York: Warner Books, 1983], p. 136).

29. Holland, *Psychoanalysis and Shakespeare*, p. 41.

30. Sachs's theories of beauty in *The Creative Unconscious* are sometimes said to extend those of Freud. For Sachs, the indispensable condition for beauty is the absence of anxiety: "in other words, that neither the conscious nor the unconscious contents provoke moral condemnation. The distance, marked by conscience, between the ideal which the Super-ego demands and the actual ego, with all its vices and infirmities, has disappeared, and no objection is raised even to the Id and its drives" (p. 273). This, though, is quite similar to what Freud implies in his emphasis on disguise and distortion, and Sachs only goes beyond Freud when he talks of the perfection of form as a way of relieving writers from guilt about their fantasies—what Sachs calls the "narcissistic bribe" offered by the work of art. According to Sachs, poets give up a good deal when they abandon the narcissistic satisfactions of an asocial daydream for the necessary disguises and distortions of art. The aesthetic bonus is the author's (and reader's) reward, the replacement or recompense he or she receives for overcoming narcissism. Freud has only one passage close to this, from *The Future of an Illusion*, in which he says that acts of artistic creation "heighten [the artist's] feelings of identification, of which every cultural unit stands in so much need, by providing an occasion for sharing highly valued emotional experiences. And when those creations picture the achievements of his particular culture and bring to his mind its ideals in an impressive manner, they also minister to his narcissistic satisfactions" (21:14). Rank will make much of this point.

31. Wollheim, "Freud and the Understanding of Art," p. 221.

32. Johan Huizinga, *Homo Ludens* (London: Temple Smith, 1971), pp. 28–29.

33. Anthony Storr, *The Dynamics of Creation* (New York: Atheneum, 1972), p. 118.

34. Spector, *Aesthetics of Freud*, p. 117.

35. Philip Rieff, *Freud: The Mind of the Moralist* (New York: Viking Press, 1959), p. 351.

36. This later view of Freud's is shared, among others, by Storr, who disapproves of most of what Freud has to say about play before his late phase. For Storr, "it seems highly likely that one biological function of play is to teach young animals how to ritualize their primitive impulses of aggression in such a way that they can fit into a social group. . . . If it can be shown, as I think it can, that the apparently superfluous, 'extra' activity of the play in fact fulfills an essential function, it will not be difficult to extend this notion to art" (*Dynamics of Creation*, p. 125). In this theory, play itself, the simple

exercise of one's imaginative capacities, becomes the purpose of art; Freud's earlier notion of art as a means, through an aesthetic bonus, of allaying ungratified wishes is left behind. But this notion is left behind not by Freud himself (he never developed the later theory), but by some of his followers.

Holland points to a different connection between art and play, though whether this connection relates to Freud's theory of the aesthetic bonus is difficult to say. To be successful, an artist, like a child at play, must create a space or dimension that, though unreal, is also believable. As Freud says in "Creative Writers and Day-Dreaming," "many things which, if they were real, would not give him enjoyment, can do so in the play of phantasy, and many excitements which, in themselves, are actually distressing, can become a source of pleasure for the hearers and spectators at the performance of a writer's work" (9:144). The source of the pleasure Freud is talking of here is neither catharsis nor the work's fulfillment of one's wishes, but rather the writer's ability to create a coherent and believable world, a "reality" that, in Holland's words, "serves to reduce some of the egoistic quality of the daydream by simply objectifying it—although at the same time sharply distinguishing it from 'real' reality" (*Psychoanalysis and Shakespeare*, p. 17). This view of art or culture is very close to that of Winnicott, and it clearly helps to differentiate the artist from the neurotic or daydreamer.

37. See Charles Rycroft, *A Critical Dictionary of Psychoanalysis* (Harmondsworth, Middlesex: Penguin, 1972), p. 72: "In psycho-analysis the term is usually used to refer to instances in which the state of inhibition can be regarded as a symptom."

38. Ella Sharpe, "From *King Lear* to *The Tempest*," *International Journal of Psycho-Analysis* 27, nos. 1 and 2 (1946):29. For Sachs, see *The Creative Unconscious*, pp. 289–323.

3. After Freud

1. Frederick Crews, "Analysis Terminable," *Commentary* 70, no. 1 (July 1980):26. In "Psychotherapies for Writer's Block," in *When a Writer Can't Write: Studies in Writer's Block and Other Composing-Process Problems*, ed. Mike Rose (New York: Guildford Press, 1985), pp. 182–226, Robert Boice, a clinical psychologist interested in behavioral techniques, lists six varieties of treatment for blocked writers, in addition to psychoanalysis. One of these, though, is automatic writing; a second is not a psychotherapy at all, merely a reminder that "anecdotal information" about blockage is available from authors themselves; and a third deals with treatments for writer's cramp rather than block. That leaves transactional and gestalt therapies (grouped together by Boice), behaviorist therapies, and the findings of cognitive psychology. The cognitive approach is that of Rose and the educational psychologists mentioned earlier.

In transactional therapy, which attributes writer's block to inhibiting authority figures, such as teachers, the therapist aims to "retain writers in situations where criticism is minimized, where exploration and play are safe" (p. 196); in gestalt therapy, the technique employed is "paradoxical treatment": in Boice's words, "by stating a doubt that the client can succeed, the therapist motivates the client to prove him/her wrong" (p. 196).

The theoretical formulations of behavioral therapy are no fuller or more interesting: as Boice himself admits, "all these techniques derive from common sense strategies that had long before been established by successful writers" (p. 198) (he has Irving Wallace principally in mind). But they are funnier. One technique, "productive avoidance," was devised in 1970 by J. T. Nurnberger and J. Zimmerman and reported in the article "Applied Analysis of Human Behaviour; an alternative to conventional motivational inference and unconscious determination in therapeutic programming." This technique "virtually assured writing by having the client write out cheques for a meaningful sum to a hated organization (e.g., the Ku Klux Klan) which would be mailed on any scheduled writing day when the preset number of pages was not completed. Not only did Nurnberger and Zimmerman produce a reliable increase in the writing output of their patient, but his related problems including marital dissatisfaction showed parallel improvements" (p. 198).

Boice's own experiments in this field are only marginally less resourceful. The technique he advocates is "contingency management," which involves the construction of "contracts" with patients: for example, a certain number of pages per day, or no shower—the shower being what Boice calls a "contingency reward." Not all these contracts work, though, because "some clients begin by insisting on contingencies that have little chance of succeeding" (p. 201). One especially devious client of Boice's, a professor turned administrator, came up with a plan to "earn his lunches by meeting writing goals; that way, he reasoned, he would either write or lose weight" (p. 201). Boice relates this proposal and his response to it without a flicker of irony or amusement: "Once the ineffectiveness of this contingency plan had been demonstrated he agreed to establish separate rewards for writing and dietary programs, both with good results" (p. 201).

2. "On the Relation of Analytical Psychology to Poetry" (1922), in *The Collected Works of C. G. Jung*, trans. R.F.C. Hull; ed. H. Read, M. Fordham, and G. Adler, 20 vols. (London: Routledge and Kegan Paul, 1953–78), 15, par. 110. This is one of two brief but influential essays on literary creativity by Jung, the equivalents of Freud's "Creative Writers and Day-Dreaming" and "The Paths to the Formation of Symptoms." The other essay is "Psychology and Literature" (1930; revised and expanded, 1950). The essays' accounts of the creation of works of art and literature are then confirmed or exemplified in two subsequent essays: one on Joyce's *Ulysses* and another on Picasso, both of which were published in 1932. On the whole, the many incidental references to literary creativity and blockage elsewhere in Jung's writings conform to these explicit formulations. (Unless otherwise specified, subsequent references to Jung's writings are to volume and paragraph number of the *Collected Works*. Dates refer to the earliest published editions in German.)

3. Hence a book such as Barbara Hannah's *Striving Towards Wholeness* (New

York: Putman, 1971), with its attempts to show how the Brontës and Robert Louis Stevenson, among others, wrote from pure inspiration, from the unconscious, as in Charlotte Brontë's remark that "the writer who possesses the creative gift owns something of which he is not always master" (p. 195). Also of relevance to the autonomy of creative power is Jung's account of the inception of Nietzsche's *Zarathustra*, in which consciousness "plays the role of slave to the daemon of the unconscious, which tyrannizes over it and inundates it with alien ideas. . . . Only this elemental force can wrench from oblivion the oldest and most delicate traces in a man's memory, while yet he retains his full genius" ("Cryptomnesia" [1905], 1, par. 184). As Jung says in "Psychology and Literature,"

> a specifically artistic psychology is more collective than personal in character. Art is a kind of innate drive that seizes a human being and makes him its instrument. The artist is not a person endowed with free will who seeks his own ends, but one who allows art to realize its purposes through him. As a human being he may have moods and a will and personal aims, but as an artist he is "man" in a higher sense—he is "collective man," a vehicle and moulder of the unconscious psychic life of mankind. (15, par. 157)

According to Erich Neumann, perhaps the best known of Jung's followers in the aesthetic realm, this is a truth discoverable within the careers of individual artists and writers. Although a writer or artist may begin in self-expression, as he matures "he becomes the heir and son of his cultural tradition, so that his maturest works are those that are least personal" (*Art and the Creative Unconscious* [New York: Pantheon Books, 1959], p. 179)—a point Jung himself suggests when he calls the first part of *Faust* psychological and the second part visionary ("Psychology and Literature," 15, par. 138). Nor are the divisions between personal and impersonal hard and fast, or the testimonies of writers themselves reliable. According to Marie-Louise von Franz, Jung's longtime collaborator, "some artists feel that they themselves mainly give *gestalt* to what they write, that they consciously choose every word, every turn of the story, drama, or poem. Others feel that they are completely under the dictate of an unknown force, and every word is a surprise to them. But this is only how the writer himself feels; even in the former case the unconscious factor may also have influenced the work, only the writer acquiesced so completely to it that he did not experience it as a 'foreign' force" (in "Analytical Psychology and Literary Criticism," *New Literary History* 12, no. 1 [Fall 1980]:119–20).

4. As for whether visionary poets do anything with their revelations except assent to them—how, if at all, they make them comprehensible or palatable—Jung says little. And what he does say is usually negative. In this respect, he is even further from the actual experiences of writers—and thus from an acceptable account of their difficulties—than Freud. The autonomous complex is not subject to conscious control, even when the writer thinks otherwise. In Jung's words, "the poet's conviction that he is creating in absolute freedom" would then be "an illusion: he fancies he is swimming

but in reality an unseen current sweeps him along" ("On the Relation of Analytic Psychology to Poetry," 15, par. 113). This sense of the all-importance of what Freud would call the primary process makes Jung, according to Herbert Read, no better than Freud. "Exactly like Freud," writes Read, "and in spite of his sense of broader implications, Jung is primarily interested in what he can abstract from a work of art and interpret in terms of his theory of the unconscious" (quoted by Morris Philipson, in *Outline of a Jungian Aesthetic* [Evanston: Northwestern University Press, 1963], p. 167. For Read's view of the Jungian aesthetic, see "Poetic Consciousness and Creative Experience," in vol. 25 of *Eranos-Yearbook 1956,* ed. Olga Fröbe-Kapteyn [Zurich: Rhein-Verlag, 1957], pp. 357–89). Jung does not, for instance, tell us why in some cases the collective unconscious issues only in fantasies, whereas in others it produces poems. Such a question simply "cannot be fathomed" (*Modern Man in Search of a Soul* [London: Kegan Paul, 1955], p. 189).

5. Although the visionary artist or poet can do little to facilitate creation, he or she has to be of a certain character or type—by which is meant something quite different from the formal "types" of Jungian psychology (the extrovert and introvert, or those characterized in terms of the four basic psychic functions—intuition, thinking, feeling, sensation). To begin with, the visionary artist or poet must be open to what are often perceived as quite alien impulses. The archetypes of the collective unconscious are often either monstrous-seeming, irrational, or ineffable; the poet who transmits them will be tainted with their strangeness, both in his or her own and others' eyes. True art, in Jung's high-flown Romantic idiom, is

> Sublime, pregnant with meaning, yet chilling the blood with its strangeness, it arises from timeless depths, glamorous, daemonic, and grotesque, it bursts asunder our human standards of value and aesthetic form, a terrifying tangle of eternal chaos, a *crimen laesae majestatis humanae.* On the other hand it can be a revelation whose heights and depths are beyond our fathoming, or a vision of beauty which we can never put into words . . . the primordial experiences rend from top to bottom the curtain upon which is painted the picture of an ordered world. (15, par. 141)

Clearly, the writer who communicates such visions is bound to seem odd. And he is also bound to have difficulties. "His life cannot be otherwise than full of conflicts," writes Jung of the true poet:

> On the one hand the justified longing of the ordinary man for happiness, satisfaction, and security, and on the other a ruthless passion for creation, which may go so far as to override every personal desire. . . . The creative impulse can drain him of his humanity to such a degree that the personal ego can exist only on a primitive or inferior level and is driven to develop all sorts of defects—ruthlessness, selfishness ("auto-eroticism"), vanity, and other infantile traits. ("On the Relation of Analytical Psychology to Poetry," 15, par. 102)

These are traits from which Jung himself has suffered: "I had no patience with people," he writes, "I had to obey an inner law. . . . In this way I made many enemies. A creative person has little power over his own life. He is not free. He is captive and driven by his daemon" (*Memories, Dreams and Reflections* [1962; reprint, New York: Vintage, 1973], pp. 356–58). And he consequently endures external forms of isolation, such as Jung describes in the following passage from *Psychological Types:*

> The poet who has the greatest and most immediately suggestive effect is the one who knows how to express the most superficial levels of the unconscious. . . . But the more deeply the vision of the creative mind penetrates, the stranger it becomes to mankind in the mass, and the greater is the resistance to the man who in any way stands out from the mass. . . . The more thoughtful of the nation certainly comprehend something of his message, but, because his utterance coincides with processes already going on in the mass, and also because he anticipates their own aspirations, they hate the creator of such thoughts, not out of malice, but merely from the instinct of self-preservation. . . . The fame of these creators, if it arrives at all, is posthumous and often delayed for several centuries. (6, par. 323)

The sort of writer or artist Jung has in mind here is William Blake, who was willing to be not only lonely but scorned as odd and incomprehensible, a "man with a different face"—a quote that recalls Jung's own experiences of "estrangement," from school days onward (*Memories, Dreams and Reflections*, p. 41). The true writer is thus a Romantic Outsider, a figure for whom contemporary life is unendurably limited or partial.

6. Here, for example, is Frieda Fordham on the treatment of a nonartistic autonomous complex: "It may . . . happen that the patient becomes aware of a split-off part of the personality—an autonomous complex—and yet has the greatest difficulty in integrating it, since it expresses something absolutely contradictory to the conscious personality. At this point the understanding and the sympathy of the analyst are of the utmost importance, helping to reinforce the powers of consciousness until it is able to assimilate the disturbing factor." Fordham then quotes Jung from *The Practice of Psychotherapy:* the patient does not "stand alone in his battle with these elemental powers, but someone whom he trusts reaches out a hand, lending him moral strength to combat the tyranny of uncontrolled emotions" (*An Introduction to Jung's Psychology* [Harmondsworth, Middlesex: Penguin, 1953], p. 92).

7. Rosemary Gordon, *Dying and Creating* (London: Library of Analytical Psychology, 1978), pp. 140 and 158.

8. See E. James Lieberman, *Acts of Will: The Life and Works of Otto Rank* (New York: Free Press, 1985), p. 202.

9. These works include *Technik der Psychoanalyse* (1926–31), vols. 2 and 3 of which were published in English in 1936, under the title *Will Therapy* (vol. 1, *Die Analytische Situation*, is yet to be translated); *Grundzuge einer genetischen Psychologie auf Grund der Psychoanalyse der Ich-Struktur* (1927–29), vol. 3 of which was also published in 1936, under the title *Truth and Reality;* and *Mod-*

ern Education, which appeared in English in 1932, the same year as *Art and Artist,* the crucial text in any discussion of Rank's account of literary blockage or inhibition. In 1945 *Will Therapy* and *Truth and Reality* were republished in 1 vol.

10. Otto Rank, *Art and Artist* (1932; reprint, New York: Alfred A. Knopf, 1968), p. 26.

11. Lieberman, *Acts of Will,* p. 119.

12. Anaïs Nin, *Diary,* ed. Gunther Stuhlmann, 3 vols. (New York: Harcourt Brace Jovanovich, 1966–69), 1:289.

13. Rank, *Art and Artist,* p. 26.

14. Ibid., p. xxiii.

15. Otto Rank, *"Will Therapy" and "Truth and Reality,"* trans. Jessie Taft (1936; reprint, New York: Alfred A. Knopf, 1945), p. 222, as quoted in Esther Menaker, *Otto Rank: A Rediscovered Legacy* (New York: Columbia University Press, 1982), p. 25.

16. Otto Rank, *The Trauma of Birth* (New York: Harcourt Brace, 1929), p. 210.

17. Ibid., pp. 17, 18, and 10.

18. Quoted in Lieberman, *Acts of Will,* p. 235.

19. Ernest Jones, *The Life and Work of Sigmund Freud,* 3 vols. (New York: Basic Books, 1953–57), 3:58.

20. Rank, *"Will Therapy" and "Truth and Reality,"* pp. 223–24.

21. Otto Rank, *The Myth of the Birth of the Hero,* trans. F. Robbins and Smith Ely Jelliffe (1913; reprint, New York: Brunner, 1952), p. 76. The original German edition was published in 1909.

22. Susanne K. Langer, *Mind: An Essay on Human Feeling,* 3 vols. (Baltimore: Johns Hopkins University Press, 1967–82), 1:76.

23. Rank, *Trauma of Birth,* p. xiii.

24. Quoted in Lieberman, *Acts of Will,* p. 278. The lecture, "Beyond Psychoanalysis," was reprinted in *Psychoanalytic Review* 16, no. 1 (January 1929):1–11.

25. Rank, *Art and Artist,* p. 416.

26. Translated and quoted by Lieberman, *Acts of Will,* p. xxviii.

27. Rank, *Art and Artist,* pp. 39 and 14. Subsequent references are cited by page numbers in the text.

28. Charles Rycroft, *A Critical Dictionary of Psychoanalysis* (Harmondsworth, Middlesex: Penguin Books, 1972), p. 176.

29. Rank, *"Will Therapy" and "Truth and Reality,"* p. 212.

30. Ibid.

31. Menaker, *Otto Rank,* p. 43.

32. Rank, *Art and Artist,* p. 84.

33. Menaker, *Otto Rank,* p. 43.

34. Quoted in ibid., p. 35.

35. Quoted in Lieberman, *Acts of Will,* pp. 7 and 62, from the first (and only) English translation of *The Artist,* by Eva Solomon, assisted by E. James Lieberman, in *Journal of the Otto Rank Association* 15, no. 1 (Summer 1980): 1–63.

36. Rank, *Art and Artist*, p. 40.

37. Fay Karpf, *The Psychology and Psychotherapy of Otto Rank* (New York: Philosophical Library, 1953), p. 51.

38. Quoted in Jones, *Life and Work of Sigmund Freud*, 3:77.

39. Jacques Lacan, "The Direction of the Treatment and the Principle of Its Power," in *Écrits: A Selection*, trans. Alan Sheridan (New York: W. W. Norton, 1977), pp. 230–31.

40. Ernest Becker, *The Denial of Death* (New York: Free Press, 1973), p. 96.

41. Rank, *Art and Artist*, p. 41.

42. Ibid., p. 64.

43. Ibid., p. 65.

44. Ibid., pp. 28 and 37.

45. Menaker, *Otto Rank*, p. 36.

46. See ibid., p. 43; also Irvin D. Yalom, *Existential Psychotherapy* (New York: Basic Books, 1980), pp. 293–97.

47. Menaker, *Otto Rank*, p. 53.

48. Rank, *Art and Artist*, pp. 328–29.

49. Menaker, *Otto Rank*, p. 60.

50. Rank, *Art and Artist*, p. 386.

51. Menaker, *Otto Rank*, pp. 110–12.

52. Rank, *Art and Artist*, p. 387.

53. Quoted in Lieberman, *Acts of Will*, p. 302.

54. See Ira Progoff, *The Death and Rebirth of Psychology* (New York: Julian Press, 1956); see also Lieberman, *Acts of Will*, pp. 1–32.

55. Rank, *Art and Artist*, p. xvi.

56. Quoted in Lieberman, *Acts of Will*, p. 73.

57. Jones, *Life and Work of Sigmund Freud*, 3:58.

58. Quoted in Lieberman, *Acts of Will*, p. 18.

59. See Paul Ornstein, ed., *The Search for the Self: Selected Writings of Heinz Kohut, 1950–1978*, 2 vols. (New York: International Universities Press, 1980), 1:89.

60. Heinz Hartmann, *Psychoanalysis and Moral Values* (New York: International Universities Press, 1960), p. 40.

61. Although Anna Freud and Hartmann went to great pains to anchor their theories in Freud's own writings—often, for instance, treating theoretical modifications as though they were merely additions—ego psychology is usually distinguished from classical Freudianism, which focuses on the id, the instincts, and instinctual conflict. As Freud himself admits and explains in *The Ego and the Id*, "pathological research has directed our interest too exclusively to the repressed" (19:19). Yet this concern with pathology, as Anna Freud argues (*The Ego and the Mechanisms of Defence* [London: Hogarth Press, 1942], p. 4), can also be thought to have led psychoanalysis beyond the repressed:

From the earliest years of our science, its theory, built up as it was on an empirical basis, was pre-eminently a psychology of the unconscious or, as we should say today, of the id. But the definition immediately loses all claim to accuracy when we apply it to psychoanalytic therapy. From the beginning analysis as a therapeutic method, was concerned with the ego and its aberrations: the investigation of the id and its mode of operation was always only a means to an end. And the end was invariably the same: the corrections of these abnormalities and the restoration of the ego to its integrity.

In other words, psychoanalysis has always been concerned with adaptation and health, as well as with the vicissitudes of infantile fantasy. There is nothing, many followers of ego psychology argue, especially rebellious or heterodox about its attempt to develop what Hartmann calls a "general psychology," rather than a psychology focused exclusively on psychopathology.

62. Although there are several ways to explain the dominance of ego psychology in the second generation, part of the answer, at least on a superficial level, can be attributed to the editorial authority of Kris and Hartmann: in 1933 Hartmann became coeditor of the *Zeitschrift*, and Kris of *Imago*; in 1945 they cofounded the influential theoretical journal *Psychoanalytic Study of the Child*.

63. Jay R. Greenberg and Stephen A. Mitchell, *Object Relations in Psychoanalytic Theory* (Cambridge, Mass.: Harvard University Press, 1983), p. 248.

64. From Rycroft's account of "energy" in *A Critical Dictionary of Psychoanalysis*, p. 43.

65. Roy Schafer, "Regression in the Service of the Ego: The Relevance of a Psychoanalytic Concept for Personality Assessment," in *Assessment and Human Values*, ed. Gardner Lindzey (New York: Rinehart, 1958), p. 123.

66. J. Laplanche and J.-B. Pontalis, *The Language of Psychoanalysis*, trans. Donald Nicholson-Smith (New York: W. W. Norton, 1973), p. 171.

67. "Once the ego has accumulated a reservoir of neutralized energy of its own," writes Heinz Hartmann, "it will—in interaction with the outer and inner world—develop aims and functions whose cathexis can be derived from this reservoir, which means that they have not always to depend on *ad hoc* neutralizations" ("Notes on the Theory of Sublimation" [1955], in *Essays on Ego Psychology* [New York: International Universities Press, 1964], p. 229).

68. At some points, Hartmann even posits the existence of unneutralized ego energy, though he never fully works out this possibility. See Greenberg and Mitchell, *Object Relations*, p. 260; and Heinz Hartmann, Ernst Kris, and Rudolph M. Lowenstein, "Comments on the Formation of Psychic Structure," in *Psychoanalytic Study of the Child* 2 (1946):15 and 14.

69. Greenberg and Mitchell, *Object Relations*, p. 238.

70. Heinz Hartmann, "Technical Implications of Ego Psychology" (1951), in *Essays on Ego Psychology*, p. 145.

71. See Hartmann, *Ego Psychology and the Problem of Adaptation*, p. 23.

72. Ibid., p. 12.

73. Although Norman Holland begins, in his best-known book, *The Dynamics of Literary Response* (1968; reprint, New York: W. W. Norton, 1975), with the orthodox Freudian view of art as a compromise formation, he proceeds along ego-psychology lines. Freud's simple "disguise" and "aesthetic bonus"

are replaced by a much more detailed and elaborate range of defenses, in the manner of Anna Freud's *The Ego and the Mechanisms of Defence;* these defenses, in turn, are seen as responses to a comparably elaborate range of inaugurating id impulses. "Certain impulses seem to call forth certain defenses" (*Psychoanalysis and Shakespeare* [New York: McGraw-Hill, 1964], p. 131) is Holland's theory, and these impulses and defenses are carefully mapped and charted in his early books.

Although Holland sees literary defenses as the products of conscious, as well as unconscious, ego functions (which is why he prefers the terms "defensive mastery" or "adaptive strategy" or "defense maneuver" to "defense mechanism"), he says relatively little about the relations between literary form and the development of autonomous ego functions—by which is meant, in part, the ego-psychology version of mature object relations. Only in a later book, *Five Readers Reading* (New Haven: Yale University Press, 1975), do questions of development enter in, by way of Heinz Lichtenstein's influential concept of "identity" in "Identity and Sexuality: A Study of Their Interrelationship in Man," *Journal of the American Psychoanalytic Association* 9, no. 2 (April 1961):179–260.

By ignoring questions of development in his earlier work, Holland left himself open to the criticism that his theory of defensive transformation (rather than "disguise"), in Alan Roland's words, "simply results in a newer, much more subtle, and more thorough reductivism" ("Towards a Representation of Psychoanalytic Criticism," in *Psychoanalysis, Creativity, and Literature: A French-American Inquiry,* ed. Alan Roland [New York: Columbia University Press, 1978], pp. 258–59). Or, as Frederick Crews says, with characteristic pungency: "Glossaries of readers' fantasies and defenses, illustrations of their possible combinations, and proof that any work can be assigned to the scheme do not capture the literary enterprise much better than manuals of sex postures capture love. In both cases the inadvertently fostered attitude is resignation: Here we go again, what will it be this time?" (*Out of My System: Psychoanalysis, Ideology and Critical Method* [New York: Oxford University Press, 1975], p. 82). Yet Holland's writings have improved matters in other respects: he *has* helped to shift attention from content to form, encouraging others to locate creativity and blockage in the secondary, as well as the primary, process (e.g., in the business of plotting, or rhyme, or the ability—or inability—to deal with mythic or other conventions).

74. Ernst Kris, *Psychoanalytic Explorations in Art* (New York: International Universities Press, 1952), pp. 59 and 60.

75. See ibid., pp. 39–42, for "reality testing."

76. Ibid., p. 60.

77. Heinz Hartmann, "The Concept of Health" (1939), in *Essays on Ego Psychology,* p. 13. Freud introduced and elaborated the term *regression,* at first in relation to dream phenomena, in the last theoretical chapter of *The Interpretation of Dreams* and later, in Schafer's words, "to help account for neurotic and psychotic psychopathology and the disruption of infantile and adolescent development" ("Regression in the Service of the Ego," p. 199). In orthodox or classical theory—that is, before ego psychology—the implications of

the term were conflictual and negative. Only once does Freud give regression a positive valuation, despite its obvious connections with catharsis ("This happened—of all places—in a passage of his 'History of the Psychoanalytic Movement' [1914]," according to Michael Balint, in *The Basic Fault: Therapeutic Aspects of Regression* [New York: Brunner/Mazel, 1979], p. 123)—which may in part be because of the checkered history of regression as a therapeutic technique. It was Ferenczi who first experimented with regression, or what he called "the principle of relaxation," within therapy. "In contrast to the active technique," writes Balint, Ferenczi's use of regression, or relaxation, "aimed at avoiding any unnecessary increase of tension, Ferenczi thought that responding favorably to the patient's expectations, demands, or needs . . . might change the lifeless situation of a long drawn-out analysis" (p. 151). The technique helped lead to a bitter break with Freud, whose initial reaction, in Balint's words, "was withdrawal. By tacit consent, regression during analytic treatment was declared a dangerous symptom and its value as a therapeutic ally . . . repressed" (p. 151).

78. Crews, *Out of My System*, p. 77.

79. Quoted in Kris, *Psychoanalytic Explorations in Art*, p. 254.

80. Ibid.

81. Crews, *Out of My System*, p. 77.

82. Kris, *Psychoanalytic Explorations in Art*, p. 63.

83. Elizabeth Wright, *Psychoanalytic Criticism: Theory in Practice* (London: Methuen, 1984), p. 61.

84. Kris, *Psychoanalytic Explorations in Art*, p. 45.

85. Ibid., p. 59. These notions of artistic creation, it is worth stressing, quickly found their way into psychoanalytic criticism, though the orthodox account remained dominant. In 1957, five years after the publication of Kris's *Psychoanalytic Explorations in Art*, Simon Lesser's influential *Fiction and the Unconscious* argued that literature was essentially integrative and adaptive and that its tendency was always "to balance demands, to harmonize claims and counter claims" ([Boston: Beacon Press, 1957], p. 84). For Lesser, the best poetry "invites resistances and achieves its goodness by overcoming them" (p. 85); so also does the best fiction. And they do so with a new and characteristic serenity: the serenity of the mature adult for whom the superego is kindly and tolerant rather than harsh and punitive. For Lesser, fiction is "a kind of confession based upon acceptance and love"; it is a way of allowing for—incorporating and accommodating—fantasies while implicitly acknowledging inevitable limits. To Freud and his immediate followers, art was a way of expressing forbidden instinctual material; Lesser sees it quite differently, "as an outlet for idealistic and contemplative tendencies thwarted in our daily experiences" (p. 82). In ego-psychology terms, which are drawn from Freud's later, structural theory,

> the ego withholds nothing and it asks for nothing, neither for extenuation of punishment nor even for forgiveness. The superego voluntarily gives the ego something it evidently values even more than these, understanding and the assurance of continued love. It notes the stir-

rings of the ego which have got it into difficulty, but without revulsion or censure. Like a fond parent, the superego assures the ego: "I see your faults very clearly. But I do not condemn you. And I love you still." (P. 92)

Fiction is thus "integrative" and can heal "intra-psychic tensions." The writer of fiction needs to be able to adapt and harmonize conflicting claims. "In trying to balance these claims," writes Lesser, in the manner of the ego psychologist, "fiction is engaging in one of the activities which occupies the ego itself" (p. 93).

86. Schafer, "Regression in the Service of the Ego," p. 129. Subsequent references are cited by page numbers in the text.

87. Gilbert J. Rose, *The Power of Form: A Psychoanalytic Approach to Aesthetic Form,* monograph 49 in the series *Psychological Issues* (New York: International Universities Press, 1980), p. 211.

88. In such essays as "Beyond the Bounds of the Basic Rule" (1960) and "Forms and Transformations of Narcissism" (1966); also in essays on Thomas Mann, Beethoven, and creativity and childhood, all reprinted in vol. 1 of *The Search for the Self,* ed. Ornstein.

4. British Object-Relations Theory

1. Klein was born in Vienna and trained in Budapest and Berlin, first with Sandor Ferenczi and then with Karl Abraham. She moved to London in 1926 at Ernest Jones's invitation (Jones had heard her lecture in a conference at Salzburg the year before), and she soon became a dominant and controversial figure in the British Psychoanalytic Society.

2. Melanie Klein, "The Psychological Principles of Early Analysis" (1926), in *The Writings of Melanie Klein,* 4 vols. (London: Hogarth Press, 1975), 1:134.

3. Klein's account of infancy was based on very little direct contact with pre-Oedipal children: her youngest patient was two and three-quarters years old.

4. Hence, in part, Klein's move from Vienna to London in 1926. Within the British Psychoanalytic Society, the conflict became especially pronounced after 1935, when Klein introduced the concept of the "depressive position." Nor was the conflict helped by Anna Freud's own arrival in London in 1938. When Jones tried to clear the air by initiating the so-called controversial discussions of 1943–34, the split only widened. "The discussions resulted in the clearer emergence of three distinct schools of thought," writes Hanna Segal (*Melanie Klein* [New York: Viking Press, 1980], p. 110):

The followers of Anna Freud, those of Melanie Klein, and the majority, a large group of British analysts prepared to accept some of Melanie Klein's findings, but not all. This scientific division led also to structural changes in the British society. . . . The training analysts and their candidates were divided into two groups—the B group (Anna Freud and her followers) and the A group (the rest of the society). . . . The candidates attended a common theoretical course, in which there was, in the third year, a course on Melanie Klein's work, but they attended separate clinical seminars.

This so-called gentleman's agreement still exists, though the split is no longer as bitter. As for the reception of Klein's views in the United States, opinion has been overwhelmingly negative (this is not true of South America). "For some years," wrote one British observer in 1974, "it seemed that the work of Klein had been declared an un-American activity" (J. D. Sutherland, "Object-Relations Theory and the Conceptual Model of Psychoanalysis," *British Journal of Medical Psychology* 36, no. 2 [1963]:109). In, for example, Otto Fenichel's *The Psychoanalytic Theory of Neurosis* (1945), which has something of the status of a textbook in American analytic circles, Klein receives only a few passing references, all of them negative. Until recently (thanks in part to the writings of Otto Kernberg and Edith Jacobson), American training institutes largely ignored her work, bracketing it with that of other "deviant" theorists, such as Karen Horney and Franz Alexander. For an account of the differences between Klein and Anna Freud, see Segal, *Melanie Klein*, pp. 42–44; Anna Freud, "A Short History of Child Analysis" (1966), reprinted in *Problems of Psychoanalytic Technique and Therapy, 1966–1970* (London: Hogarth Press, 1972), pp. 48–58; and Phyllis Grosskurth, *Melanie Klein: Her World and Her Work* (New York: Alfred A. Knopf, 1986), pp. 164–69.

5. See Susan Isaacs, "The Nature and Function of Phantasy," in *Developments in Psycho-Analysis*, ed. M. Klein, P. Heimann, S. Isaacs, and J. Riviere (London: Hogarth Press, 1952), pp. 67–121; see also Harry Guntrip, *Psychoanalytic Theory, Therapy and the Development of the Self* (New York: Basic Books, 1977), pp. 52–68.

6. Melanie Klein, "On Identification," in *New Directions in Psycho-Analysis: The Significance of Infant Conflict in the Pattern of Adult Behaviour*, ed. M. Klein, P. Heimann, and R. E. Money-Kyrle (London: Tavistock Publications, 1955), p. 312. See also Joan Riviere: "An intense fear of dying by active aggression or passive neglect is a fundamental element of our emotional life, is as deeply rooted in our unconscious minds as life itself and is barricaded off from conscious expression by every known mechanism of defense" ("The Unconscious Phantasy of an Inner World Reflected in Examples from Literature," in ibid., p. 357).

7. "Introjection" is the term coined by Freud in *The Ego and the Id* to account for the development of the superego, which for him was based primarily on the paternal figure.

8. Segal, *Melanie Klein*, p. 123.

9. Ibid., p. 117.

10. Klein, *Writings*, 1:219–20.

11. Joan Riviere, "On the Genesis of Psychical Conflict in Early Infancy," *International Journal of Psycho-Analysis* 17, no. 4 (October 1936):407.

12. This shift in meaning signals an important difference between Klein and Freud. As Jay R. Greenberg and Stephen A. Mitchell suggest, for Freud bodily process instigates drive, whereas for Klein "the drives, psychological

in nature, give meaning to bodily events to express their aims" (*Objects Relations in Psychoanalytic Theory* [Cambridge, Mass.: Harvard University Press, 1983], p. 140).

13. Klein, "On Identification," p. 312.

14. Melanie Klein, "On the Theory of Anxiety and Guilt" (1948), in *Writings*, 3:32.

15. Because the paranoid-schizoid position begins from birth, this means that Klein conceives of the prelinguistic infant as having enough ego or self to express anxiety and to protect himself or herself through defense mechanisms. Her view is quite different from that of Freud, who uses the word "organism" instead of "ego" when describing the newborn infant's reactions to threat. To Freud, the infant, in Segal's words, is "a biological and not yet a psychological entity" (*Melanie Klein*, p. 114).

16. Segal, *Melanie Klein*, p. 80.

17. The term D. W. Winnicott prefers is "the stage of concern." See "A Personal View of the Kleinian Contribution" (1962), in *The Maturational Processes and the Facilitating Environment* (London: Hogarth Press, 1965), p. 176. This stage also marks another departure from Freud, because it suggests that the Oedipal wishes that develop in the depressive position can be dealt with not only by anxiety—that is, fear of castration or death—but by a love of the parents and a wish to protect and not to hurt them.

18. Segal, *Melanie Klein*, p. 132.

19. Ibid., pp. 132–33.

20. In Klein, *Writings*, 1:270.

21. The most important of these essays were four written between 1929 and 1963: "Infantile Anxiety-situations in a Work of Art and in the Creative Impulse" (1929), "The Importance of Symbol-Formation in the Development of the Ego" (1930), "On Identification" (1955), and "Some Reflections on *The Oresteia*" (1963). The essays of 1929, 1955, and 1963 are simply Kleinian versions of the sort of symbol-hunting characteristic of first-generation Freudian critics; the essay of 1930, a Kleinian theory of symbolism, is, in several respects, comparably orthodox.

22. Hanna Segal, "A Psycho-Analytical Approach to Aesthetics," in *New Directions*, ed. Klein, Heimann, and Money-Kryle, p. 388.

23. Quoted in ibid., p. 389.

24. Ibid., p. 398.

25. Ibid.

26. Hanna Segal, *The Work of Hanna Segal* (New York: Jason Aronson, 1981), p. xiv.

27. Hanna Segal, "A Psycho-Analytical Approach to Aesthetics," in *New Directions*, ed. Klein, Heimann, and Money-Kryle, p. 391. In like manner, the journalist patient who complained to Segal of having no style of his own was inhibited, sometimes to the point of blockage, by a tormenting "bad internal father-figure," whom he sought to defend himself against by placating (ibid., p. 392). His dream material revealed that one way of doing so was to write. But because he did not want his tormentor to be alive—and writing was a way of keeping him alive—he was blocked. In specifically Kleinian terms,

when depressive or reparative feelings were aroused, and he sought in his art to restore the lost internal image, paranoid feelings, which were still ultimately predominant, rose up and overwhelmed him—and he could not write.

28. Ibid., p. 295.
29. Ibid.
30. Ibid., p. 298.
31. Ibid.
32. Ibid., p. 400.
33. Ibid., pp. 404–5.
34. In Segal, *Work of Hanna Segal*, p. 213.
35. Ibid., p. 214.
36. Ibid., p. 216.
37. This symposium was the source of Segal's "A Psycho-Analytical Approach to Aesthetics" and Klein's "On Identification," as well as of important contributions by Adrian Stokes and Joan Riviere. The symposium was also meant to contain a contribution from Winnicott, but he and Klein fell out over the paper he offered, "Transitional Objects and Transitional Phenomena" (*International Journal of Psycho-Analysis* 34, no. 2 [1953]:89–97), subsequently to become one of Winnicott's most influential works (it is reprinted as chap. 1 of Winnicott's best-known book, *Playing and Reality* [London: Tavistock Publications, 1971], pp. 1–25). The published proceedings, *New Directions* (1955), mark the birth of object-relations aesthetics as something very like a movement.
38. Marion Milner, "The Role of Illusion in Symbol Formation," in *New Directions*, ed. Klein, Heimann, and Money-Kyrle, p. 85.
39. Marion Milner, *An Experiment in Leisure* (London: Chatto and Windus, 1937), p. 49. Milner is as likely to have Klein in mind at this point as Freud because, in "The Importance of Symbol-Formation in the Development of the Ego," Klein reveals as ambivalent an attitude to symbolization as Freud himself. The essay is probably the most important of Klein's writings on creative or aesthetic issues and is worth outlining briefly. It begins with Freud's assumption that symbolism is the transference of interest from an original object—an object toward which action or desire is directed—to an object that is in reality different from it but felt to be somehow the same. This transference is produced by instinctual conflict, though for Klein, of course, the conflicting instincts are the pre-Oedipal life and death instincts. The fear we have of our aggressive or death instincts, the sort of instincts at work in both the paranoid-schizoid and depressive positions, is so intense that we transfer the instincts onto the original objects: the threatened breast becomes the threatening breast. In normal development, though, this initial transference is eventually followed by other, less frightening ones: less threatened and thus less threatening substitutes are sought out. "Anxiety," writes Klein of one of her patients, "contributes to make him equate the organs in question [they stand for threatened part objects] with other things; owing to this equation these in turn become objects of anxiety, and so he is impelled constantly to make other and new equations" (*Writings*, 1:220).

The process of symbolization gradually constructs the subject's relation to the outside world; without it, no such relation is possible. This is illustrated by Klein's patient Dick, an autistic four year old, who could neither play, talk, nor express love or fear. Klein's observations confirm her theories (as is usual in psychoanalytic writing), revealing Dick to be terrified of his aggressive impulses toward his mother. So intense is his terror, Klein concludes, that it paralyzes Dick's fantasy life; he is too frightened even to employ the initial symbolic defenses of the paranoid-schizoid position. As Hanna Segal puts it, "he had not endowed the world around him with any symbolic meaning. . . . He therefore took no interest in it" ("Notes on Symbol Formation," in *International Journal of Psycho-Analysis* 38, no. 5 [1957]:392).

To begin with, then, the developing subject must be able to symbolize, but if the subject is to develop a mature or adult relation to the environment, to "reality," symbolization of this sort must cease. This cessation is necessary because in such symbolization "the child's earliest reality is wholly phantastic," a mass of fearful projections and omnipotent delusions, which are the products of intolerable persecutory fears and splitting. Development of the ego and an adult subject's true relation to a true reality "depend on the degree of the ego's capacity at a very early period to tolerate the presence of the earliest anxiety situations" ("The Importance of Symbol-Formation in the Development of the Ego," in *Writings*, 1:238)—that is, to confront rather than project (a form of symbolization) its fears and to tolerate ambivalent feelings (about the newly recognized whole object) rather than to idealize or denigrate their objects. The unspoken assumption behind this view is that symbolization is a species of evasion or distortion; the view recalls the pejorative implications of the orthodox Freudian account, which Klein's followers—especially Segal and Winnicott, as well as Milner—seek to revise.

The essay moves both ways: it implicitly denigrates the symbolic impulse, but it sees that impulse as essential to development. Without symbolization, the development of the ego is arrested. This latter point Klein makes in ringingly positive terms, echoing a statement from the 1923 essay "Early Analysis," in which symbolism is called "the driving force in the cultural evolution of mankind" (*Writings*, 1:104). It is precisely this faith in the positive value of symbolization that Klein's followers emphasize in their rehabilitation of the creative impulse.

40. Milner, "The Role of Illusion in Symbol Formation," p. 97.

41. Ibid., p. 88. To Milner, such experiences are what an ego psychologist might call productive regressions. Much of what she says about these experiences recalls Kris on inspiration, a phenomenon that he conceives of as the passive reception of something from the "outside" and that he associates with either oral or pregenital states, when passiveness is a precondition of total gratification, as in nursing. Milner's account of the experiences also recalls Winnicott (the question of priority is a difficult one) and Rank—as in Rank's belief, which Milner quotes, that "art and play both link the world of 'subjective unreality' and 'objective reality,' harmoniously fusing the edges but not confusing them" (ibid., p. 98).

Finally, the closeness of Milner's theories to those of Rank raises the larger question of his influence on post-Kleinian theory in general—something post-Kleinians rarely acknowledge. Anton Ehrenzweig, for example, agrees with much of what Rank says about the importance and ubiquity of the birth trauma in creative production, yet he claims not to have found Rank's theories of much use, turning instead, via Milner, to Frazer's theories of the dying god (see *The Hidden Order of Art: A Study in the Psychology of Artistic Imagination* [London: Weidenfeld and Nicholson; Berkeley and Los Angeles: University of California Press, 1967], p. 173): "The ordered progress of a complex science like psychoanalysis is not helped by boldly anticipating leaps," writes Ehrenzweig in explanation of his attitude to Rank. "I myself was not really helped by Rank, Graves, or Jung"—all of whom, he admits, anticipate important aspects of his theory (ibid., p. 181).

42. Milner, "The Role of Illusion in Symbol Formation," p. 101.

43. Ibid., pp. 101–2.

44. Ibid., p. 104.

45. Ibid.

46. Marion Milner, *On Not Being Able to Paint* (1950; reprint, London: Heinemann, 1981), p. xvii. Subsequent references are cited by page numbers in the text.

47. Winnicott, "A Personal View of the Kleinian Contribution," p. 172.

48. Ibid., p. 177.

49. See D. W. Winnicott, "Appetite and Emotional Development" (1936), in *Collected Papers: Through Pediatrics to Psycho-Analysis* (1958; reprint, London: Hogarth Press, 1975), p. 36.

50. Winnicott, "Transitional Objects and Transitional Phenomena," 90. Subsequent references are cited by page numbers in the text.

51. Elizabeth Wright, *Psychoanalytic Criticism: Theory in Practice* (London: Methuen, 1984), p. 93. It is also important to emphasize that Winnicott talks of transitional phenomena as well as transitional objects, a point that Wright overlooks when she objects to Winnicott's theories as a paradigm of art because they "import into all forms of creativity and interpretation a prejudice for objects assumed to be ready for human recognition" (ibid., p. 95).

52. Winnicott, "Transitional Objects and Transitional Phenomena," p. 91. Adam Phillips, in *Winnicott* (London: Fontana Press, 1988), finds something missing in this essay: "Winnicott . . . never makes clear how the child gets from the private experience [the essentially unsharable transitional object] to a more communal experience, from a personal teddy-bear to a pleasure in reading Dickens" (p. 115). Charles Rycroft criticizes the essay from another perspective: "Even if one accepts Winnicott's idea that the capacity to play originates in the infant's initial interactions with its mother, the extension and imaginative elaboration of play into culture and religion must, it seems to me, involve the father as a person who performs some function other than that of an auxiliary mother—which is how Winnicott all too often conceives of fathers" (*Psychoanalysis and Beyond* [London: Chatto and Windus, 1985], p. 142).

53. Winnicott, "Transitional Objects and Transitional Phenomena," p. 91.

54. Ibid., p. 96.

55. Ibid., p. 95. The importance Winnicott attaches to the behavior of the actual parent is a key element in his revision of orthodox Kleinian theory. "Klein claims to have paid full attention to the environmental factor," writes Winnicott, "but it is my opinion that she was temperamentally incapable of this ("A Personal View of the Kleinian Contribution," p. 177). Almost from the start, Winnicott places more stress on the strengths and weaknesses of environmental provision than does Klein, who derives object relations from innate, constitutional drives, the phylogenetically transmitted life and death instincts. Klein approaches pre-Oedipal development, writes Winnicott, *"apart from the study of child-care.* She has always admitted that child-care is important but has not made special study of it" ("Class" [1958], in *Maturational Processes*, p. 126). This assessment is, in one sense, unfair, because Klein greatly stresses the positive influence of the parent during the period when the child is working through the depressive position. Klein believes that the parent can soften the child's destructive impulses and assuage his or her despair (about the murderous potential of those impulses)—though it is true that Klein says relatively little about the effect of inadequate or defective parental care.

Greenberg and Mitchell offer a social or biographical account of this difference between Klein and Winnicott: "As a pediatrician and director of a child psychiatric clinic," they write, "Winnicott was much more aware of battering and neglecting mothers than was Klein, who had a fashionable West End practice" (*Object Relations*, p. 202). This awareness may also help to account for the differences in style in their respective theoretical writings. Although the precise meaning of the aphorisms and simple, unselfconscious-seeming terminology (for example, "good-enough mothering") of Winnicott can be elusive, his style is remarkably clear and welcoming. One always hears the clinician in his writing, and the clinician who is used to talking in an unpatronizing manner to children and worried parents. Klein's writing, however, is often opaque and *ex cathedra,* as if issuing from a not only higher but often Delphic authority. (For a more sympathetic account of Klein's "turgid" style, see Grosskurth, *Melanie Klein: Her World and Work,* pp. 195–96.)

56. Winnicott, "A Personal View of the Kleinian Contribution," p. 177. Coleridge himself was as attentive to developmental as to artistic "suspensions." While in Germany in 1798, he was especially struck by one aspect of the ritual surrounding Knecht Rupert, Father Christmas's mysterious forerunner: "The way that the children have been 'let into the secret' of Knecht Rupert's real identity at the age of seven or eight, instinctively continued the charade for their smaller brothers and sisters" (Richard Holmes, *Coleridge: Early Visions* [London: Hodder and Stroughton, 1989], p. 215).

57. Ibid., p. 190.

58. D. W. Winnicott, "Communicating and Not Communicating Leading to a Study of Certain Objects," in *Maturational Processes*, p. 192.

59. D. W. Winnicott, "The Location of Cultural Experience," *International Journal of Psycho-Analysis* 48, no. 3 (1967):371 (the essay is reprinted in *Playing and Reality*, pp. 95–103).

60. Ibid., 370.

61. Winnicott, *Playing and Reality*, p. 62. Although Winnicott rarely refers directly to the Romantic poets, Adam Phillips thinks Winnicott's writing "has its roots in the romanticism of Wordsworth, Coleridge, and Lamb" (*Winnicott*, p. 15), whereas Richard Poirier even detects resemblances to American romanticism ("Frost, Winnicott, Burke," *Raritan* 2, no. 2 [Fall 1982]:114–27).

62. Winnicott, *Playing and Reality*, p. 57.

63. Albert Hutter, "Poetry in Psychoanalysis: Hopkins, Rossetti, Winnicott," *International Review of Psycho-Analysis* 9, no. 3 (1982):310.

64. Ibid.

65. D. W. Winnicott, "Ego Distortion in Terms of True and False Self" (1960), in *Maturational Processes*, p. 148.

66. Greenberg and Mitchell, *Object Relations*, p. 201.

67. For a useful synopsis of the differences between Lacan and Winnicott, see Tony Pinckney, *Women in the Poetry of T. S. Eliot* (London: Methuen, 1983), pp. 15–17.

68. Hutter, "Poetry in Psychoanalysis," p. 311.

69. Gerard Manley Hopkins to Robert Bridges, 1 September 1885, in *The Letters of Gerard Manley Hopkins*, ed. C. Abbott (London: Oxford University Press, 1935), p. 222.

70. Winnicott, *Playing and Reality*, p. 62.

71. Hutter, "Poetry in Psychoanalysis," p. 312.

72. Winnicott, *Playing and Reality*, p. 62.

73. Ibid., p. 117.

74. "It was the interest of the artists which sent this book on its way," wrote Anton Ehrenzweig in the "Preface" to the second printing of the American edition of *The Psychoanalysis of Artistic Vision and Hearing* (1953; reprint, New York: George Braziller, 1965), pp. vii–viii.

75. In gestalt theory, beauty or satisfactory pattern, as Ehrenzweig points out, belongs "only to the surface layers of the mind," layers that are "foreign to the 'gestalt-free' depth mind" (ibid., p. xvi).

76. Ehrenzweig, *Hidden Order of Art*, p. 6. Subsequent references are cited by page numbers in the text.

77. Entries of 16 February 1930, 26 December 1929, and then 16 February 1930 again, in *The Diary of Virginia Woolf*, ed. A. O. Bell, 5 vols. (London: Hogarth Press, 1980), 3:287, 275, and 287.

78. Ehrenzweig, *Hidden Order of Art*, p. 58.

79. Ibid., p. 59.

80. For Ehrenzweig, this is the case with most modern art, which is either "all intellect or all spontaneity, hardly ever both at the same time" (ibid., p. 64). Today's artists swing wildly from one extreme to another: material, controlling elements are drastically overturned, only to be followed by a defensive rationality, which "in turn stifles further spontaneity and has to be overcome by another burst from the depth" (ibid., p. 66). Ehrenzweig points to the fate of action painting as an example of this vicious cycle: what is at first meant to be a liberating "eruption of art's unconscious substructure" provokes so extreme a defensive reaction from the attached surface faculties that "overnight the spontaneous breakthrough from below is turned into another

deliberate, manneristic device": action painting deteriorates into a "very deliberate exercise in decorative textures with little sensitivity to the unconscious form discipline that first animated it" (ibid., pp. 66–67, in which the term "form discipline" reminds us that for Ehrenzweig spontaneity and dedifferentiation are means to a work's unconscious or hidden *order*).

So common is this cycle in modern art that Ehrenzweig feels that the spirit of deliberate destruction characteristic of the art of the 1960s will soon die out, to be replaced by "something more positive . . . aiming at constructive results rather than demolishing existing formulae and clichés" (ibid., p. 70). And in his own practice as an art teacher, Ehrenzweig hoped to encourage such a death by stressing the importance of a return to "the objective factors" most modern art of his era sought to destroy or deny. As early as 1960, he was attacking the concept and practice of "free expression" for its tendency to produce not what is unique, but "a general orderly style taught at many art schools" ("Alienation versus Self-Expression," *Listener* 63 [February 1960]:345–46 and 368).

81. Ehrenzweig, *Hidden Order of Art*, p. 79. Subsequent references are cited by page numbers in the text.

82. Ibid., p. 174. Ehrenzweig also finds this theme—the drama or conflict of creation—in the myth of the Dying God, which he sees as both a metaphor for the creative process and a sign of its ubiquity as "content." Ehrenzweig came to a sense of the importance of the motif of the Dying God indirectly, through Milner's early book *An Experiment in Leisure*. What surprised Milner about her fascination with the motif of divine death and rebirth—as in the myths of Adonis, Attis, Osiris, or Jesus—is that sadomasochistic impulses played little part in its impact upon her. As Ehrenzweig says, in a lengthy review of Milner's book, the theme "did not so much represent id fantasy as certain ineffable changes in the ego during the onset of creativeness. This Milner aptly calls 'creative surrender.' What is felt emotionally as surrender to self-destruction in the image of the Dying God is really a surrender to the disintegrating action of low-level imagery, which dissolves the hardened surface clichés while consciousness sinks towards an oceanic level" ("The Creative Surrender," in *The Practice of Psychoanalytic Criticism*, ed. L. Tennenhouse [Detroit: Wayne State University Press, 1976], pp. 139–40). Or, as Ehrenzweig later states in *Hidden Order of Art*, "death and rebirth mirror the ego's dedifferentiation and re-differentiation"; this double rhythm can be seen as "an interaction between basic life and death instincts active within the creative ego" (p. 177).

For Ehrenzweig, as for Milner, the motif of the Dying God is more than a mere symbol: it also inspires creativity. Hence Milner's talk of "the still glow that surrounded some of these images in my mind . . . the feeling of greatest stillness and austerity" (quoted in *The Practice of Psychoanalytic Criticism*, ed. Tennenhouse, pp. 137–38). We are to believe that such a feeling encourages or facilitates "creative surrender," as well as representing it.

83. John Keats to George and Tom Keats, 21, 27 (?) December 1817, in *The Letters of John Keats*, ed. Hyder Edward Rollins, 2 vols. (Cambridge, Mass.: Harvard University Press, 1958), 1:193 and 194.

84. Ehrenzweig, *Hidden Order of Art*, p. 24.

85. Ibid., p. 124.

86. Ibid., p. 278.

87. Ibid., p. 179.

88. Ibid., p. 223.

89. "Introduction," in *The Image in Form: Selected Writings of Adrian Stokes*, ed. Richard Wollheim (New York: Harper and Row, 1972), pp. 26–27. Stokes's importance to object-relations aesthetics lies not only in his writings but in his role as founder of the Imago Society, an important group that began to meet regularly in the fifties to discuss art from a Kleinian or object-relations perspective. Members of the group included Roger Money-Kyrle, Wilfred Bion, Donald Meltzer, and J. O. Wisdom. Subsequent references are cited by page numbers in the text.

90. Adrian Stokes, "Form in Art," in *New Directions*, ed. Klein, Heimann, and Money-Kyrle, pp. 410–11.

91. Ibid., p. 408.

92. Excerpted in *Image in Form*, ed. Wollheim, p. 149.

93. Ibid., p. 150.

94. As excerpted in ibid., p. 48.

95. Ibid.

96. Stokes, "Form in Art," p. 419.

97. Stokes extends the distinction between carving and modeling to painting as well as sculpture because, just as some sculpture arises out of a reverence for stone and elicits its meaning from it, "similarly in painting there is the canvas, the rectangular surface and the whiteness to fructify, a preexistent minimum structure that not only will be gradually affirmed but vastly enriched by the coalescence with other meanings" (*Painting and the Inner World* [1963], as excerpted in *Image in Form*, ed. Wollheim, p. 99). This tradition in painting is rare, but its exponents include Piero della Francesca, Georges de la Tour, and Vermeer—artists for whom color is conceived of, as Stokes says in *Colour and Form*, as "the division of white." Such an artist "carves the white canvas, divides that white . . . opens it to show the strength of colour that may evolve from it" (ibid., p. 54). For Vermeer and de la Tour, color seems to come from within the life of the form, rather than to reflect temporary lights from outside.

98. Adrian Stokes, "The Luxury and Necessity of Painting," in *Three Essays on the Painting of Our Time* (1961), as excerpted in *Image in Form*, ed. Wollheim, p. 91.

99. Adrian Stokes, *The Invitation in Art* (1965), as excerpted in *Image in Form*, ed. Wollheim, p. 106.

100. Adrian Stokes, *Reflections on the Nude* (1967), as excerpted in *Image in Form*, ed. Wollheim, pp. 117–18.

101. Pinckney, *Women in the Poetry of T. S. Eliot*, p. 65.

102. Ibid., p. 58.

103. Ibid.

104. Ibid., p. 67.

105. Stokes, "The Luxury and Necessity of Painting," p. 89.

106. Ibid., p. 91.
107. Ibid., p. 111.
108. Ibid.
109. Stokes, "Form in Art," p. 420.

5. Theories of Origin

1. W. J. Bate, *The Burden of the Past and the English Poet* (Cambridge, Mass.: Harvard University Press, 1970).
2. Ibid., p. 4.
3. Quoted in Thomas McFarland, "The Originality Paradox," in *Originality and Imagination* (Baltimore: Johns Hopkins University Press, 1984), p. 7. Keyes Metcalf estimated some decades ago that the ideal modern library would contain "perhaps thirty million books" (quoted in ibid., p. 8). Nor are sheer numbers the only source of print-induced anxiety. According to Walter J. Ong, print fosters a sense of writing as an individual and unique communication: "Typography had made the word into a commodity. The old communal oral world had split up into privately claimed freeholdings. The drift in human consciousness toward greater individualism had been served well by print" (*Orality and Literacy: The Technologizing of the Word* [London: Methuen, 1982], p. 131).
4. John Dryden, "To My Dear Friend Mr. Congreve" (line 5), quoted in Bate, *Burden of the Past and the English Poet*, p. 26.
5. Bate, *Burden of the Past and the English Poet*, p. 4.
6. Ibid., p. 16.
7. Ibid., pp. 43–44.
8. Quoted in ibid., p. 44.
9. Pat Rogers, *The Augustan Vision* (London: Weidenfeld and Nicholson, 1979), p. 57.
10. Matthew Arnold, "The Study of Poetry" (1880), quoted in *The Eighteenth Century,* ed. Pat Rogers (London: Methuen, 1978), p. 7.
11. Geoffrey Hartman, "Evening Star and Evening Land," in *The Fate of Reading* (Chicago: University of Chicago Press, 1975), pp. 147–78; and Jean-Pierre Mileur, *Literary Revisionism and the Problem of Modernity* (Berkeley and Los Angeles: University of California Press, 1982), p. 198.
12. Mileur, *Literary Revisionism and the Problem of Modernity,* p. 199.
13. Rogers, *Augustan Vision,* pp. 138–39, cites lines 29–32 as syntactically representative: "Let not ambition mock their useful toil / Their homely joys, and destiny obscure; / The short and simple annals of the poor." "Typically," he writes, of the rude forefathers in these lines, "a personified abstraction governs their being. . . . Their very breath is vainly called by urn and bust; their heart is laid (once more) in a neglected spot."
14. Mileur, *Literary Revisionism and the Problem of Modernity,* p. 204.
15. Rogers, *Augustan Vision,* p. 134.
16. Quoted in *The Poems of Gray, Collins, and Goldsmith,* ed. Roger Lonsdale (New York: Longman, 1969), pp. 110 and 113.

17. Rogers, *Augustan Vision*, pp. 136–37.
18. Samuel Johnson, "Life of Gray," in *Rasselas, Poems, and Selected Prose,* ed. Bertrand H. Bronson (New York: Holt, Rinehart and Winston, 1958), p. 440.
19. Rogers, *Augustan Vision*, pp. 140–41.
20. Samuel Johnson, *Life of Collins,* in *Rasselas,* ed. Bronson, p. 502. Before his breakdown, Collins busied himself in London in the 1740s with numerous literary enterprises—projected translations, tragedies, treatises, periodicals—all of which came to nothing. The one work that he completed and published, the slim volume of a dozen *Odes on Several Subjects* (1746), was unpopular, and Collins is said to have bought up and destroyed the unsold copies. Many of these poems are about not only poetry but its degeneration and the present age's weakness. The "Ode to Fear" begs of its personified subject the power "to read the Visions old, / Which thy awak'ning Bards have told" (54–55), a power that Shakespeare preeminently possessed. "Hither gain the fury deal," Collins prays at the poem's conclusion, "Teach me but once like Him to feel" (68–69). Such grandeur, though, in Johnson's words, had "the character rather of his inclination than his genius" (ibid.).
21. Quoted in *Eighteenth Century,* ed. Rogers, p. 62.
22. Quoted in Bate, *Burden of the Past and the English Poet,* p. 46.
23. Rogers, *Augustan Vision*, p. 140.
24. Ibid., p. 142.
25. Roger Lonsdale, ed., *Thomas Gray and William Collins: Poetical Works* (Oxford: Oxford University Press, 1977), p. xxi.
26. William Wordsworth, Preface to *Lyrical Ballads* (1800), in *The Prose Works of William Wordsworth,* ed. W.J.B. Owen and Jane Smyser, 3 vols. (Oxford: Clarendon Press, 1974), 1:128.
27. See Roger Shattuck, "The Demon of Originality," in *The Innocent Eye: On Modern Literature and the Arts* (New York: Farrar, Straus and Giroux, 1984), p. 91.
28. William Duff, *An Essay on Original Genius in Philosophy and the Fine Arts, Particularly in Poetry* (1767), quoted in Bate, *Burden of the Past and the English Poet,* p. 50.
29. Richard Hurd, *The Golden Age of Queen Elizabeth* (1759), quoted in Bate, *Burden of the Past and the English Poet,* p. 59.
30. Joseph Warton, *Essay on Pope* (1756), quoted in Bate, *Burden of the Past and the English Poet,* p. 55.
31. Samuel Taylor Coleridge to Thomas Curnick, 9 April 1814, in *Collected Letters of Samuel Taylor Coleridge,* ed. Earl L. Griggs, 6 vols. (Oxford: Clarendon Press, 1959–71), 3:914.
32. Samuel Taylor Coleridge, *Biographia Literaria,* ed. James Engell and W. Jackson Bate, in *The Collected Works of Samuel Taylor Coleridge,* ed. Kathleen Coburn, (a projected 16-vol. work) (London: Routledge and Kegan Paul, 1983), 2:151.
33. The episode is recounted by Mary and Charles Lamb in a letter of 22 May 1815, as quoted in Stephen Gill, *William Wordsworth: A Life* (Oxford: Clarendon Press, 1989), pp. 314–15.
34. William Hazlitt, "On the Living Poets" (1819), in *Lectures on the English Poets and the Spirit of the Age,* ed. A. R. Waller (London: Dent, 1914), p. 163.

35. John Keats to J. H. Reynolds, 3 February 1818, in *The Letters of John Keats*, ed. Hyder Edward Rollins, 2 vols. (Cambridge, Mass.: Harvard University Press, 1958), 1:224.

36. Quoted in Bate, *Burden of the Past and the English Poet*, p. 5.

37. John Keats to J. H. Reynolds, 3 May 1818, in *Letters of John Keats*, ed. Rollins, 1:278–82.

38. See Lawrence Lipking, *The Life of the Poet: Beginning and Ending Poetic Careers* (Chicago: University of Chicago Press, 1981), pp. 3–11.

39. John Keats to Benjamin Bailey, 8 October 1817, in *Letters of John Keats*, ed. Rollins, 1:169–70.

40. John Keats to J. A. Hessey, 8 October 1818, in ibid., 1:374.

41. John Keats to Benjamin Haydon, 10, 11 May 1817, in ibid., 1:141–42.

42. John Keats to George and Georgiana Keats, 17–27 September 1817, in ibid., 2:186.

43. In the BBC Radio 4 program "Writer's Block," a "Kaleidoscope Extra" broadcast on 26 March 1986. Amis's advice has a fine comic pedigree, as in the following passage from chap. 13 of vol. 9 of Laurence Sterne, *Tristram Shandy* (1760; New York: New American Library, 1960), pp. 501–2:

> Now in ordinary cases, that is, when I am only stupid, and the thoughts rise heavily and pass gummous through my pen—
>
> Or that I am got, I know not how, into a cold un-metaphorical vein of infamous writing, and cannot take a plumb lift out of it *for my soul;* so must be obliged to go on writing like a Dutch commentator to the end of the chapter, unless something be done—
>
> —I never stand conferring with pen and ink one moment; for if a pinch of snuff or a stride or two across the room will not do the business for me —I take a razor at once; and have tried the edge of it upon the palm of my hand, without further ceremony, except that of first lathering my beard, I shave it off; taking care that if I do leave hair, that it not be a grey one: this done, I change my shirt—put on a better coat— send for my last wig—put my topaz ring upon my finger; and in a word, dress myself from one end to the other of me, after my best fashion.

44. John Keats to George and Georgiana Keats, 14–31 October 1818, in *Letters of John Keats*, ed. Rollins, 1:404.

45. Bate, *Burden of the Past and the English Poet*, pp. 129–30.

46. Ibid., p. 132.

47. Ibid., p. 130.

48. Ibid., p. 127.

49. Ibid., pp. 133–34.

50. Quoted in M. H. Abrams, *The Mirror and the Lamp: Romantic Theory and the Critical Tradition* (Oxford: Oxford University Press, 1953), p. 159.

51. Quoted in James Engell, *The Creative Imagination* (Cambridge, Mass.: Harvard University Press, 1981), p. 72.

52. Quoted in Abrams, *Mirror and the Lamp*, p. 159.

53. Isaac Newton, *Principia Mathematica* (1687), quoted in Abrams, *Mirror and the Lamp*, p. 164.

54. See Abrams, *Mirror and the Lamp*, pp. 193–94.

55. Thomas Rymer, "Answer to Davenant" (1650), quoted in ibid., p. 190.

56. Ibid., p. 191.

57. René Rapin, *Reflections on Aristotle's Treatise of Poesie* (1674), trans. Thomas Rhymer, quoted in ibid.

58. Quoted in ibid.

59. Jonathan Swift, *The Tale of the Tub*, ed. A. C. Guthkelch and D. Nichol Smith (1920; reprint, Oxford: Clarendon Press, 1958), p. 146.

60. Arthur Waugh, ed., *Lives of the English Poets*, 2 vols. (London: Oxford University Press, 1952), 2:34.

61. Abrams, *Mirror and the Lamp*, p. 187.

62. These sources can be found in the work of Bate, Abrams, and Engell, to whose accounts of Romantic theories of creativity I am deeply indebted, as the surrounding notes attest. That these accounts are themselves infused with what Jerome McGann calls "Romantic Ideology" may well be true, and McGann and others are correct to call attention to the need for distance from that ideology. "The Romantic Age is so-called," writes McGann, "not because all its works are Romantic, but rather because the ideologies of Romanticism exerted an increasingly dominant influence during that time" (*The Romantic Ideology: A Critical Investigation* [Chicago: University of Chicago Press, 1983], p. 19). It is precisely the influence of those ideologies which matters in this study, though, including the influences they had on writers, critics, and thinkers of the so-called post-Romantic period.

63. Quoted in Abrams, *Mirror and the Lamp*, p. 199.

64. Quoted in ibid., p. 200.

65. Hoffman figures not only in Freud's accounts of literary creativity but also in his theory of the *Todestrieb*. For example, in "The Uncanny" Freud draws on Hoffman's stories of terror and the supernatural—in which the feelings evoked are those of "having been here before," or of getting stuck in the same situation (or returning to the same spot) over and over again—for examples of compulsive repetition. The actual term "repetition-compulsion" first appears in "The Uncanny" as the last of the themes associated with Hoffman's novel *The Devil's Elixir* (1813–16).

66. Quoted from Hoffman's story "Princess Brambilla," in Robert Currie, *Genius: An Ideology in Literature* (London: Chatto and Windus, 1974), p. 57.

67. Currie, *Genius: An Ideology in Literature*, p. 73. Hoffman's sense of genius as confined to the few was something of a mid-eighteenth-century invention. For a detailed account of the history of the term, see Christine Battersby, *Gender and Genius* (London: Women's Press, 1989), particularly pp. 71–76 and 103–15, on Romantic notions of genius.

68. McFarland, *Originality and Imagination*, p. 48. Richard Holmes, in *Coleridge: Early Visions* (London: Hodder and Stroughton, 1989), notes that "the shift of interest from France to Germany also marks the move away from political radicalism to more purely intellectual interests. The German universities were coming to be regarded as the research-centres of Europe" (p. 117n).

69. Quoted in Thomas McFarland, *Romanticism and the Forms of Ruin: Wordsworth, Coleridge, and Modalities of Fragmentation* (Princeton: Princeton University Press, 1981), p. 13.

70. Quoted and translated by McFarland in ibid.

71. Quoted in ibid., p. 20.

72. Quoted in ibid., p. 21.

73. Ibid., p. 25.

74. Mario Praz, *The Romantic Agony,* 2d ed. (1933; London: Oxford University Press, 1970), pp. 14–15.

75. Longinus, *Dionysos Longinus on the Sublime,* trans. William Smith, 4th ed. (London, 1770). This translation, which first appeared in 1739, was the standard edition during the period in which Longinus attained his greatest influence in England. Quoted in Samuel H. Monk, *The Sublime: A Study of Critical Theories in Eighteenth-Century England* (1935; reprint, Ann Arbor: University of Michigan Press, 1962), p. 12.

76. Monk, *The Sublime,* p. 12.

77. Quoted in ibid., p. 13.

78. "A cliché echoed from Boileau," writes Monk in ibid., p. 22. See also Neil Hertz, "A Reading of Longinus," in *The End of the Line: Essays on Psychoanalysis and the Sublime* (New York: Columbia University Press, 1985), pp. 1–20.

79. Monk, *The Sublime,* p. 23.

80. Ibid., p. 29.

81. Thomas Weiskel, *The Romantic Sublime: Studies in the Structure and Psychology of Transcendence* (Baltimore: Johns Hopkins University Press, 1976), p. 4.

82. Ibid., p. 13.

83. Monk, *The Sublime,* p. 4.

84. Quoted in ibid., p. 7.

85. Weiskel, *Romantic Sublime,* p. 8.

86. Neil Hertz, "The Notion of Blockage in the Literature of the Sublime," in *Psychoanalysis and the Question of the Text,* ed. Geoffrey H. Hartmann, Selected Papers from the English Institute, 1976–77, n.s., no. 2 (Baltimore: Johns Hopkins University Press, 1978), pp. 62–85 (the essay is reprinted in Hertz, *The End of the Line*).

87. Ibid., p. 76.

88. Elizabeth Bruss, *Beautiful Theories: The Spectacle of Discourse in Contemporary Criticism* (Baltimore: Johns Hopkins University Press, 1982), p. 288.

89. Harold Bloom, *Poetry and Repression* (New Haven: Yale University Press, 1976), p. 2.

90. Harold Bloom, *The Anxiety of Influence: A Theory of Poetry* (New York: Oxford University Press, 1973), p. 5.

91. Ibid., p. 30.

92. Geoffrey Hartman, "War in Heaven" (review of *The Anxiety of Influence*), *Diacritics* 3, no. 1 (Spring 1973):26.

93. Bloom, *Anxiety of Influence,* p. 31.

94. Ibid., p. 7.

95. Ibid., p. 11.

96. Ibid., p. 30.

97. Harold Bloom, *A Map of Misreading* (Oxford: Oxford University Press, 1975), p. 18.

98. In Ann Wordsworth, "An Art That Will Not Abandon the Self to Language: Bloom, Tennyson, and the Blind World of the Wish," in *Untying the Text*, ed. Robert Young (London: Routledge and Kegan Paul, 1981), pp. 214–15.

99. Hartman, "War in Heaven," p. 29.

100. Bloom, *Anxiety of Influence*, p. 5.

101. Ibid., p. 15.

102. Bruss, *Beautiful Theories*, p. 357.

103. Bloom, *Poetry and Repression*, p. 25.

104. McFarland, *Originality and Imagination*, pp. 46–47.

105. Bloom, *Anxiety of Influence*, p. 8.

106. Ibid., p. 26.

107. Ibid., p. 148.

108. Bloom, *A Map of Misreading*, pp. 18 and 76.

109. Ibid., p. 18.

110. Bloom, *Poetry and Repression*, p. 7.

111. Harold Bloom, *Agon: Towards a Theory of Revisionism* (Oxford: Oxford University Press, 1982), p. 49.

112. Harold Bloom, *Kabbalah and Criticism* (New York: Seabury Press, 1975), p. 84.

113. Bloom, *Anxiety of Influence*, p. 22.

114. Bloom, *Poetry and Repression*, p. 2.

115. Bloom, *Anxiety of Influence*, p. 22. In Bloom's earliest investigations of Romanticism, this rebellious impulse is everywhere apparent. Both Shelley and Blake, the subjects of Bloom's first two books, are seen as desperate to break free from "formulated myth" (*Shelley's Mythmaking* [New Haven: Yale University Press, 1959], p. 8), or what Blake calls the "other man's system" (Bloom's book on Blake is *Blake's Apocalypse* [Ithaca: Cornell University Press, 1970]). Romanticism in general is seen as a "revolt not only against orderly creation, but against compulsion, against conditioning, against all unnecessary conditioning that presents itself as being necessary" ("To Reason with a Later Reason: Romanticism and the Rational," in *The Ringers in the Tower: Studies in Romantic Tradition* [Chicago: University of Chicago Press, 1971], p. 298). Wordsworth's "Resolution and Independence" is a poem "about not being able to do what Blake's Milton does, to cast off the coverings of anxiety and of self-torturing analysis" (ibid., p. 326), and its talk of "despondency and madness" is, in Hartman's account of Bloom's reading, the "dark obverse of the quest for originality and autonomy" (*Criticism in the Wilderness: The Study of Literature Today* [New Haven: Yale University Press, 1980], p. 51).

For Bloom, then, all Romantic poetry is "about" writer's block because the past, whether conceived as a person, as in Bloom's later theoretical writings, or as convention, as in his early work, is always the poem's (or poet's) hidden antagonist or inhibitor. What marks the break between Bloom's early writings and the works that follow *The Anxiety of Influence* is less his emphasis on the inhibiting power of the past than a growing disillusion with Romantic faith in the transfiguring powers of nature and the imagination. Neither provides escape from a fallen world, that which the Gnostics call the "Demiurge," which is why Bloom identifies himself as a believer in gnosis rather than a Gnostic; for Bloom, though Creation is fallen, salvation—the return to light—is impossible.

116. Bloom, *Anxiety of Influence*, p. 10.

117. Ibid., p. 25.

118. Bloom, *A Map of Misreading*, pp. 37, 35, 71, and 38.

119. Bruss, *Beautiful Theories*, p. 333.

120. Ibid., pp. 343 and 333.

121. The mappings of *Poetry and Repression*, in Bruss's words, "have a theatrical power first and a function to perform only after that. . . . The balance between literature and theory is just enough to give the theory, as poetry, a certain pleasant (painful) mien of strictness and 'severe' ratiocination, while also allowing it, as poetic speculation, the freedom to forego documentation and demonstration. . . . One understands more about the nature and narrowness of strength as a criterion of value by observing Bloom's tactics as a writer than by any formulations he actually presents—and especially by seeing how his need for outrage grows from book to book" (*Beautiful Theories*, pp. 345, 351, and 354).

122. Ibid., pp. 339.

123. Bloom, *Agon*, pp. 38–39. The question of Bloom's own predecessors or blocking agents is an inevitable one, given such a passage. To William Pritchard, the great precursor with whom Bloom wrestles is F. R. Leavis, against whom he had already done battle by championing Shelley in his first book ("Mr. Bloom in Yeatsville," *Partisan Review* 38, no. 1 [1971]:107). Like Bloom, Leavis was a critic of powerfully held and eccentric opinions, a proponent of "great" (as in Bloom's "strong") poets and traditions, and of a narrow and narrowing range. McFarland notes of Bloom's unargued acceptance of the canon that "aside from such personally generous gestures by which he includes his own friends—John Ashbery, A. R. Ammons, Angus Fletcher, Paul de Man—in his listings of canonical figures, he is docile in accepting the valuations already given by literary history" (*Originality and Imagination*, p. 42). In other words, Bloom is really—or underneath—a child of Leavis; which is to say, of Eliot and Arnold. Bruss points to Bloom's vision of literary theory as a sort of "negative theology," and to the "priestly" or Arnoldian air with which he goes about his business as critic and theorist (*Beautiful Theories*, pp. 292–93). The deep hostility in Bloom's relatively rare references to Leavis, Eliot, and Arnold only confirms the suspicion of indebtedness.

Of other possible precursors, McFarland mentions Bloom's teacher W. K. Wimsatt, whose notion of the autonomy of art works Bloom obviously challenges (*Originality and Imagination*, p. 42), and Geoffrey Hartman and others identify Northrop Frye, whom Bloom acknowledges as his master in *The Visionary Company*. Frye is a suitable candidate for several reasons: he offers a reinterpretation of not only Romanticism but poetry in general; he is the author of a grand theory; he is much given to elaborate schematizing; and he has done more than any other contemporary Anglo-American critic to foster a view of poetry as a product of other poems rather than experience, even employing a metaphor of familial struggle to characterize influence (as in "the new poem, like the new baby, is born into an already existing order of words, and is typical of the structure of poetry to which it is attached. The new baby *is* his own society appearing once again as a unit of individuality, and the new poem has a similar relation to its poetic society" [quoted in *Originality and Imagination*, p. 45]). Bloom "corrects" Frye in the same way he corrects Arnold, Eliot, and Leavis: by arguing for the inhibiting, rather than the enhancing, effect of influence. "Freedom for Frye," writes Bloom in *A Map of Misreading*, "as for Eliot, is the change, however slight, that any genuine single consciousness brings about in the order of literature simply by joining the simultaneity of such order" (p. 30). Even if Bloom accepted the possibility of a "genuine single consciousness," he would see such a joining as anxiety-inducing.

Finally, one other sort of influence is worth mentioning: the "theory" revolution in Continental and then Anglo-American criticism. Although Bloom consciously opposes key deconstructive assumptions—about distinctions of value and the claims of personal autonomy—the manner of his later, increasingly opaque writings bears witness to their influence. Nor is this influence solely stylistic. As Joseph Riddell and others have argued, Bloom's theories clearly alter in response to specific deconstructive objections; that is to say, in defiance of his own theories, which stress past rather than present influence (Riddell's arguments about Bloom's debt to theory can be found in an untitled review of *Kabbalah and Criticism* and *Poetry and Repression*, in *Georgia Review* 30, no. 4 [Winter 1976]:989–1006). Part of what threatens Bloom about contemporary Continental skepticism is, as Bruss points out, its obvious belatedness. In the past, theorists did not labor "so thoroughly in the shadow of a monumental master" (*Beautiful Theories*, p. 314)—for example, as Lacan does with Freud, or Althusser with Marx, or Derrida with the actual words of his philosophical predecessors. For Bloom, to resist the present fashion is to continue the fight for "identity," originality, all that makes strong poetry possible—and blocks all but the strongest.

124. McFarland, *Romanticism and the Forms of Ruin*, p. 5.

125. McFarland, *Originality and Imagination*, p. 3. McFarland also quotes Eugene M. Waith, *The Herculean Hero: In Marlowe, Chapman, Shakespeare and Dryden* (New York: Columbia University Press, 1967).

126. Quoted in E. A. Havelock, *Preface to Plato* (Cambridge, Mass.: Harvard University Press, 1963), p. 201.

127. McFarland, *Originality and Imagination*, p. 21.

128. Renato Poggioli, *The Theory of the Avant-Garde*, trans. Gerald Fitzgerald (Cambridge, Mass.: Harvard University Press, 1968), p. 52, quoted in ibid., p. 8. Subsequent references to McFarland, *Originality and Imagination*, are cited by page numbers in the text.

129. Quoted in ibid., p. 11.

130. According to Helen Darbishire, the line "echoes Ariosto's 'cosa non detta in prosa mai ne in rima'" (*The Poetical Works of John Milton*, ed. Helen Darbishire, 2 vols. [Oxford: Clarendon Press, 1952], 2:283).

131. McFarland, "Field, Constellation, and Aesthetic Object," in *Originality*

and Imagination, p. 58. The Johann Gottfried Herder quotation is McFarland's translation from *Ideen zur Philosophie der Geschichte der Menschheit* (1784–91).

6. Wordsworth and Writer's Block

1. Matthew Arnold, "On Translating Homer" (1861), in *Matthew Arnold: On the Classical Tradition,* ed. R. H. Super (Ann Arbor: University of Michigan Press, 1960), p. 145. This is vol. 1 of *The Complete Prose Works of Matthew Arnold,* ed. Super, 11 vols. See also Paul Sheats's description of the progress of *The Prelude* as "retrograde," in "Wordsworth's 'Retrogrades' and the Shaping of *The Prelude,*" *Journal of English and German Philology* 71, no. 4 (October 1973):473–90.

2. Kenneth R. Johnston, *Wordsworth and "The Recluse"* (New Haven: Yale University Press, 1984), p. 119.

3. James K. Chandler, *Wordsworth's Second Nature: A Study of the Poetry and Politics* (Chicago: Unversity of Chicago Press, 1984), p. 189.

4. Robert Rehder, *Wordsworth and the Beginnings of Modern Poetry* (London: Croon Helm, 1981), p. 72. Chandler agrees: "The poet's freedom about where to take up residence must be understood as a metaphorical adumbration of his decision about which subject he will freely choose . . . for his poems" (*Wordsworth's Second Nature,* p. 192).

5. See William Wordsworth, *"The Prelude," 1798–1799,* ed. Stephen Parrish (Ithaca: Cornell University Press, 1977), p. 6.

6. From chap. 22 of the *Biographia Literaria,* ed. James Engell and W. Jackson Bate, in vol. 2 of no. 7 of *The Collected Works of Samuel Taylor Coleridge* (a projected 16-vol. work), ed. Kathleen Coburn (London: Routledge and Kegan Paul, 1983), 2:129.

7. Geoffrey Hartman, *Wordsworth's Poetry, 1787–1814* (New Haven: Yale University Press, 1964), p. 38.

8. Hanna Segal, "A Psycho-Analytical Approach to Aesthetics," in *New Directions in Psycho-Analysis: The Significance of Infant Conflict in the Pattern of Adult Behaviour,* ed. M. Klein, P. Heimann, and R. E. Money-Kyrle (London: Tavistock Press, 1955), p. 390.

9. Simon Stuart, *New Phoenix Wings: Reparation in Literature* (London: Routledge and Kegan Paul, 1979), pp. 106–7.

10. Hanna Segal, "Notes on Symbol Formation," *International Journal of Psycho-Analysis* 38, no. 5 (1957):395.

11. Thomas McFarland, *Romanticism and the Forms of Ruin: Wordsworth, Coleridge, and Modalities of Fragmentation* (Princeton: Princeton University Press, 1981), p. 152.

12. D. W. Winnicott, "Transitional Objects and Transitional Phenomena," *International Journal of Psycho-Analysis* 34, no. 2 (1953):96.

13. The phrase comes from an essay Wordsworth wrote after completing *The Borderers.* The subject of the essay is the psychology of such people as Oswald, the play's villain. The essay was undiscovered until 1934. See *The*

Poetical Works of William Wordsworth, ed. E. de Selincourt and Helen Darbishire, 5 vols. (Oxford: Clarendon Press, 1940–49), 1:345.

14. McFarland, *Romanticism and the Forms of Ruin*, p. 76.

15. Geoffrey Hartman, *Criticism in the Wilderness* (New Haven: Yale University Press, 1980), p. 30.

16. *The Letters of William and Dorothy Wordsworth: The Early Years, 1787–1805*, ed. E. de Selincourt; rev. ed., Chester L. Shaver (Oxford: Clarendon Press, 1967), p. 366. There are 7 vols. of letters altogether, all published by Clarendon Press. After *The Early Years, 1787–1805* comes *The Middle Years. Part 1, 1806–1811*, ed. E. de Selincourt; rev. ed., Mary Moorman (1969); *The Middle Years. Part 2, 1812–1820*, ed. E. de Selincourt; rev. ed., Mary Moorman and Alan G. Hill (1970); *The Later Years. Part 1, 1821–1828*, ed. E. de Selincourt; rev. ed., Alan G. Hill (1978); *The Later Years. Part 2, 1829–1834*, ed. E. de Selincourt; rev. ed., Alan G. Hill (1979); *The Later Years. Part 3, 1835–1839*, ed. E. de Selincourt; rev. ed., Alan G. Hill (1982); and *The Later Years. Part 4, 1840–1853*, ed. E. de Selincourt; rev. ed., Alan G. Hill (1988). Subsequent references use the abbreviations *EY* (Early Years), *MY* (Middle Years), and *LY* (Later Years), followed by editors, part, and page numbers.

17. The charge of inconstancy is explained in chap. 22 of the *Biographia Literaria*, ed. Engell and Bate, 2:121; the deleted stanza from "Resolution and Independence" is quoted in 2:125.

18. Michael G. Cooke, *The Romantic Will* (New Haven: Yale University Press, 1976), p. 211.

19. The "old Man" is likened to a huge "stone" (57) couched on the "bald top" of an eminence, then a "sea beast" (62) isolated "on a shelf / Of rock or sand" (thus recalling the "pool" of the previous stanza, which is "bare to the eye of heaven").

20. From the Fenwick notes dictated late in Wordsworth's life for Isabella Fenwick, his friend and amanuensis. See *The Poetical Works of William Wordsworth*, ed. de Selincourt and Darbishire, 4:463–64.

21. William Hazlitt, "My First Acquaintance with Poets" (1823), in *"Sketches and Essays" and "Winterslow,"* ed. W. Carew Hazlitt (London: George Bell, 1902), p. 271.

22. Lionel Trilling, "The Immortality Ode," in *The Liberal Imagination: Essays in Literature and Society* (Harmondsworth, Middlesex: Penguin Books, 1970), p. 154.

23. To Harold Bloom, the "Tree" of line 51 is "not an archetypal or Platonic tree, but simply a particular tree whose individual appearance Wordsworth had noticed" (from a footnote to the poem in vol. 4 of the 6-vol. paperback edition of the *Oxford Anthology of English Literature* entitled *Romantic Poetry and Prose*, ed. Harold Bloom and Lionel Trilling [New York: Oxford University Press, 1973, p. 178]); however, this is only partly the case. For how can one not associate so singular a capitalized "Tree" with its biblical archetype, and thus with fallen Creation, the world of time and loss? That one cannot accounts for the impression that the lost gleam or glory is somehow the fault of the "Tree." The external world does not so much drown or overwhelm poetic power (as it will later in the poem) as symbolize its powerlessness in the face of the brute facts of nature, which force it to fade.

24. *Romantic Poetry and Prose,* ed. Bloom and Trilling, pp. 148 and 126.

25. Thomas McFarland, in *Originality and Imagination* (Baltimore: Johns Hopkins University Press, 1984), p. 73, points to a particularly egregious example of this process in the following lines from stanza 9 of "Ode: Intimations":

> O Joy! that in our embers
> Is something that doth live,
> That nature yet remembers
> What was so fugitive!
> The thought of our past years in me doth breed
> Perpetual benediction: not indeed
> For that which is most worthy to be blest;
> Delight and liberty, the simple creed
> Of Childhood, whether busy or at rest
> With new-fledged hope still fluttering in his breast.
>
> (130–39)

26. Ibid.

27. William Wordsworth to Catherine Clarkson, January 1815, in *MY,* ed. de Selincourt; rev. ed. Moorman and Hill, 2:189.

28. Quoted in Willard L. Sperry, *Wordsworth's Anti-Climax* (Cambridge, Mass.: Harvard University Press, 1935), p. 29.

29. *Romantic Poetry and Prose,* ed. Bloom and Trilling, p. 186n.

30. See Richard Onorato, *The Character of the Poet: Wordsworth in "The Prelude"* (Princeton: Princeton University Press, 1971), pp. 323–32.

31. William Wordsworth to Isabella Fenwick, 28 July 1842, in *LY,* ed. de Selincourt; rev. ed., Hill, 4:361, quoted in McFarland, *Romanticism and the Forms of Ruin,* p. 166.

32. John Jones, *The Egotistical Sublime* (London: Chatto and Windus, 1954), p. 187.

33. See Hartman, *Wordsworth's Poetry,* pp. 333–34. Hartman reminds us that in the past religion itself seemed "too much a product of that same apocalyptic consciousness"—that is, an expression of poetry or plastic power taken to an extreme. "In the later poetry, however, religion has changed its role. It now protects rather than threatens nature. . . . Wordsworth is suspicious of everything that could raise the apocalyptic passions" (ibid.).

34. Quoted in F. W. Bateson, *Wordsworth: A Re-interpretation* (London: Longman, 1956), p. 171.

35. Ibid., p. 110. According to Karl Kroeber, in his survey of criticism of Wordsworth in *The English Romantic Poets: A Review of Research and Criticism,* ed. Frank Jordan (New York: Modern Language Association of America, 1985), p. 264, "a decline in the quality of his poetry is denied by no influential critic." For a recent defense of later Wordsworth—and a lively account of the debate about the merits of the later poems and revisions—see Jack Stillinger, "Textual Primitivism and the Editing of Wordsworth," in *Studies in Romanticism* 28, no. 1 (Spring 1989):3–28.

36. Stephen Gill, *Wordsworth: A Life* (Oxford: Clarendon Press, 1989), pp. 319–20.

37. The "compositional hedges" that rescue Wordsworth from these gulfs and abysses are, in Johnston's words, "simple and desperate" (*Wordsworth and "The Recluse,"* p. 241).

38. *Specimens of the Table Talk of the Late Samuel Taylor Coleridge*, 2 vols. (London, 1835), 2:70–71, quoted in Jonathan Wordsworth, *Wordsworth: The Borders of Vision* (Oxford: Oxford University Press, 1982), p. 352.

39. Samuel Taylor Coleridge to William Wordsworth, 30 May 1815, in *Collected Letters of Samuel Taylor Coleridge*, ed. Earl L. Griggs, 6 vols. (Oxford: Clarendon Press, 1956–71), 4:574.

40. Samuel Taylor Coleridge to William Wordsworth, 12 October 1799, in ibid., 1:538.

41. Samuel Taylor Coleridge to Thomas Poole, 14 October 1803, in ibid., 2:1013.

42. Jonathan Wordsworth, *Wordsworth: The Borders of Vision*, p. 356.

43. William Wordsworth to Samuel Taylor Coleridge, 6 March 1804 and 29 March 1804, in *EY*, ed. de Selincourt; rev. ed., Shaver, pp. 452 and 464, respectively.

44. William Wordsworth to Thomas De Quincey, 6 March 1804, in ibid., p. 454.

45. William Wordsworth to Sir George Beaumont, 25 December 1804, in ibid., p. 518.

46. William Wordsworth to Sir George Beaumont, 3 June 1805, in ibid., p. 594.

47. Dorothy Wordsworth to Lady Beaumont, 25 and 26 December 1805, in ibid., p. 664.

48. William Wordsworth to Thomas De Quincey, 6 March 1804, in ibid., p. 454.

49. This is a point that Johnston makes in *Wordsworth and "The Recluse,"* p. 248.

50. In Johnston's words, "a final, apocalyptic reading of human and national talents is evoked and drawn back" (in ibid.).

51. "For the fourth time running," comments Jonathan Wordsworth (*The Borders of Vision*, pp. 374–75),

he was bringing out a collection precisely when he might have been expected to be getting on with the central part of the building: the first volume of the *Lyrical Ballads* had followed his original announcement of *The Recluse* in March 1798, and work on the second had begun when *Home at Grasmere* was abandoned in April 1800. *Poems 1807* had been put together when it became obvious . . . that Coleridge was not going to be able to provide the material that was so urgently needed; and now Wordsworth was surely putting off the day when the consequences of his recent Preface would have to be faced. As in the period following the completion of *The Prelude* in 1805, we begin to hear of family anxieties. By February 1815 there is the same ominous talk of the poet's reading for the nourishment of his mind: "William has had one of his weeks of rest," Dorothy writes on the eighteenth, "and we now begin to wish that he was at work again, but as he intends completely to plan the first part of *The Recluse* before he begins the composition, he must read many books before he will fairly set to labour again."

52. Mary Wordsworth to Edward Quillinan, 26 October 1824, in *The Letters of Mary Wordsworth*, ed. Mary E. Burton (Oxford: Clarendon Press, 1958), p. 119.

53. Dorothy Wordsworth to Henry Crabb Robinson, 13 December 1824, in *LY*, ed. de Selincourt; rev. ed., Hill, 1:292.

54. Dorothy Wordsworth to Catherine Clarkson, 27 March 1821, in ibid., 1:150.

55. Quoted from unpublished papers at Dove Cottage, in Jonathan Wordsworth, *The Borders of Vision*, p. 450n.54.

56. Quoted from the same unpublished papers, in ibid.

57. Quoted in ibid., p. 376.

58. Johnston, *Wordsworth and "The Recluse,"* p. 238. Jonathan Arac, in "Bounding Lines: *The Prelude* and Critical Revision," *Boundary 2* 7, no. 3 (Spring 1979):31–48, offers an alternative account of the benefits of incompletion: "There is a humane liberation in letting go—even with indecision, anxiety, and guilt—such a project as *The Recluse*, in deferring the end, keeping the self suspended in receptivity like the Boy of Winander. There is a reward too in replacing the end, letting the interpretation stand for the achievement, the wandering for the goal: 'something evermore about to be' (VI, l. 608), 'The budding rose above the full rose blown' (XI, l. 121). The revisions to *The Prelude* demonstrate the continuing liveliness of response in Wordsworth, his continuing power to find between the lines of the earlier text the places where imagination will come to him" (p. 37). And later: "If *The Prelude* fulfills the ambition it expresses, it is not because it has reached the goal but rather . . . the means had become the end" (p. 40).

A more recent account of Wordsworth's difficulties with *The Recluse* is offered by Stephen Gill in *Wordsworth: A Life*, when he calls Coleridge "quite wrong" (p. 202) to claim that epic was Wordsworth's "natural Element": "Lyrical utterance was for Wordsworth [the] natural mode," though epic "remained his 'last and favorite aspiration'" (p. 202). Although Gill does not see the unfinished *Recluse* as enabling, as do Johnston and Arac in their different ways, he believes that "twentieth-century preoccupation with what he did not publish" has obscured the fact that "what he was actually doing between 1798 and 1807 was identifying himself publicly with the lyric, and ennobling it in the hierarchy of genres by the claims made in the Prefaces of 1800 and 1802" (p. 202). For Gill, Wordsworth's "is a poetry of questioning, of gleams, flashes, intimations, visionary Moments. Wordsworth was not, and could not become, the poet of Coleridge's imaginings" (p. 146).

7. The Case of Coleridge

1. E. K. Chambers, *Samuel Taylor Coleridge: A Biographical Study* (Oxford: Clarendon Press, 1950), p. 331.

2. Norman Fruman, *Coleridge: The Damaged Archangel* (London: Allen and Unwin, 1972), p. 260.

3. These later poems reveal, in Fruman's words, "a fitful energy quickly exhausted . . . genius shows itself in flashes, but he seems to have no subject but a momentary spasm of feeling, and no secure or settled technique upon which to lean for support" (in ibid.). For a quite different assessment of the late lyrics, see Edward Kessler, *Coleridge's Metaphors of Being* (Princeton: Princeton University Press, 1979).

4. W. J. Bate, *Coleridge* (New York: Macmillan, 1968), p. 136.

5. Thomas McFarland, *Romanticism and the Forms of Ruin* (Princeton: Princeton University Press, 1981), p. 6.

6. Quoted in Bate, *Coleridge*, p. 130.

7. See chap. 13 of the *Biographia Literaria*, ed. James Engell and W. Jackson Bate, in vol. 1 of no. 7 of *The Collected Works of Samuel Taylor Coleridge* (a projected 16-vol. work), ed. Kathleen Coburn (London: Routledge and Kegan Paul, 1983), 1:304 and 300; henceforth cited as *CW*, ed. Coburn.

8. Both quotes are in McFarland, *Romanticism and the Forms of Ruin*, pp. 21 and 22.

9. Ibid., p. 21.

10. From Samuel Taylor Coleridge's 1809 "Prospectus" to *The Friend*, ed. Barbara E. Rooke, in vol. 2 of no. 4 of *CW*, ed. Coburn, 2:16.

11. Samuel Taylor Coleridge to Thomas Poole, 31 March 1800, in *The Collected Letters of Samuel Taylor Coleridge*, ed. Earl L. Griggs, 6 vols. (Oxford: Clarendon Press, 1956–71), 1:329; henceforth cited as *CL*, ed. Griggs.

12. From Coleridge's "Prospectus" to *The Friend*, ed. Rooke, in vol. 2 of no. 4 of *CW*, ed. Coburn, 2:16.

13. Entry of 10 May 1804, in *The Notebooks of Samuel Taylor Coleridge*, ed. Kathleen Coburn, 3 vols. (Princeton: Princeton University Press, 1957–73), 2:2086; henceforth cited as *CN*, ed. Coburn.

14. Kristine Dugas, "Struggling with the Contingent: Self-conscious Imagination in Coleridge's Notebooks," in *Coleridge's Imagination*, ed. Richard Gravil, Lucy Newlyn, and Nicholas Roe (Cambridge: Cambridge University Press, 1985), p. 61.

15. Samuel Taylor Coleridge to Daniel Stuart, 7 October 1800, in *CL*, ed. Griggs, 1:629, quoted in McFarland, *Romanticism and the Forms of Ruin*, pp. 61–62.

16. Samuel Taylor Coleridge to John Thelwall, 17 December 1800, in *CL*, ed. Griggs, 1:656.

17. Entry of 9 January 1804, in *CN*, ed. Coburn, 1:1832.

18. Samuel Taylor Coleridge to Sir George Beaumont, 1 February 1804, in *CL*, ed. Griggs, 2:1054.

19. Samuel Taylor Coleridge to J. J. Morgan, 14 May 1814, in ibid., 3:489.

20. Samuel Taylor Coleridge to Joseph Cottle, 26 April 1814, in ibid., 3:477.

21. Quoted in Bate, *Coleridge*, p. 121.

22. McFarland, *Romanticism and the Forms of Ruin*, p. 106.

23. Samuel Taylor Coleridge to Thomas Poole, c. 11 October 1800, in *CL*, ed. Griggs, 1:356.

24. Samuel Taylor Coleridge to Joseph Cottle, [early February] 1797, in ibid., 1:309.

25. Samuel Taylor Coleridge to James Webbe Tobin, 17 September 1800, in ibid., 1:351.

26. Entry of 21 October 1804, in *CN*, ed. Coburn, 2:2237.

27. Quoted in *Coleridge's Shakespearian Criticism*, ed. Thomas M. Raysor, 2 vols. (Cambridge, Mass.: Harvard University Press, 1930), 2:181. It is Henry Crabb Robinson who recounts the comment in a letter of 3 January 1812 to Mrs. Thomas Clarkson. After quoting Coleridge on action, Crabb Robinson continues: "Somebody said to me, 'This is a satire on himself.'—'No,' said I, 'it is a eulogy'" (2:181–82).

28. Quoted in Bate, *Coleridge*, p. 111.

29. Entry of 23 December 1804, in *CN*, ed. Coburn, 2:2368.

30. Sara Coleridge to Hartley Coleridge, 5 August 1834, in *CL*, ed. Griggs, 6:992.

31. Samuel Taylor Coleridge to James Gillman, 13 April 1816, in ibid., 4:630.

32. Quoted in Bate, *Coleridge*, p. 11.

33. The contemporary was Humphrey Davy, quoted in ibid., p. 115.

34. Quoted in McFarland, *Romanticism and the Forms of Ruin*, p. 111.

35. Entry of 11 January 1805, in *CN*, ed. Coburn, 2:2398.

36. Samuel Taylor Coleridge to Thomas Poole, 9 October 1797, in *CL*, ed. Griggs, 1:347.

37. McFarland, *Romanticism and the Forms of Ruin*, p. 113.

38. Samuel Taylor Coleridge to Thomas Poole, March 1797, in *CL*, ed. Griggs, 1:310, quoted in ibid., p. 114.

39. Campbell and Gillman are quoted in McFarland, *Romanticism and the Forms of Ruin*, p. 117. Richard Holmes's assessment of Coleridge's mother is from *Coleridge: Early Visions* (London: Hodder and Stoughton, 1989), p. 4.

40. Quoted in Holmes, *Coleridge: Early Visions*, p. 9.

41. Samuel Taylor Coleridge to Derwent Coleridge, 7 February 1807, in *CL*, ed. Griggs, 3:1–2.

42. Quoted in Fruman, *Damaged Archangel*, pp. 21 and 25.

43. Samuel Taylor Coleridge to G. L. Tuckett, 6 February 1794, in *CL*, ed. Griggs, 1:63.

44. Quoted in Holmes, *Coleridge: Early Visions*, p. 15n.

45. Entry of 18 May 1808, in *CN*, ed. Coburn, 2:3321. Fruman connects Coleridge's fearfulness about adulthood with a lifelong "anxiety to please, the habit of assentation . . . [a product of] his ceaselessly gnawing self-doubts and fear of rejection. . . . He simply could not believe that he could be liked for himself alone. . . . Adverse criticism in any form was neurotically painful to him, which is one of the many reasons why he submitted his work to the public with such anxious and misleading prefaces" (*Damaged Archangel*, p. 418).

46. McFarland, *Romanticism and the Forms of Ruin*, p. 123.

47. Entry of 10 April 1805, in *CN*, ed. Coburn, 2:2543.

48. Entry of 27 October 1803, in ibid., 1:1616, and of 19 April 1804, in ibid., 2:2026.

49. Samuel Taylor Coleridge to John Thelwall, 14 October 1797, in *CL*, ed. Griggs, 1:349.

50. See Dugas, "Struggling with the Contingent," p. 59.

51. To Raimonda Modiano, the richness of nature in Coleridge's later writings makes his own "absence of . . . genial spirits so much more evident and painful to endure" (*Coleridge and the Concept of Nature* [London: Macmillan, 1985], p. 43).

52. Modiano says that, throughout "The Picture," "the narrator is subject to conflicting responses to nature. He is by no means indifferent to nature for he repeatedly tries to remain faithful to nature's true identity. . . . But at the same time, the side of nature that is revealed in the absence of human projections is often so harsh and unappealing [it is a landscape of 'weeds,' 'thorns,' 'matted underwood' and 'rustling snakes,' lines 1–6] that it almost invites personal fantasy" (ibid., p. 93).

53. This is a point that Anthony John Harding makes: "The inability to speak one's thought because of disunity in the inward being is a theme common to several poems of Coleridge that abjure the prophetic stance" ("Mythopoesis: The Unity of Christabel," in *Coleridge's Imagination*, ed. Gravil, Newlyn, and Roe, p. 211).

54. In Coleridge's prose account of the night, in a letter of 24 September 1796 to Thomas Poole, his blockage dissolves at the sight not so much of the child as the nurturing mother: "When two hours after, I saw it at the bosom of it's Mother; on her arm; and her eye tearful & watching it's little features, then I was thrilled & melted, & gave it the Kiss of a FATHER" (*CL*, ed. Griggs, 1:236). The episode is recorded in a subsequent sonnet on the birth, "To A Friend Who Asked, How I Felt When The Nurse Presented My Infant To Me" (1796).

55. Harding, "Mythopoesis," p. 212.

56. For Harding, the conclusion to pt. 2 "appears to be a commentary not on a moral truth . . . but on a truth about speech, and about its frightening disconnectedness from willed thought and meaning" (ibid.).

57. The first of Furman's instances is quoted in *Inquiring Spirit*, ed. Kathleen Coburn (London: Routledge and Kegan Paul, 1951), p. 68; the second is from an entry of 21–24 November 1803, in *CN*, ed. Coburn, 1:1679. The 1805 plea to Wordsworth is from an entry of 20 October–20 November 1805, in ibid., 2:2712. The plea to Thomas Poole is from a letter of 5 November 1796, in *CL*, ed. Griggs, 1:249.

58. McFarland, *Romanticism and the Forms of Ruin*, p. 119.

59. Entry of August 1805, in *CN*, ed. Coburn, 2:2647, quoted in ibid., p. 121.

60. Ibid., p. 122.

61. Samuel Taylor Coleridge to George Coleridge, 1 May 1794, in *CL*, ed. Griggs, 1:80. Holmes points out that "of the first fifty letters Coleridge is known to have written, thirty-five were to George; and the *Poems* of 1797 would be dedicated to him, with an epigraph from Horace, 'notable among brothers for his paternal spirit'" (*Early Visions*, p. 14).

62. "In all these relationships," writes McFarland, "he assumed something of the situation of a child, for the neurotic nature of his needs froze him into certain infantile attitudes" (*Romanticism and the Forms of Ruin*, p. 123).

63. Ibid., p. 128.

64. In Martin Greenberg's words, plagiarisms "lay like a lump inside him, a part of that being blocked and stopped—of that 'sense of stifled power!'— which was his lifelong experience" (*The Hamlet Vocation of Coleridge and Wordsworth* [Iowa City: University of Iowa Press, 1986], p. 23]).

65. Quoted in McFarland, *Romanticism and the Forms of Ruin*, p. 127.

66. The letter, dated 4 April 1802, about thrice the length of "Dejection," was addressed to Sara (or "Asra," as Coleridge sometimes called her), the sister of Wordsworth's fiancée. Although its starting point was metaphysical—the loss of that "visionary gleam" Wordsworth complains of in the stanzas he had read to Coleridge—its manner was much more personal and less explicitly philosophical than the later, finished version, for at its heart was a sense of the doomed nature of Coleridge's love for Sara and of the unhappy marriage that stood in its way. For an account of the verse letter "both on its own terms and as an antithetical completion of Wordsworth's Ode" (p. 103), see Gene W. Ruoff, *Wordsworth and Coleridge: The Making of the Major Lyrics, 1802–1804* (London: Harvester Wheatsheaf, 1989), pp. 59–103.

In *Early Visions*, Holmes connects the verse letter to a new thrust in Coleridge's Notebooks and correspondence: "toward self-consciousness. . . . His whole instinct was turning towards this form of confessional writing, in his letters, his Notebooks, and his poetry." Holmes also sees this writing as especially powerful: "Hence the paradox that is so often in the letters and poems of the 1801–4 period . . . [Coleridge] describes this apparent loss of creativity in the most brilliant and imaginative new ways" (p. 290). The Notebook entries for the 1801–4 period make Coleridge "one of the great English diarists" (p. 363).

67. Samuel Taylor Coleridge to Mary Evans, 7 February 1793, in *CL*, ed. Griggs, 1:49.

68. It is wholly characteristic of Coleridge that at such a moment, in what is, after all, almost a paraphrase of Wordsworth's "Lucy Gray," the one "revision" he introduces, in Modiano's words, is "the change of focus from the parents' to the child's despair," a change that "indicates Coleridge's own self-projection as a dependent and helpless being, rather than an actual rebirth of poetic vigor at the heels of his poet-master" (Modiano, *Coleridge and the Concept of Nature*, p. 49).

69. McFarland, *Romanticism and the Forms of Ruin*, p. 75.

70. Wordsworth's crucial role in this abandonment is suggested by a letter of 25 March 1801 to William Godwin: "The Poet is dead in me—my imagination . . . lies, like Cold Snuff on the Circular Rim of a Brass Candlestick. . . . If I die, and the Booksellers will give you any thing for my life, be sure to say—'Wordsworth descended on him, like the Γνῶθι σεαυτόν from heaven; by shewing to him what true poetry was, he made him know, that he himself was no Poet" (*CL*, ed. Griggs, 2:714).

71. Samuel Taylor Coleridge to Robert Southey, 29 July 1802, in ibid., 2:831, and to Robert Southey, 11 December 1794, in ibid., 1:137.

72. Samuel Taylor Coleridge to Robert Southey, 19 July 1802, in ibid., 2:814.

73. Samuel Taylor Coleridge to Thomas Poole, October 1797, in ibid., 1:354.

74. Samuel Taylor Coleridge to Robert Southey, 29 July 1802, in ibid., 2:831.

75. McFarland, *Romanticism and the Forms of Ruin*, p. 251.

76. Fruman, *Damaged Archangel*, pp. 330–32.

77. For a more detailed account of this distinction, see K. M. Wheeler, *The Creative Mind in Coleridge's Poetry* (London: Heinemann, 1981), pp. 22–24. The "Preface" concludes with a corroborating quotation from "The Picture." The lines quoted are those in which the forlorn lover, imagining his beloved's face reflected in a "desert stream" (72), "Worships the watery idol, dreaming hopes / Delicious to the soul" (83–84). The beloved is then imagined scattering flowers on her reflection, and the image vanishes. The lines Coleridge actually quotes express hope and longing:

> . . . all the charm
> Is broken—all that phantom-world so fair
> Vanishes, and a thousand circlets spread,
> And each mis-shape['s] the other. Stay awhile,
> Poor youth! who scarcely dar'st lift up thine eyes—
> The stream will soon renew its smoothness, soon
> The visions will return! And lo, he stays,
> And soon the fragments dim of lovely forms
> Come trembling back, unite, and now once more
> The pool becomes a mirror . . .
> (91–101)

In their original context, these lines are followed by a passage, already quoted, in which the "Ill-fated youth" is destined to "waste thy manly prime" in search of the maiden; to be "bewitched" by a "shadow" of her shadow. The image is unrecoverable. Here, its unrecoverability is left unspoken, but the lines quoted have the same poignancy as the conclusion of "Dejection: An Ode." The "Preface" ends with a sentence that reinforces the mood: "Yet from the still surviving recollections in his mind, the author has frequently purposed to finish for himself what had been originally, as it were, given to him. Σαμερον αδιον ασω [Αὔιον ἄδιον ἄσω 1834]: but the tomorrow is yet to come."

78. Ibid., p. 31.

79. Bate, *Coleridge*, p. 76. Holmes, on the other hand, argues that "there is no reason to disbelieve the basic truth of Coleridge's wonderful story of the 'lonely farmhouse,' the opium, and the old folio" (*Early Visions*, p. 168).

80. See Beverly Fields's conclusion that the poem is "about action, of whatever kind, including poetic. The first thirty-six lines describe Kubla Khan's action, a *fait accompli*, and the rest of the poem describes the persona's incapacity for action" (*Reality's Dark Dream: Dejection in Coleridge* [Kent, Ohio: Kent State University Press, 1967], p. 92).

81. David Beres, "A Dream, A Vision and a Poem: A Psycho-Analytic

Study of the Origins of the Rime of the Ancient Mariner," *International Journal of Psycho-Analysis* 32, no. 2 (1951):97–115, quoted in McFarland, *Romanticism and the Forms of Ruin*, p. 116.

82. Fruman (*Damaged Archangel*, pp. 346 and 399) relates the poem not only to Coleridge's creative inhibitions but also to his sexual ones:

> The startling contrast of a sunny pleasure dome and caves of ice may well suggest the dual nature of the dome in the dreamer's mind. It is sunny and dedicated to pleasure, and yet there are caves of ice: cold, frozen, underground, perhaps forbidding. When we remember the caverns measureless to man and the lifeless ocean, the ominous chasm, and the ancestral voices heard from fear, it is not hard to suppose that the caves of ice reveal . . . his deep, interior recoil from an act which "taken by itself," he was to write later, "was both foolish and debasing." (P. 399)

Or, as Greenberg states, "the free run of paradise (witness the fate of Adam and Eve, and Satan) risks a compensatory retribution" (*Hamlet Vocation of Coleridge and Wordsworth*, p. 149)—one that, in this context, has Oedipal overtones.

83. Maud Bodkin, *Archetypal Patterns in Poetry* (Oxford: Oxford University Press, 1934), p. 143.

84. Greenberg, *Hamlet Vocation of Coleridge and Wordsworth*, p. 51.

85. Entry of September-October 1803, in *CN*, ed. Coburn, 1:1515.

86. George Watson, in the "Preface" to his edition of the *Biographia Literaria* (London: Dent, 1965), p. xii.

87. Bate, *Coleridge*, p. 131.

88. Ibid., p. 186.

89. *Biographia Literaria*, ed. Engell and Bate, 1:233–34.

90. Ibid., 1:300.

91. Samuel Taylor Coleridge to Thomas Curtis, 29 April 1817, in *CL*, ed. Griggs, 4:728.

92. *Biographia Literaria*, ed. Engell and Bate, 1:302–4.

93. Ibid., 1:304.

94. Here, for example, is McFarland on the letter: "The invocation of the *magnum opus* neatly divests Coleridge of the onerous responsibility of formal deduction, and, so relieved, he is able simply to deposit—to dump, really— the distinction of primary imagination, secondary imagination, and fancy. The key point in the whole bizarre business, however, is that without such invocation, the distinction could not have appeared at all" (*Romanticism and the Forms of Ruin*, p. 352).

95. Ibid., pp. 351 and 349.

96. To Jean-Pierre Mileur, for example, "Coleridge is being driven by the evidence of his own poetic productions to regard poetry in a negative light. It would appear that Coleridge's failures to complete poems are less independent causes than statements in themselves of his poetic condition" (*Vision and Revision: Coleridge's Art of Immanence* [Berkeley and Los Angeles: University of California Press, 1982], p. 62).

97. Entry of 20 October–20 November 1805, in *CN*, ed. Coburn, 2:2711.
98. Entry of October-November 1806, in ibid., 2:2921.
99. *Miscellaneous Criticism*, ed. Thomas M. Raysor (Cambridge, Mass.: Harvard University Press, 1936), pp. 163–64.
100. Edward Kessler, *Coleridge's Metaphors of Being* (Princeton: Princeton University Press, 1979), p. 5.
101. Ibid., p. 6.
102. Samuel Taylor Coleridge to George Coleridge, 10 March 1798, in *CL*, ed. Griggs, 1:399.
103. Entry of September 1807, in *CN*, ed. Coburn, 2:3158.
104. Kessler, *Coleridge's Metaphors of Being*, p. 4.
105. Ibid., p. 5n.5.
106. Bate, *Coleridge*, p. 118.
107. Samuel Taylor Coleridge, *Hints Towards the Formation of a More Comprehensive Theory of Life*, ed. Seth B. Watson (London: John Churchill, 1848), p. 17.
108. Entry of September 1808, in *CN*, ed. Coburn, 3:3401.
109. Kessler, *Coleridge's Metaphors of Being*, p. 47.
110. Entry of February 1807, in *CN*, ed. Coburn, 2:2998.

8. Writing, Speech, and Culture

1. E. A. Havelock, *The Literary Renaissance in Greece and Its Cultural Consequences* (Princeton: Princeton University Press, 1982), p. 6.
2. Walter J. Ong, *Orality and Literacy: The Technologizing of the Word* (London: Methuen, 1982), p. 84.
3. Ibid., p. 85. Although according to Oswyn Murray, *Early Greece* (Brighton: Harvester Press, 1980), "the first datable evidence for the existence of the Greek alphabet comes from the pottery of the period 550–700" (p. 93). The Greek alphabet seems to have been a modification of the Phoenician writing system. Murray speculates that "the adaptation from Phoenician is likely to have taken place in a mixed Phoenician-Greek community." He suggests Crete or "a trading post such as Al Mina" (p. 93).
4. See E. A. Havelock, *Preface to Plato* (1963; reprint, Cambridge, Mass.: Harvard University Press, 1983), p. 40. The clearest reference to writing in *The Frogs* occurs when the chorus tells Dionysus not to worry about the audience. In David Barrett's translation: "As for the audience, / You are mistaken / If you think subtle points / Will not be taken. / Such fears are vain, I vow; / They've all got textbooks now" (Aristophanes, *The Wasps, The Poet and the Women, The Frogs*, trans. David Barrett [Harmondsworth, Middlesex: Penguin Books, 1964], p. 196). In the original Greek, the line numbers for Aristophanes' antibook references in *The Frogs* are 943 and 1409. In *Early Greece*, Murray points out that "by the late sixth century an institution like ostracism in Athens . . . presupposes large numbers of citizens able to write at least the name of a political opponent" (p. 95). And later: "By the fifth century it is clear that the average male Athenian citizen could read and write" (p. 96).

5. Havelock, *Preface to Plato*, p. 40. Murray, *Early Greece*, disagrees. If by the fifth century most male Athenians could read and write, "it is therefore wrong to speak of craft or restricted literacy in the seventh and sixth centuries" (p. 96). Still, when Murray goes on to admit that "literacy is itself a vague term" and that at a "higher level [of literacy] Greece in many respects long remained an oral culture" (p. 96), he does not seem to be differing much from Havelock.

6. Edith Hamilton and Huntington Cairns, eds., *The Collected Dialogues of Plato* (New York: Pantheon Books, 1963), p. 476. The translation of the *Phaedrus* is by R. Hackforth. Further reference to the *Phaedrus*, and later to the *Seventh Letter*, translated by L. A. Post, will be given by page numbers from *The Collected Dialogues of Plato*, accompanying the citations.

7. Walter Hamilton, ed., *Plato: Phaedrus and Letters VII and VIII* (Harmondsworth, Middlesex: Penguin Books, 1973), p. 11.

8. Iris Murdoch, *The Fire and the Sun: Why Plato Banished the Artists* (Oxford: Oxford University Press, 1977), p. 23. Some of Plato's contemporaries share these views about writing. Oenopides, the mathematician, rebuked a young man who had a great many books, saying "not in a bookshelf but in the heart." Antisthenes, the philosopher, consoled a friend who had lost his notes by arguing that knowledge should be in the soul, not on paper (see Rosalind Thomas, *Oral Tradition and Written Record in Classical Athens* [Cambridge: Cambridge University Press, 1989], p. 33). Charles L. Griswold, Jr., in *Self-knowledge in Plato's "Phaedrus"* (New Haven: Yale University Press, 1986), sees Phaedrus himself as a victim of the druglike properties of writing: "At the start of the dialogue we find that Phaedrus is intent on memorizing, in the solitary splendor of the countryside and without critical reflection or effort to question the author or himself, the text with which he has fallen in love" (p. 213).

9. Ong, *Orality and Literacy*, p. 81.

10. Murdoch, *The Fire and the Sun*, p. 81.

11. See Jacques Derrida, *Of Grammatology*, trans. Gayatri Chakravorty Spivak (Baltimore: Johns Hopkins University Press, 1976), pp. 7 and 14, and, more generally, 165–268. For Derrida's fantastically rich and detailed reading of the *Phaedrus*, see "Plato's Pharmacy," in *Dissemination*, trans. Barbara Johnson (Chicago: University of Chicago Press, 1981), pp. 61–155. Stanley Fish takes a Derridean approach to the *Phaedrus* in *Self-consuming Artifacts: The Experience of Seventeenth-Century Literature* (Berkeley and Los Angeles: University of California Press, 1972), pp. 5–21.

12. Derrida sees such activity in psychoanalytic terms—as transgressive, a form of not only parricide but masturbation (all that "twisting" and "pulling" to no productive end). In *Of Grammatology*, writing and masturbation are "supplementary." They are simultaneously destructive of presence (the supplemental is not the thing itself, just as the written and the masturbatory fantasy are "proxies"), yet they originate out of a desire to attain presence, a desire born out of a sense of the inadequacy of nature or "the real"—as in speech's inadequacy (to truth), in the case of writing; or the unavailability of the desired person or beloved, in the case of masturbation. Writing, like mas-

turbation, is thus associated with a "traditional culpability" (p. 150) and inevitably calls forth "the threat of castration" (p. 151). Both inspire feelings of frustration and disillusion as well as Oedipal anxieties: "The presence that is thus delivered to us [in either writing or masturbation] is a chimera. . . . The sign, the image, the representation, which come to supplant the absent presence are the illusions that sidetrack us. To culpability, to the anguish of death and castration, is added or rather is assimilated the experience of frustration" (p. 154).

Derrida's recourse, here, to psychoanalytic—specifically Freudian—terms is carefully qualified. Psychoanalytic and deconstructive readings differ from, as well as resemble, each other. "In spite of certain appearances," Derrida writes, "the locating of the word *supplement* is here not at all psychoanalytical if by that we understand an interpretation that takes us outside of the writing towards a psychobiological signified" (p. 159). For Derrida, of course, there is no getting outside the writing: *il n'y a pas de hors-texte*—there *is* no "real mother" to get back to. This is in part why he finds "the reading of the literary 'symptom' [as in orthodox psychoanalytic interpretation] most banal, most academic, most naive" (p. 159).

13. Murdoch, *The Fire and the Sun*, p. 31.

14. Havelock, *Preface to Plato*, p. 5.

15. Ibid., p. 31.

16. The description comes from the 103-line "Preface" to the *Theogony*, which dates from "a period not later than the end of the seventh century" (ibid., p. 61). The quotation itself, from line 66, is from Havelock's translation in ibid., p. 62. Havelock's view of oral cultures and the oral state of mind is seconded in important respects by a famous article, also first published in 1963, coauthored by Jack Goody and Ian Watt. The article, "The Consequences of Literacy," is reprinted in *Literacy in Traditional Societies*, ed. Jack Goody (Cambridge: Cambridge University Press, 1968), pp. 22–68. It argues not only for writing's role in the development of logic and rational thought, but in the growth of individualism and democracy. Havelock and Goody have been criticized by Murray in *Early Greece* for exaggerating the independent power of writing as a force for change: "Literacy works to strengthen tendencies already present in a society, rather than altering it fundamentally" (p. 98). Thomas, in *Oral Tradition and Written Record in Classical Athens*, criticizes Goody, Watt, and Havelock in particular, for implying "a strict division between 'oral' and 'literate' characteristics and 'oral' and 'literate' societies" (p. 3). She also cites the work of Ruth Finnegan—especially *Oral Poetry: Its Nature, Significance and Social Content* (Cambridge: Cambridge University Press, 1977)—as challenging the sharpness of the distinction between "oral" and "literate" societies, as well as what Thomas characterizes as the "technological determinism" (p. 24) implied by Goody and Watt. I find Thomas's criticisms unfair. Neither Goody and Watt nor Havelock are as naïvely unqualified or extreme in their assertions as she implies, even in their early work.

17. Ong, *Orality and Literacy*, p. 40.

18. Havelock, *Preface to Plato*, p. 303. For an interesting account of Plato's

decision to write and to write in the dialogue form, see Griswold, *Self-knowledge in Plato's "Phaedrus,"* pp. 219–29. Griswold points to numerous features of the dialogue form which allow Plato to overcome Socrates' strictures against writing. Among these features are its "unsystematic and noncatechistic character; Platonic anonymity and irony; the presence of several layers of meaning contained within one another, the more difficult lying underneath the simpler; the interplay between drama and argument and so between showing and saying; the mimetic and mirroring nature of the dialogues; and the absence of a dialogue between mature philosophers" (p. 220). Stanley Fish takes a similar stance in *Self-consuming Artifacts,* arguing that the *Phaedrus* escapes Socrates' "condemnation . . . of anything written or formally delivered" because it "does not exhibit the characteristics of a written artifact" (pp. 9 and 14). To Ronna Burger, in *Plato's Phaedrus: A Defense of the Philosophic Art of Writing* (Tuscaloosa: University of Alabama Press, 1980), the dialogue form resolves a crucial problem for Plato. In spoken discourse, "the self-moving motion of soul is always an obstacle to reaching . . . perfect fixity and stability." In writing, "the perfect fixity of the written word seems to exclude the possibility of living thought." The Platonic dialogue represents "the ideal meeting point . . . the convergence of the two paths of *erōs* and death, of living speech and writing" (pp. 107–8).

For a shrewd summary of these and other readings of the *Phaedrus,* see G.R.F. Ferrari, *Listening to the Cicadas: A Study of Plato's Phaedrus* (Cambridge: Cambridge University Press, 1987), especially pp. 204–22. Ferrari sees the dialogue as examining "the gulf between the pursuit of wisdom and the pursuit of the effects of wisdom" (p. 217).

19. Ong, *Orality and Literacy,* p. 72.

20. Ibid., p. 24.

21. Havelock, *The Literary Renaissance in Greece,* p. 11.

22. Quoted in Christopher Lehmann-Haupt, "Struggling to Crack Writer's Block," *New York Times,* 3 November 1983. For a more detailed account of the impact of the new technology on writing, see Michael Heim, *Electric Language: A Philosophical Study of Word Processing* (New Haven: Yale University Press, 1988), and Edward Mendelson's skeptical review-article, "The Corrupt Computer," in *New Republic* 198, no. 8 (February 1988):36–39.

23. Ong, *Orality and Literacy,* p. 131.

24. Ibid., p. 132.

25. Ibid., p. 133.

9. Blockage and Externality: The Woman as Writer

1. Anne Finch, Countess of Winchilsea, "Ardelia's Answer to Ephelia" (1713), line 209, quoted in Cora Kaplan, *Sea Changes: Essays on Culture and Feminism* (London: Verso, 1986), p. 82. I have retained Kaplan's modernized spelling in the quotation. The couplet from which the quotation comes reads: "Why should we from that pleasing art [poetry] be ty'd, / Or like State Pris-'ners, Pen and Ink deny'd" (208–9). See Myra Reynolds, ed., *The Poems of*

Anne Countess of Winchilsea (Chicago: University of Chicago Press, 1903), p. 45.

2. Virginia Woolf, *A Room of One's Own* (London: Collins, 1977), p. 46. Simone de Beauvoir imagines a comparably melancholy fate for a female Van Gogh: "How could Van Gogh have been born a woman? A woman would not have been sent on a mission to the Belgian coal mines in Borinage, she would not have felt the misery of the miners as her own crime, she would not have sought a redemption; she would therefore have never painted Van Gogh's sunflowers. Not to mention that the mode of life of the painter—his solitude at Arles, his frequentation of cafés and brothels, all that nourished Van Gogh's art . . . would have been forbidden her" (*The Second Sex*, trans. H. M. Parshley [1949; Harmondsworth, Middlesex: Penguin Books, 1972], p. 722).

3. Woolf, *A Room of One's Own*, p. 47.

4. Ibid., p. 48.

5. Ibid., pp. 48 and 49.

6. Ibid., p. 108. For a different reading of the opening pages of *A Room of One's Own*, see Mary Jacobus, *Reading Woman: Essays on Feminist Criticism* (London: Methuen, 1986), pp. 37–40.

7. Mary Ellmann, *Thinking about Women* (London: Macmillan, 1968), p. 81.

8. Ann Bradstreet, "The Prologue" (lines 25–26), in *The Tenth Muse* (1650); reprinted in *The Norton Anthology of Literature by Women*, ed. Sandra M. Gilbert and Susan Gubar (New York: W. W. Norton, 1985), p. 62.

9. Margaret Cavendish, Duchess of Newcastle, *A True Relation of My Birth, Breeding, and Life* (1656), quoted in Sandra M. Gilbert and Susan Gubar, *The Madwoman in the Attic: The Woman Writer and the Nineteenth-Century Literary Imagination* (New Haven: Yale University Press, 1979), p. 63. For the complete *True Relation*, see *The Life of William Cavendish, Duke of Newcastle to which is added The True Relation of My Birth, Breeding, and Life by Margaret, Duchess of Newcastle*, ed. C. H. Firth (London: John C. Nimmo, 1886). Selections from the *True Relation* are found, usefully contextualized, in *Her Own Life: Autobiographical Writings by Seventeenth-Century Englishwomen*, ed. Elspeth Graham, Hilary Hinds, Elaine Hobby, and Helen Wilcox (London: Routledge and Kegan Paul, 1989).

10. Kaplan, *Sea Changes*, p. 82. The name of Kaplan's anthology is *Salt and Bitter and Good: Three Centuries of English and American Women Poets* (New York: Paddington Press, 1975).

11. Both *On the Generation of Animals* and the *Politics* are found in *The Basic Works of Aristotle*, ed. Richard McKeon (New York: Random House, 1966), pp. 676 and 1144–45.

12. For Aristotle, Galen, and the legacy of their ideas about creativity and the female body, see Christine Battersby, *Gender and Genius: Towards a Female Aesthetic* (London: Women's Press, 1989), pp. 28–34. Battersby is also good on the obstructing powers of nonmedical "science," as in "the naïvety of the statistical methods" used in much social-scientific and psychological research on creativity and women (see pp. 124–33). For more general studies of the role of science in the construction of sex roles and gender differences, see

Ludmilla Jordanova, *Sexual Visions: Images of Gender in Science and Medicine between the Eighteenth and Twentieth Centuries* (New York and London: Harvester Wheatsheaf, 1989), and Cynthia Eagle Russett, *Sexual Science: The Victorian Construction of Womanhood* (Cambridge, Mass.: Harvard University Press, 1989).

13. John Winthrop, *The History of New England from 1630 to 1649*, ed. James Savage (Boston, 1826), quoted in Wendy Martin, "Ann Bradstreet's Poetry: A Study of Subversive Piety," in *Shakespeare's Sisters: Feminist Essays on Women Poets*, ed. Sandra M. Gilbert and Susan Gubar (Bloomington: Indiana University Press, 1979), p. 26.

14. Elaine Showalter, *A Literature of Their Own: British Women Novelists from Brontë to Lessing* (London: Virago Press, 1978), p. 77. Showalter also quotes Geraldine Jewsbury's view that the female body is "liable to collapses, eclipses, failures of power . . . unfitting [the woman writer] from the steady stresses of ever-recurring work" (p. 77). That this was true in Jewsbury's own case is a sign of the power of internalization. After the completion of each of her novels, Jewsbury fell ill with a variety of stress-related symptoms. She finally gave up writing fiction entirely, on her doctor's orders (see ibid., pp. 81–82).

15. Elizabeth Barrett to Robert Browning, 11 August 1845, in *The Letters of Robert Browning and Elizabeth Barrett Browning, 1845–46*, ed. Elvan Kintner, 2 vols. (Cambridge: Harvard University Press, 1969), 1:151.

16. Anne Finch, Countess of Winchilsea, "The Spleen," quoted in *Norton Anthology of Literature by Women*, ed. Gilbert and Gubar, p. 108.

17. Quoted in Gilbert and Gubar, *Madwoman in the Attic*, p. 8.

18. "Preface" to *The Lucky Chance* (1687), in *The Collected Works of Aphra Behn*, ed. Montague Summers, 6 vols. (London: Heinemann, 1915), 3:187.

19. Quoted in Gilbert and Gubar, *Madwoman in the Attic*, pp. 3 and 9, and Battersby, *Gender and Genius*, pp. 69 and 41. The lines quoted are from *The Romance of the Rose*, trans. Harry W. Robbins (New York: Dutton, 1962), p. 414. For a more considered, if only marginally less inflaming, account from Anthony Burgess of the role of gender in creativity, see "Grunts from a Sexist Pig," in *Homage to Qwert Yuiop: Selected Journalism, 1978–85* (London: Abacus, 1987), pp. 1–4.

20. Roland Barthes, *Sade/Fourier/Loyola*, trans. Richard Miller (New York: Hill and Wang, 1976), p. 182, quoted in Gilbert and Gubar, *Madwoman in the Attic*, p. 10.

21. Gilbert and Gubar, *Madwoman in the Attic*, p. 7.

22. Nina Auerbach, in an untitled review of Gubar and Gilbert, *Madwoman in the Attic*, in *Victorian Studies* 23, no. 4 (Summer 1980):506. For the metaphor of literary maternity, see also Ellmann, *Thinking about Women*, p. 63; Nina Auerbach, "Artists and Mothers: A False Alliance," *Women and Literature* 9 (Spring 1978):3–5; and Terry Castle, "Lab'ring Bards: Birth *Topoi* and English Poetics 1660–1820," *Journal of English and German Philology* 78, no. 2 (April 1979):193–208. Other criticisms of Gilbert and Gubar for their stress on inhibiting patriarchal metaphors of authorship include Mary Jacobus, "Review of *The Madwoman in the Attic: The Woman Writer and the Nineteenth-Century Imag-*

ination," in *Signs: Journal of Women in Culture and Society* 6, no. 3 (Spring 1981):517–23; and Toril Moi, *Sexual/Textual Politics: Feminist Literary Theory* (London: Methuen, 1985), p. 64.

23. Elaine Showalter, "Feminist Criticism in the Wilderness," in *The New Feminist Criticism: Essays on Women, Literature and Theory,* ed. Elaine Showalter (London: Virago Press, 1986), p. 251.

24. Terry Lovell, "Writing Like a Woman: A Question of Politics," in *Feminist Literary Theory: A Reader,* ed. Mary Eagleton (Oxford: Basil Blackwell, 1986), p. 84. Battersby, in *Gender and Genius,* cites Jackson Pollock and Henry Miller as artists who "stressed their maleness precisely in order to compensate for the essentially passive and intuitive nature of their own working methods" (p. 40). For a witty account of comparable anxieties among male literary theorists, see Elaine Showalter, "Critical Cross-Dressing," in *Raritan* 3, no. 2 (Fall 1983):130–49.

25. Gilbert and Gubar, *Madwoman in the Attic,* p. 12.

26. Susan Gubar, "'The Blank Page' and the Issues of Female Creativity," *Critical Inquiry* 8, no. 2 (Winter 1981):256; the examples are also from Gubar (245–46). Many more such examples can be found in vol. 1 of the projected 3-vol. successor to Gilbert and Gubar's *Madwoman in the Attic,* entitled *No Man's Land: The Place of the Woman Writer in the Twentieth Century* (New Haven: Yale University Press, 1988), 1:3–62. The volume is subtitled *The War of the Words.*

27. Reprinted in Virginia Woolf, *Women and Writing,* ed. and intro. Michèle Barrett (London: Women's Press, 1979), p. 58.

28. Quoted in Ellen Moers, *Literary Women* (London: Women's Press, 1978), p. 17.

29. Quoted in Gilbert and Gubar, *Madwoman in the Attic,* p. 24.

30. Woolf, *Women and Writing,* ed. and intro. Barrett, p. 59.

31. Ibid., p. 62.

32. Gilbert and Gubar, *Madwoman in the Attic,* pp. 29–30.

33. Hélène Cixous, "The Laugh of the Medusa," trans. Keith Cohen and Paula Cohen, *Signs* 1 (Summer 1976):875–93; excerpted in *Feminist Literary Theory,* ed. Eagleton, pp. 226–27.

34. Catherine Gallagher, "George Eliot and *Daniel Deronda:* The Prostitute and the Jewish Question," in *Sex, Politics, and Science in the Nineteenth-Century Novel,* ed. Ruth Bernard Yeazell, Selected Papers from the English Institute, 1983–84, n.s., no. 10 (Baltimore: Johns Hopkins University Press, 1986), p. 40. Subsequent references are cited by page number in the text.

35. Kaplan, *Sea Changes,* p. 220.

36. Ibid., p. 221.

37. Ibid.

38. Ibid.

39. For Lacan's account of language, acculturation, and the figure of the father in the family, see, especially, "The Function of Speech and Language in Psychoanalysis," in *Écrits: A Selection,* trans. Alan Sheridan (New York: W. W. Norton, 1977), pp. 30–113; and Anika Lemaire, *Jacques Lacan,* trans. David Macey (London: Routledge and Kegan Paul, 1977), pp. 66–92.

40. "It is one and the same system: the erection of paternal logos . . . and of the phallus as 'privileged signifier' (Lacan)," quoted and translated by Jonathan Culler in *On Deconstruction: Theory and Criticism* (Ithaca: Cornell University Press, 1982), p. 172.

41. For Freud's view of female development, see Sarah Kofman, *The Enigma of Woman: Woman in Freud's Writings*, trans. Catherine Porter (1980; Ithaca: Cornell University Press, 1985). For an account of the differences between Freud's view of female development and those of Lacan and Klein, see the essays in pt. 3 of Juliet Mitchell, *Women: The Longest Revolution. Essays in Feminism, Literature and Psychoanalysis* (London: Virago Press, 1984), pp. 221–313. For other psychological and psychoanalytic accounts of female development, see Carol Gilligan, *In a Different Voice: Psychological Theory and Women's Development* (Cambridge, Mass.: Harvard University Press, 1982); and Jean Strouse, ed., *Women and Analysis: Dialogues on Psychoanalytic Views of Femininity* (New York: Grossman, 1974).

42. Juliet Mitchell, *Psychoanalysis and Feminism* (New York: Vintage, 1975), p. 405.

43. From canto 29 of *The Cantos of Ezra Pound* (London: Faber and Faber, 1968), p. 149.

44. Kaplan, *Sea Changes*, pp. 77–78.

45. Ibid., p. 83. See also Jan Montefiore, *Feminism and Poetry: Language, Experience, Identity in Women's Writing* (London and New York: Pandora Press, 1987); and Irene Taylor and Gina Luria, "Gender and Genre: Women in British Romantic Poetry," in *What Manner of Woman: Essays in English and American Life and Literature*, ed. Marlene Springer (New York: New York University Press, 1977), pp. 98–123.

46. Robert Halsband, "Women and Literature in Eighteenth-Century England," in *Women in the Eighteenth Century and Other Essays*, ed. Paul Fritz and Richard Morton (Toronto: Hakkert, 1976), p. 55. See also Ian Watt, *The Rise of the Novel: Studies in Defoe, Richardson and Fielding* (1957; reprint, Berkeley and Los Angeles: University of California Press, 1965): "The majority of eighteenth-century novels were actually written by women, but this had long remained a purely quantitative assertion of dominance" (p. 298).

47. Kaplan, *Sea Changes*, p. 83. For an account of the identification of novels and novel-writing with women, and of the novel's gradual growth in esteem (from "commodity" to "literature"), see Terry Lovell, *Consuming Fictions* (London: Verso, 1987), pp. 47–94.

48. Samuel Taylor Coleridge, *Biographia Literaria*, ed. James Engell and W. Jackson Bate, in vol. 2 of no. 7 of *The Collected Works of Samuel Taylor Coleridge*, ed. Kathleen Coburn (London: Routledge and Kegan Paul, 1983), 2:304. For the complicated and intriguing relationship of Romantic theories of creativity and the woman writer, see Battersby, *Gender and Genius*, pp. 3–8, 35–47, 89–92, 98–103, 111–19, and 159–60. Also worth noting in this regard are Alan Richardson, "Romanticism and the Colonization of the Feminine," and Marlon B. Ross, "Romantic Quest and Conquest: Troping Masculine Power and the Crisis of Poetic Identity," both in *Romanticism and Feminism*, ed. Anne K. Mellor (Bloomington: Indiana University Press, 1988), pp. 13–25 and 26–51.

For more general studies of Romanticism from a feminist perspective, see Margaret Homans, *Women Writers and Poetic Identity: Dorothy Wordsworth, Emily Brontë, and Emily Dickinson* (Princeton: Princeton University Press, 1980), and *Bearing the Word: Language and Female Experience in Nineteenth-Century Women's Writing* (Chicago: University of Chicago Press, 1986); see also Mary Jacobus, *Reading Woman,* and Mary Poovey, *The Proper Lady and the Woman Writer: Ideology as Style in the Works of Mary Wollstonecraft, Mary Shelley, and Jane Austen* (Chicago: University of Chicago Press, 1984).

49. Kaplan, *Sea Changes,* p. 83. Anaïs Nin turned to the diary form in part out of a sense that it would allow her to write in the first-person singular and still be female. Writing a diary is "a feminine activity, it is a personal and personified creation, the opposite of the masculine alchemy" (quoted in Battersby, *Gender and Genius,* p. 45).

50. N. Flowers, ed., *The Journals of Arnold Bennett,* 2 vols. (London: Cassell, 1932), 1:6, as quoted by Stephen Heath in *Feminist Literary Theory,* ed. Eagleton, p. 221.

51. From Heath's translation of a passage from "Le Sexe ou la Tête" (1976), in *Feminist Literary Theory,* ed. Eagleton, p. 221.

52. Gillian Beer, "Beyond Determinism: George Eliot and Virginia Woolf," in *Women and Writing about Women* (London: Croom Helm, 1979), p. 95, as quoted in *Feminist Literary Theory,* ed. Eagleton, p. 221.

53. Ann Rosalind Jones, "Writing the Body: Toward an Understanding of l'Écriture féminine," in *New Feminist Criticism,* ed. Showalter, p. 363. For more detailed accounts of *l'écriture féminine,* see Elissa D. Gelfand and Virginia T. Hules, eds., *French Feminist Criticism: Women, Language and Literature, an Annotated Bibliography* (London and New York: Garland, 1985). Also noteworthy is the overview provided by Gilbert and Gubar in *No Man's Land,* 1:227–71.

54. For "jouissance," see Stephen Heath's "Translator's Note" in Roland Barthes, *Image-Music-Text* (New York: Hill and Wang, 1978), p. 9.

55. Ellmann, *Thinking about Women,* p. 166.

56. Kaplan, *Sea Changes,* pp. 226, 227, and 228.

57. Margaret Cavendish, Duchess of Newcastle, *A True Relation of My Birth, Breeding, and Life* (1656), as quoted in Patricia M. Spacks, *The Female Imagination* (New York: Alfred A. Knopf, 1975), p. 193.

58. Ibid. Valerie Sanders, *The Private Lives of Victorian Women: Autobiography in Nineteenth-Century England* (Brighton: Harvester, 1989), pp. 32–33, reads this passage differently: "There is no false humility in the Duchess's writing. She says frankly that she delights in her singularity, is ambitious, and has written her *True Relation* for her own sake and not that of her readers."

59. The Countess of Winchilsea, that is, wrote, "still with contracted wing" (line 61), "The Introduction" (1689?); reprinted in *Norton Anthology of Literature by Women,* ed. Gilbert and Gubar, p. 101.

60. Showalter, *A Literature of Their Own,* p. 17.

61. "Memoirs of the Life of Mrs. Mary Brunton by Her Husband," which forms the "Preface" of *Emmeline* (Edinburgh, 1819), p. xxxvi, as quoted in ibid., pp. 17–18.

62. Showalter, *A Literature of Their Own*, p. 13.
63. Woolf, *A Room of One's Own*, p. 70.
64. Showalter, *A Literature of Their Own*, pp. 154 and 180.
65. Woolf, *A Room of One's Own*, p. 71.
66. Showalter, *A Literature of Their Own*, p. 21.
67. Ibid., pp. 30 and 194.
68. Ibid., p. 197.
69. Ibid. Kathleen Blake, in *Love and the Woman Question in Victorian Literature* (Brighton: Harvester, 1983), gives qualified approval to Showalter's remarks about obesity, though "at times" Shreiner can see a large woman "in positive terms. . . . Still, in her own style Shreiner characteristically 'belittles' women as a way of making them attractive" (p. 218).
70. Virginia Woolf, "Romance and the Heart" (1923), in *Contemporary Writers* (London: Hogarth, 1965), pp. 124–25. The essay and an earlier review are reprinted in Virginia Woolf, *Women and Writing*, ed. and intro. Barrett, pp. 188–92.
71. Showalter, *A Literature of Their Own*, p. 261.
72. Ibid.
73. Ibid. Dorothy Richardson defends her experimental techniques in the "Foreword" to the collected edition of *Pilgrimage*, 4 vols. (London: Dent, 1938), 1:9 and 12. For a more sympathetic account of those techniques than Showalter offers, see Gillian E. Hanscombe, *The Art of Life: Dorothy Richardson and the Development of Feminist Consciousness* (London: Peter Owen, 1982), esp. 39–62, on "a woman's sentence."

Index

Abrams, M. H., 128, 129, 288n.62
Addison, Joseph, 134
Adler, Alfred, 56, 76
Adventures of Huckleberry Finn, The (Twain), 12–15
Aesthetics, psychoanalytic. *See* Psychoanalytic aesthetics
African-Americans, blockage of, 234
Aids to Reflection (Coleridge), 187
Akenside, Mark, 119
Alison, Archibald, 134
Allendy, René, 64
Amis, Kingsley, 125
Anaxagoras, 68
"Ancient Mariner, The" (Coleridge), 192, 193, 194, 197
  glosses to, 197, 202, 213
  as unsatisfactorily completed, 186
"Andrea del Sarto" (Browning), 18, 22
Andreas-Salomé, Lou, 107
Anxiety of Influence, The (Bloom), 137–41.
  See also Influence anxiety
"Apologia pro Vita sua" (Coleridge), 195
Arbuthnot, John, 236
"Arctic Summer" (Forster), 11, 27–28
Aristophanes, 219, 304n.4
Aristotle, 235, 240
Arnheim, Rudolf, 22
Arnold, Matthew, 117, 146
Art and artists
  carving and modeling traditions in (Stokes), 108–11, 284n.97
  Coleridge on, 98
  ego psychologists' view of, 78
  Ehrenzweig on, 104–6
  Freudian view of, 34–37, 39–48, 223, 262n.13
  Jung on, 56–57, 57–58, 59, 268n.5
  Doris Lessing on, 40–41
  Milner on, 93–94, 95
  modern (Ehrenzweig), 282–83n.80
  painter or visual artist vs. writer, 22–23

as play, 47–48, 264–65n.36
  Segal on, 90
  subject-object struggle of, 23
Artistic creation. *See* Creation and creativity
Auden, W. H., 19
Auerbach, Nina, 237

Babbitt, Irving, 143
Bahr, Hermann, 19–20
Bailey, Benjamin, 124
Baillie, John, 134
Balint, Michael, 82, 273–74n.77
Barrett, Elizabeth (later Elizabeth Barrett Browning), 235, 246, 248
Barthes, Roland, 16, 237, 245
Bate, W. J., 115, 116, 122, 125–26, 252
  and Bloom, 138
  on Coleridge, 186, 206, 210, 214
  and decline of poetry, 140–41, 143
  on Johnson, 15–16
  Keats and decline, 123, 124
  on neoclassicism 127, 131
  on self-consciousness, 120
Bateson, F. W., 179
Battersby, Christine, 235, 236
Beaumont, Sir George, 175, 182
Beauty. *See also* Art and artists
  Freud on, 45–47
  Sachs on, 264n.30
  Segal on, 90–91
Beauvoir, Simone de, 245, 308n.2
Becker, Ernest, 69–70
Beer, Gillian, 244
Benn, Aphra, 236
Bennett, Arnold, 244
Beres, David, 208
Bergler, Edmund, 1, 2–4, 6, 7, 19, 46, 55
Beyond the Pleasure Principle (Freud), 37, 38, 66
Biographia Literaria (Coleridge), 24, 186–87, 209–12

Biographia Literaria (continued)
  poet-God comparison in, 243
  Wordsworth stanza criticized in, 168
Birth trauma, Rank and Freud on, 64–66
Blair, Robert, 120
Blake, William, ix, 132, 137, 269n.5
Blockage. *See* Writer's block
Blocking agents
  for Bloom, 138, 291–92n.123
  for Coleridge, 211
  for Freud, 37
  in *A Room of One's Own*, 234
Bloom, Harold
  and anxiety of influence, 137–42
  and McFarland, 143, 144
  predecessors of, 291–92n.123
  on Romanticism, 290–91n.115
  and Weiskel on sublime, 136
  and Wordsworth, 137, 173, 175
"Blossoming of the Solitary Date Tree,
  The" (Coleridge), 186, 192
Bodkin, Maud, 208
Bonaparte, Marie, 20, 44
Bouhours, Dominique, 127
Boileau, Nicolas, 127, 134
Braddon, Mary, 247
Brandes, George, 42
Bridges, Robert, Hopkins letter to, 102
Brill, A. A., 4
British object-relations theory. *See* Object-
  relations theory
Brontë, Charlotte, 236, 239, 246, 247, 248
Brontë, Emily, 246, 248
Brown, Norman O., 69–70
Browning, Elizabeth Barrett, 235, 246, 248
Browning, Robert, 18, 22
  and open-endedness, 231
  as "strong poet," 137
Brunton, Mary, 246
Bruss, Elizabeth, 137, 139, 141
Bürger, Gottfried, 139
Burgess, Anthony, 15, 236
Burke, Edmund, 134
Butler, Marilyn, 24
Byron, Lord George Gordon
  Don Juan, incompletion of, 132
  and "Kubla Khan," 205
  and writer's isolation, 129

"Cain" (Coleridge), 194
Campbell, James Dykes, 191
Camus, Albert, 25–26
Cavendish, Margaret (Duchess of New-
  castle), 234, 235, 245–46, 250
Cézanne, Paul, 110
Chambers, E. K., 186
Child analysis, 83–88

"Christabel" (Coleridge), 132, 186, 189,
  192, 194, 196–97, 213
Civilization and Its Discontents (Freud), 39,
  45
Cixous, Hélène, 239, 244
"Coeli Enarrant" (Coleridge), 186
Cognition, 16
Cognitive science, 16–18
Coleridge, Derwent (son), 191
Coleridge, George (brother), 198, 213
Coleridge, Mary, 248
Coleridge, Samuel Taylor, 24–25, 145,
  186–89, 215
  and blockage in *Biographia Literaria*,
    209–12
  blockage poetry of ("Dejection: An
    Ode"), 199–203
  conversational fluency of, 190, 229
  incomplete works of, 24, 132, 186–87,
    230
  and incompletion, 231
  influence of, 130
  Keats on, 106–7
  and "Kubla Khan," 205–9
  and language, 212–15, 219, 222, 225
  and McFarland, 142
  and object relations, 193–97
  and originality, 99–100, 121
  and philosophy, 24–25, 183, 187, 200–
    201, 202–3, 205, 209–11, 212
  plagiarisms by, 99–100, 197–98, 205,
    210, 215, 229
  poet-God comparison by, 243–44
  psychology of, 189–93
  and "willing suspension of disbelief,"
    98
  and Wordsworth, 155, 167, 168, 173,
    180–81, 182, 193, 197, 198, 202, 203–5
  and writer's isolation, 129
  and written word, 251
Coleridge, Sara (wife), 190
Collins, William, 117, 118–19, 120, 121,
  129, 130
Communication. *See* Language
Conrad, Joseph, 15, 16
Contingency management, 266n.1
Countess of Winchilsea (Anne Finch), 236,
  246, 250
Creation and creativity. *See also* Art
  Bate on, 126
  Bloom's theory of, 137–42
  cognitive scientists' interest in, 16
  ego psychology on, 74, 77, 78–79, 274–
    75n.85
  Ehrenzweig on, 106, 107
  and Freud, 33, 34, 140, 264n.30
  Jung on, 60–62

Klein on, 88
Milner on, 92, 94
and Rank, 55, 63, 65, 68–69, 70, 71
and Rank on Freud, 68
and Philip Roth character, 5
Segal on, 88–89, 90
Winnicott on, 98
and Wordsworth in *Prelude*, 154, 157, 159
Creative exhaustion, 27–29
"Creative Writers and Day-Dreaming" (Freud), 34, 35, 36, 39, 42, 43, 45, 46
Crews, Frederick, 36, 55, 78
Currie, Robert, 131

Darwin, Charles, 22
Davenant, William, 127
Death
Menaker on fear of, 72
Rank on fear of, 69–70, 73
Death instinct
and Freud, 37–38, 53–54, 83, 84, 261n.12, 288n.65
and Klein, 83, 84, 85
Segal on, 91
"Dejection: An Ode" (Coleridge), 24, 99, 167, 186, 199–203, 301n.66
Delusions and Dreams in Jensen's "Gradiva" (Freud), 39, 42, 48
Dennis, John, 134
De Quincey, Thomas, 132, 183, 189, 198
Derrida, Jacques, 223, 224, 225, 237–38, 242, 305–6n.12
Dickinson, Emily, 243, 244
Dionysius the Younger (tyrant of Syracuse), 224
Doolittle, Hilda, 33, 237
Dostoevsky, Fyodor, Freud on, 51
Dryden, John, 116, 117–18, 127
Duchess of Newcastle (Margaret Cavendish), 234, 235, 245–46, 250
Duff, William, 121
Dugas, Kristine, 188

Ecclesiastical Sonnets (Wordsworth), 179
Egerton, George, 248
Ego
Freud on, 34, 50–51, 75
for Rank vs. Freud, 68
Ego psychology, 55, 74–81, 271–72n.61
"Americanism" of, 69
and Lesser, 274–75n.85
and neoclassicism, 128, 144
and Rank, 69
second generation of American, 56
and writer as autonomous, 242
Ehrenzweig, Anton, 103–7, 112

and Jung, 61
and Rose, 80
and Wordsworth in *Prelude*, 155
"Ejaculation" (Wordsworth), 179
"Elegiac Stanzas" (Wordsworth), 174–80
Eliot, George
on "chilling ideal," 26, 95
"feminine" style of, 244
and women writers, 240–41, 242, 247
Eliot, T. S., 111, 116, 143
Ellman, Mary, 234, 245
Emerson, Ralph Waldo, as "strong poet," 137
Empedocles, 68
Empson, William, 20
English School of Psychoanalysis, 82. *See also* Object-relations theory
"Eolian Harp, The" (Coleridge), 193
Erikson, Erik, 79
Evening Voluntaries (Wordsworth), 179
Excursion, The (Wordsworth), 178–79, 183, 184
"Preface" to, 183, 212
"Exile, An" (Coleridge), 192

Fairbairn, W. R. D., 56, 82, 85–86
"Fears in Solitude" (Coleridge), 192
Fechner, G. T., 45
Federn, Paul, 21
Feelings and reason. *See* Reason-feelings relation
Fenichel, Otto, 2, 79, 208
Fenwick notes of Wordsworth, 170, 294n.20
Ferenczi, Sandor, 83
Finch, Anne (Countess of Winchilsea), 236, 246, 250
Fischer, Kuno, 47
Fliess, Wilhelm, 34, 41
"Force of Destiny, The" (Coleridge), 189
Forster, E. M., 11, 27–28, 58
Fragment
"Kubla Khan" as, 205
as literary type, 132
French Revolution, and Wordsworth, 163–65
Freud, Anna, 75, 83, 271–72n.61
Freud, Sigmund
and artists as patients, 33
on limits of psychoanalytic aesthetics, 19
on Rank's style, 73
on those "wrecked by success," 27
as writer, 33
Freudian theory, 33, 54
and aesthetic bonus, 44–47, 264n.30
aesthetics secondary in, 54, 88

Freudian theory *(continued)*
  and artist's disguise, 43–44
  and art-neurosis relation, 39–41, 42–43
  on art and reality, 223
  and art as wish fulfillment, 34–37, 41
  and Bergler, 2, 3, 4
  and birth trauma, 64–65
  and Bloom, 139–40
  and child analysis, 83, 84
  and death instinct, 37–38, 53–54, 83, 84,
    261n.12, 288n.65
  and ego psychology, 75, 76, 271–72n.61
  and flexibility of repression, 48, 53
  and German idealist philosophy, 130
  on *Hamlet*, 41–42, 44
  Hoffman's influence on, 130, 131
  and illusion, 101
  on immortality, desire for, 70
  and "Kubla Khan," 208
  on Leonardo, 43, 48, 51–53, 71
  and meaning vs. formal or technical
    qualities, 19–20
  on Michelangelo's Moses, 261–62n.12
  and Milner, 92
  and play, 47–48, 264–65n.36
  and pleasure from psychic activity, 78–
    79
  and Rank, 63, 64
  and Twain, 14
  and will, 68
  and women, 49, 54, 243, 311n.41
  and writer's block, 48–54, 80
Fricker family, 198
Friend, The (Coleridge), 187, 212
"Frost at Midnight" (Coleridge), 194
Fruman, Norman, 186, 205
Fry, Roger, 19, 20
Fuchs, Daniel, 29
Furbank, P. N., 27

Galen, 235
Gallagher, Catherine, 239–41
Garrod, H. W., 174
Gaskell, Elizabeth, 246
Gass, William, 236
Gay, John, 236
Genius
  and Coleridge, 121, 204–5
  as ideal, 121
  Romantic view of, 130–31
Gerard, Alexander, 128
Gestalt therapy, 266n.1
Gilbert, Sandra M., 236, 237, 239, 241, 250
Gill, Stephen, 179
Gillman, James, 187, 191, 193
Gillman family, 193, 198
Gissing, George, 21

Godwin, William, 121–22, 189
Goethe, Johann Wolfgang von, 41, 44
Golden Notebook, The (Lessing), 40–41
Golding, William, *The Spire*, 91–92, 112
Gombrich, E. H., 103
Goodman, Paul, 24
Gordon, Rosemary, 61–62
Grand, Sarah, 248
Graves, Robert, 237
Graveyard School, 120
Gray, Thomas, 117–18, 119–20
  and originality or genius, 121
  and Romanticism, 129, 130
  and Wordsworth, 153, 180, 184
Greenacre, Phyllis, 56, 97
Greenberg, Jay R., 75, 100–101
Gregg, W. R., 240
Grillparzer, Franz, 20
Gubar, Susan, 236, 237, 238, 239, 241, 250
Guilford, J. P., 16–17
Guilliame de Loris, 236–37
Guntrip, Harry, 82

Hagstrum, Jean, 132
Hall, John, 133
Hamlet (Shakespeare)
  Coleridge on, 189
  Freudian account of, 41
Hammett, Dashiell, 15, 26–27, 28
Hartley, David, 126–27
Hartman, Geoffrey, 138, 139, 155, 168, 178
Hartmann, Heinz, 74–75, 76, 78, 79, 128
Havelock, Eric A., 142, 226–27, 228, 229
Hawthorne, Nathaniel, and Melville, 28,
  29
Haydon, Benjamin, 125
Hazlitt, William, 116, 122, 170, 187, 190,
  212
H.D. *See* Doolittle, Hilda
Hebbel, Friedrich, 63
Heidegger, Martin, 22
Heimann, Paula, 82
Helmholtz, Hermann von, 16
Herbert, George, 102
Herder, Johann, 144–45
Hertz, Neil, 136–37
Hesiod, 226
Hidden Order of Art, The (Ehrenzweig),
  103–7
Hitschmann, Eduard, 2, 63, 74
Hoffman, E. T. A., 130–31, 288n.65
Holland, Norman, 4, 35–36, 46, 77, 272–
  73n.73
Holmes, Richard, 191, 301n.66, 302n.79
Home, Henry, Lord Kames, 127, 134
Home at Grasmere (Wordsworth), 179, 181,
  183, 184

"Homeless" (Coleridge), 192
Homer
   Coleridge's invocation of, 195
   and Plato on poetry, 227
Hopkins, Anne, 235
Hopkins, Gerard Manley, 10, 20, 101, 102, 236
"Hour when we shall meet again, The" (Coleridge), 192
Howells, W. D., Twain letter to, 13
Hug-Hellmuth, Hermine von, 83
Huizinga, Johan, 47
Hulme, T. E., 111, 143
"Human Life" (Coleridge), 186
Hume, David, 134
Humor. *See* Jokes, Freudian treatment of
Hurd, Richard, 121, 124
Hutchinson, Sara, 168
Hutter, Albert, 100, 101, 102
"Hymn Before Sunrise, in the Vale of Chamouni" (Coleridge), 186

Ibsen, Henrik, 44, 73
Idealist aesthetics, and play, 47
Idealist philosophy
   and Coleridge's *Biographia*, 209
   and Romantic account of writer, 130
Imagination
   Coleridge on, 210, 211
   in Romantic theory, 130
Individuation
   Jung on, 55, 59–60, 62
   Rank on, 66–67, 71
   Winnicott's account of, 102
Influence anxiety, 126, 139–40, 235. *See also* Literary history
   and Bate, 115–22
   and Bloom, 137–42
   and Coleridge, 145
   and Keats, 122–26
   and McFarland, 142–45
Inhibitions, Symptoms, and Anxiety (Freud), 50–51
Inspiration
   and early-eighteenth-century poets, 127–28
   and Keats, 123
   Kris on, 77
   Schafer on, 80
   Schreiner, 248
Interpretation of Dreams, The (Freud), 20, 41, 49, 64
Irving, Washington, 115
Isaacs, Susan, 82
Iscove, Melvyn, 3

Jacobson, Edith, 56
James, Alice, 248

James, William, 69, 78
Jameson, Frederic, 35
Jeffrey, Francis, 116
Jean de Meun, 236–37
Jensen, Wilhelm, 39
Johnson, Diane, 27
Johnson, Samuel, 15, 129
   on Collins, 120
   on Gray, 119–20
   on sublime, 134
Johnston, Kenneth, 185
Jokes, Freudian treatment of, 45, 262n.13
Jokes and Their Relation to the Unconscious (Freud), 45, 46, 47
Jones, Ann Rosalind, 244
Jones, Ernest, 19, 35, 40, 41, 65, 73, 92
Jones, James, 237
Jones, John, 177
Jonson, Ben, 116, 139
Joyce, James, 57
Jung, Carl, 48, 55, 56–62
   aesthetics secondary for, 88
   and Freud, 84
   and Hoffman, 131
   and "Kubla Khan," 208
   and "symbolic" poet, 130
   and visionary artist, 57–58, 59, 268–69n.5

Kafka, Franz, 21, 154
Kames, Lord. *See* Home, Henry
Kant, Immanuel
   and Coleridge's *Biographia*, 209, 210
   and sublime, 135
Kaplan, Cora, 234, 241, 242, 243, 244, 250
Karpf, Fay, 69
Kazin, Alfred, 4
Keats, John, 10, 24, 106, 122–25, 126
   and Bloom, 138
   fragments of, 132
   on "muddy stream" of reality, 131
   as "strong poet," 137, 138
   and wish for blockage, 137
   on Wordsworth, 155
   and writer's isolation, 129
"Keepsake, The" (Coleridge), 195
Kernberg, Otto, 56
Kessler, Edward, 213, 214, 215
Kierkegaard, Søren, 222
King Lear (Shakespeare)
   and Freud on death instinct, 37–38, 261n.12
   and Wordsworth *Prelude*, 148
Klein, Melanie, 82–88, 92, 93, 112, 275–76n.4
   on art and literature, 177n.21
   and Ehrenzweig, 104

Klein, Melanie *(continued)*
  on paranoid-schzoid-depressive pro-
    gression, 101
  and Stokes, 108
  and symbolization, 159–60, 278–79n.39
  and Winnicott, 96, 281n.55
Kohut, Heinz, 74, 80
Körner, C. G., 49
Kris, Ernst, 20, 75, 77–79, 80
  and Ehrenzweig, 103–4
  on painters and sculptors, 22
  and Rank, 69
  and Philip Roth character, 6
Kristeva, Julia, 244–45
"Kubla Khan" (Coleridge), 99–100, 132,
  186, 194, 205–9
  preface to, 205–7, 211, 213

Lacan, Jacques, 69, 101, 242
Lamb, Charles, 121–22, 187
Langer, Susanne K., 66
Language
  and Coleridge, 212–15, 219, 222, 225
  and Plato's objection to writing, 220–28
  Rank on formation of, 67
  written vs. spoken, 219–20, 222, 230–31
Language community, and women, 242–
  44
Laplanche, J., 36–37, 75
Larkin, Philip, 7–9
Leonardo da Vinci, Freud on, 43, 51–53,
  71
*Leonardo da Vinci and a Memory of His Child-
  hood* (Freud), 34, 43, 48, 49, 51–53
Lessing, Doris, 40–41
Lewis, Wyndham, 111
"Life with a Hole in It, The" (Larkin), 8–9
"Limbo" (Coleridge), 186, 201
"Lines Left upon a Seat in a Yewtree"
  (Wordsworth), 162
"Lines Written in the Album at Elbinger-
  ode" (Coleridge), 195
Literary history
  Bloom on, 137–42
  and Coleridge, 121, 145, 186–89, 215
    (*see also* Coleridge, Samuel Taylor)
  limits of, 122–26
  McFarland on, 142–45
  neoclassicism, 116–17, 121, 126, 128,
    144
  Romanticism, 116, 126–37, 242, 252,
    280n.62, 290–91n.115 (*see also* Roman-
    ticism)
  and source of blockage, 115
  and Wordsworth, 121–22, 145 (*see also*
    Wordsworth, William)
Literature. *See* Art and artists; Poetry

Locke, John, and Wordsworth, 180
Longinus, 133–35, 136
Lonsdale, Roger, 120
Lottman, Herbert, 26
Lowenstein, Rudolf, 75

McCarthy, Mary, 1
McCarthy, Patrick, 26
McFarland, Thomas, 132, 142–45, 252
  and Bloom, 139
  and Coleridge, 189
    Biographia Literaria, 212
    childhood, 191
    and "Dejection: An Ode," 202
    and genius, 205
    at Gillmans', 193
    plagiarisms, 197, 198, 229
    and "Resolution and Independence,"
      167
  and sublime, 136
  on Wordsworth, 162, 173, 177
McLuhan, Marshall, 229
Mailer, Norman, 11, 245
Malatesta, Sigismondo, 111
Malthus, Thomas, and Coleridge, 188
Man, Paul de, 138
Martin, Wendy, 235
Martineau, Harriet, 246
Melville, Herman, 28–29
"Melville's Withdrawal" (Updike), 28–29
Menaker, Esther, 71, 72
Merchant of Venice, The (Shakespeare), and
  Freud on death instinct, 37–38
Mileur, Jean-Pierre, 117, 118
Miller, George, 16
Miller, Henry, 63
Milner, Marion, 82, 92–96, 112
  and adaptation, 100
  and creative process as minimum, 106
  on desire for ease and pleasure, 40
  and Ehrenzweig, 103, 104
  on importance of ground or medium,
    105
  and Jung, 61
  and originality vs. tradition, 99
  and Rose, 80–81
  and Wordsworth in *Prelude*, 155
  and writers vs. painters, 23
Milton, John, 124
  and Coleridge allusion, 207
  and Longinus, 133–34
  and tradition, 144
  Wordsworth allusion to, 148
Mitchell, Juliet, 243
Mitchell, Stephen A., 75, 100–101
Moby-Dick (Melville), 28

Modernism, and modeling vs. carving tradition, 110–11
Monk, Samuel, 133, 134, 135, 136
Morgan, John, 209
"Moses of Michelangelo, The" (Freud), 19, 41, 261–62n.13
Murdoch, Iris, 222, 226
My Life as a Man (Roth), 5–7

Neoclassicism, 116–17, 121
    and ego psychology, 128, 144
    and Romantic theories, 126
"Ne Plus Ultra" (Coleridge), 186, 201
Neurosis and neurotics
    and Bate on artistic creation, 126
    of Coleridge, 190, 198
    and Freud on art, 39–41, 42–43, 57
    Milner on, 95
    Rank on, 66–67, 73
    of Wordsworth, 174
Neurotic styles, Federn on, 21
Newton, Isaac, 127
Nietzsche, Friedrich, 71, 73, 104, 267n.3
"Nightingale, The" (Coleridge), 194
Nin, Anaïs, 63–64, 68, 73
"Not at Home" (Coleridge), 192
Novalis, 130

Object-relations theory, 20–21, 82, 251–52
    and Coleridge, 193–97
    and ego psychology, 76, 80
    of Ehrenzweig, 103–7
    and form-content reconciliation, 20–21
    of Klein, 82–88 (*see also* Klein, Melanie)
    and McFarland's theory, 144, 145
    of Milner, 92–96 (*see also* Milner, Marion)
    and Rank, 66
    and Schreiner heroines, 249
    of Segal, 88–92 (*see also* Segal, Hanna)
    of Stokes, 108–12
    and sublime, 136–37
    of Winnicott, 96–103 (*see also* Winnicott, D. W.)
    and Wordsworth (*Prelude*), 155
"Ode: Composed upon an Evening of Extraordinary Splendor and Beauty" (Wordsworth), 179
"Ode: Intimations of Immortality" (Wordsworth), 10, 170–74, 175–76, 177, 199
Oedipus complex
    and analysis of young children, 83
    and Coleridge, 198
    and Freud's view of art, 35–37, 49
    Klein on, 87

and Rank, 65
    and sublime, 136
Oedipus myth, Rank on, 70
Oedipus Rex (Sophocles), 41
Olsen, Tillie, 1
"On Chapman's Homer" (Keats), 124, 138
Ong, Walter J., 219, 222, 228, 229, 231
On Not Being Able to Paint (Milner), 23, 92, 94–96
"Opus Maximum" (Coleridge), 24, 187, 212
Oral culture
    Plato's objections to, 226–28
    and word processors, 230
Originality
    and Coleridge, 99–100
    Hazlitt on, 122
    McFarland on, 142–44
    and neoclassicism, 116, 121
    Romantic view of, 126, 131
    Winnicott on, 99
Osorio (Coleridge), 194
"Outcast, The" (Coleridge), 192
Outline of Clinical Psychoanalysis (Fenichel), 2

"Pains of Sleep, The" (Coleridge), 186, 196
Parrish, Stephen, 150
Pater, Walter, on Coleridge, 187
"Paths to the Formation of Symptoms, The" (Freud), 34, 39, 42, 48
Phaedrus (Plato), 22, 220–21, 222–24, 227–28
"Phantom or Fact" (Coleridge), 214
Philosophy. *See also* Aristotle; Plato; Wittgenstein
    and Coleridge, 24–25, 180–81, 183, 187, 200–201, 202–3, 205, 209–11, 212
    and Wordsworth, 163, 180–81
Picasso, Pablo, 57
"Picture, The" (Coleridge), 186, 195
Pinckney, Tony, 110–11
Plagiarism
    by Coleridge, 99–100, 197–98, 205, 210, 215, 229
    Winnicott's account of, 100
Plague, The (Camus), 25–26
Plato
    McFarland on, 142–43
    on poetry, 22
    Rank on, 72
    and written language, 213, 220–28, 231, 239–40, 242, 306–7n.18
Play
    Freud on, 47–48, 264–65n.36
    Klein on, 83
    Winnicott on, 97

Poe, Edgar Allan, 44
Poetry. *See also individual poets*
  decline of, 140–41
  Plato on, 22, 226–28
  and poets as makers, 127–28
  of strong poets, 137–40
  and women as writers, 234, 243–44
Poggioli, Renato, 143
Poincaré, Jules, 16
Pontalis, J.-B., 36–37, 75
Poole, Thomas, 24, 181, 191, 197
Pope, Alexander, 116, 128–29, 134, 236
Pound, Ezra
  and poet as poem, 237
  and Stokes, 110–11
  on women, 243
Praz, Mario, 132
Prelude (Wordsworth), 146, 147–67, 173
  anxiety and inadequacy in, 131
  and Hopkins, 10
  and outer world, 201
  and *The Recluse*, 181, 182, 183, 184, 185, 212
  and "To William Wordsworth," 203, 204
Printing, mass, writers inundated by, 115–16
"Processions. Suggested on a Sabbath Morning in the Vale of Chamouny" (Wordsworth), 178
Productive avoidance, 266n.1
"Professions for Women" (Woolf), 238
Proust, Marcel, 89
Psychoanalytic aesthetics, 4
  and formal or technical qualities of art, 19–22
  and Forster remarks, 12
  Freud on limits of, 19
  and Klein, 88, 277n.21
  second generation of, 55
  and Twain, 14
Psychoanalytic theory. *See also individual authors*
  American acceptance of, 4
  and deconstructionism, 306n.12
  English school of, 82 (*see also* Object-relations theory)
  Freud vs. Winnicott on, 101
  and institutionalized prohibitions, 232
  scientific status of, 56
  and sublime, 136
Psychoanalytic Theory of the Neuroses, The (Fenichel), 2
Psychology of forms, 80
Psychology of neoclassicism, 126–27
"Psychopathic Characters on the Stage," 19
Psychotherapy. *See also specific authors*

Winnicott on, 102
  for writer's block, 55–56, 265–66n.1
Putnam, James Jackson, 69

Quillinan, Edward, 184

Rank, Otto, 55, 56, 62–74
  and Bloom, 140
  and ego, 76
  and Milner, 92
  and Oedipus complex, 36
  and symbolism, 40
Rapin, René, 127, 128
Rapaport, David, 79
Read, Herbert, 103
Reason vs. feeling
  and eighteenth-century view of poetry, 127–28
  and Plato on poetry, 228
  for Wordsworth, 163
Recluse, The (Wordsworth), 132, 180–85, 212
Reductionism
  of Freudian aesthetics, 36
  of Hitschmann, 74
  and Holland, 273n.73
Reid, Forrest, 11
Reid, Thomas, 134
Reik, Theodore, 36
Remorse (Coleridge), 194
Republic (Plato), 220, 226, 227–28. *See also* Plato
"Resolution and Independence" (Wordsworth), 9–10, 167–70, 171, 172
  concluding lines of, 173
  creative precariousness in, 149–50
  leech-gatherer's intrusion in, 151, 166, 167–69
Reynolds, J. H., 123, 124
Rhymer, Thomas, 116, 127
Richardson, Dorothy, 249–50
Richard III (Shakespeare), 44
Ricks, Christopher, 4
Rieff, Philip, 47–48
Rilke, Rainer Maria, 107
"Rime of the Ancient Mariner." *See* "Ancient Mariner, The"
Riviere, Joan, 82, 85, 96
Robins, Elizabeth, 248
Robinson, Henry Crabb, 184
Rogers, Pat, 119, 120
Romanticism, 126–33, 280n.62
  Bloom on, 290–91n.115
  of "Kubla Khan" preface, 205, 207
  and print culture, 231
  slow generation of, 116

and sublime, 133–37
and writer as autonomous, 242
Romantic self-consciousness, 252
Room of One's Own, A (Woolf), 232–34, 250
Rose, Gilbert, 80
Rose, Mike, 1, 16–18
Rosmersholm (Ibsen), 44
Rossetti, Christina, 244
Rossman, Joseph, 16
Roth, Henry, 29
Roth, Philip, 5–7
Rousseau, Jean-Jacques, 132
Ruskin, John, 238
Rycroft, Charles, 68

Sachs, Hanns, 20, 264n.30
and Freud on beauty, 46
and Freud on Goethe, 44
in Milner essay, 92
and Shakespeare, 54
and symbolism, 40
Sade, Marquis de, 237
Salinger, J. D., 29
Schafer, Roy, 75, 79, 80
Schelling, Friedrich, 210
Schiller, Johann, 49–50, 56
Schlegel, Friedrich, 132
Schmitz, Otto A. H., 57
Schopenhauer, Arthur, 68, 69, 73
Schreiner, Olive, 248–49
Schweitzer, Albert, and Kohut on Hitschmann, 74
Segal, Hanna, 82, 88–92, 112
and artistic quality, 21
and creative process as artistic content, 106
on "de-fusion," 93
and Ehrenzweig, 103, 104
on guilt, 87
and originality vs. tradition, 99
and symbolic transference, 160, 161
and Wordsworth *(Prelude)*, 157
Semiotic, the (Kristeva), 244–45
"Separation" (Coleridge), 192
Seventh Letter (Plato), 224, 225, 227–28
Seven Types of Ambiguity (Empson), 20
Shakespeare, William, 42, 44, 53, 54. See also *Hamlet; King Lear; Merchant of Venice; Richard III*
Bloom on, 138
Sharpe, Ella, 54
Shattuck, Roger, 120
Shaw, Lemuel, Jr., 28
Shelley, Percy Bysshe
fragments by, 132
as "strong poet," 137

and Wordsworth, 179
and writer's isolation, 129
Shenstone, William, 117, 119
Showalter, Elaine, 235, 236, 237, 246–49, 250
Silences (Olsen), 1
Smith, Henry Nash, 13, 14
Sonnets upon the Punishment of Death (Wordsworth), 179
Southey, Robert, 190, 193, 198, 204, 236
Spector, Jack, 47
Spire, The (Golding), 91–92, 112
Sterne, Laurence, 287n.43
Stevens, Wallace, as "strong poet," 137, 138
Stokes, Adrian, 103, 106, 108–12
Storr, Anthony, 47
Strachey, James, 96
"Stranger Minstrel, A" (Coleridge), 195
Stuart, Simon, 157
Sublimation
Bloom on, 140
Freud on, 140
Klein on, 88
and Romantic sublime, 134
Sublime
and "the semiotic," 245
and Wordsworth, 161, 166, 168
and writer's block, 133–37
Sullivan, Harry Stack, 56
Sutherland, James, 120
Swift, Jonathan, 128
Sybiline Leaves (Coleridge), 209
Symbolism and symbolization
Freud/Jones on, 35, 278n.39
in Kleinian theory, 159–60, 278–79n.39
and Milner, 92–93, 94
Sachs and Rank on, 40
and Segal, 89, 160, 161
for Wordsworth, 160

Technology, vs. isolation of composing process, 229–30
Temple, Sir William, 116
Tennyson, Alfred, as "strong poet," 137
Thackeray, William Makepeace, 10–11
Thelwall, John, 194
"This Lime-tree Bower my Prison" (Coleridge), 194, 202
"Thou art indeed just, Lord" (Hopkins), 10, 102
"Three Graves, The" (Coleridge), 194
Ticknor, George, 184
"Tintern Abbey" (Wordsworth), 10, 148, 151, 170, 173, 175, 202
"To the Rev. George Coleridge" (Coleridge), 193

"To William Wordsworth" (Coleridge), 186, 203–4
Transactional therapy, 265–66n.1
"Transcendent Function, The" (Jung), 60–62
Trilling, Lionel, 3, 39, 172
"Tuft of Primroses, The" (Wordsworth), 183
Twain, Mark, 10, 12–15, 256nn. 40, 41, 257n.44
Tyler, Anne, 29

Unconscious
 and Freudian theory, 271n.61
 Jung on, 57–59, 60–62, 267n.3
 and Rank's revision of Freud, 64
 and Romantic account of writing, 130
Updike, John, 28–29, 34–35

Vasari, Giorgio, 51, 52
Vernal Ode (Wordsworth), 179
Vico, Giovanni Battista, 140
Voltaire, 120

Wallas, Joseph, 16
Walpole, Horace, 119
"Wanderings of Cain, The" (Coleridge), 192
Warton, Joseph, 117, 119, 121
Warton, Thomas, 117, 119
Weiskel, Thomas, 134, 136
Whitman, Walt, as "strong poet," 137
Will
 Freud on, 68
 and Rank, 68, 71
"Windhover, The" (Hopkins), 20
Winnicott, D. W., 82, 96–103, 112, 280n.52, 281n.55
 and Coleridge, 191
 and "depressive position," 87
 and ego psychology, 76
 and Ehrenzweig, 104
 and "facilitating environment," 160
 and Jung, 61
 on objective perception, 162
 and Rose, 80
Winthrop, John, 235
Wish fulfillment, writing as (Freud), 34–37, 42
Wittgenstein, Ludwig, 222
Wollheim, Richard, 45, 47, 108
Wollstonecraft, Mary, 238
Women writers, 244–50
 and Freud, 49, 54, 243
 inhibiting pressures on, 234–35
  false biology, 235–36
  patriarchal metaphors, 236–38

stereotypes, 238–42
symbolic order, 242–44
and Shakespeare's sister (Woolf), 232–34
Wood, Mrs. Henry, 247
Woodhouse, Richard, 123
Woolf, Virginia, 104–5, 232–34, 238–39, 244, 249
Word processors, 229–30
Wordsworth, Ann, 138–39
Wordsworth, Dora (daughter of William), 184
Wordsworth, Dorothy (sister of William), 162–63, 166–67, 168
 and Coleridge, 189, 193, 198
 letters on Wordsworth by, 182, 184
 and "Tintern Abbey," 202
Wordsworth, William, 9–10, 18, 131, 145, 146. *See also specific poems*
 and Coleridge, 155, 167, 168, 173, 180–81, 182, 193, 197, 198, 202, 203–5
 complaint by, 120
 influence of, 130
 McFarland on, 144–45
 Milton compared with, 124
 and originality, 121–22
 poetical accounts of childhood, 191
 Recluse, incompletion of, 132
 as "strong poet," 137
 and sublime, 136
 and writer's block
  blockage experience (*Prelude*), 147–57
  blockage and externality ("Ode"), 170–74
  blockage and subjective need, 162–67
  generic blockage (*Recluse*), 180–85
  infancy and origins of creative power (*Prelude*), 157–62
  qualitative blockage ("Elegaic Stanzas"), 174–80
  "Resolution and Independence," 167–70
 and writer's isolation, 129
 "Work Without Hope" (Coleridge), 186
Wright, Elizabeth, 97
Writer and Psychoanalysis, The (Bergler), 1, 3
Writer's block
 advice for overcoming (Keats/Amis/Sterne), 125, 287n.43
 and age of tradition or convention, 144
 alternative terms for, 7–8
 and authors
  Browning, 231
  Camus, 26
  Coleridge, 24–25, 186, 199, 215 (*see also* Coleridge, Samuel Taylor)

Conrad, 15, 16
Forster, 11–12, 27–28
Freud, 33
Gray, 119
Hammett, 26–27, 28
Hopkins, 10
Larkin, 7–9
Philip Roth, 5–7
Twain, 12–15
Wordsworth, 9–10, 146, 157 (*see also*
    Wordsworth, William)
Bate on, 126
breakthrough from, 211–12, 245, 252
cognitive explanation of, 16–18
vs. creative exhaustion, 27–29
in early vs. late career, 25–27
ego psychology on, 74, 80 (*see also* Ego
    psychology)
Ehrenzweig on, 106
familiarity of term, 4
Freud on, 48–54, 80
historical dimension to, 115, 252 (*see also*
    Influence anxiety; Literary history)
Hutter on, 100
institutionalized prohibitions as, 232
Jung on, 57–59, 62
and Klein, 88
looseness of term, 18
Menaker on, 72–73

Milner on, 94–95, 95–96
and oral vs. written culture, 228–31
origin of term, 1–2, 254n.4
vs. other types of block, 22
as psychoanalytically treatable condi-
    tion, 4
psychotherapies for, 55–56, 265–66n.1
as qualitative, 18–19, 21
questions on, ix–x
Rank on, 71, 73
and Rank's break with Freud, 63
and Romantic sublime, 133–37
and Romantic theories, 126, 131, 132–33
Segal on, 89
Stokes on, 111–12
types of, 23–25
and Winnicott's views, 98–99, 103
and women, 233–35, 245, 248–50
and Wordsworth, 18, 173, 174–80
Writer's Block: The Cognitive Dimension
    (Rose), 1, 16–18
Writer's cramp, 2
Written language, 219–20, 222, 230–31
    Coleridge's distrust of, 213–14
    Plato on, 220–28, 306–7n.18

Yeats, William Butler, as "strong poet,"
    137
Young, Edward, 120, 130, 143

Designed by Laury A. Egan

Composed by Graphic Composition, Inc., in Palatino text and display type.
Printed by R. R. Donnelley and Sons Company on 55-lb. Cream White Sebago.

DATE DUE

GAYLORD			PRINTED IN U.S.A.